DEDICATION

This book is dedicated to my first grandchild, CONNOR JAMES HORNE, born September 28, 2013. I have so enjoyed watching you grow, and can't wait to see all that the Lord has in store for you! Pop's prayer for you is that you will be a faithful servant of the Lord, fully devoted to Him, and exceedingly *"powerful in the Scriptures"* (Acts 18:24).

AUTHOR'S NOTES

All of the quotes in these devotions, unless otherwise noted, are from the Modern English Version, which I recommend highly. If I were beginning my ministry today, the MEV might very well be my "go-to" translation for both personal study and preaching. All other quotes are from the 1984 edition of the New International Version, and are marked "NIV 84."

You will note that I use a generous amount of verse references in these devotions. That is on purpose. I never want you to read a sentence I've written and wonder, "Where did he come up with that?" My suggestion would be to read the chapter in the Bible, then go to the devotion with Bible kept open, looking back at those references as you read.

You will also no doubt note quickly that some of these devotions are longer and some are shorter. Some chapters of the New Testament just lent themselves to more writing than others. In some of them, I wrote about basically the whole chapter. In others, I focused on one or two verses that captured my attention. That was just the nature of the various chapters and how the Lord spoke to me through them.

I would love to hear from you about how the Lord uses these thoughts in your life. I can be contacted by email at drbrody123@gmail.com. You can also order additional copies from me at this email address.

Donnie C. Brannen
September 2015

INTRODUCTION

I am convinced that the most important thing you can do for your spiritual life is to set aside regular, disciplined time to spend with the Lord in prayer and in His Word. You can call it "daily devotions" or your "quiet time" or "God time" or "prayer time" or whatever. It doesn't much matter what you call it, but it does matter that you do it! I usually call it my "quiet time," but I don't know why, because there's certainly no requirement I know of that it be quiet!

Let me tell you my story. I was saved at the age of nine, but when I was saved, nobody gave me any guidance in what I could do to grow in Christ other than go to church and Sunday School (my church didn't have any kind of specified youth group other than the Sunday School and Training Union departments). I've often said that when I came forward to profess faith in Christ, the pastor told me to have a seat on the pew, and that's what I thought the Christian life was all about! In Sunday School, there were places to check off on our Sunday School record, like "Read Bible Every Day" and "Studied Sunday School Lesson," but nobody really stressed to me (at least not that I can remember; maybe I missed it) the importance of spending time with the Lord, and so I didn't, other than dutifully going to Sunday School and church almost every Sunday. As a result, my relationship with God during my teen years was like a casual dating relationship, and not a marriage. I hung out with the Lord a few hours every weekend, but we didn't have very much contact between those "dates." Given that the church is called the bride of Christ, it's obvious that God wants our relationship with Him to be more like a marriage, a constant, intimate, personal interaction with Him on a daily basis.

To be honest, even after I went to seminary and started in ministry, my prayer life was spotty and undisciplined at best, and even in seminary, I don't think any class ever stressed the importance of daily time spent with the Lord. They taught me about the Bible, about parsing Greek and Hebrew verbs, about church history, and about preaching to feed other people, but nobody said one word to me about how I could feed my own soul. After I graduated and went to my first full-time church, I was praying more and I was in the Word more (preparing sermons and such), but still my interactions with the Lord were in a spotty, unfocused, undisciplined way, catch-as-catch can. I prayed when I needed something. I prayed a lot on the run from this thing to that thing. I knew I needed a more disciplined approach, but as a young pastor and young father, I made the excuse, who has the time? If I had continued the way I was going, I have no doubt that I would have eventually burned out or washed out of the ministry.

But thank God, one day I got a crack in my windshield and had to stay at the shop for several hours while it was repaired. The only thing I had to read that day was a book by Bill Hybels called *Too Busy Not to Pray*. Out of hundreds of books I've read, there are very few that I would call "life-changing," but that one was. In that book, he talked about the importance of setting aside time every day to focus on the Lord in prayer and in His Word, and he spoke of it not so much as a duty and a discipline, but as a delight. I was both convicted and inspired by that book.

About that same time, Lane Adams, who had retired as an associate evangelist with the Billy Graham organization and who was a representative of Scripture Union, came and spoke at our minister's conference about the importance of the daily quiet time, and about Scripture Union's quiet time resources. That was 24 years ago. I was 29 years old, and I had wasted the first 20 years of my Christian life without a consistent time with the Lord. I can't help but wonder how different my teen years might have been, and how different my early ministry might have been, if my walk with the Lord hadn't been so casual and spotty.

I started spending time with the Lord in prayer and in His Word on a regular basis, using Scripture Union's *Encounter with God* and Moody Bible Institute's *Today in the Word* as devotional guides. For over two decades, that quiet time discipline - though waxing and waning in consistency at times - had indeed become a delight. By the end of 2014, though, I had hit a wall spiritually. I was still praying, still reading the Word and the devotional readings, probably with greater consistency than ever, but it had become dry, rote ritual. I felt like I was just going through the motions, but not truly communicating with God.

As I was praying about those feelings and frustrations, I clearly sensed the Lord saying to me, "Quit reading them, and start writing them." Sometime along that same time, I ran across the statistic that there are 260 chapters in the New Testament, and immediately, the thought came to my mind, "At five a week, that's 52 weeks." I knew I had my assignment. I would write a devotion on each chapter of the New Testament.

And so this journey began in January of 2015. It has been a blessed journey for me, and I pray that as you read these thoughts, it will be a blessed journey for you as well.

I would suggest that you go through the New Testament at the rate of five chapters a week. Take the entire year. Use Saturday as a make-up and review day, and of course, Sunday as a corporate worship day. You can go straight through from Matthew to Revelation, or you can skip around, but make it your goal to engage the entire New Testament in the coming year. You will never be the same after you have finished this journey!

MATTHEW

FEARFULLY AND WONDERFULLY MADE
MATTHEW 1

Joseph is one of the great unsung heroes of the birth narratives and beyond. For Jesus to be qualified to be our Savior meant that He had to fulfill the Law perfectly, including such matters as being circumcised on the eighth day by His legal father and being presented and dedicated at the Temple several weeks later. The legal father of a child was whoever was married to his mother at the time of his birth. Children born to unwed mothers, and thus without legal fathers, were cut off from the Temple, so Joseph's submission to God's Word here is no less necessary, and no less striking in its implications - both negative for Joseph, and positive for the world - than Mary's submission recorded in Luke. We might wonder at the purpose of the genealogy of chapter one. After all, why trace the ancestry of Joseph, given that Joseph was not Jesus' biological father? Being that Matthew is a distinctively Jewish gospel, written primarily to Jews to convince them that Jesus is the Messiah, it was important for him to establish Jesus' legal right to the throne of Israel, a legal right that comes not only biologically through his mother (whose genealogy is in Luke), but through his legal father, Joseph. All of those generations, both their genetic makeup and their experiences that formed them and influenced their parenting, combined to made Joseph the man he was, a man God could trust to take care of His child. In a sense, they are unsung heroes as well.

PRAYER: When the Bible says that we are *"fearfully and wonderfully made"* (Psalm 139:14 NIV 84), we often think only of the biological union of our parents that God used to form us. But it goes much deeper and further than that. We are all the products of all the genetic combinations of all of our ancestors, all of them combining to form our own unique genetic soup. Imagine that! God has used and ordained all of the couplings of every previous generation to create you just the way you are! Thank Him that you are indeed *"fearfully and wonderfully made."*

KNOWING THE SCRIPTURES AND MISSING THE SAVIOR
MATTHEW 2

Those who are academically inclined have to guard against becoming "puffed up" by knowledge (I Corinthians 8:1) in their spiritual walks. It is very easy to slide into a belief that the smartest one in the room, in terms of Biblical knowledge, is the most spiritual in the room, when in fact, the opposite may be true. Greater knowledge *can* lead to greater spirituality, but it can also lead to an arrogant carnality that is intimately familiar with the Word of the Lord, but woefully distant from the Lord of the Word. The magi from the east were no doubt "wise men" in many areas, but their knowledge of the Messiah and of the Scriptures was limited. Because of their knowledge of astronomy, when they saw a strange phenomenon in the sky, they believed a king had been born in Israel, and they assumed that a king would naturally be born in the capital city of Jerusalem and in the household of the current king, Herod the Great. They were mistaken in those assumptions, but the Bible scholars of the day, no doubt eager to display their superior knowledge of the Scriptures to these ignorant foreigners, set them straight. They knew from the Old Testament prophecy of Micah that the Messiah was to be born in Bethlehem, a mere five miles away. The wise men made their way to Bethlehem, but the Bible scholars stayed in Jerusalem, no doubt scoffing at the notion that the Messiah had been born. Surely, if the Messiah had been born, God would have revealed it to us, they may have thought, and not to foreigners from a distant land with a sign in the sky! And so it was that the "ignorant" magi worshiped Him and brought Him gifts in homage, while the "brilliant" scholars missed out on what the Scriptures they studied pointed to: the birth of a Savior, the long-awaited and long-prophesied Christ. The wise men had come a great distance, at great expense and difficulty, to see the newborn King; the Bible scholars wouldn't travel a mere five miles to see if it were true. Who were really the "wise men," those who knew the Scriptures inside and out, or those who came to worship the Savior?

PRAYER: God certainly puts no premium on ignorance, but He is absolutely appalled at pride. Indeed, He tells us in His Word that He actively opposes the proud, but gives grace to the humble (I Peter 5:5). Pray that God will fill you with the knowledge of Himself and His Word. Pray also that your increasing knowledge will not lead to pride, but rather to a greater love of God and others, because *"Knowledge produces arrogance, but love edifies"* (I Corinthians 8:1), or the NIV 84 puts it, *"Knowledge puffs up, but love builds up."*

FATHERS AND SONS
MATTHEW 3

There are two sons in Matthew 3, one with an earthly father, and one the Son of God. About His Son Jesus, God the Father said, *"This is my beloved Son, in whom I am well-pleased."* I wonder if Zechariah (or as his name could also be rendered, Zacharias) felt that way about John? Zechariah was a priest, from a long line of priests going all the way back to the first High Priest, Aaron. For many years of his life, his greatest disappointment was that he and his wife Elizabeth had been unable to have children. He had no son to pass the priesthood on to, and that long line of priests, it seemed, would end with him. But then, at the high point of his ministry, as he was burning incense in the Temple, the angel Gabriel had appeared to him, telling him that he would have a son in his old age, a son who would go forth in the spirit and power of Elijah to bring revival to the nation. I wonder if Zechariah expected that those predictions would come true within the bounds of a priestly ministry? If he lived long enough to see John grow to manhood, I wonder if he was taken by surprise when John rejected the vestments of the priesthood in favor of a camel hair garment and a leather belt? I wonder if he was appalled when John went to the wilderness rather than serving in the Temple? I wonder if he was confused by this "new baptism" that his son was preaching? I wonder if I understood fully the role that John was chosen to perform in salvation history? There's something about fathers and sons, an all-too-common pattern of fathers seeking to squeeze their sons into a mold, usually their own mold, and sons seeking to break the mold and go their own way. John, of course, didn't go his own way, but God's way. Whatever Zechariah's response, John was faithful to the call of God, and he was highly commended for it by the One who matters most (Luke 7:24-28).

8

PRAYER: By this time in Israel's history, there were 20,000 priests in Israel, but only one man would be the forerunner of the Messiah. Israel didn't need another priest; it needed a prophet to prepare the way of the Lord, and after 400 years of prophetic silence, John was that prophet. God's plan for Zechariah's son was so much bigger than anything Zechariah could have imagined in all those years he longed for an heir. Pray for your children (or perhaps your grandchildren or future children) today, that they will follow God's path in all things. If it's God's path, it will be *"exceedingly abundantly beyond all that <you> ask or imagine"* (Ephesians 3:20).

WHAT HAPPENS WHEN WE SAY YES
MATTHEW 4

Having been baptized, Jesus is now ready to begin his public ministry. Perhaps you are stepping out into a new area of ministry or leadership, saying "yes" to a call from God. Here's a checklist for what you can expect as you follow His call to ministry:

> *Divine Leadership (v. 1):* Jesus was led by the Spirit into the wilderness.

> *Intensified Opposition (v. 1b):* I'm sure this was not the first time Jesus had dealt with temptation, but this was temptation of an intensity He had likely not seen before. Knowing who He was, and knowing that He had come to destroy his works, the devil himself came after Him. Most of us speak of being "tempted by the devil." It's good shorthand to speak of the whole of the kingdom of darkness arrayed against us, but in truth, most of us have never been within miles of the devil. Our spiritual warfare is most often conducted against low-level demon functionaries,

against the flow of the world under the sway of the evil one, and against our own sin nature. Jesus dealt with the king-demon himself. Those who stand higher than their brethren, who are committed to seeking and serving the Lord diligently, who move into leadership roles, can expect to receive greater hostile attention from the forces of darkness. As someone well put it, "new levels, new devils."

Increased Awareness of Weakness (v. 2): After fasting for forty days, Jesus was hungry. I would imagine so! Serving the Lord will invariably bring us to the end of our strength. It will test us spiritually, mentally, emotionally, and sometimes physically. But always remember, *"<God's> strength is made perfect in weakness"* (II Corinthians 12:9).

Temptations to Selfishness, Pride, and Power (vv. 3-10): The three particular temptations Jesus faced are temptations that come, in a lesser sense, to all who assume any degree of leadership: the temptation to use one's position and authority to serve oneself rather than to serve others, to pursue the attention, applause and admiration of people, and to accumulate personal power.

Angelic Assistance (v. 11): Angels came and ministered to Jesus, and they minister to us as well (Hebrews 1:14).

New Beginnings (v. 12): It's interesting that Jesus' first act after the temptations was to move from his hometown to Capernaum. Sometimes, serving the Lord will take us to new areas, sometimes literally, but always figuratively in terms of learning and faith. Serving Him will stretch us beyond our normal comfort zones, show us, again, our areas of weakness, and cause us to trust the Lord more.

New Comrades (vv. 18-21): Jesus began gathering His disciples together, and they went out to do ministry together. Not even Jesus was a Lone Ranger. He calls us to work together with fellow believers in doing His work.

Changed Lives (vv. 23-25): What makes the effort, the opposition, and the difficulties all worthwhile is the joy of seeing God change lives through our work!

PRAYER: In prayer today, say yes to Him. If he's leading you into a new area of ministry, and you may have been hesitant, say yes. If you're not currently serving Him in ministry, say yes in advance, asking Him to show you where He would have you serve. If you're in the thick of the battle, facing opposition and temptation, and feeling your strength failing, look to Him for leadership and angelic assistance. Lean on your fellow servants in the church, and look ahead to the joy of changed lives to come!

SALT AND LIGHT
MATTHEW 5

As Jesus begins His Sermon on the Mount in Matthew 5, the key to the chapter is in verses 13-16, where He tells us that we are the salt of the earth and the light of the world. Salt had a variety of uses in the ancient world. It was used to add flavor to food, but it was most valuable in the ancient world for cleaning wounds and keeping meat from spoiling. Salt was so valuable in the first century that Roman soldiers received an allotment of salt as part of their pay. If you've ever heard it said of someone that he's "not worth his salt," that phrase goes all the way back to the Roman army; a sorry soldier was said to be not worth even his salt allotment, much less the rest of his pay. In declaring us the salt of the earth, Jesus gave us some idea of how we are to relate to the world we live in. We are to bring a "pleasant" taste to the world around us. It should never be the case that everyone silently groans when "the Christian" walks into the room. We are to promote healing - emotional healing, physical healing, and spiritual healing. Like salt going into a wound, the message of the gospel may sting going into the open wounds of sin, but it is the only source of healing for those wounds. And certainly, we're to bring our influence to bear on the society around us. The world we live in is a dead, rotting carcass, and the only thing that can preserve it from complete ruin is the "salty" influence of Christian people and Christian principles. We are also the light of the world. Jesus said in John 8:12 that He was the light of the world. The two passages are not in conflict. Jesus goes on in John 8:12 to say that *"Whoever follows me shall not walk in the darkness, but shall have the light of life."* He also said in John 9:5, *"While I am in the world, I am the light of the world."* Jesus was the light shining into the darkness of this world (John 1:3); since His Ascension, He has left that task to His body, the church made up of believers in Him. It is our job to shine His light into our world. When we don't shine as believers, the world gets ever darker. We live as salt and light when we display the characteristics of the Beatitudes: recognizing our poverty of spirit, mourning over our own and others' sins, hungering and thirsting for righteousness, and walking in meekness, mercy, purity, and peace (vv. 3-9). To truly live as salt and light means that we do not respond to life and circumstances in the normal and "natural" ways that the world does (vv. 17-48). This counter-cultural lifestyle brings us both blessing from God and persecution from the world (vv. 10-12, 13b, 43-48).

PRAYER: Reflect on the truth that living for the Lord brings both blessing from God and persecution from the world (II Timothy 3:12). If you are in the midst of persecution, thank Him that the blessing will far outweigh the suffering. Ask Him to open your eyes today to how you can be a more salty influence and a brighter light in your world.

NOW OR LATER?
MATTHEW 6

Much of Matthew 6 concerns itself with where our focus lies. Are we focused on the now, or on the eternal? It's an important question, because our focus determines the entire course of our lives (vv. 22-23). Jesus speaks first to us about our *"acts of righteousness"* (NIV 84) or *"charitable giving."* It was customary upon exiting the Temple or the synagogue to give alms to the poor, the blind and the crippled who would gather there. Jesus had evidently been appalled at those who made a grand production out of their giving, likening it to satirically to sounding a trumpet to announce one's giving. While many have taken His command to give in secret to an extreme (unwillingness to use offering envelopes or take charitable donations off one's taxes, for example), we would all do well to examine our motives. Do we give for an earthly reward, or for a heavenly reward? If the Internal Revenue Service one day no longer allows a deduction for giving to the church (not at all an improbable possibility), will you keep giving? Jesus also mentions prayer as an activity that can have an earthly reward and a heavenly one. Again, we could take this to an extreme, refusing to lead in prayer in church for example. But again, it is our motives that are in question. We've all heard those whose public prayers seemed focused far more on themselves and the congregation's reactions than on the Lord. Fasting comes in for a similar treatment. The Pharisees fasted twice a week, on Tuesdays and Thursdays, despite the fact that the Law only required fasting one day a year, on the Day of Atonement. Many of them would neglect their normal grooming and disfigure their faces on fast days to show the misery they were enduring for the Lord, hoping that by doing so people would notice and commend their piety. Jesus urges us to seek the rewards of heaven, not the rewards of our fellow men. He urges us to store up treasures in heaven - treasures that are permanent - rather than temporary treasures on Earth. Verses 25-34 tell us how we can know if our focus is heavenly or earthly. What do we most worry about - earthly things, or seeking the kingdom of God?

PRAYER: Focus your prayer time today around Jesus' model prayer in verses 9-13. Rather than simply repeating the Lord's Prayer, personalize it. What "daily bread" do you need for today? Is there someone you need to forgive? What temptations are you facing? Where do you most see a need for kingdom influence in your world?

THE WORLD'S FAVORITE SCRIPTURE
MATTHEW 7

There was a more Biblically literate time when most people could quote various passages of Scripture: Psalm 100, Psalm 23, and John 3:16, for example. Today, few people can quote Scripture, but one Scripture that almost everyone can quote is Matthew 7:1: *"Judge not, that you be not judged."* It is an oft-quoted, but seldom understood Scripture, thrown out as a weapon to silence anyone daring to use the Bible to defend a moral position. In a world that rejects godly values, the only value that is venerated above all others is a radical tolerance that proclaims all positions as equally valid and all decisions as morally neutral. But Jesus was clearly not telling us to put all moral discernment aside, and to declare all things as morally neutral. He tells us just a few verses later, in verse 6, not to give what is holy to dogs, or throw pearls before swine. That indicates the necessity of moral judgment. What Jesus was condemning was the subjective judgmentalism that condemns others based on one's personal preferences rather than the revealed will of God. I personally don't like earrings on men, but I don't see any Biblical injunction against it, so to condemn someone for having an earring would be an example of judging based on personal preference. On the other hand, if I point out to someone who's cheating on his wife that the Bible condemns adultery, *I'm* not judging him; I'm merely announcing the verdict of the righteous judge. Jesus was also condemning the kind of judgment that harshly condemns others for their sins and pays no attention to one's own (vv. 3-5). Let us remember that there is a judgment to come, and a fearful one at that (vv. 21-23). We who have entered the narrow gate that leads to life (vv. 13-14) do those who are on the broad path to destruction no favors by leaving them undisturbed in their sin, the victim of false prophets assuring them of salvation as they barrel down the superhighway to hell (vv. 15-20). Nor do we do our fellow believers any favors by not confronting them when they stray from the truth (vv. 24-27).

PRAYER: As you pray today, re-read verses 7-11. Bask in the truth that our Father in heaven longs to give us good things when we ask. He may not always give us what we ask, because in our ignorance we are sometimes foolish enough to actually ask for stones and snakes instead of bread and fish. Trust Him always to know what's best, and to do what's best, in response to your prayers.

THE FINAL AUTHORITY
MATTHEW 8

At the end of the Sermon on the Mount, we're told that the people were amazed at Jesus' teaching, because He taught as one having authority, and not as the scribes (7:28-29). The full extent of His authority, though, goes far beyond His teaching. Contrary to the modern cynics who desire to dismiss Him as nothing more than a great teacher, His full authority begins to be revealed in chapter 8. First, we read of the cleansing of the leper. Leprosy was the most dreaded disease of the ancient world, a disease that first isolated a person from society, and then slowly caused the person to literally fall apart. No one would touch a leper, but Jesus did. The leper displayed absolute faith in Jesus' ability to heal him, his only concern being whether He would be willing. He discovered to his delight that Jesus was not only able, but absolutely willing. All of us have been infected with a "disease" called sin. Those who are deep in the throes of the worst kinds of sin may wonder if Jesus is willing to touch them with forgiveness and eternal life. The Word of God is clear that He is willing. He always responds to the cry of faith, and the level of sin's decay is no impediment to His healing and forgiving power. The next account in the chapter is of the healing of the centurion's servant. This Roman soldier was part of the occupation army of Rome, a Gentile. To most Jews of the day, Gentiles were detestable, untouchable. They believed that even to enter a Gentile's home would make them unclean. But Jesus was willing to enter the Roman officer's home to heal his servant, even though the centurion, showing remarkable faith (v. 10), said that His presence would not be necessary. He had faith that Jesus could give the word where He was, and the servant would be healed some distance away. There are no social barriers or distance barriers that Jesus is unwilling or unable to overcome (v. 11). In verses 23-27, Jesus shows His mastery over even the forces of nature by stilling a storm at sea. Truly, there is no situation in life that is beyond His control (v. 27). Finally, in verses 28-34, Jesus delivers the two demoniacs in the Gergasenes, also known as the Gadarenes. Mark and Luke speak of only one demoniac, apparently focusing their attention on the more vocal, or perhaps the more well-known, of the two men, who called himself "Legion." Because Matthew was writing his gospel to Jews, he was always careful to mention when there were two of anything, because of the Jewish standard of every fact being established by two or more witnesses. The account certainly raises more questions than it answers. Why did Jesus do as the demons asked? Why did He allow them into the pigs? Why did the pigs then drown themselves? Regardless of the unanswered questions it raises, it demonstrates one thing beyond doubt: Jesus has absolute power over every spiritual force. Even a "double legion" of demons is dispatched with one word! Jesus is willing and able to overcome every barrier save one: He will not violate a person's free will. A person must decide freely to believe in Him and follow Him (vv. 18-22).

PRAYER: Today in prayer, thank the Lord for His authority that is above and beyond disease, sin, culture, circumstances and the demonic. If you are a Gentile (non-Jewish) believer, thank Him that you are part of those mentioned in verse 11 who *"come from the east and the west and will dine with Abraham, Isaac and Jacob in the kingdom of heaven."*

THE RISE OF OPPOSITION
MATTHEW 9

Thus far in Matthew, we've seen Jesus preaching, healing and delivering demoniacs, in most cases to the amazement and delight of the crowds (the exception being in Gentile territory when the deliverance of the two demoniacs resulted in the loss of the swine). Now, for the first time, we see opposition to Him and His ministry arising among the Jews. The first hint of it comes when a paralytic is brought to Him, and He says to Him, *"Your sins are forgiven you"* (v. 2). Had He said merely, "Rise and walk," there would have been no problem. The scribes were no doubt there to see the miracles of healing they had heard about, but His claim to forgive sin was more than they could handle. Given that only God can forgive sin, they concluded that He was blaspheming, rather than concluding the truth, that He is God! After the healing of the paralytic, the crowds were amazed and glorified God, but the scribes remained angry over the perceived blasphemy. From there, we're told of Jesus' call to Matthew to follow Him, and the banquet Matthew arranged for Him with all of his tax-collector and sinner friends. Tax-collectors were greatly despised in Israel. They were Jews, but they worked for the hated Romans, and they were known to be unscrupulous and dishonest in their treatment of their fellow Jews. The Pharisees were appalled that Jesus would share a meal with such people, but Jesus told them that these were exactly the people who needed Him most: *"Those who are well do not need a physician, but those who are sick"* (v. 12). And those were not the only incidents of opposition. Even John's disciples questioned Him about the fact that His disciples did not fast in the manner of the Pharisees and John's followers. When Jesus went to the ruler's house to heal his daughter, His statement that *"The girl is not dead, but is sleeping"* (v. 24) elicited laughter and scorn from the professional mourners. Finally, the healing of the demonized mute elicited an accusation that Jesus was in fact commanding demons because He was in league with the ruler of demons, the devil himself. Opposition in doing the work the Lord is inevitable. Sometimes, it comes in the form of people misunderstanding our words or our motives, such as in the case of the scribes when Jesus healed the paralytic. Sometimes, when we "get our hands dirty" ministering to those who need it most, self-righteous people will object. Sometimes, even people of faith will not understand when God is pouring out new wine and requiring new wineskins to hold it: new methods and strategies and vehicles for communicating the same glorious gospel. Sometimes, when we live by faith, those who live by sight will ridicule and scorn us as foolish. Sometimes, even the obvious good we do for others will be called evil by those who are themselves deceived and under the sway of the evil one. How do we respond to such ill treatment in the service of the Lord? We could respond by quitting, which is the response the evil one hopes for. But far better is when we take our focus off of what the opposition is doing and rejoice in what God is doing. In spite of the opposition Jesus faced, a paralytic could walk, a tax-collector (and most likely some of his friends) received new life, a woman was healed from a twelve year illness, a child was raised from the dead, two blind men could see, and a mute man could talk, now free from the demon who had silenced him. Jesus didn't let opposition stop Him from going *"throughout all the cities and villages, teaching in their synagogues, preaching the gospel of the kingdom, and healing every sickness and every disease among the people"* (v. 35) because *"He was moved with compassion for them, because they fainted and were scattered, like sheep without a shepherd"* (v. 36).

PRAYER: Pray today for a heart of compassion that overcomes all opposition to doing the Lord's work. Remember Jesus' words of verses 37-38: *"The harvest truly is plentiful, but the laborers are few. Therefore, pray to the Lord of the harvest, that He will send out laborers into His harvest."*

THE MISSION
MATTHEW 10

In order to prepare them for their lifelong task of taking the gospel to the world, Jesus commissions and sends out His apostles on a preliminary mission, limited only to Israel (v. 6), and apparently for a specified time (v. 23, which is best seen as speaking of the duration of this assignment, not promising that Jesus would return during the lifetime of the apostles). They had traveled with Jesus and observed His teaching and ministry; now, He calls them to do the same works and preach the same message they had seen and heard (vv. 7-8). They were to go out without extensive supplies to teach them to rely upon God to provide for their needs (vv. 9-10). Jesus prepares them for what they will face on this journey by telling them that response to their message and ministry will be mixed. In some places they will be received gladly; in others, they will be rejected strongly (vv. 11-15). This preliminary mission is not only preparing them to minister, but "toughening them up" for their later mission after Jesus' resurrection and ascension, a mission in which the opposition will be much more intense (vv. 16-22). A disciple must recognize that such opposition is to be expected. After all, if Jesus faced such opposition (see Matthew 9), who are we to think that we will be spared as we minister and preach in His name (vv. 24-25)? In the face of potential, impending, or realized persecution, we must not draw back in fear, but go forward with even greater boldness (vv. 26-27), knowing that those to whom we proclaim the gospel are facing the much more fearful prospect of standing before the eternal, righteous Judge unprepared, and knowing that our Father is intimately involved and watching over us (vv. 29-31). When the temptation comes to deny our Lord in order to avoid persecution, we must speak up all the louder, confessing Him boldly before men (vv. 32-33). We should not be surprised if persecution arises even from among our closest relationships, from within even our own families (vv. 34-37), a most devastating level of betrayal to be sure. However, in spite of all the opposition, difficulty and persecution that the world and the evil one may throw at us, there are eternal rewards awaiting those who take up their crosses and follow Him (vv. 38-42).

PRAYER: Have you ever denied or downplayed your Christian faith in the face of ridicule, difficulty or opposition? If so, ask the Lord's forgiveness. Pray for boldness to stand strong even in the face of persecution, and for a willingness to die to self (the true meaning of taking up one's cross) in order to live for Him.

DISAPPOINTMENT WITH JESUS
MATTHEW 11

John the Baptist had recognized in Jesus a righteousness greater than his own even before he baptized Him. At His baptism, he had seen the Holy Spirit descend on Him as a dove (John 1:32-34), and had heard the voice of the Father proclaim, *"This is my beloved Son, in whom I am well pleased"* (Matthew 3:17). In light of this revelation of Jesus as the Messiah, John's preaching changed from "The Messiah is coming!" to "The Messiah is here, and His name is Jesus!" He publicly declared that *"He must increase, but I must decrease"* (John 3:30), urging those who had followed him to turn their ultimate allegiance to Jesus. But now, John has been thrown in prison after publicly condemning Herod's unlawful marriage. Languishing there day after day, he must have thought, "Surely, Messiah Jesus will soon rescue me from this prison. Surely, He can miraculously deliver me. I'm His relative, after all, and His forerunner." Perhaps John, like many of his time, misunderstood the mission of the Messiah and expected Him to be a military hero who would overthrow the Roman occupation of Israel. What was He waiting for? When no rescue came, doubts began to arise in his mind and heart. Did I miss it? Was I wrong about Him? Did I identify the wrong man as Messiah? Did I mislead my followers in telling them to follow Him? In his doubt, he sent two of his disciples to ask of Jesus, *"Are you the one who was to come, or should we expect someone else?"* (v. 3, NIV 84). Bitter disappointment has a way of eroding even the strongest faith. God doesn't always respond to our situations the way we think He should, in the timing we hoped He would, or in the manner we think we somehow "deserve." In our disappointment, we may begin to doubt our relationship with Him, or to doubt His goodness. The foul-breathed voice of the accuser whispers at times, and screams at other times, his accusations against us and against God: "God doesn't love you. If God loved you, you wouldn't be in this fix. If you were a better Christian, God would rescue you." And on and on it goes. Jesus answered that sharp query by telling John's disciples to go and tell John what they were witnessing even at the time they came to Jesus: *"The blind receive their sight and the lame walk, the lepers are cleansed and the deaf hear, the dead are raised up, and the poor have the gospel preached to them"* (v. 5). Maybe Jesus hadn't responded to John's current situation the way he thought the Messiah should have, but there was no doubt that John had been right about Him. His actions showed beyond a doubt that He was indeed the Lord's Christ. When we find ourselves disappointed with God's response to a current situation, we would be wise to remember all the many times He's shown Himself faithful and powerful on our behalf in the past. Rather than rebuke John for his doubts, Jesus bolstered his faith, and encouraged him to stand strong and not fall away (v. 6). Then, He spoke words of highest commendation of John to all who would hear (vv. 7-19). When John in his disappointment said the worst about Jesus, Jesus said the best about him.

PRAYER: Are you dealing with frustrating situations, difficult challenges, or even doubts about God and His goodness today? Jesus' words in verses 28-29 are especially for you: *"Come to Me, all you who labor and are heavily burdened, and I will give you rest. Take my yoke upon you, and learn from Me. For I am meek and lowly in heart, and you will find rest for your souls. For my yoke is easy, and my burden is* *light."* Rather than merely asking for relief from your situation, ask Him for His rest, His yoke (His control and guidance), and His lessons even in the midst of the situation.

LORD OF ALL
MATTHEW 12

As Jesus travels about ministering and teaching in Matthew 12, He continues to encounter opposition, primarily at this point from the Pharisees, a Jewish religious sect that had taken the Biblical commands in the Law and come up with all kinds of rules interpreting how to be obedient to them. To break one of their "Pharisee Rules," in their minds, made a person guilty of breaking the Law itself. When Jesus' disciples were going through the grainfields on the Sabbath, breaking off heads of grain as they made their way to the synagogue, the Pharisees protested that what they were doing was not lawful. Their problem was not that the disciples were breaking off the heads of grain, which was permissible as a person passed through the fields, but the fact that they were doing it on the Sabbath. Under the Pharisee Rules, even an act so simple constituted illegal work; they were, in the estimation of the Pharisees, "harvesting grain" on the Sabbath. Jesus made it plain, and showed Biblical precedent, that necessity at times would allow for such activity with no divine sanction. Going on from there to the synagogue, a "test case" was put before Jesus by those who were already growing in their opposition to Him. A man with a withered hand was brought to Him with the question, *"Is it lawful to heal on the Sabbath?"* (v. 10). Jesus' answer was masterful, exposing both their hypocrisy and His own compassion. He points out to them that all of them, if they had a sheep fall into a pit on the Sabbath, would labor to rescue the sheep, but yet they would condemn Him for using His power to heal a man on the Sabbath day. *"How much more valuable is a man than a sheep!"*

he declared (v. 12, NIV 84), and then set forth this principle, *"Therefore, it is lawful to do good on the Sabbath."* When He healed the man with the withered hand, the Pharisees, bested twice by Him in a single morning, were so angry they wanted Him dead, but He had proved His point that *"the Son of Man is Lord even of the Sabbath"* (v. 8). Soon after, Jesus delivered a demonized man from the demon that had made him both blind and mute, a notable miracle that led many people to believe that He could in fact be the long-awaited Messiah (v. 23). The Pharisees, though, still stinging over His violations of their rules, grumbled that *"This Man does not cast out demons except by Beelzebub the ruler of the demons"* (v. 24). His power over the demonic, they concluded, was evidence that He was in league with Satan himself. Jesus showed how warped their logic was. If He were truly doing the devil's work, He wouldn't be taking demons *out* of people, but putting them *into* people. If Satan (through Jesus) were casting demons out of people, they should rejoice and be glad, because the devil's kingdom would be fighting against itself and could not long stand. He proposes a much more likely scenario: that He is in league not with Satan, but with one mightier than Satan, the Holy Spirit, and it is through His power that demons flee and men are set free (vv. 25-32). Jesus shows Himself as Lord over the Spirit world, and He declares that He will judge those whose blind hatred has caused them to blaspheme the Holy Spirit by attributing His work to the devil (vv. 31-32). Indeed, He will judge all men for every idle word they speak (vv. 33-37). In verses 38-42, Jesus declares Himself greater than the prophet Jonah and King Solomon. He is Lord of the Sabbath, God's beloved Servant (v. 18), more powerful than the devil and all his forces, the one who will judge all men, and greater than the prophets and kings who came before Him (or all who came after Him, for that matter). And the wonder of wonders - this Sovereign Lord of All wants to be in an intimate, personal, family relationship with you and me (vv. 46-50)!

PRAYER: As Christians, we do not keep the Sabbath (the Sabbath is Saturday), but we do honor the Lord's Day, Sunday, as a day of rest and worship. Necessity sometimes takes us out of our normal Sunday routine, but if we were honest, some of our "necessities" really aren't all that necessary. Ask the Lord today where you may have dishonored His day, and how you can better honor Him by doing good on the Lord's Day.

PARABLES
MATTHEW 13

Jesus begins teaching the people in parables, stories taken from life from which spiritual lessons may be drawn. His reason is given in verses 10-17. Given the level of opposition that He has already endured, using parables allows Him to communicate spiritual truth to His followers without providing additional ammunition to those who have already decided that He deserves to die. To the initiated, the parables contained *"the mysteries of the kingdom of heaven"* (v. 11); to the uninitiated, they were just stories of mundane, everyday things like cooking, commerce or farming. Proverbs 25:2 says that *"It is the glory of God to conceal a thing, but the honor of kings is to search out a matter."* God's ultimate desire is not to conceal the truth from us, but to create in us a hunger for the truth. Jesus explains these first few parables, but later on, having shown His disciples the interpretive principles behind them, He for the most part stops explaining them. The first parable is the familiar story (and the familiar image for those who first heard it) of a sower going out to sow seed. In our day, farmers plow the ground and then plant seed in nice neat rows. Back then, farmers would first "broadcast" the seed, covering the ground with it, and then plow it under. Such a process invariably meant a loss of some of the seed. Some seed would be devoured by birds. Some would fall on rocky ground with just a little bit of topsoil above rock. These plants would spring up quickly, because the roots could only go so deep, but without that good root system, they would be unable to get enough moisture to survive the heat of the summer. Some seeds would fall among thorns, and the plants that grew would be choked out by the thorns. However, the seed that fell on good ground would produce a harvest, thirty, sixty or 100 times what was sown. Jesus explained that some people hear the Word, and the evil one immediately snatches it away. Others hear the Word and receive it on some level, but don't truly have any root in Christ. They fall away when it costs to be a Christian. Others hear the Word, but the cares of the world and the deceitfulness of riches choke it out, and it never comes to fruition. But then there are those who truly receive the Word, who are rooted in Christ and Christ alone. They produce fruit for the Kingdom - some more than others - but all produce fruit. A similar parable about the weeds and the wheat teaches us that the church will always be a mixed bag, with true believers and false professors occupying the same pew. In the ancient world, if a person had a grudge against another, he might seek revenge on his rival by oversowing his wheatfields with darnel, a weed that is almost indistinguishable from wheat until harvest time. The weeds would choke out much of the wheat, and take valuable moisture and nutrients away from the wheat that survived, resulting in a lesser yield. Darnel is similar enough to wheat that no one would risk trying to weed it out, lest in doing so he uproot the wheat entangled in its root system as well. The oversowing of fields was a common enough occurrence that there were laws enacted against it in the ancient world. Jesus is telling us that we may not always be able to tell the true believers from the false, but there will be a final judgment and a final separation at the time of the harvest, the end of the age. The two short parables in verses 44-45 have confused some. After all, salvation is free, but these parables seem to indicate that it is very costly. So, which is it? It's both. Salvation is free for all to receive, paid for by the blood of Jesus on the cross of Calvary. But receiving it costs us everything, as all that we are and all that we have are surrendered to His Lordship. Many are those (like the rich young ruler) who balk at such a price, but consider the parables. Why would any man sell all he had to buy a field with a treasure in it, or a precious pearl? The answer is obvious: the treasure or the pearl must be of far greater value than everything he has. Likewise, the gift of God - forgiveness of sin and eternal life in heaven - is of far greater value than anything we could ever obtain.

PRAYER: II Corinthians 13:5 (NIV 84) says, *"Examine yourselves to see whether you are in the faith; test yourselves."* Jesus' parables in this chapter should give us pause, especially in light of His earlier teachings that many of the mis-sown seed and darnel are blissfully unaware of their condition, believing fully that they are wheat sown in good soil and on their way to heaven (see Matthew 7:21-23). Is your faith truly in Christ and His sacrifice on the cross for salvation, not in good works you've done or religious ritual you've experienced or family background or church membership you hold? Have you surrendered your life fully to His Lordship? Is there evidence of fruit in your life? Pray that the Lord will show you if you are not in the faith. If you are not, call upon Him now in repentance and faith for salvation. If you are, thank Him that *"blessed are your eyes, for they see, and your ears, for they hear"* (v. 16).

WHEN STORMS ARE STILLED (AND WHEN THEY'RE NOT)
MATTHEW 14

The story of the second stilling of the storm (the first one was in Matthew 8:23-27) is an exciting account of Jesus' rescue of the disciples from a powerful storm at sea. Ferocious squalls are not unusual on the Sea of Galilee. It is a relatively small lake (13 miles long and seven miles wide), but it is very deep (150 feet) and is situated in a basin 680 feet below sea level surrounded by mountains. Storm systems come in suddenly over the mountains, stirring the waters to levels that can swamp a fishing boat, but those who sailed those waters regularly (and at last five of the disciples were Galilean fishermen) knew that such storms generally come in suddenly but blow out quickly. The wisdom of the day said to take down the sails, bail water like crazy, pray fervently, and hope it goes away quickly! But this storm seemed to be sitting on top of the disciples. It had gone on for hours, and unlike the last time they had faced such a storm, Jesus wasn't in the boat with them. Jesus had commanded the disciples to get into the boat, knowing full well that this storm was coming. Don't miss that point. They were in the storm not because they were out of the will of God, but precisely because they were in the will of God. There are some who will tell you that obedience to God produces nothing but "clear skies and smooth sailing," but that is simply not true. As we read the Bible, we find that there are three kinds of storms a believer can find himself in. The first kind is a storm of opposition, where the devil comes against us. Then there are storms of correction, when God disciplines us to bring us back in line with His will. That's the kind of storm Jonah sailed into when he disobeyed God. Then there is this kind of storm, a storm of perfection, where God teaches us lessons about Himself and helps us to grow. The disciples found themselves in this storm not because they were disobedient, but because they were obedient; not because God was disciplining them, but because God was discipling them, expanding their faith. After seeing the miracle of Jesus walking on the water, and His stilling of the storm, it is obvious that the storm has done its work. The faith of the disciples was growing. After the first stilling of the storm, they had proclaimed, *"What kind of Man is this that even the winds and the sea obey Him!"* (8:27). Now, they worship Him and proclaim, *"Truly, You are the Son of God"* (v. 33). As we celebrate the miraculous rescue of the disciples from their storm, though, let us not miss the fact that there is another storm in this chapter, recorded in verses 1-12, a storm without a miraculous rescue. John the Baptist found himself in a perfect storm of political intrigue, caught between a weak and vacillating leader and the machinations of a vicious, vengeful woman. The result was his gruesome death by beheading. Nowhere does the Word of God promise that we will never suffer for our faith, or that we will never face death in the cause of Christ. Many of our brethren today, particularly those in many Muslim-dominated areas, are being killed in horrible ways each day. Why them and not us? Why were the disciples rescued and John executed? Certainly, John was no less loved and no less committed to Christ than the disciples were. There is a mystery in who is rescued (or who is healed, for that matter) and who is not. That mystery calls us to trust, a trust best expressed by Shadrach, Meshach and Abednego to King Nebuchadnezzar: *"...our God whom we serve is able to deliver us from the burning fiery furnace...But even if He does not, be it known to you, O king, that we will not serve your gods, nor worship the golden image which you have set up"* (Daniel 3:17-18).

PRAYER: Are you in a storm today? Ask the Lord to reveal to you what kind of storm it is, and what He is trying to teach you. Is He teaching you to stand strong against the enemy? Is He trying to teach you that you made some poor decisions, some decisions that placed you outside His will? Or is He trying to stretch your faith, to teach you to trust Him more? Declare to Him that you will trust Him in the midst of the storm, and you will trust Him with the outcome of the storm.

CLEAN AND UNCLEAN
MATTHEW 15

Once again, Jesus and His disciples run afoul of "The Pharisee Rules," this time in regard to ritual washing before eating. All of us have been taught to wash our hands before eating as a matter of hygiene, but the concern of the scribes and Pharisees was not hygiene, but rather *"the tradition of the elders"* (v. 2) handed down to them from previous generations. The washing they speak of was a complicated ritual washing, and it was a matter of pure tradition, with no root whatsoever in the Scripture. The Pharisees had elevated their rules, regulations and rituals to the level of Scripture, even to the point of declaring that neglecting their washing ritual brought ritual defilement (v. 20). Indeed, as Jesus illustrates, they had even elevated their traditions *above* the level of Scripture. The specific example He gives is of the "Corban Vow," which again was a matter of pure tradition with no root in Scripture. When a person took the Corban Vow, he made a public announcement that upon his death, all of his goods would be sold and the proceeds given to the Temple treasury. After that vow, he would be free to use his wealth any way he deemed appropriate, but he could not give any of it away, for that would be "robbing the Temple." It seemed a pious thing to do, but Jesus pointed out that it was really just an excuse for greed, a loophole to avoid helping one's parents in their old age. Thus, in keeping their man-made tradition, they were breaking the Biblical commandment to honor their parents. Jesus goes on to explain that what defiles us is not some failure to adhere to outward rituals; true defilement comes from our corrupt hearts. The disciples were concerned that the Pharisees were offended by Jesus' teaching, but Jesus tells them to leave the Pharisees, that they are blind guides leading the blind. That must have been a shock to the disciples' system. All of their lives, they had been taught to respect the Pharisees, to look up to them as paragons of righteousness, and to listen to them as teachers of God's Law. As they continue to travel and minister, Jesus shows them by word and deed that much of what they had been taught their whole lives was false, particularly the ingrained prejudice they carried against non-Jews. Departing from Israel into the Gentile region of Tyre and Sidon, Jesus encounters a woman who begs Him to deliver her daughter from demonization. Taking together her descriptions in Matthew and Mark, she was a Greek-speaking woman of Canaanite ancestry living in a Gentile area. She may be the most Gentile person in the whole gospel! Why did He treat her with such harshness? Certainly, He was testing her faith, but He already knew the level of her faith (and He knew that He could treat her this way without her giving up on her request). This was an acted-out parable for the sake of the disciples. They had been taught their whole lives that Gentiles were unclean, and that the Messiah was for the Jews alone. Jesus treats her as all of the Pharisees and most Jewish men (including, no doubt, the disciples at this point of their lives) would have, but in the end, He grants her request and speaks to her kindly. From there, Jesus begins healing many people in that region. Verse 31's statement that "...*they glorified the God of Israel*" indicates that these were Gentiles He was ministering to. Jesus is teaching the disciples that He is not just the Messiah for the Jews, but for all people. Finally, there is the feeding of the 4000. The disciples had seen Jesus feed 5000 previously, but those were Jews. Eating with Gentiles was absolutely taboo among Jews (a taboo so ingrained, in fact, that long after he should have known better, Peter still struggled with this issue - see Galatians 2:31-34). Eating with Gentiles, they had been taught, would make them unclean. Would Jesus break even that cultural taboo? The answer was yes, and taking seven loaves and a few small fish, He fed the multitude.

PRAYER: Ask the Lord today to show you any area of your life where you might be elevating church tradition or religious tradition to the level of Scripture, or even beyond the level of Scripture. Ask Him to point out to you any areas of religious, racial or social prejudice you may have inherited from your elders. What people who are not like you is the Lord calling you to reach out to today?

THE SHOCKING CALL OF DISCIPLESHIP
MATTHEW 16

One of the great evidences for the truthfulness of the gospels is the fact that if the disciples had conspired together to make up the story, surely they would have made themselves look better. Throughout the gospels, they often come across as selfish, angry, vengeful, jealous, and slow to understand. Indeed, their inability to comprehend Jesus' comment to *"Take heed and beware the yeast of the Pharisees and Sadducees"* (v. 6) certainly makes them appear exceedingly dull. But let us not be too hard on the disciples. After all, within a short span of time, their lives and beliefs had been turned completely upside-down. They had found the long-awaited Messiah, and they had been taken into His inner circle as His closest followers, leaving behind homes, families and jobs to follow Him. They had seen Him do amazing miracles that showed Him as Lord over nature, over need, over sickness and over spirits. They had listened to His teaching, teaching that was fresh and new and different from any they'd ever heard, and indeed, they had seen Him reject (and tell them to reject) most of what they had been taught before and those who had taught it. They could see the hostility of the Pharisees and Sadducees, important and powerful people, rising against Him. Perhaps it wasn't that they were so dull. Perhaps they were just in shock. Earth-shattering things were happening in rapid succession, and the pace would only increase. At Caesarea Philippi, Jesus asked them what the crowds were saying about Him and His identity. Some in the crowds were identifying Him with John the Baptist, perhaps as Herod had done (14:2). Others said that He was Elijah, a reference to the Old Testament prophecy that said that Elijah would precede the Messiah's coming (Malachi 4:5-6), a prophecy fulfilled by John the Baptist. Still others were saying that Jesus was Jeremiah (there was a widespread Jewish belief that Jeremiah would return before the Messiah's coming), or that He was a prophet like the prophets of old. When Jesus asked (v. 15), *"But who do you say that I am?"* Peter spoke for them all in proclaiming, *"You are the Christ, the Son of the Living God."* What a revelation! And what a commendation from Jesus Peter received in response to this answer (vv. 17-19). Now that they had settled in their minds His identity as the Messiah, He must teach them His purpose for coming. If their heads were swimming before, imagine the impact of hearing that *"He must go to Jerusalem and suffer many things from the elders and chief priests and scribes, and be killed, and be raised on the third day"* (v. 21). We who know the full story can't fully appreciate what a shock it must have been to hear those words, and Peter reacts vehemently against this news, only to be rebuked harshly (compare v. 17 with v. 23). If Jesus' words about His own future were not disturbing enough, His words about their futures were no less ominous: *"If anyone will come after Me, let him deny himself, and take up his cross, and follow Me. For whoever would save his life will lose it, and whoever loses his life for My sake will find it."* Again, for us, those words have lost much of their meaning, lost in a sea of figurative speech (not that they don't have figurative meaning), but the disciples, living in that Roman-dominated culture, knew that anyone who carried a cross was carrying it to the place of execution, and was soon to be nailed to it to die a grisly death. Jesus certainly promised that it would be ultimately worth it (vv. 26-27), but it is a testament to the disciples' faith that they weren't running for the door!

PRAYER: Dietrich Bonhoeffer once said, "When Jesus calls a man, He bids him 'Come and die.'" We are all called to die to sin, to self, and to the world and its many enticements, and many down through the centuries and in various places today are called to die literally for the cause of Christ as martyrs. The word "martyr" (*martyrion* in Greek) originally meant simply "a witness." It picked up the connotation of one who dies for the faith because so many in those early centuries who witnessed faithfully of Christ were killed as a result. But what greater witness to our faith could there be than going to our deaths in full confidence of Jesus' words about eternal life? Pray today for the strength to give the ultimate testimony of your faith should circumstances demand it of you. Pray for those who are facing persecution and martyrdom around the world, that they will stand strong for Christ. Pray for the courage not only to die for Christ, but to die to self and live for Him each day.

THE TRANSFIGURATION
MATTHEW 17

The last verse of the previous chapter is fulfilled in verses 1-13, as Peter, James and John accompany Jesus to a high mountain where they see Him in all of His glory. It is an amazing sight, as His garments and His face shine with heavenly light, and Moses and Elijah appear to speak to Him. The sight is so mind-boggling that Peter begins to babble about building three shelters, one for Jesus, one for

Moses, and one for Elijah. By the way, isn't it interesting that in this heavenly vision, Peter instantly recognized Moses and Elijah? That should settle once and for all the age-old question many have about whether we will know our loved ones in heaven. Why *wouldn't* we know our loved ones in heaven? After all, there we will know even as we have been known (I Corinthians 13:12), knowing not only loved ones, but everyone! Peter's reaction to this magnificent experience parallels our own all too often. When God does something spectacular in our lives (or in our church), we want to "camp" there forever, when God wants us to move on with Him from glory to glory (II Corinthians 3:18). Many a denomination has been birthed out of revival fire, formed out of the desire to institutionalize a move of God, and the structure remains long after the fire has moved on. It has been said that throughout church history, some of the greatest obstacles to what God is doing in a current move are those God most used in a previous move. God the Father's statement to the disciples that *"This is my beloved Son, with whom I am well pleased. Listen to Him"* (v. 5) served to assuage their doubts about Him and the frightening direction His teaching had taken (see previous devotional). Jesus would continue to prepare them for His impending death and resurrection (vv. 22-23) from this point on in His ministry, and though they were sorrowful over it, they never abandoned Him. When they came down the mountain to the crowds, a man came to Jesus begging Him to heal his son, an epileptic who often fell into water and fire during his seizures. The disciples had been unable to heal him, which brought a cry of despair from Jesus (v. 17). The measure of a mature disciple is that he can carry on his master's work in the master's absence. The disciples' failure to deal with the situation, or even apparently to properly diagnose it not as a physical ailment needing healing, but as a spiritual ailment needing deliverance, demonstrated how far they still had to go. Jesus cast out the demon causing the disease, and the boy was healed instantly. So-called "mountaintop" experiences in our Christian lives (revivals, conferences, camps, powerful worship experiences, etc.) are wonderful times of refreshing, equipping and inspiration, but the distance from the mountain to the valley can be a precipitous drop indeed. But the real work of ministering to the hurting and discipling those younger in the faith (vv. 19-23) happens in the valley of day-to-day living. Even something as mundane as paying taxes can contain a spiritual lesson, a practical lesson and a faith-building exercise (vv. 24-27). The two-drachma tax was collected from all Jewish adult males yearly for the upkeep of the Temple in Jerusalem. Jesus made the point to Peter that as the Son of God, He of all people should be exempt from a tax levied for the upkeep of His Father's house. However, He taught Peter a practical lesson in paying the tax. Jesus, as we have seen, was never afraid of offending those whose teaching contradicted His own, but in many lesser matters, it is better to take the loss than to prove the point at the cost of unnecessary offense.

PRAYER: Have you been guilty of trying to "camp out" on the mountaintop of experiences with God? Ask the Lord today where you can minister to the hurting and disciple the younger in your everyday walk. Ask Him also to give you wisdom to know when to prove a point, and when to avoid unnecessary offense.

FORGIVENESS AND UNFORGIVENESS
MATTHEW 18

In Hebrews 12:15 (NIV 84), we are told to *"See to it that...no root of bitterness grows up to cause trouble and defile many."* Bitterness is like a weed that starts small but eventually chokes out the fruitbearing plants, and that root of bitterness can strangle the spiritual life and usefulness of even the most committed Christian. In response to how we should handle offenses committed against us, Peter asked the question, *"Lord, how often shall I forgive my brother who sins against me? Up to seven times?"* Peter was willing to forgive seven times, which he no doubt thought was pretty good considering that the rabbis taught their disciples to forgive only three times. When Peter suggested seven, he probably thought that Jesus would commend him. How magnanimous he was! How spiritual! Twice as much as expected, plus one more for good measure! But then Jesus took the wind right out of his sails. "No, Peter, not seven times, but 70 times seven." Even with that huge number, Jesus didn't mean that we are to count off 490 times, and then stop forgiving. What he was saying was, "Peter, if you're counting, you're not truly forgiving." True forgiveness takes away *all* of the anger, *all* of the bitterness, *all* of the desire for revenge. Peter wanted to hold onto 1/7 of the bitterness of each offense, just enough to keep a record, and after seven offenses, then he would feel justified in getting his revenge. True forgiveness, though, issues a full pardon, not a partial, incomplete one. Jesus then told a story about a man who owed the king 10,000 talents that he could not pay, so the king ordered the man and his family sold into slavery. The debtor begged the king for patience and promised that he would repay the money. He may have been sincere, but there is no way he could have repaid that amount. We're talking about 600,000 day's wages; it would take almost 2000 years to pay off that sum! But the king had compassion, and completely canceled his huge debt. He took the financial loss himself and let the man go free. But verse 28 says that this slave went out and found a fellow slave who owed him a trifling amount in comparison to what he had owed. This fellow slave responded in the same manner that he had, asking for more time, but he refused to forgive as he had been forgiven, and he threw the man into debtor's prison. The point of the parable is obvious. Like the man in the parable, we owed a sin debt that we could not possibly pay. No amount of good works or effort could have ever repaid that debt. But God in His mercy, because of Jesus' sacrifice on the cross, freely forgave us when we came to Him in repentance, placing our faith in Christ and surrendering our lives to His Lordship. Jesus paid the price for our sins so we could go free. In light of how much we've been forgiven, it is inexcusably wicked for us to refuse to forgive others. Whatever they may have done to us, it pales in comparison to what our sins did to Christ. Refusing to forgive locks us away in a prison of our own bitterness, removed from fellowship (though not relationship) with God, and bereft of many of the joys of being a Christian. Three quick points need to be made about forgiveness. Number one, true forgiveness is not just external. Jesus said we must forgive from the heart. We can tell someone, "I forgive you" and act like all is well even while still harboring thoughts of bitterness or revenge. Second, true forgiveness is an act of the will. We think of the heart as the seat of the emotions, but the Greeks saw it as the seat of the will. If you're waiting for some wonderful feeling, some emotional wave of forgiveness to just wash over you, you'll never forgive. Forgiveness is not a feeling. We choose to forgive out of obedience to God's command, not because we feel like forgiving, but when we truly forgive, the feelings will follow. Third, forgiveness is a decision made today that must be reiterated tomorrow. After the decision to forgive is made, at some point in the future, something will bring that offense to mind yet again. At that point, we must decide whether to reiterate that forgiveness or revoke that forgiveness.

PRAYER: Ask the Lord today to show you any "bitter weed" of bitterness that may be growing in your heart. Ask Him to show you anyone you are harboring a grudge against, refusing to forgive. Thank Him for His forgiveness of you, and extend that same amazing grace to whoever has offended you. If you are struggling to forgive, ask the Lord to give you the willingness to forgive.

TEACH YOUR CHILDREN WELL
MATTHEW 19

"Jesus loves the little children, all the children of the world..." Most of us learned that song as children, but the gospel of Matthew shows us the truth of it. Think of all the children mentioned so far in the gospel. Jesus raised a 12-year-old girl from the dead (9:25), a little boy (John 6:9) surrendered his lunch to feed the multitude (14:13-21), a Canaanite girl was delivered from demonization after her mother fought through an initial rebuff (15:21-28), and a boy was healed from demonically-inspired seizures when his father refused to get discouraged by the disciples' failure and brought the boy to Jesus (17:14-18). In the previous chapter, Jesus used a child to teach the apostles about true greatness in the Kingdom (18:1-5). He stated that *"whoever welcomes a little child like this in my name welcomes me"* (18:5 - NIV 84) and He went on to issue two grave warnings to those who would harm children: *"But if anyone causes one of these little ones who believe in me to sin, it would be better for him to have a large millstone hung around his neck and to be drowned in the depths of the sea"* and *"See to it that you do not look down on one of these little ones. For I tell you that their angels in heaven always see the face of my Father in heaven"* (18:6, 10 - NIV 84). How shocking then, considering Jesus' example and teaching, that the disciples would rebuke the children who were coming to Jesus, which then drew a sharp rebuke from Him to them! Don't ever overlook children, viewing them as unimportant. God views them with delight as enormously valuable and dear to Him. I find it interesting that this incident is sandwiched between Jesus' teaching on divorce and His encounter with the rich young ruler. The most effective vehicle for passing the faith along to future generations is the home, but one of the most destructive forces impacting many children today is divorce. Numerous studies show that the best environment for a child to grow and prosper is an intact home with his biological mother and father. The ease of divorce in Jesus' time (some rabbis of the day would grant a divorce for such trivialities as the wife oversalting her husband's eggs or burning a meal) had conspired no doubt to rob many children of an intact home. Many men were taking advantage of the liberal rabbis' lax standards to divorce their wives, who had borne their children, in order to marry younger or more attractive women. Jesus said that although they had made it technically legal, to divorce one's wife for some reason other than marital unfaithfulness on her part and marry another was still adultery in the eyes of God. The disciples' next statement (v. 10) is a testament to how deeply ingrained this easy divorce was in that culture. If a man can't get out of a marriage, they were saying, it is better not to marry! In our day, decades of "no fault divorce" has likewise created a culture of divorce, a culture where people actually go into marriage with the attitude of "if this doesn't work out, we can always get a divorce." The statistics are often repeated that 50% of all marriages end in divorce, and that the rate of divorce among church members is the same or higher than the unchurched. Neither statistic is true. The ratio of divorce to marriages hit 50% for one year back in the 70s; today, the divorce rate is hovering somewhere around 30%, and the rate of divorce among professing Christians is actually quite a bit lower than that. But every divorce represents a colossal human tragedy, and the collateral damage when a family implodes always falls disproportionately upon the children. And divorce is often passed down generationally. Those who come from broken homes are more likely to experience divorce themselves, if indeed they ever marry. Clearly, one of the best thing parents can do for their children is to love their spouses!

The rich young ruler's story is a tragedy of a young man who, for whatever reason, had not been properly taught in childhood. As a result, he believed that eternal life is a prize to be earned through good deeds (v. 16). He was trained to be "good," but was never shown that he was a sinner in need of God's mercy (vv. 18-20), and he was deceived into believing that earthly riches are of greater importance than spiritual things (v. 22). I wonder how many parents today are training their children to behave in socially acceptable ways, and to pursue "the American dream" of a good education, a good job, a good salary, and a nice home, rather than training them to seek first the Kingdom of God and His righteousness (Matthew 6:25-34). What a tragedy when someone gains the whole world (or everything the world says is important) and loses his soul (16:26)!

PRAYER: Think about the children in your life - your children, grandchildren, nieces, nephews or others. Ask the Lord to open your eyes that you might never overlook them. Ask Him how you can be a part of training the next generation of children through your church or otherwise. Pray for the marriages of those couples you know with children.

THE UPSIDE-DOWN KINGDOM
MATTHEW 20

Jesus' statement that *"the first will be last, and the last first"* (19:30, see also 20:16), seems strange to our ears, but it points to a powerful truth: the Kingdom of God functions very differently from the values and thinking of the world. Jesus' parable of the workers in the vineyard cannot help but arouse a response of "That's not fair!" We sympathize with the workers in the story who worked hard all day, only to be paid the same wage as those who worked only an hour. Even if we understand the logic of the landowner's reasoning in verses 13-15, that he was not cheating the early workers, but merely exercising his right to be generous to the later workers, it still seems an affront to justice somehow. And it would be, if the parable were a treatise on labor relations, but it's not. Rather, it's a statement about the Kingdom of Heaven (v. 1), and the magnificent truth it teaches us is that entry into the Kingdom is not a matter of how long we've worked or how hard we've worked in the Lord's vineyard; salvation is a matter of hearing and heeding the Master's call! If it were a matter of works, of doing enough good works to somehow outweigh the bad, some would be hopelessly lost, too old in getting to the starting point to make sufficient headway against the lifetime of sin they've accumulated. But it's not a matter of works, but of the generosity (grace) of the Master toward those who answer His call, *whenever* they answer it (v. 15). It is never too late to answer the Lord's call to salvation, but it is foolish to put off answering it until a later time. There was a point in the story where the landowner stopped gathering more workers and turned His attention to rewarding those previously called. Likewise, there will come a day when the Lord's call to salvation ends (and it may end at any moment for any of us through our deaths), and the result will be rewards for those who answered that call, and judgment for those who didn't. James and John's request of Jesus, voiced through their mother, serves to illustrate again how Kingdom values cut cross-grain to worldly values. Jesus had already promised the Twelve the top spots in the Kingdom (19:28), but James and John were not satisfied with being in the top twelve. They wanted to be number one and number two. Their attempt to do an end-around the others caused the others to be indignant with them, but Jesus explained another facet of the upside-down nature of the Kingdom. Unlike the world (*"the Gentiles"*), where rulers *"lord it over them, and those who are great exercise authority over them"* (v. 25), the greatest in the

Kingdom are not those barking orders at others, but those who are servants of all; not those who are served, but those who serve. Our prime example of that truth? Jesus Himself, who *"did not come to be served, but to serve and to give His life as a ransom for many"* (v. 28).

PRAYER: We are living in a world that urges us to "look out for number one," a dog-eat-dog world that applauds the ruthless ambition to be the top dog. Even in the church, servanthood often gives way to "serve-me-hood," an entitlement mentality that says that if everything's not to my liking, I'm taking my ball and bat (or rather, my tithe and attendance) and going elsewhere where I can get a "better deal." Pray that the Lord will show you any areas of your life where you have bought into the world's value system. Ask Him to open up opportunities for you to pursue true greatness in His eyes through serving others.

CLEANING HOUSE
MATTHEW 21

When Jesus made His Triumphal Entry into Jerusalem to begin Passion Week, it was a provocative act to be sure, full of Messianic overtones. Many no doubt at the time recalled the Messianic prophecy of Isaiah recorded in verse 5: *"Look, your King is coming to you, humble, and sitting on a donkey."* The crowd's waving of palm branches, hailing Him as the "Son of David" (a Messianic title) and crying out "Hosanna" ("save us") all pointed to the belief of many of them that He was the Messiah, coming to Jerusalem to lead a rebellion against the hated Romans and set up His Kingdom. That was not His intent, of course. He was not a warrior-Messiah satisfied with a mere earthly kingdom; He was coming to set up a much different kind of Kingdom. But make no mistake. This *was* an invasion. He was coming to Jerusalem to clean house, beginning with His house (v. 13), the Temple. The cleansing of the Temple of the money-changers and sacrifice-sellers addressed an abuse of the worshipers that had been going on for years. The priests at the Temple would sell "pre-approved" animals for sacrifice at exorbitant prices, and would routinely disqualify animals brought in from the outside as somehow blemished and unacceptable for sacrifice. Not only were they overcharging for the sacrificial animals, the priests had come up with another scheme to squeeze profit from those sincere worshipers who desired to obey God's commands: Temple money. Because Roman money had a portrait of Caesar on one side, and his claim to divinity on the other, Roman money was considered idolatrous and could not be used in the Temple. Those desiring to purchase an animal would have to trade their Roman money for inoffensive Tyrian shekels, at a high exchange rate, of course. Jesus' violent expulsion of the money-changers and sacrifice-sellers shows His determination that, if only for a few days, the Lord's Temple would be what He desired it to be: a place of prayer, a place of healing, a place of worship, and a place of truth (vv. 13-16). This act of disrupting the commerce of the Temple, during the busy and lucrative Passover week no less, began an ongoing conflict between Jesus and the Jewish authorities for the rest of the week, culminating in their having Him arrested and crucified. The cursing of the fig tree (vv. 18-19) is an acted-out parable about what is to come in Israel's future. Because fig trees put forth their fruit before their leaves, the fact that the tree was in leaf (Mark 11:13) held forth the promise of fruit, but upon inspection, it had none. Because the tree had not produced fruit, it was cursed and withered away. The same was true of the Jewish nation (often symbolized as a fig tree) and particularly its leadership, which looked good on the outside, but had not produced the fruit of true inner righteousness God required. They would soon bring a curse on themselves through their rejection of the Messiah (27:25), and then the nation would wither for a generation until it was finally destroyed by the Romans in A.D. 70. Jesus predicts this house-cleaning to come: *"the kingdom of God will be taken from you and given to a nation bearing its fruits,"* i.e., the church. The authorities' failed attempts to trap Jesus (such as in verses 23-27), and His not-so-veiled references to them in His parables (vv. 28-44) only served to heighten their frustration and anger (vv. 45-46).

PRAYER: The Bible teaches that judgment, and revival, always begin in the Lord's house, among His people. Ask the Lord to show you any areas of your "Temple" where there is a need of "house-cleaning." Ask Him to show you any areas of your life where you may look good to others, but under the all-seeing inspection of Christ, there is no fruit being produced for Him.

ULTIMATE LOYALTY
MATTHEW 22

In the first 14 verses of chapter 22, Jesus tells another parable whose meaning could not be missed by His enemies standing close by, a parable that expanded on his statement of 21:43: *"...the kingdom of God will be taken from you and given to a nation bearing its fruits."* The parable concerns a king holding a wedding feast for his son. He issued invitations to many, but they laughed off the invitation and refused to come. If that weren't bad enough, they seized the servants issuing the invitations, treated them terribly, and even killed them. The king in his anger sent his army to destroy those murderers and burn their city. As with many of Jesus' teachings during these final days before the crucifixion, this parable foreshadows Israel's imminent rejection of Him as Messiah and the not-so-distant destruction of Jerusalem as a result. It should be noted that most of Jesus' early followers were in fact Jews, and there have been Jewish believers in

Him in every generation, but the nation as a whole, influenced by their leadership, rejected Him, resulting in God's judgment on them at the hands of the Romans in 70 A.D. In the story, when those originally invited to the feast refused to come, the invitation was then extended to others, representing the fact that the gospel would go to the Gentiles, and the Gentiles would be the primary ones who received it. But there is a word of caution in the latter part of the story. When the king came in to view his guests, one man was in the banquet hall without wedding garments. Given that wedding garments were supplied by the host, there was no excuse not to have wedding garments on, and this man in his regular clothing was an affront to the king. He was therefore bound hand and foot, and thrown out of the banquet hall *"into outer darkness, where there will be weeping and gnashing of teeth"* (v. 13). The lesson for us is that it is not enough to hear God's invitation to salvation, or even to answer it in a superficial way (see Matthew 13:20-21). A true internal change must take place that only comes through true faith in Christ, an internal change that clothes us in the righteousness that the Father provides. No Christian will be sinlessly perfect on this side of heaven, but those who claim to be born again, yet still walk in the same patterns of sin as before they were "saved," need to seriously question whether they are just hanging around the banquet hall still clothed in the rags of sin, destined to be cast into the outer darkness and horrible agony of hell. In light of the parable's devastating prediction of their near future, the Pharisees and the Herodians come to Jesus to try to trap Him. These two groups normally hated each other, but they had found a common enemy in Jesus. The Pharisees hated Roman rule in Israel, whereas the Herodians were supportive of it. After trying to set Him up with flattery (v. 16), the loaded question they posed to Jesus in verse 17 was, *"Is it lawful to pay taxes to Caesar, or not?"* The Pharisees knew that many of those in the crowd bristled at

Roman rule and the high taxes they were forced to pay to the empire. This Jewish resentment of the Roman occupation would eventually lead to the rebellion that resulted in the destruction of the nation and the dispersing of the people in 70 A.D. The Pharisees taught that it was wrong to pay taxes to Caesar, because Caesar claimed to be a god, but it was an abstract theological argument, voiced no doubt behind closed doors. They dared not cross the Roman authorities by actually refusing to pay the taxes. The Herodians if course, supported paying taxes to Caesar. By posing this question to Jesus publicly, they thought they had Him in a no-win situation. If he declared that it was right to pay taxes to the hated Romans, the Pharisees knew that many in the crowd would be disappointed, and would stop following Him. If He said that it was wrong to pay taxes to Caesar, the Herodians could have Him arrested for inciting rebellion against Roman law. Jesus asked for a Roman denarius. On one side of the coin was a portrait of Caesar, and on the other his inscription that claimed divinity: "Caesar is Lord." Many scholars believe that when Jesus said, *"Render therefore to Caesar the things that are Caesar's"* (v. 21), He held the coin up with the face of Caesar showing, but when He went on to say, *"and to God the things that are God's"* He turned it to show Caesar's blasphemous inscription. In this one line, Jesus taught once and for all that we do owe a certain degree of loyalty and support to earthly governments, even corrupt ones, but our ultimate loyalty is to God and God alone. We are called to obey the laws of human governments until and unless they require of us what God forbids or forbid us to do what God requires. In those cases, God's commands come first.

PRAYER: You have been invited to the marriage supper of the Lamb (Revelation 19:5-9). Have you received that invitation and the pure white wedding garments that go with it? Or are you still walking in the rags of the old life of sin? Ask the Lord into your heart today as your Lord and Savior, repenting of your sin and placing your faith in His sacrifice on the cross. Ask the Lord to show you anywhere your appropriate loyalty to your government may be lacking, or where your ultimate loyalty to Him may be.

WOE TO YOU!
MATTHEW 23

Matthew 23 shows us Jesus at His most intense. After numerous efforts of the Jewish authorities to trap Him, He rings out with a scathing indictment against His main antagonists, the teachers of the Law (or scribes) and Pharisees. He begins by speaking to the crowds about them in verses 2-12, but from verse 13 on He addresses them directly in the form of seven woes, all marked by the opening expression, *"Woe to you, teachers of the law and Pharisees, you hypocrites!"* (v. 13 NIV 84). There are actually eight woes in the passage if we include *"Woe to you, blind guides"* in verse 16, but the passage is commonly called "The Seven Woes" because of the seven that begin with that characteristic refrain. Jesus excoriates the Pharisees for their hypocritical false religion, a false religion that looked good on the outside, but yet produced no fruit (see Matthew 21:18-19 and the previous devotion on it). We often hear the word "hypocrite" thrown around lightly, but the origin of the word is instructive to us. It was a word taken from the ancient Greek theatre. In Greek plays, actors wore large masks that covered their entire heads and rested on their shoulders. If a play had several parts that were not on stage at the same time, the director would hire a single actor to play them all. That actor, who would go off-stage, change masks, and emerge as someone else entirely, was called "the hypocrite" (which means "under a mask"). In time, the word came to mean someone who wears masks figuratively, someone who is one thing in one situation and something else in another, or, as in the case with the Pharisees, someone who shows forth a veneer of righteousness that covers up the corruption in their hearts. Jesus condemns them for their arrogance and pompous piety (vv. 5-12), their teaching of falsehood that leads people to hell (v. 13), their abuse of the helpless (v. 14), their "fingers-crossed-behind-the-back" oath-taking (vv. 16-22) and their laser focus on minor points of the Law even while oblivious to more important matters (vv. 23-24). All of these offenses, though, are merely symptoms of the real problem (vv. 25-28). The Pharisees' ongoing conflict with Jesus throughout His ministry was over the nature of true righteousness. To the Pharisees, righteousness was a matter of keeping the commandments and their corollary rules. They had convinced themselves that they *could* keep the Law perfectly, even though it was given to show people their sin and need of a Savior. Keep the external rules, they taught, and God will overlook your sinful heart. Jesus taught that true righteousness is not from the outside in, but from the inside out. Our only hope of attaining the true inner righteousness that God demands is to approach Him in repentance and faith, allowing Him to cleanse our wicked hearts. The last woe (vv. 29-35) contains yet another prophecy of the impending destruction of the nation, the city and the Temple, and tells the reason for that judgment to come. That generation was about to do something so heinous that it would *"Fill up...the measure of <their> fathers' guilt"* (v. 32), an act that would be as evil as all previous evil combined (see also verse 35-36). Their forefathers had murdered the prophets (v. 31), but they were going to murder the Son of God Himself. Their judgment for that crime would not be immediate (about 40 years would pass), and during that time, God, despite the horrible nature of their sin against Him, would continue to hold forth the offer of mercy through His servants (v. 34). Though many individuals would repent and be saved (see Acts 2, for example), the nation as a whole would not repent, and God's awful judgment would fall. Verse 37 is a poignant indicator that what initially appears to be an angry tirade of Jesus against His persecutors is in fact the broken-hearted final appeal of a spurned lover. When Jesus had cleansed the Temple earlier in the week, He had declared that *"My house shall be called a house of prayer"* (21:13). Now, as He exits the Temple, he declares, *"Look, your house is left to you desolate"* (v. 38). For just a few days, the Temple had been what God always desired it to be, but now, as Jesus leaves it, never to return during His first sojourn on Earth (v. 39), it is left desolate of the presence of God, awaiting its eventual destruction. There is in verse 39, however, a hint of the still-future turning of the Jewish people to Him (Romans 11:25-27; Revelation 7:1-8), a turning that seems to be related to the Lord's future coming (Zechariah 12:10, Revelation 1:7).

PRAYER: Are there any areas of your life where you wear a religious mask? Are you consistent in your faith-walk, or does your faithfulness vary with your settings and circumstances? Ask the Lord to forgive you for any hypocrisy in your life, and to reveal any area of mask-wearing you may not be able to see.

AND THEN THE END WILL COME
MATTHEW 24

The study of eschatology (last things) tends to be controversial in our age. Numerous interpretive schemes have been put forth to explain and systematize the teachings of Jesus, Old Testament prophecies, references in the epistles, and of course, the difficult-to-understand final book of the Bible, Revelation. Anytime there is such a degree of disagreement among reputable scholars, it usually points to the fact that the Bible itself is not abundantly clear. Such is usually the case with predictive prophecy; it only comes into sharp focus after its fulfillment. Jesus came the first time exactly as the Word predicted, but not fully like anyone expected. I suspect that His second coming will be the same: exactly as predicted, but like no one expects. Whatever your particular beliefs about the end times, there are some truths that are evident from Jesus' teachings in Matthew 24:

> *Suffering is not an anomaly; it is the nature of life on this fallen planet.* Everything Jesus talks about in verses 4-14 were present in the first century (*"this generation"* - v. 34) and have been present in every generation since, including ours. We in America know little of the persecution and suffering that our brethren down through the centuries have faced and that our brethren in various places around the world today are still facing.

> *Jesus IS going to return to Planet Earth.* His first coming was marked by suffering, pain and death as He fully entered into the horrors of this fallen planet. When He comes again, He will come *"with power and great glory"* (v. 30), a public, absolute, final vindication of Him and His people (vv. 30-31). Christ's future coming, His Millennial reign on Earth, and the final state of heaven comprise the church's blessed hope.

> *We will meet the Lord in the air, not on the ground.* Anyone claiming to be Christ on Earth (vv. 23-28) is a false Christ. There have been such false Christs in all generations, and they have fooled many, but the true believers will not be fooled (v. 24); they know that His coming will be absolutely unmistakable (v. 27).

> *No one knows the day or the hour of His coming.* Despite the statement of Jesus in verse 36, many date-setters down through the centuries have claimed to be

the exception to the rule. The Father and the Father alone knows when Christ's coming will be.

The world will be caught by surprise by His coming, but believers are to live in expectation of His coming. The so-called "signs of the times" are such that all believers in every age could reasonably expect that His coming could be at any time. Therefore, they should not be surprised when His coming happens (vv. 42-44). This knowledge of the possibility of His "any moment" appearing is an incentive for holy living and consistent, diligent service to Him in the here and now (vv. 45-51). The unbelieving world, though, will be completely taken by surprise by His coming (vv. 37-41).

While we watch and wait for His appearing, our task is to evangelize the world. "And this gospel of the kingdom will be preached throughout the world as a testimony to all nations, and then the end will come" (v. 14). There is a certain degree of gospel penetration into the world that must take place prior to the end. We do not know at what point the evangelization of the world will be sufficient to fulfill this prophecy, but we do know this: if the Lord has not returned, our task is not yet finished.

PRAYER: Pray today for worldwide evangelism efforts, and ask the Lord how you can be involved in evangelizing *your* world. Who do you know who needs to hear the gospel?

GIVE ME OIL IN MY LAMP
MATTHEW 25

Jesus' Olivet Discourse concludes with two parables of warning and a teaching on judgment. In the Parable of the

Ten Virgins, ten virgins went out to meet the bridegroom carrying lamps, but only five of them had oil for their lamps. The five foolish virgins missed the bridegroom's coming and were left out of the wedding banquet. Even though they reference him as "Lord," he states, *"Truly I say to you, I do not know you"* (v. 12). What is the symbolic meaning of these two groups of virgins? I believe that the wise virgins are those who are truly born again and indwelt by the Holy Spirit. They have oil (a common Biblical image for the Holy Spirit) in their lamps. The unwise virgins represent those who have some connection to the faith, but are not truly born again. They may have given mental assent to the truth of the gospel, but they have not been truly converted, and therefore are not indwelt by the Holy Spirit (see also 7:21-23). The two groups were indistinguishable from each other – they were all virgins, and all carrying lamps - until it came time to light the lamps at the approach of the bridegroom, and then the truth, so to speak, came to light. Jesus taught us often that the church would be a mixed bag of true believers and deceived unbelievers dwelling side-by-side, but at the time of His coming, "the weeds and the wheat" will be separated (13:24-30). Jesus' concluding words to *"Watch therefore, for you know neither the day nor the hour in which the Son of Man is coming"* (v. 13) is another warning that His coming can be at any time. Foolish indeed are those who recognize the truth of the gospel and yet put off responding in faith to it. This parable is a call to *"Examine yourselves, seeing whether you are in the faith: test yourselves"* (II Corinthians 13:5) to *"make your calling and election sure"* (II Peter 1:10) - before it's too late! The Parable of the Talents and the vision of the judgment of the nations both give us clues about how we can make our calling and election sure. All of us have different levels of gifts, talents and abilities. Those who are truly in Christ recognize that they are stewards of all that they have been given, and can be counted upon to invest the Lord's gifts in the work of the

Kingdom, with the hope of "Kingdom profit" following. Those who invest their lives in other things show that they don't really know the Master (does verse 24 truly reflect what we see of the master earlier in the parable?). Likewise, those who are truly in Christ are willing to minister, as Jesus did, to *"the least of these"* - the poor, the hurting and the sick - knowing that in doing so, they are ministering to the Lord Himself.

PRAYER: The teaching of Matthew 25 should give all of us pause. Are we truly in the faith, truly born again and indwelt by the Holy Spirit, or are we just dwelling in the vicinity of those who are, a close counterfeit, but not the real thing? Do our lives show forth the signs that accompany true salvation, the giving of ourselves and our possessions as stewards in the work of the Kingdom, and the willingness to love and minister to the least of these? Pray for discernment of your spiritual condition today. If the Lord reveals to you that you're not truly saved, then for heaven's sake (literally!), ask Jesus into your heart as Lord and Savior, turning from your sins and in faith receiving what He did for you on the cross of Calvary. If you are truly in the Kingdom, ask Him to show you how you can be a more faithful steward of all He's given you, and how you can have a more active ministry to the lost and hurting.

REACTING TO JESUS
MATTHEW 26

The die is cast. The Jewish authorities have made up their minds: Jesus must die. They decide to seize Him covertly and hand Him over to the Romans for execution at some point after the Passover Feast. Their fear is that with the city swelled with thousands of Passover pilgrims, word of Jesus' arrest might cause a riot that would jeopardize their position with the Roman authorities. When Judas comes forward, offering to betray Jesus into their hands at a time and place away from the crowds, they determine to go forward with their plot. It is interesting to note the different ways those around Jesus react to Him in this chapter. For the woman with the alabaster box of perfume (John tells us it was Mary of Bethany), her reaction to Him is one of absolute adoration, expressed in expensive sacrifice, no doubt fueled by Jesus' raising of her brother from the dead (John 11). Judas, angered by what he viewed as a waste (and more so a wasted opportunity for him to have more money to steal - John 12:5-6), and concerned lest he get caught up in the authorities' murderous ambitions against Jesus, decides it is time to switch sides. He has tagged along with Jesus thus far, stealing from the money box, enjoying the "show," and hoping to be a mover and shaker in an earthly kingdom. Now that it's obvious that there is no earthly kingdom forthcoming (at least not imminently), he formulates a plan to leave Jesus, ingratiate himself to the Jewish authorities and get a new start on life by betraying Him for money. That He would betray Jesus with a kiss, a sign of affection, just highlights the heinousness of the betrayal. For the disciples, there is a vacillation between confidence (v. 35) and question (vv. 21-22) about their own commitment. For Peter, James and John, the weakness of the flesh takes over (v. 41) and they slumber during Jesus' most difficult hour, when He most needed the comfort and companionship of His closest friends. For Peter, in particular, there is a boastful arrogance (v. 33), and a violent effort at defense (v. 51, again, John's gospel gives us his name as the sword-wielding assailant), followed by the three denials before sunrise that Jesus had predicted. And of course, there are the false accusations and violent reactions levied against Jesus by the Sanhedrin (vv. 59-68). Many today respond in the same ways to Jesus. There are those who are violently opposed to Him, leveling against Him, His teachings and His followers all manner of false charges. Oftentimes, arguments and animosity give way to violence against His body, the church. There are believers like Peter, who are boastful about their relationship to Him, and always seeking to "defend" Him in the strongest of terms, but also those who, like Peter, deny Him (either implicitly or explicitly) when the pressure is on. There are those who are slumbering while God's directives (such as the Great Commission) go unheeded, seduced by the lure of the flesh rather than the call of the Spirit. There are those who are unsure of their commitment, confident today and wavering tomorrow, and others who make a show of following Jesus out of a desire for some kind of earthly benefit, but whose true colors come out when the demands of true discipleship emerge. And then there are those like Mary - absolutely sold out, laying their all on the altar, so enamored in their love and gratitude to Him that no one's criticism matters and no sacrifice is too extreme. Such followers often garner criticism from the world (and even from within the church - vv. 8-9) but receive high praise from the Lord; indeed, even in this devotion, we are fulfilling a loving promise and prophecy made about Mary by Jesus (v. 13).

PRAYER: Where will you stand when "crunch time" comes? When the call of true discipleship comes, will you answer, or will you be slumbering and oblivious to that call? Will you waver in your commitment? Will you deny your Lord under pressure? Will you be shown not to be a true disciple after all? Or will you be like Mary, completely sold out to Him and His cause, no matter the cost? Pray for grace to stand strong under whatever pressure the world brings against you. Pour upon Him your best praise and thanksgiving today.

TRIAL AND CRUCIFIXION
MATTHEW 27

With the long night now over, the Sanhedrin meets in official session to condemn Jesus. Their meeting the night before had been illegal for at least two reasons: it was held at night, and it was held in the High Priest's home, rather than in the official meeting place, the Chamber of Hewn Stone in the Temple. It was also illegal to render a verdict in capital cases on the same day as hearing the evidence, but legalities take a back seat to their murderous agenda. The Sanhedrin, having condemned Him for blasphemy, takes Him to Pontius Pilate, the Roman governor, who alone can order His execution. The Romans reserved the right of execution to themselves, and only for crimes that *they* considered capital offenses. Blasphemy would not have registered on Pilate's radar screen, so they changed the charges to something a Roman governor would be greatly concerned about, accusing Him of sedition against the Roman Empire, of claiming to be a king in opposition to Caesar (see Luke 23:1-2). Pilate found no evidence of this charge against Jesus, and discerned that the Jewish authorities were seeking His death out of jealousy (v. 18). He wanted to release Jesus because of His obvious innocence, and at his wife's urging (v. 19), but found himself in a difficult position. He was on shaky political footing with Rome; any uprising, or any accusation lodged by the Jews against him might be enough to lead to his ouster (see John 19:12). He tried to have Jesus released, but the crowd, at the urging of their leaders, chose Barabbas (whose name, ironically, means "Son of the Father"). Jesus, in a further injustice, was found innocent by the judge (vv. 23-24) but *still* sentenced to a brutal flogging and the most horrible method of execution imaginable, crucifixion. We might look at the particulars of this chapter and conclude that Jesus was caught up in a web of Jewish religious hatred and Roman political intrigue, another man among many falsely accused, condemned and put to death. But if we view it only from this human angle, we miss the big picture. Jesus was not caught up in matters beyond His control; He was fully in control of the situation, right up to and including the moment of His death (v. 50). The fact that He cried out with a loud voice at His death indicates that His strength was not exhausted (those who died of crucifixion usually died of asphyxiation as the weight of their bodies created pressure on their lungs), and the fact that He released His spirit indicates that He chose that moment to die. He had suffered long enough to purchase our redemption, but He would suffer no more. The tearing of the Temple veil (v. 51) symbolized that His once-for-all sacrifice had been accepted, opening the way for sinful human beings to be forgiven and come before a Holy God. The preliminary resurrection of verses 52-53 showed that death, which came into the world through sin, had been completely conquered by Jesus. The centurion's statement that *"Truly He was the Son of God"* (v. 54) foreshadows the gospel's future expansion into the Gentile world. Finally, Joseph of Arimathea's burial of Jesus, and the Roman contingent placed at the tomb to guard it, set the scene for the most amazing event in history, the resurrection of the Lord Jesus Christ!

PRAYER: Had Jesus not chosen to go to the cross, the entire Roman army could not have placed Him there. He freely chose that horrible fate for a world of lost sinners. Spend some time thanking Him today for His great gift of salvation, and for the great price He was willing to pay for it.

THE GREAT COMMISSION
MATTHEW 28

Chapter 28 begins with the most incredible event in all of history, the resurrection of Jesus Christ from the dead, and ends with the most powerful assignment in all of history: His Great Commission to take the message of His atoning death and resurrection to the whole world. His resurrection shows us beyond a reasonable doubt (although some, amazingly, who saw Him afterward *still* doubted - v. 17) that He was who He said He was, and that He had accomplished what He said He would accomplish. Jesus claimed to be able to give eternal life to those who believe in Him; if He could not conquer death for Himself, what reason would we have to believe He could do it for us? In rising from the dead, He showed that He has indeed conquered death and the grave. In raising Him from the dead, God put His seal of approval on His sacrifice, showing that it was both acceptable and accepted, the way opened for us to receive forgiveness of sins and eternal life. That is a message worth sharing, and the Great Commission gives us that assignment of sharing it. Jesus' words in verses 18-20 were not just for His first disciples; it is a command incumbent upon all who have come to know Him as Lord and Savior, all disciples in all ages. He begins His Great Commission with a statement of His authority: *"All authority has been given to Me in heaven and on earth."* If He has all authority in heaven and on earth, clearly He has the authority to give us this command, and we have the responsibility of obeying it! There is no higher authority in heaven or earth that can supercede this assignment! The first part of the Great Commission deals with **making disciples**: *"Go therefore and make disciples of all nations"* (v. 19a). Our modern translations make it sound as if there are two commands there: *"Go"* and *"make disciples,"* but in fact, *"Go"* is a participle, not a command, and the sentence would be best rendered, *"As you are going, make disciples."* The difference is important. Often, we attribute the Great Commission solely to those who *"go"* somewhere, particularly to those who go to foreign lands to spread the gospel as missionaries. Jesus was making a much bigger challenge, one that applies to us all. He says that wherever we go, and whatever else we do while we're there, we should be looking for ways to make disciples through the preaching, teaching and witnessing of the gospel. We don't have to go somewhere to make disciples; there are plenty of opportunities to spread the gospel just in the course of our normal going - going to work, going to school, going about our daily tasks, going among our family, friends, co-workers and neighbors. Even the translation *"all nations"* can confuse us into thinking of the Great Commission only in terms of those who go to foreign lands, but the word used here does not refer to nations in terms of political entities. In Greek, it's *panta ta ethne*; literally, "all the ethnics." Jesus was telling His disciples that the gospel was not just for the Jews, but for all people of all people groups, no matter their ethnic, racial or social backgrounds. The second part of the Great Commission deals with **marking disciples** through the ordinance of baptism. Those who have received Christ as their Lord and Savior are called to publicly acknowledge Him through being baptized in the name of the Father, the Son and the Holy Spirit. That formulation of the singular *"name"* with the plural Father, Son and Holy Spirit is a strong statement of the nature of God as a Trinity (from "tri" meaning three, and "unity" meaning one). The Bible teaches us that there is one God eternally revealed in three persons, God the Father, God the Son and God the Holy Spirit. It is appropriate that we baptize in the name of the Father, the Son and the Spirit, as all three persons of the Godhead are involved in our salvation. As someone once put it, the Father *thought it* as He set in motion His plan of salvation, the Son *bought it* through His death on the cross, and the Spirit *brought it* through His ministry of conviction and conversion. After we have made disciples through the gospel, and marked them as disciples through baptism, then we have the task of **maturing disciples** by *"teaching them to observe all things I have commanded you"* (v. 20). Becoming a disciple happens in an instant, at the moment of placing one's faith in Christ, but living out the implications of that decision is a lifelong process of learning and growing. The Great Commission is a remarkable assignment, one far bigger than our abilities, but Jesus promises that He has not left us to accomplish it in our own strength. Through the Holy Spirit, He has promised to be with us always, even to the end of the age.

PRAYER: While the Great Commission is not just for the missionaries, it certainly *is* for the missionaries. Take a few moments to pray for missionaries around the world who are spreading the gospel, and especially for any missionaries you may know personally. Pray that your eyes will be open for opportunities to share the gospel in the course of your normal "going," and that you will have boldness to do so. If you have not been baptized since you became a believer, pray a prayer of repentance for neglecting that command of the Word, and commit yourself to being baptized at the earliest opportunity. Pray for your spiritual growth, that you might become a fully mature follower of Christ, a doer of God's Word, and not just a hearer of it (James 1:22).

MARK

THE RECOVERY ZONE
MARK 1

Most scholars believe the gospel of Mark was the first one written, with Matthew then supplementing the basic outline he found with his own memories of Jesus. Afterward, Luke used both of the earlier documents, along with his own research and eyewitness interviews, to craft a comprehensive gospel. Finally, John, not wanting to go over the same ground as the others, wrote a supplementary gospel, focusing his attention on aspects of Jesus' ministry and teachings that the others were not led to record. Early church history records that Mark, who was a close associate of the apostle Peter, wrote this gospel based on the stories he had heard Peter share about Jesus. It is the simplest, shortest, and fastest-moving of the four gospels, as you've probably already determined just from reading the first chapter. Events that took several chapters of the gospel of Matthew to record are recorded in rapid succession in this first chapter of Mark. The "frenzy" of how it is written creates for us a sense of the busyness of Jesus' ministry. Verses 21-34 give us a glimpse of a typical day, at least a typical Sabbath day, in Jesus' ministry. He entered the synagogue and taught, and a demonized man began to cry out in His presence. I find it fascinating that this demonized man was in the synagogue, sitting on the same pew he'd probably occupied for years. It is doubtful that anyone there (other than Jesus, of course) knew that he was demonized; indeed, he himself may have been unaware of the malevolent entity dwelling inside him. There were no doubt negative ramifications in his life from being demonized, but in all likelihood, he had not associated them with demonic influence. Demons, despite their depictions in Hollywood movies, prefer to do their foul deeds in secret, but in the presence of the Holy One of God, this demon could not maintain his disguise, and he cried out in abject terror. Jesus cast out the demon and set the man free from his bondage. From there, He went to Simon Peter's house, where Peter's mother-in-law lay sick with a fever. Jesus healed her, and she began to serve them. Note that Jesus had no qualms about healing on the Sabbath, despite the fact that "the Pharisee Rules" forbade healing on the Sabbath. In their bizarre, legalistic world of rules and regulations, it was acceptable to do what was necessary to keep someone from getting worse on the Sabbath, but doing anything to make them better was sin! In the evening, after the sun set and the Sabbath was over (they obviously thought that Jesus would not heal on the Sabbath), the whole city came to Peter's house, bringing with them the sick and the demonized for Jesus to minister to. We're told that *"He healed many who were sick with various diseases and cast out many demons"* (v. 34), probably doing so until late in the evening. What a busy day, and no doubt a drain on Him physically, emotionally, mentally and spiritually. We would expect Jesus to sleep in or take a day off after such a taxing day, but instead, we see in verse 35, *"In the morning, rising up a great while before sunrise, He went out and departed to a solitary place. And there He prayed."* How did Jesus recover from His busy, draining day? By starting the next day alone with His

Father, praying. It's no doubt the best way to start the day, but we need not be legalistic about the morning. For some, a morning devotional time just doesn't work; they are better suited for an afternoon or evening quiet time. There are other times in the gospels that we see Jesus departing from the crowds in the evening to pray, sometimes even praying all night. *When* we spend time with the Lord is not the issue; *that* we spend time with Him is. If the very Son of God needed time alone with His Father, how much more do we? Jesus' time with His Father helped clarify His mission. When the disciples found Him, He announced that they would not be staying there in Capernaum, but going to other nearby towns to preach there also, *"For that is why I have come"* (v. 38). That time alone with the Father also re-energized Him. And so *"He preached in their synagogues throughout Galilee and cast out demons"* (v. 39). Do you find your days to be busy and draining? Commit yourself to spending time with the Lord on a daily basis. Far from being one more thing on the never-ending list, that time with the Lord will give you guidance to know what is most important, what God would have you leave in and take out of your schedule. In that time in His presence, you will also receive strength to get back up and into the fight again.

PRAYER: Is your time with the Lord regular and consistent, or hit and miss? Too busy, you say? Jesus was extraordinarily busy, but still carved out time to spend with His Father. Not enough time? You have 24 hours in a day, just like everyone else. It's not a matter of time, but a matter of priorities. Pray that your time with Him might become the great non-negotiable of your day. Pray that in your quiet times, you might receive guidance for your steps and strength for your days.

THE UNEXPECTED JESUS
MARK 2

After a preaching tour around Galilee, Jesus returned to His base of operations in Capernaum. When the people of the town heard that He was there, they came and so crowded the house that no one else could get in. Four men came, carrying a paralytic on a mat. Having seen Jesus heal before, they had faith that He would heal their friend of his paralysis, and they would not be deterred by the crowd. They went up on the roof, moved aside the tiles and lowered the man into the room where Jesus was. They no doubt expected Jesus to say to the man, "Your paralysis is lifted," but Jesus had a deeper and more profound agenda, and His words to the man were completely unexpected: *"Son, your sins are forgiven"* (v. 5). I wonder if the man's friends were disappointed? We brought him all the way here, they may have thought, and He's not going to be healed? We're not told what kinds of illnesses Jesus had healed in Capernaum before. Perhaps none were as serious as this one, and when He said these words, their hearts may have sunk, thinking that paralysis might be beyond His abilities. Of far greater importance to Jesus than the state of the man's body was the state of his soul. Far better to live out his life in paralysis and spend eternity in heaven than to be healed here on Earth and spend eternity in hell. That's why for Jesus, the healing miracles, as incredible as they were, were always secondary to the preaching of the gospel (see v. 2). Not only were the paralytic and his friends surprised by Jesus' unexpected words, the scribes who where there were likewise surprised, even to the point of being appalled, at Jesus' words. Only God can forgive sins, they reasoned, and this man claims to forgive sins; therefore, He is a blasphemer, claiming the prerogatives that only belong to God. They had the right premise, but came to the wrong conclusion. It is true that only God can forgive sins, and that Jesus declared this man's sins forgiven, but the conclusion they should have drawn was that in forgiving sins, Jesus was demonstrating that He was God in the flesh! Even though they didn't say anything, Jesus knew what they were thinking and responded to their thoughts (which must have been quite unexpected indeed!). Then, to show His authority to forgive sins, which only God can do, He did something else that only God can do: He healed the man of his paralysis. In verses 13-17, Jesus acts in unexpected ways again, calling a tax collector named Levi (also known as Matthew) as one of His disciples. Tax collectors were hated by the Jews. They were seen as collaborators with the Roman occupation forces, and traitors to the Jewish nation. For Jesus to call this man, and then to go to supper at his house, was unexpected behavior. Few Jews would eat with a tax collector, and the scribes and Pharisees let their distaste over it be known. Jesus responded that *"Those who are well have no need of a physician, but those who are sick. I came not to call the righteous, but sinners to repentance"* (v. 17). In the rest of the chapter, Jesus acts in unexpected ways in terms of fasting and "the Pharisee Rules" about "harvesting" grain on the Sabbath. He is not like other "religious leaders," and He will not be confined by the expectations placed on Him by others and their man-made religious rules. Jesus still often acts in unexpected ways in our lives. Just when we think that we have Him and His ways figured out (what arrogance of finite minds to believe they have figured out an infinite God!), He moves in a new and different way to reveal more of Himself to us. Jesus' words in verses 21-22 encourage us to be open to new ways and new approaches. While His message never changes, the ways it is presented can, do, and should change. Often, unfortunately, those who were most used of God yesterday can be the biggest stumbling-blocks to what He wants to do today, if they become set in their ways, holding stubbornly to methodologies that have long ago lost their effectiveness.

PRAYER: Back then, wine was stored in skins made of animal hide. The gasses that resulted from the fermentation process caused the wineskins to swell. New, never-before-used wineskins could handle that stretching. Old wineskins that had previously been stretched to their limits could not handle the pressure and would burst. However, winemakers eventually discovered a way to reuse the old wineskins. If the old wineskins were soaked thoroughly in olive oil, it would renew their suppleness. Oil in the Bible is often symbolic of the Holy Spirit. Ask the Spirit to thoroughly soak you through and through, making you flexible to receive the new wine He wishes to pour into you.

THE MISUNDERSTOOD JESUS
MARK 3

If you've ever been falsely accused or misunderstood, even by those closest to you, you're in good company. Mark 3 shows how dramatically those around Him completely misunderstood Jesus - His purpose, His priorities and His power. Mark's rendering of the healing of the man with the withered hand draws a sharp contrast, evident in Jesus' question in verse 4, *"Is it lawful to do good or to do evil on the Sabbath, to save life or to kill?"* So faulty were the Pharisees' priorities, placing Sabbath-keeping above almost all else, that they couldn't see Jesus' point: what better use of the Sabbath could there be than doing good to someone? How could it be wrong to save a life on the Sabbath? And how great an evil is it to do wrong, to kill, or to plot someone's murder on the Sabbath (v. 6)? The crowds also had misplaced priorities. They came from a wide area, seeking Him out not because of His teaching, but because *"they heard what great things He did"* (v. 8). Those desperate for healing pressed against Him with such force that they threatened to crush Him in their efforts to touch Him. Jesus calls twelve of His disciples, designating them apostles, but as later passages will show, their understanding of Jesus and His mission were questionable as well, at least at this point. They wanted to be "big wigs" in an earthly kingdom they believed He was going to set up, and Judas, who would later betray Him, found in following Him an opportunity for the embezzlement of ministry funds. Even Jesus' mother and brothers display a faulty understanding of Him and His ministry. Believing that *"He is out of his mind,"* they come to *"take charge of him"* (v. 21 - NIV 84). Mary's concern for Him seems to be driven by a mother's worry about His well-being (v. 20); the brothers, as other Scriptures indicate, did not believe in Him until after the resurrection. They might have had a better understanding of Him had they chosen to join in with those who were *"seated in a circle around him"* (v. 34 - NIV 84), rather than *"standing outside"* (v. 31). The Pharisees saw Him as a lawbreaker (although it was not God's Law that He broke, but their man-made interpretations of it), and declared Him as demonized, attributing the works of the Holy Spirit to unclean spirits (vv. 20-30). So, the crowds saw Him as a healer, the apostles saw Him as a future earthly king, Judas saw Him as a convenient source of illicit revenue, His family saw Him as out of His mind, and the Pharisees saw Him as a lawbreaker. Amazingly, the only ones who knew the truth about Him in the entire chapter were the demons, who declared *"You are the Son of God"* (v. 11).

PRAYER: Verse 14 contains a powerful statement of the disciple's priority: *"He ordained twelve to be with Him, and to be sent out to preach."* Our first priority as disciples is just to be with Him, to spend time in His presence. Only then are we qualified to be sent out to serve Him and minister for Him. Pray that the Lord will keep your priorities straight, that your service to Him will grow out of your devotion to Him, and that your service to Him might never crowd out your time spent with Him.

THE GROWTH OF THE KINGDOM
MARK 4

When God shares some truth with us, it is both a blessing and a tremendous responsibility. *"Do you bring in a lamp to put it under a bowl or a bed? Instead, don't you put it on its stand? For whatever is hidden is meant to be disclosed, and whatever is concealed is meant to be brought out into the open...With the measure you use, it will be measured to you - and even more. Whoever has will be given more; whoever does not have, even what he has will be taken from him."* (vv. 21-25, NIV 84). When God pours truth into us, we have a responsibility to share it in both word and deed and not to keep it to ourselves. Hoarding His Word or His blessings is counter-productive. In keeping it to ourselves, we ultimately lose it. In sharing it with others, we retain it and are given more! Too many Christians are like saturated sponges. Unless a sponge is squeezed out, it sits, and it soaks, and it sours and it stinks. But when it is squeezed out, it can receive more water, fresh water that keeps it clean and useful. How many believers sit week after week in Sunday School classes and on church pews, soaking it all in, so to speak, but never having it "squeezed out" in service and sharing with others? We are called not only to be doers of the Word (James 1:22), but to be sharers of the Word (Matthew 28:20). The more we practice and share what God teaches us, the more it lodges in our hearts, and the more God will teach us. A similar truth is communicated in the next parable, which speaks of a man sowing seed. A person might be able to accumulate enough seed to feed himself for a season, but once he's eaten them, what then? By spreading the seed, he gains a much larger crop for himself, and he also gains seed to plant for the next harvest. Notice that *"when the grain is ripe, immediately he applies the sickle because the harvest has come"* (v. 29). When the grain comes to maturity, if it is not harvested in a timely manner, it will rot and be lost. The next parable teaches us not to underestimate the power of the smallest seed God plants within us (vv. 30-32). The smallest of insights or the slightest grain of an idea, empowered by God, can grow and become something great that blesses us and others.

PRAYER: The Kingdom grows in us and through us not by accumulation, but by distribution; not by hoarding, but by scattering. Pray that the Lord will open your eyes to opportunities to speak the truth He's revealed to you into others' lives, to share a word of Biblical counsel, to speak a word of Biblical comfort, or to articulate a word of Biblical witness.

THREE GREAT ENEMIES
MARK 5

In Mark 5, we see Jesus encountering (and vanquishing) three great enemies of humanity: demons, disease, and death. Verses 1-20 tell of Jesus' encounter with the demonized man Legion. Jesus had dealt with demons previously, but this was an extreme case of demonization, a "hive" of demons swarming in this afflicted man. Those who are demonized often exhibit such symptoms as obsession with death (v. 3a), outbursts of rage marked by supernatural strength (v. 3b-4), isolation (v. 5a), misery (v. 5b), and self-destructive tendencies (v. 5c) to a lesser or greater degree, depending upon the level of demonic influence. Note clearly that the demons that had so totally taken control of this man and had terrified the entire region through him now kneel before Jesus, recognizing Him as *"Jesus, Son of the Most High God,"* and crying out and cringing in abject terror. They knew who He is, and they knew that He had all power and authority over them. Jesus cast the demons out of the man, and they went into the herd of pigs nearby. The pigs then rushed into the sea and drowned. As a result, Jesus was asked to leave the region, but He would not be without a witness there. Legion desired to go with Jesus, but Jesus would not let him. Instead, He told him to go home and testify to his friends about what God had done for him. Apparently, Legion became quite the witness, as we're told he *"began to proclaim in the Decapolis* ("Ten Cities") *what great things Jesus had done for him. And everyone was amazed."* Amazed indeed. The depth of his previous bondage and the extent of his current freedom all testified in this largely Gentile area (only a Gentile area would have had such a large herd of pigs) of the amazing power of Jesus. The story of Jairus' daughter and the woman with the issue of blood show Jesus' mastery over death and disease, respectively, as Jesus restores to life a twelve-year-old girl, and ends a twelve-year-old illness. The woman who touched Jesus' clothes showed an incredible faith, faith that came by hearing the testimony of others (vv. 27-28). Her reluctance to ask Jesus for help directly probably stems from the nature of the disease. Her bleeding issue was like a menstrual cycle that would not end, and menstruating women, under the Jewish Law, were considered unclean. When Jesus asked about who had touched His garments, she fell before Him fearful and trembling, perhaps expecting a rebuke. Instead, He spoke tender words of kindness to her, assuring her that her healing was real and permanent (v. 34). We can only imagine Jairus' reaction to all this. His daughter was at the point of death (v. 23), and Jesus was wasting time, or so it must have seemed in his eyes. And then, messengers brought him the news that his child was dead. At that point, he thought, it was all over. It was too late. If only Jesus hadn't delayed! But Jesus spoke words of encouragement to Jairus, encouraging him to believe, and continued on with him to the house. There, He performed a far greater miracle than the healing of a disease as He raised the little girl from the dead.

PRAYER: God is in control. There are no spiritual forces more powerful than He is. There is no disease beyond His ability to heal. Even death is subject to His control. Pray for anyone you know today who is struggling with spiritual issues, dealing with habitual sin, or blinded to the truth of the gospel. Pray that the demonic forces driving their addiction or deception will be broken in the name and power and authority of Jesus. Pray for those you know who are dealing with illnesses of various kinds, particularly long-term intractable illnesses. Pray also for those you know who are dealing with death: the impending or recent death of a loved one, or their own looming deaths. Pray for healing if it be the Lord's will, and if not, that dying grace will be bestowed upon them in fullness. Thank Him that He is Lord over the demonic, Lord over disease, and Lord over death (John 11:25). Pray for opportunities to testify of the great things Jesus has done for you, and that others might come to faith in Him through your testimony.

REJECTION AND RECEPTION
MARK 6

Mark 6 shows Jesus ministering in miraculous power everywhere, but in some places more than others. There is a certain sadness in Jesus' rejection in His hometown and home synagogue. He had spent most of the first thirty years of His life in Nazareth. The people of that small village had known Him as a child. They had seen Him grow to manhood. They had worshiped beside Him in the synagogue. Some of them had been His customers when He worked as a carpenter. They knew His mother, His four brothers and His sisters (which, by the way, indicates that Joseph and Mary had at least six children after Jesus was born), and many of them were related to Jesus. We would expect His return to Nazareth to be nothing less than a triumphant homecoming, but rather than celebrate "a hometown boy made good," they resented Him, even though they recognized His wisdom and had heard of His miracles performed elsewhere. Jesus responded to their rejection with His famous saying that *"A prophet is not without honor, except in his own country, and among his own relatives, and in his own house"* (v. 4). Note the painful progression of that verse. It hurts to be rejected in your own country. It hurts more to be rejected among your relatives. It hurts even more to be rejected by those within your own household! Sometimes those closest to us, the ones whose opinions we most value and the ones from whom we most desire approval, are the last and the least to give it. As a case in point, we're told that none of Jesus' brothers came to faith in Him until after the resurrection. How painful it must have been for Him to feel their disapproval of Him and His ministry, or even their mere indifference. As a result of their rejection and lack of faith, *"He could not do any miracles there, except that He laid His hands on a few sick people and healed them. And He was amazed because of their unbelief"* (v. 5). What a statement that is! No miracles, just a few healings! Most of us would consider an instantaneous healing to be an incredible miracle. It makes us wonder what kinds of things He normally did when He found faith among a people, and what wonderful demonstrations of love and power Nazareth missed out on because of their unbelief born of familiarity. Verses 30-43 (the only miracle recorded in all four gospels) show just one example of Jesus performing a non-healing miracle: the feeding of the five thousand. Jesus sends the disciples out on a mission soon after His rejection at Nazareth (vv. 7-13). They had seen how He was treated in His hometown, and He prepares them for similar treatment as they travel about (v. 11). It is a sad thing when we and the message we bring are rejected, but we must not give up in despair when we are rejected. Instead, we must "shake it off" and move forward, for there are those who will receive us and our divinely ordered message gladly (vv. 12, 33-34, 54-56).

PRAYER: Have you experienced rejection as a Christian? Have those close to you been unhappy about your decision to follow Christ, or about decisions you've made in following Him? Have those you've witnessed to refused the invitation to salvation? While we grieve that rejection (and I cannot read verses 4 and 11 in any tones other than grief, not anger), we cannot allow rejection to stop us. There are others who need our witness, our example, and our ministry, and many of them will receive it gladly. Pray for those who have rejected the message of the gospel, that in the future they will reconsider and receive Christ. And pray for perseverance in your own life to keep going forward, living and proclaiming the truth even in the face of rejection, ridicule or persecution.

GOOD IDEAS?
MARK 7

The early part of Mark 7 is ground we've previously covered in Matthew 15. Jesus is running afoul of the Pharisees because He and His disciples do not adhere to their rules, in this case, the complicated ritual washing they engaged in before meals. Mark, writing for Roman readers, gives a much fuller description of this ritual washing than does Matthew, whose original Jewish readers would have been familiar with it. He shows that it not only involved the washing of hands, but also the *"cups and pitchers and bronze vessels and dining couches"* (v. 4). Special attention was given to washing before eating when returning from the marketplace. As modern readers, knowing what we do about hygiene and preventing the spread of disease, we cannot help but be struck by the fact that all of these practices seem to be very good ideas. After all, as we've all heard, "cleanliness is next to godliness." Or is it? It is worth noting that the Pharisees were not doing this as a matter of hygiene, and while it may have had positive benefits, their motivation was to try to please God by conducting this man-made ritual, and their judgment was that anyone who did not engage in this ritual could not possibly be pleasing to God. The lesson for us is that just because something seems to be a good idea (or, in our pragmatic culture, just because it "works") does not mean it's from God, and we must not judge others for not adhering to our good ideas, our way of doing things. As in Matthew, Jesus illustrates the danger of elevating human ideas to that level. In practice, we can become so enamored with our "good ideas," thinking that they're pleasing God, that they actually get in the way of obeying God-prescribed commands, which truly does please Him. The example Jesus gave is of the Corban Vow. In keeping the Corban Vow, which was a man-made "good idea" for supporting the Temple, the Pharisees violated God's explicit command to honor their fathers and mothers. That was true defilement on the part of the Pharisees (vv. 20-23), even if every bite of food they put in their mouths was absolutely clean by their standards. The last account in the chapter, that of Jesus healing the deaf and mute man, has some interesting and curious details. Notice that Jesus is in the region of the Decapolis, the very region where Legion had gone, telling his story throughout the ten cities of that area. Jesus receives a much different reception from the time He was "run out of town" after Legion's deliverance. Probably because of Legion's testimony, He is received there gladly. Matthew speaks here of great crowds bringing numerous sick people to Him; Mark concentrates on one such healing, but he indicates that it is one among many (note the crowd in verse 33 and the words *"them"* and *"they"* in verses 36-37). Jesus' methods for healing people vary widely. Some He heals with a touch, others with words, and still others with different actions. In this healing, He put His fingers into the man's ears, and then spat and touched his tongue before commanding his ears to *"Be opened"* (v. 34). Perhaps the variety in the methods He used is a lesson to us. It is not the method that matters, but the Lord behind the method. All too often, we chase after methods (again, looking for "good ideas" that "work"), and we can become so tied to our methods that we begin to trust them rather than trust Him. God wants us chasing after Him, looking to His power and guidance, not chasing after methods. There's nothing wrong with methods, as long as they're not ungodly methods, but we must always hold them loosely, and we must place our trust in the Lord who energizes them, not in the methods themselves.

PRAYER: We are to use methods and trust God. If we're not careful, we can begin to trust our methods and try to use God to make our methods work. Pray that God will reveal to you not only what He wants done, but how He wants it done. Pray that He will reveal any area of your life where you've elevated man-made "good ideas" above His Word. Pray that He will show you any area of your life and service where you've become more focused on the method than the Lord behind the method.

A SECOND TOUCH
MARK 8

The healing of the blind was an unmistakable sign of Jesus' Messiahship. The Old Testament had predicted that the Messiah would heal the blind (Isaiah 35:5-6), and while various prophets had healed other diseases and had even raised the dead, only Jesus to this time had made the blind see. This healing is unique in all of the accounts of Jesus' healings in that it occurred in stages rather than all at once. After spitting on the blind man's eyes and laying His hands on him, Jesus asked if he could see anything, to which the man replied, *"I see men as trees, walking"* (v. 24). Apparently, he had not always been blind, and he knew enough to know that what he was seeing, while better than total blindness, was not total sight either. Once again, Jesus laid His hands on his eyes, and this time *"made him look up."* At that point, *"he was restored and saw everyone clearly"* (v. 25). What is the point of this two-stage healing? Did Jesus fail in His first attempt? Did He somehow miscalculate the amount of healing power it would take to deal with this case? I think we must reject any notion that Jesus failed and had to try again. After all, He is God incarnate, and He knew exactly what was needed to effect this healing. He *could* have healed the man instantly, as He had done with many before, but He *chose* to do it this way. I've heard it said that a good lawyer never asks a question unless he already knows the answer. When God asks a question (as in verse 23), it is not because He is seeking information; He always knows the answer. I see Jesus' question here in much the same light as the question posed to the crippled man at the Pool of Bethesda (John 5:6), a question designed to help him probe his own motivations and desires. Just to go from total blindness to blurred vision was a remarkable miracle. Would this blind man be satisfied with this partial healing? Would he say to himself, "Well, I'm better off than I was before," and move on? Would he assume that this was the best Jesus could do? Or would he press in for the complete healing? Sometimes in life, as we are praying about a situation, we get a partial answer, a degree of relief from whatever is plaguing us, but not a complete "healing," so to speak. The question at that point is, will we be satisfied with the partial, or will we continue to press in to God for the full answer? Will we settle for "better," or will we continue to seek for God's best? Will we let the partial define the limit of our faith, believing that's the best God can do or is willing to do, or will we let the partial bolster our faith to believe for the full answer to come?

PRAYER: Is there any area of your life where God has given you a partial answer, but not the full answer yet? Have you given up on that answer, deciding that the partial is as good as it's going to get? Perhaps God has designed this situation to "make you look up" in greater dependence upon Him. Confess to the Lord that you have been too satisfied with too little. Thank Him for the partial answer, but trust Him and beseech Him for a second touch.

ALL THINGS POSSIBLE
MARK 9

The father of the demonized boy in verses 14-29 is a portrait of frustration. He has dealt for years (v. 21) with a horrible, demonically caused ailment (v. 18), frustrated no doubt by his inability to help his son or to find any help for him. He had brought his son to Jesus, having heard about Jesus' power over disease and demons, only to find that Jesus wasn't available, and His disciples weren't up to the task. Rather than leaving in disappointment, he stays to try to see Jesus, despite the huge crowd that is also waiting for Him (v. 15). When he finally speaks to Jesus, his statement that *"if You can do anything"* (v. 22) is met by an "if" from Jesus: *"If you can believe, all things are possible to him who believes"* (v. 23). His frustration overflows in tears as He cries out in verse 24, *"Lord, I believe. Help my unbelief!"* When we face serious, long-term, ongoing problems in our lives or in the lives of those we love, sometimes it is hard to believe that anything will ever change. The father's cry is one that we should mimic. When our faith is wavering, we should cry out to the Lord in an honest appeal for more faith! Jesus, in response to the father's cry for help, his tears, and his faith - weak though it was - came through for him, rebuking the demon and bringing his son to complete health. The disciples certainly don't come across very well in this chapter. When Jesus comes down from the mountain, he finds them locked in an argument with the scribes (v. 14). They have failed to cast out a demon, apparently because of a lack of prayer and fasting (v. 29). Jesus foretells His death and resurrection in the most straightforward of terms, and yet they do not understand Him and are afraid to ask Him (vv. 30-32). In verses 33-37, in spite of their failure and their lack of understanding, they actually pass the time as they travel by debating which of them is the greatest! Finally, we see them rebuking someone who was casting out demons in Jesus' name, because he was not in their group (v. 38). Strangely enough, they were critical of someone else for doing effectively what they had just utterly failed to do! Jesus told them to leave this successful exorcist alone, that he was obviously on the same side as they were (vv. 39-40). So, we have a portrait of a group of men who, despite having spent a couple of years with Jesus, are marked by contentiousness, lack of discipline, lack of success, lack of understanding, and no lack of ego, jealousy and clannishness. Not to mention the fact that one of them would eventually betray Jesus! Not a pretty picture at all! Yet, compare that picture with what these men would later become, and the distance between the two is mind-boggling. What made the difference? These men had faith in Jesus, and *"all things are possible to him who believes"* (v. 23).

PRAYER: Are you dealing with long-standing, frustrating issues of one kind or another? Do you despair of ever finding an answer? Cry out to God, saying, "Lord, I believe. Help me in my unbelief!" Are you frustrated by how slow your progress as a disciple seems? Pray for the Lord to do a work in you such as what He did in those first disciples in bringing them from great immaturity to Spirit-filled maturity, power and usefulness in His Kingdom.

THE MARRIAGE TEST
MARK 10

The Pharisees came to Jesus to test Him in regard to marriage. The issue in Jesus' day was ease of divorce, with liberal rabbis granting divorce for almost any reason. Since "no fault" divorce became the norm nation-wide in America in the early 1970s, ease of divorce is certainly an issue in our day, driven most often by the hardness of human hearts that insist upon their own way. But the greatest test Christians face when it comes to marriage in our day has to do with the redefining of marriage to include so-called "gay marriage," polygamy, and any number of other interpersonal arrangements between consenting adults. If marriage is defined as anything and everything, then marriage has no meaning at all. Jesus' answer to the Pharisees is the answer that we must embrace, and declare, in this age of attacks upon the institution of marriage. Jesus, rather than debating the Law, took them back beyond the Law to the Creator's original design and intent for marriage, quoting from Genesis 1 (*"God made them male and female"*) and Genesis 2 (*"For this cause..."*). The provision in the Law for divorce was made to regulate (not to facilitate!) the failure of human beings to live up to God's standard, the ideal relationship He desires to create in marriage, because of the hardness of our hearts. These foundational Scriptures teach us that marriage, in God's original plan, is a male and female arrangement. The principals in a marriage relationship are one male and one female, not two or more males or two or more females, or any multiple combination thereof. His ideal is one man and one woman - *"For this cause a man* (singular)*...shall cleave to his wife* (singular) *and the two* (and only two in an exclusive relationship) *will become one flesh."* A man cannot become one flesh with another man, nor a woman with another woman, because that one-flesh unity comes from the male and female complementing each other (most clearly seen in the necessity of male and female to reproduce), each one bringing to the relationship what the other lacks, not only physically, but emotionally and mentally as well. God has created male and female such that they are not only built differently, but wired differently, by design. It is only in the joining of the male and female, in an exclusive relationship of greater priority and closeness even than the relationship with one's parents, that the highest form of fulfillment (becoming one flesh) can occur. When you need a complement, a duplicate will not suffice. No two women, no matter how much they may be compatible, can bring into the relationship what God designed a man to bring. No two men, no matter how much they may be attracted to one another, can bring into a relationship what a woman is designed to bring. No two men, and no two women, no matter how much they may love the children they have adopted or artificially conceived, can bring both a male and female influence into the life of those children, and for their optimum growth and development, children need both kinds of influence. As Christians, we must cling to God's definition of marriage. It is not "traditional marriage" that we are defending. Traditions can and do change, so if marriage is just a "tradition," then it can be changed on a whim. It is "Biblical marriage," or "God-ordained marriage" that we defend, the standard that we must uphold. That is the definition of marriage we must insist upon, no matter how the world, its courts, or its governments may co-opt and pervert the word.

PRAYER: Pray for any married couples that come to mind, for the strengthening of their marriages. Pray for any couples who are heading toward marriage, that they might build a strong foundation in God's Word for their marriages. Pray for those you may know whose marriages are in trouble. Ask God to soften hard hearts and bring them to reconciliation. Pray for those who are confused by Satan's attempts to counterfeit God's good gift of marriage, that they might come to a knowledge of, and acceptance of, the truth.

WHAT'S HINDERING YOUR PRAYERS?
MARK 11

Verses 12-21 comprise what scholars call a "Markan sandwich," a literary device in which Mark starts an account, interposes another connected account, and then returns to the first one (another example is in 5:21-43, where the story of the woman with the issue of blood is contained within the story of Jairus' daughter). Here, Jesus curses a fig tree that had leaves but no figs. Mark's statement that *"it was not the season for figs"* (v. 13) makes it sound like an immature temper tantrum on the part of Jesus; after all, why would He expect to find figs on the tree if it was not fig season? The reason is because of the leaves. Most trees put forth leaves first, and then fruit comes later; the fig tree, by contrast, puts forth its fruit, and then its leaves, and then the fruit ripens. Even though it was not quite time for figs, an especially vibrant tree in especially good soil could produce figs early. The leaves gave forth the promise that this was just such a tree. If there were leaves, there should be figs. They would not have been mature yet, and they would have been bitter to the taste, but they would have still been edible. Jesus could have handled immature, bitter fruit, but *no* fruit among the leaves indicated that the tree was a non-productive tree. It was occupying good ground, using up its nutrients and soaking up its moisture, but only producing leaves. While it looked good, it produced nothing of value. From there, the scene shifts to the Temple, where Jesus drives out the moneychangers and the sellers of sacrifices (vv. 15-19). His statement that *"Is it not written, 'My house shall be called a house of prayer for all nations'? But you have made it a den of thieves"* (v. 17) gives us insight into his motivations for this provocative act. *"All nations"* here, as in

Matthew 28:19, does not refer to nations in terms of geographical and political borders, but to all ethnic and people groups. Many scholars believe that the market was set up in the outermost court of the Temple, the court of the Gentiles, the only place in the Temple complex where non-Jews were allowed. God wanted Gentiles to come to the Temple so that they might hear about Him from His people in that court of the Gentiles. But imagine some Gentile, perhaps from a distant land. He has heard about the one true God, and desires to know about Him, so He makes his way to Jerusalem. As he approaches the city, he sees the beautiful Temple of God, gleaming gold in the sunlight, dominating the skyline, and he just knows that here he will get the answers that he seeks. But as he approaches that beautiful Temple, he begins to notice a bad smell. It smells like animals, along with all the wonderful aromas that accompany them. As he enters the outermost limits of the Temple grounds, he finds himself in a noisy, smelly market. There is the sound and smell of the animals, the noise of people arguing and haggling over the exchange of money, and crowds of people engaged in commerce that this Gentile cannot imagine has anything to do with worship. He moves onward, past the market toward the beautiful Temple itself, where he is greeted by a wall, inscribed in several languages with the warning that should a Gentile dare pass that point, his life would be forfeit. Sadly, he turns and leaves the Temple, never to return. He thought that he could find someone who would tell him about this God of the Hebrews at the Temple, but upon closer inspection, he found nothing. Like the fig tree, the Temple looked good - from a distance - but those in charge of its operation were not bringing forth the fruit that God desired, bringing Gentiles to faith in Him so that they too might lift up prayers to Him (v. 17). Like the fig tree, because of the lack of desired fruit, the demise of the Temple and the nation was imminent. The next morning, Peter points out that the fig tree had withered from the roots

(vv. 20-21), and Jesus uses the incident to teach them about prayer, and in particular, two hindrances to prayer: lack of faith in God, and lack of forgiveness for others. Jesus' teaching on faith does not indicate that if we have enough faith, we can bring to pass whatever we will. Faith is always rooted in God's will, not our own, and no amount of faith can coerce God into doing something against His will. After all, we are to *"Have faith in God"* (v. 22) not in our own ability to conjure up faith. But faith is essential to bring God's will to pass on Earth, and lack of faith limits how much of His will gets done on Earth (see Mark 6:5-6 and Matthew 13:58). Likewise, our unwillingness to forgive others when they sin against us also hinders our prayers. Lack of faith and lack of forgiveness, then, can bring about a situation in us that is much like the fig tree and the Temple: the danger of looking good to others, but not truly bearing the fruit that God desires in our lives.

PRAYER: Is there anyone against whom you are bearing a grudge, holding on to unforgiveness? Forgive that person, and ask God's forgiveness for bearing that grudge as long as you did. Sometimes in our lives, a slow, steady erosion occurs, such that we expend far more energy trying to look good (or godly) to others than actually bearing fruit. This is hypocrisy, and it will wither our faith to the roots. Pray that the Lord might reveal to you any area of such hypocrisy, however slight it may be. Pray that you might bear true fruit in Him.

GIVING TO ALL WHAT'S DUE THEM
MARK 12

The agricultural image Jesus used in the parable of verses 1-12 would have been a common one, that of a landowner renting out his land to tenant farmers in exchange for a share of the harvest. When harvest time came, however, the tenants refused to pay the landowner what was due him, punctuating their refusal by abusing his servants and ultimately killing his son. The obvious solution to such mistreatment is that *"the owner of the vineyard...will come and kill the vinedressers and give the vineyard to others"* (v. 9). This parable was a reference to the Jewish nation and especially to the Jewish leaders, who had been entrusted with God's truths, but had not given God His due in producing the fruit of righteousness that God requires. The ones to whom this parable was directed *"knew that He had spoken the parable against them"* (v. 12) and desired to seize Him, but were afraid to because of the people. The stone that they rejected (Jesus) would become the cornerstone of the new entity that God would build, His church. Jesus' famous statement to *"Render to Caesar the things that are Caesar's, and to God the things that are God's"* (v. 17) raises a question for us: what is due to Caesar (human government) and what is due to God? Romans 13:7 is instructive to us in terms of "rendering to Caesar": *"For this reason you also pay taxes, for they are God's servants, devoting themselves to this very thing. Render to all what is due them: taxes to whom taxes are due, respect to whom respect is due, fear to whom fear is due, and honor to whom honor is due."* In terms of giving to God the things that are His, verse 30 tells us clearly that our obligation to Him is an absolute one, a call to *"love the Lord your God with all your heart, and with all your soul, and with all your mind, and with all your strength"* (v. 30). In other words, we are to submit our emotions, our wills, our intellects and our abilities to Him in complete surrender, recognizing in Him our ultimate loyalty. To love Him with our entire beings in this way, we must know Him and know Him well. I am haunted by Jesus' words in verse 10 (*"Have you not read this Scripture?"*) and verse 24 (*"Do you not err, because you know neither the Scriptures nor the power of God?"*). It is only through a regular interaction with His Word that we discover what pleases Him, such that we can then surrender our entire beings to

Him, committing ourselves to the path that pleases Him. As a corollary of loving Him, we must give our fellow man what is due him by loving our neighbors as ourselves (v. 31). The widow at the end of the chapter (vv. 41-44) is a prime example of such total love and complete surrender to God. While others may have put in much more, they were merely giving out of the overflow of their abundant riches. She, on the other hand, put in all she had, two lepta, the smallest coin circulated. In terms of actual worth, it wasn't much, but it was a huge sacrifice for her, and it generated a strong commendation from Jesus.

PRAYER: While we are called to love the Lord with all of our hearts, souls, mind and strength, most people will lean to one area above the others. Some lean more toward worship (heart), others toward contemplation (soul), others toward study (mind), and still others toward service (strength). Ask the Lord to show you how to strengthen your love in the other areas as well, and look for opportunities to love Him outside your normal approach. Pray that you will show His love to all the people you encounter today by loving them as yourself. Finally, pray about what the Lord might have you sacrifice today, whether it be time, money, effort or energy.

WHAT IF IT WERE TODAY?
MARK 13

As we look at the world that is seemingly falling apart all around us, it is very easy to feel depressed and out of control. We cannot control the geopolitical intrigues that lead to wars and rumors of wars (vv. 7-8a). We are helpless in the face of natural disasters like earthquakes and famines (v. 8b) which cause untold suffering worldwide. And certainly, we have no control over when persecutions, betrayals and hatred are brought to bear upon us, or upon our brothers and sisters in other lands. Of all the "signs of the times" that Jesus gives (which have been present, to a lesser or greater extent, in all generations - v. 30), there is only one that we have any degree of control over: *"And the gospel must be preached to all nations"* (v. 10). That is our assignment, to hold forth the truth of the gospel to all people, in all circumstances, and in all times. We must not shrink back from that task in fear as we face the prospect of wars, persecutions, rejection and natural disasters; we must press forward with even greater determination to share the gospel of Christ! Indeed, it is often in the midst of the suffering wrought by such events that the gospel's message of hope rings out most clearly, both in the one speaking it and in the one hearing it. In spite of all that we face in this sin-damaged world and from sin-controlled human beings, we have the assurance that *"Heaven and earth will pass away, but My words will not pass away"* (v. 31). God's Word is far more powerful that any force that would seek its destruction. In our day, the Lord's second coming has often been the subject of needless controversy and pointless, unbiblical speculation (v. 32). What has often been lost in the shuffle of schemes and charts and predictions is the admonition that Jesus gave us in verses 33-37: *"Take heed, watch and pray. For you do not know when the time will come. For the Son of Man is like a man leaving on a far journey who left his house and gave authority to his servants and to every man his work, and commanded the porter to watch. Watch therefore - for you do not know when the master of the house is coming, in the evening, or at midnight, or at the crowing of the rooster, or in the morning - lest he come suddenly and find you sleeping. What I say to you I say to all: 'Watch!'"* When we see the world falling apart around us, it should motivate us to pray, it should motivate us to look for (and look forward) to Christ's coming, and it should motivate us to discover and do the work He has called us to, to do our part in preparing others for His coming.

PRAYER: An old gospel song asked, concerning Jesus' coming, "Oh, what if it were today?" If it were today, would you be a part of His elect gathered by angels from the four winds (v. 27)? Would you regret at His coming that you have been lulled to sleep, whether by fear, or by laziness, or by the allure of the world (v. 36)? Would there be those in your circle of influence who would not be ready for His coming because you have not shared Jesus with them? Thank the Lord today that in a world gone mad, He is coming to make things right. Pray for awareness of the work He wants you to do in the meantime, and for opportunities to tell others about Him.

DIFFICULT PRAISE, DIFFICULT PRAYER, DIFFICULT PERSECUTION
MARK 14

This long chapter starts with the Sanhedrin's plot to arrest Jesus, and ends with Him in custody, but there is much in between. Mary of Bethany (see John 12:3) performs an extravagant act of worship in pouring out very expensive perfume on Jesus, perfume worth three hundred day's wages. But she didn't just pour it out. She broke the alabaster box that it was in, which itself would have had value. Why did she break the box? Because once the box was broken, there was no turning back. It was precious perfume, no doubt the best she had to offer, perhaps her most prized possession, and the temptation might have been to pour out just a few drops, or maybe half of it, on Jesus and keep the rest for herself. Breaking the box eliminated all hesitation. Once the box was broken, there was no way to hold any of it back, no way to avoid pouring every last drop on Jesus. For this lavish gift, she was roundly condemned by those present. Sometimes, those around us, even those who should know better, don't understand our commitments to Jesus. They may rebuke us for being, in their estimation, too extravagant in our praise, too generous in our giving, or too radical in our service. Our own flesh may tempt us to hold back from surrendering all, particularly in the face of such criticism. Like Mary, our response should be to "break our boxes," making a once-for-all final decision, eliminating all possibility of turning back in the face of criticism or opposition. We should recognize that while people may misunderstand and malign, Jesus receives our gifts gladly, and He commends us for them (vv. 6-9). Mary teaches us about difficult, sacrificial praise in the face of critical voices. In Gethsemane, Jesus teaches us about difficult prayers. Being fully God, Jesus knew in full, gory detail everything that was going to happen to Him that night and the next day; being fully human, He was possessed of all the drives and instincts that make us human, including that most powerful of instincts, the instinct for survival. No wonder He struggled! Sometimes, even when we fully know God's will in a matter, it is difficult for us to go forward for fear of the consequences. Jesus' prayer is instructive to us: *"Abba, Father, all things are possible for You. Remove this cup from Me, yet not what I will, but what You will"* (v. 36). Like Jesus, in such difficult times, we should draw near to God in intimacy, reminding ourselves of our relationship to Him: He is our Father, our "Abba," an Aramaic term of endearment, like "Daddy." Then we should bow our wills to His, knowing that as our loving Father, His will is always best. Peter shows us how *not* to deal with difficult times of pressure and persecution. Peter's failure in the courtyard began much earlier, as he approached the time of pressure with great self-confidence that he would not fall away, even if all the rest did (v. 29). Even after Jesus told him that he would deny Him three times that every night, Peter insisted that he would not (v. 31). When Jesus found him sleeping, He told him, *"Simon, are you sleeping? Could you not keep watch one hour? Watch and pray, lest you enter into temptation. The spirit is willing, but the flesh is weak."* It is interesting that Jesus does not call him "Peter" ("the Rock") here, but by his old, pre-Jesus name, "Simon." Relying on his self-confidence in his own abilities, he would be Simon. Only by relying upon the Lord could he be Peter. In times of pressure and persecution, we must be diligent to watch and pray, recognizing our weakness, and calling upon Him for strength.

PRAYER: Are you facing difficult times? Are you being criticized for your walk with Christ? Are you struggling with the perceived consequences of something He's leading you to do? Are you facing pressure or persecution from the world? Pray that the Lord would shatter every box that would keep you from full surrender to Him. Admit to Him that in and of yourself, you are powerless, and pray that you might face the criticism of others, the weakness of the flesh, and the pressure of the enemy in the fullness of His strength alone.

THE VIEW OF THE SAVIOR
MARK 15

The worst of human nature is on full display in Mark's account of Jesus' conviction and crucifixion. In the hostile members of the Sanhedrin, we see the schemers, making up scandalous lies to get an innocent man sentenced to death. In the crowd, we see the easily swayed, not really knowing what was going on, but joining in because everyone else was. In Barabbas, we have a violent murderer, a notorious terrorist of his day. In Pilate, we see human weakness; he knew that Jesus was innocent, but under pressure, he condemned Him anyway. In the soldiers we see mockery and abuse at the Praetorium, and cool detachment to the suffering around them at Golgotha. In the bystanders and chief priests, we see blasphemy hurled at Jesus in His agony. We see it in Mark's account, but Jesus saw it personally played out before Him. He experienced it all: the smears on His flawless reputation, the preference of the crowd for a murdering insurrectionist rather than for the one who had healed their illnesses and taught them of God, the indignity of being found innocent and yet sentenced to die anyway, the horrendous pain of scourging followed by the abuse of the Praetorian Guard and the agony of crucifixion. Jesus heard the comments challenging Him to come down from the cross, and indeed, in the face of such horrible maltreatment, it must have been tempting to conclude, "They're not worth it" and refuse to suffer any further indignity for our salvation. But there were others there, others who reminded Him of why He was enduring this injustice and agony. At the early morning meeting of the full Sanhedrin (v. 1), Joseph of Arimathea had been there, and surely, he spoke up against this travesty of justice. Unable to stop this legalized murder from happening, Joseph did what he could afterward, rescuing Jesus' body from being burned and burying Him in his own tomb. On the cross, through a haze of pain, Jesus could see the many women who had supported Him standing there (vv. 40-41), with Him to the end, weeping for Him. In that chaotic scene, Jesus could see a hardened centurion slowly coming to faith (v. 39). Even the mocking, insincere "worship" of the soldiers (vv. 16-19) was a reminder to Him of those who would one day sincerely bow the knee to Him in worship. Hebrews 12:2 tells us that it was for the joy set before Him that He endured the cross. What was that joy? The joy of seeing those who would believe born again into His Kingdom, restored to right relationship with God, forgiven for their sins and given the gift of eternal life. As He looked on those who believed, and looked ahead to those who would believe, He found the strength to endure the agony for us, so that we might be saved.

PRAYER: Most of us at some point have heard the tired refrain that "the church is full of hypocrites." Those who hurl that accusation seem to think it is some profound revelation, as if those in the church are blissfully unaware of the presence of hypocrites there! Given that Jesus told us that would be the case, we shouldn't be surprised when we encounter hypocrites. Have you been victimized by someone's hypocrisy in the church and tempted to reject the church altogether? Always keep in mind that the presence of a counterfeit presupposes the genuine. Take your focus off of the fake, and focus on the real. Think about those genuine saints who have influenced your life. Let the life they have led before you, the sacrifices they have made for you, and the truth they have invested in you fill you with joy that will overcome your hurt, and thank the Lord for them. Express your worship and praise to the Lord Jesus, who looked beyond the agony of the cross to the joy of our salvation. While none of us individually, nor all of us collectively, were worthy of the pain He bore or the blood He shed, thank Him that His great love was such that we were worth it to Him!

IT'S NOT OVER YET!
MARK 16

The women had ministered to Jesus while He was in Galilee, and had followed Him on the journey to Jerusalem. They had stood at the foot of the cross and watched Him die the most horrible death imaginable, and then they had followed along as Joseph of Arimathea had taken His body, hastily prepared it for burial, and laid it in his own tomb. The finality of the situation was overwhelming. All of their hopes for the future were dashed on the rocks of His crucifixion. All that they had watched Him do, all that He had done personally for them (including casting seven demons out of Mary Magdalene - v. 9), all that they had heard Him teach, and now it was all over. Or so they thought. As they came to the tomb that Sunday morning, intending to redo the hasty burial preparations of Joseph, their sorrow was no doubt overwhelming. What would they do now? How could they go on without Him? And so, they focused on the task at hand. They would perform this last act of service for their Lord, and then get on with the sad business of trying to adjust to life without Him, trying to figure out what to do with the rest of their lives. Their only concern was with how to roll the huge stone away from the entrance to the tomb. Imagine their surprise when they found that the stone was rolled away already. What good fortune, they must have thought; now we can get in there to properly prepare His body. But when they entered the tomb, they did not find a beaten, battered and bloody body, but an angelic messenger telling them that the story was not over. What they thought was a period was only a semicolon. Jesus was alive! Soon they would see Him, the first being Mary Magdalene (vv. 9-11). They and Jesus' other followers would receive a new purpose for living (v. 15) and a new supernatural protection and empowerment for serving Him (vv. 17-18). God has a way of stepping into impossible situations and bringing new life out of death. Just when we think the story is over, He picks up His pen and starts writing a sequel! You may be staring at a closed door today, trying to salvage the pieces of a situation that seems totally lost. Don't give up just yet. God's still writing the story!

PRAYER: Think about times in your life when you thought the story was all over, only to have God step in with a new beginning and a much better ending. Thank Him that He is a God of such unexpected interventions. Pray about any situation where you, or someone you know, needs that kind of new beginning.

LUKE

TWO ANGELIC APPEARANCES
LUKE 1

In Luke 1, the angel Gabriel makes two appearances, to Zechariah (or Zacharias) and Mary. Their responses are very different, one a response of doubt and the other a response of faith. Zechariah was a priest, which meant that he could trace his family line all the way back to the first High Priest, Aaron. The great sorrow of his life was that he and his wife Elizabeth had been unable to have children, and now, it seemed, they were far beyond child-bearing age. That long priestly line would end with him, because he had no son to pass it on to. When he was chosen by lot to burn incense in the Temple, it was the high point of his ministry. There were over 20,000 priests in Israel, divided into 24 divisions. About twice a year, each division would report to Jerusalem for their priestly service at the Temple. A quick look at the math reveals that at any given time, there were over 800 of them on duty! The most sought-after assignments were those that actually took a priest into the Temple building itself: burning incense on the altar, lighting the candlesticks, or replacing the showbread. Those tasks were assigned by lot, and once that inside-the-Temple duty was performed, a priest would be ineligible to do it again. Many priests would go their entire ministries and never make it inside the Temple. As Zechariah burned the incense on the altar, he was startled to see Gabriel standing there, with a message that his prayers had been answered, those long ago prayed and now probably abandoned prayers for a son. He is told that his son is going to have a strategic role in salvation history as the forerunner of the Messiah. Zechariah's response is, *"How can I know this? For I am an old man and my wife is well advanced in years"* (v. 18). Looking at his situation and his resources, he doubted Gabriel's words (v. 20), and asked for a sign. Amazing. There's an angel standing there at the altar. What more of a sign could you want? In what seems to me a moment of angelic pique, Gabriel reads him his resume': *"I am Gabriel, who stands in the presence of God. And I was sent to speak to you and to bring you this good news."* Zechariah wanted a sign and he got one: inability to speak until the birth of the child. Gabriel's next appearance is to Mary in Nazareth. He likewise gives her some amazing news, that she will be the mother of the long-awaited Messiah. Mary's response is very different from Zechariah's: *"How can this be, since I do not know a man?"* (v. 34). Mary's question displays no doubt about what she has been told. Whereas Zechariah's question expressed doubt about whether God *could* overcome his limitations, her question was just a matter of asking how God *would* overcome her limitations. Oftentimes, we dismiss those who are younger, or even those who are merely younger in the faith, as unimportant and immature, but age is no indicator of superior spirituality, nor is lack of age an indicator of lack of spiritual insight and faith. It is entirely possible to grow old in Christ without really growing up in Him, and it is also possible to mature in Christ rapidly, beyond what might be expected at one's age. It is amazing that his young girl, probably no older than 14, displayed far more faith in God than an aged priest who had served the Lord for decades.

And yet, God was at work in both of them to accomplish His purposes: a young girl with an incredible faith and a willingness to serve Him come what may (v. 38), and an old man whose faith had been battered by great disappointment over the years. The one who immediately believed received immediate blessing (vv. 42 and 45); the one who doubted initially experienced discipline and then blessing (v. 20), but both of them emerged from the experience singing His praises (vv. 46-55 and vv. 67-79).

PRAYER: Is there anywhere your faith is flagging? Is there a promise of the Word that you are struggling to believe? Ask the Lord to bolster your faith and to show you how He will accomplish His Word in you and through you.

THE WALK OF THE SPIRIT
LUKE 2

Verse 25 introduces us to Simeon, and tells us that the Holy Spirit was upon Him. In this passage, we can see several characteristics that mark the Holy Spirit's presence in a person's life. First, Simeon was righteous, a word that speaks of an internal drive for personal holiness. It speaks of conformity to a standard, not some external standard set by law or culture, but an internal standard of rightness and wrongness placed there by God Himself. Not only was he righteous, he was devout. The word *"righteous"* speaks primarily of Simeon's internal devotion to God; *"devout"* speaks of his outward practice of his faith. What's on the inside comes out on the outside. Where there is inward righteousness, there will be outward devotion. Third, Simeon was a man of faith, *"waiting for the consolation of Israel"* (v. 25). He was holding in faith to the promises of God's Word that the Messiah was coming. Those three items - an internal righteousness, an external devotion, and an expectant faith in God's Word - are far more the marks of a Spirit-filled life than any spiritual gifts are. Paul said about the Corinthian church that they were lacking in no spiritual gift (I Corinthians 1:7), but yet they were far from Spirit-filled. Indeed, they were carnal to the core. They were so lacking in righteousness that the sins of the congregation were a scandal even among the pagans in Corinth (I Corinthians 5:1), and Paul said that the external practice of their faith was so chaotic that it would be better for them to disband than to keep going like they were going (I Corinthians 11:17). Because Simeon was walking in a close, intimate walk with the Holy Spirit, the Holy Spirit could make personal promises to him, including the promise that he would not die until he had seen the Christ (v. 26), and he was open to being led by the Spirit at a moment's notice (v. 27). His obedience to the prompting of the Spirit to make his way to the Temple resulted in his seeing the Savior. Not only did he see Him, he worshiped Him and testified of Him. Those who are truly walking by the Spirit will likewise display inner righteousness, outward devotion, faith in God's Word and promises, the leadership of the Spirit, a heart of worship, and a desire to tell others of Him.

PRAYER: Pray for a fresh infilling of the indwelling Holy Spirit today. Ask for His leadership in your life, and commit yourself to live by His standards and walk by His leading.

THE BAPTIST'S FAITH AND MESSAGE
LUKE 3

After 400 years of prophetic silence in Israel, the forerunner of the Messiah appeared, preaching a message much different from anything the Israelites had heard before, and, unfortunately, much different from what is being preached in many quarters today. What were the elements of John's preaching? First, he preached about *a pervasive wickedness*. That John called for repentance is evidence that he believed that man's main problem is the problem of sin, a problem not limited to a certain segment of the population. In verse 7, he called those who came to hear him *"children of vipers,"* and Matthew specifically states that he hurled that epithet even toward the Pharisees and Sadducees, the religious leaders of the day. Luke tells us that tax-gatherers were in his audience, and even Roman soldiers, and John's gospel says that common people like fishermen and people from the big city of Jerusalem alike were drawn to him, but his message of sin and his call for repentance never changed, not even when he stood before King Herod. John also preached *a proven repentance* (vv. 8a, 11-14). Repentance is a change of mind that leads to a change of direction, a change of mind about our sin, about the Savior, and about the way of salvation, and when it is real, it always leads to a changed life. That's what John means when he tells them to bring forth fruit in keeping with repentance. He illustrates in verses 11-14 what the fruit of true repentance would look like for various people. John also preached *a personal faith* (v. 8b). Many Israelites mistakenly believed that because they were biologically descended from Abraham, they must be saved. John insisted that the faith of Abraham was not sufficient to save them; that each one of them must personally exercise the same faith in God that Abraham did. Today, too many people believe that because their parents or grandparents were Christians, that they must be saved, but in truth, no one can ride the coattails of their ancestors' faith into heaven. Each person must make a personal decision to receive Christ as Lord and Savior, to exercise a personal trust in Him and what He did on the cross when He paid the price for our sins. Notice also that John preached *a powerful Savior.* Some of the people were beginning to wonder if John might be the Christ, but John quickly put down that notion (vv. 15-17). He told them that he was merely the Messiah's forerunner, and that he was not even worthy to remove the Messiah's sandals; he merely baptized with water, but Jesus would baptize with the Holy Spirit. John preached salvation to all who would receive Christ as Lord and Savior, but he also preached *a perilous judgment* to those who would not (v. 17). Those who receive Christ will spend eternity with Him in heaven; those who do not receive Him will spend eternity separated from Him in hell, a place of unquenchable fire where they will be tormented forever. Finally, notice that John called for *a public commitment*. He called for those who had repented and placed their faith in the coming Messiah to indicate it by being baptized. Likewise, today, God still calls those who repent and place their faith in Christ follow Him in baptism as an outward sign of our inward commitment.

PRAYER: Although John preached the truth, he suffered as a result (vv. 19-20). Pray for those persecuted believers in other countries and here at home who are standing for the truth against government or societal pressure. Pray for your own pastor, and for others you know who faithfully proclaim the Word of God without compromise.

CHALLENGING OUR PREJUDICES
LUKE 4

All three of the synoptic gospels (Matthew, Mark and Luke) tell of Jesus' rejection in His hometown and home synagogue. Matthew (chapter 13) and Mark (chapter 6) focus on the townspeople's familiarity with Him as the reason for His rejection. They knew Him (or thought they knew Him) too well to accept Him as a religious leader, despite what they had heard about His ministry elsewhere. Luke gives a fuller account of the situation that arose at Nazareth, and an additional insight into their rejection. Apparently, when He first began His teaching, *"All spoke well of him and were amazed at the gracious words that came from his lips"* (v. 22 - NIV 84). He was a hometown boy made good, but by the end of His sermon that day, they were so enraged that they tried to throw Him off a cliff (v. 29)! What had so angered them? Verses 25-27 tell us. Jesus was teaching about the widow of Zarephath in Elijah's time, and He made the point that while there were many widows in Israel at the time, none of them were fed miraculously, but only this Gentile (non-Israelite) woman. Then, He followed that illustration by speaking of how in Elisha's time, there were many lepers in Israel, but the only leper that was cleansed was Naaman the Syrian, another Gentile. What so aroused their wrath against Him was His teaching that God's concern stretched beyond just Israel; that He cared about Gentiles as well. That cut cross-grain to much of the teaching of the day. God's intent all along in making Israel His chosen people was so that they would be a light to the Gentiles, taking the Word of His salvation to all people. Instead, Israel had become arrogant in her special status, believing that God only cared for them. Most Jews absolutely hated the Gentiles and considered them unclean. They would not eat with a Gentile or enter a Gentile's home for fear of becoming ritually contaminated. And nowhere was that prejudice against Gentiles any more pronounced than in Nazareth, the site of a Roman army garrison in Galilee. The people of Nazareth were exposed daily to reminders of the Roman occupation of their nation. They were surrounded by the pagan worship and appalled by the immoral habits of the Roman soldiers quartered there. To suggest that God actually cared about these unclean pagans was more than they could stand, and they reacted to that message violently. No subject touches a nerve quite like having our prejudices challenged. That is probably because prejudice is ingrained deeply and early in our lives, and usually by those we love and trust the most: our parents and grandparents, who likewise had it ingrained in them by their parents and grandparents before them. Because it is ingrained so deeply, it is a vice that doesn't die easily, even in the lives of believers. To reject that prejudice handed down from those we love feels somehow like a rejection of them. But we must understand that prejudice in any form is deeply offensive to God, who created all races and people groups and loves them all equally, with an ultimate love. Never forget that the person you may have prejudice against because of his skin color or ethnic background is someone that Jesus loved enough to die for, just as He loved you. To reject that person, to look down on him, to consider him inferior, is not merely an insult to him, but to his Creator. How can we who love Him not love those He has created, and those He loves?

PRAYER: Ask the Lord today to search your heart for any traces of prejudice that may be there. If it comes to mind, repent of it, and every time you feel that old prejudice rising to the surface, reject it again. Ask Him for wisdom to view all people through the lens of His love, and to treat all people as He would treat them.

AT YOUR WORD
LUKE 5

Simon Peter had been a fisherman his entire life, plying his trade on the Sea of Galilee. I wonder if he'd ever had a night so disappointing? Keeping in mind that they were fishing with nets, and that they had fished at night when the fish were most active, and that they had been hard at it all night long, you'd think they would have caught *something*! But there was nothing. Every time they hauled those nets in that night, they came up completely empty. There were no fish to take to the market and sell, no fish even to take home for a meal. Now, there was nothing left to do but wash and mend the nets, hang them up to dry, and head home for a hot meal and some much needed rest before heading out again at sundown. While he was working on his nets, though, Jesus had need of his boat. After Peter pushed it out a bit from the shore, Jesus sat in it and taught the crowds gathered along the beach, taking advantage of this natural amphitheater. Once Jesus finished, Peter may have been saying his goodbyes to Him when Jesus told him, *"Launch out into the deep and let down your nets for a catch"* (v. 4). Peter was tired, hungry, and frustrated with his lack of success. All he wanted to do was go home and sleep. The absolute last thing he wanted to do was let down those nets again, because that would mean he would have to clean them again, and if they hadn't caught anything at night, the chances were slim they'd catch anything in the heat of the day. Jesus may have known carpentry, but Peter knew fish and fishing, and letting down the nets after just getting them cleaned was crazy. We can hear the initial hesitation in his voice, the beginning of a protest: *"Master, we have worked all night and have caught nothing"* (v. 5). But then, right in the middle of the sentence, he remembers just who this is that he's talking to, this one he was already calling "Master." If Jesus was truly his Master, Peter could not say "no" to Him. So right in the middle of his protest, he reverses course and says, *"But at Your word I will let down the net"* (v. 5). If anyone else had suggested this course of action, Peter would have laughed and headed home, but he had seen Jesus do miraculous things before, and his faith would be rewarded with the biggest catch of fish he had ever seen. Jesus then used that miraculous catch of fish as a metaphor for a new call on Peter's life, the call to catch men for the Kingdom. Never forget: the most frustrating, disappointing, discouraging night of your life can give way to the most amazing, powerful, life-changing day of your life when you obey His Word and surrender your all to Him - your belongings (v. 3), your time and effort (v. 6), and your very life (v. 11).

PRAYER: Is there some word from the Lord that you're hesitating to follow, because it seemingly doesn't make sense from your experience? Recognize that as Lord of your life, He has every right to disrupt your carefully planned schedule. Express your willingness to obey Him. Pray, as Peter did, *"At Your Word, I will..."* Are you going through a dry season, a season of failure when all your efforts are coming up empty? Pray for the Lord to reverse that situation, and to fill your nets with miraculous provision as you obey Him.

REJOICE AND LEAP FOR JOY
LUKE 6

"Blessed are you when men hate you, and when they separate you from their company and insult you, and cast out your name as evil, on account of the Son of Man. Rejoice in that day, and leap for joy..." (vv. 22-23). Hmm...not my first response. I suspect it's not yours either. We all have an innate desire to be liked rather than hated. We feel the sting of rejection when people withdraw from us and the pain of insults that are hurled our way. We recoil at the injustice of being falsely accused of evil for doing good. Jesus tells us here that because the values of the Kingdom are so diametrically opposed to the world, to be right with Him will often put us at odds with those who are in the world, resulting in hatred, insults, rejection and injustice. It may even result in poverty, hunger and weeping (vv. 20-21). How do we respond in such times of persecution? First, we must maintain a proper perspective. We are certainly not the first to experience such treatment; indeed, when we are persecuted, we are in good company, and many of that company no doubt have experienced worse (v. 23c). We are to keep in mind that no matter how good it may be, or how bad it may be (compare verses 20-22 and 24-25), this life, its hardships and its pleasures are temporary. Eternity, though, is forever, and

enduring harsh treatment here for a short time (rather than compromising our faith or the truth to avoid such treatment) results in great future rewards that last forever (v. 23b). To attempt to be popular at the expense of God's truth makes us false prophets (v. 26). But notice that we are not just to think right, stand firm, and keep a proper perspective in times of persecution. We are to actively *"do good to those who hate you, bless those who curse you, and pray for those who spitefully use you"* (vv. 27-28). We are to do unto others not as they have done to us, but to treat others as we would want to be treated (v. 31). All ancient religious codes have some form of the Golden Rule, but it is always expressed in the negative: if you don't want others doing thus-and-so to you, don't do it to them. Jesus proclaims a higher standard for His followers: not just passively refusing to do evil or retaliate, but actively doing good to others, even to those who do evil to us. His justification for such an unnatural demand that is that it is indeed unnatural; it is supernatural (vv. 32-34), a reflection of the relationship with have with God as our Father (vv. 35-36).

PRAYER: As you read today's passage and devotion, a person or persons may have come to your mind, people who have done you wrong in some way. Don't be satisfied with simply not responding in kind; God calls you to respond in kindness. Pray God's blessing upon them. Ask the Lord to show you how you can do good to all people, even to those who have done, or are doing, evil to you. Praise the Lord that *"He is kind to the unthankful and the evil"* (v. 35), for thus were all of us before we received His mercy. Praise Him for His mercy and pray that you might be a reflection and an instrument of that divine mercy to others.

FORGIVEN MUCH
LUKE 7

Despite some surface similarities, this incident is not to be confused with the anointing of Jesus by Mary of Bethany in the home of Simon the leper during His passion week. This event took place much earlier in Jesus' ministry as He dined in the home of a Pharisee who was also named Simon. Although many of the Pharisees had already rejected Jesus and were hoping, if not plotting, for His death, the fact that Simon invited Jesus to his home indicates that in his mind, the jury was still out on Jesus. Undoubtedly, he had heard the opinions of others, but he could not overlook the many amazing things that he had seen and heard that Jesus was doing. Perhaps a private audience with this teacher would help him decide what to think about Him. It was during this dinner that a certain woman came into the dining room and began anointing Jesus' feet with her tears and perfume, and wiping them with her hair. At that, Simon's mind was made up: *"If this Man were a prophet, He would have known who and what kind of woman she is who is touching Him, for she is a sinner"* (v. 39). Surely, no *true* prophet would allow such a woman to touch Him! A true prophet would kick her away from His feet, not receive this act of homage from someone like *her*. Note the present tense verbs in Simon's thoughts as compared to the description of the woman in verse 37 (NIV 84): *"a woman who <u>had lived</u> a sinful life..."* The implication is that she had once lived a sinful life, but no more, and it's fairly obvious why: Jesus had changed her life, and her act of worship was an expression of her deep, abundant gratitude. Verse 40 is remarkable in its statement that *"Jesus answered him,"* given that Simon had said nothing out loud. Jesus knew what he was thinking, and told him a story about two debtors, one of whom owed 500 denarii and the other 50. Neither could pay the debt, so the creditor forgave them both. Now, Jesus asked, which one would love the creditor more? Simon correctly answered that it would be the one who had been forgiven more. Jesus went on to point out that the woman's great love expressed in her exuberant act of worship was because she had been forgiven much. Simon, by contrast, had neglected even the common courtesies normally extended to a guest by a host: no kiss of greeting, no servant to wash His feet (or even water for Him to wash His own feet), and no offer of olive oil to anoint His face. If it is true that *"He who is forgiven little loves little"* (v. 47), what does it say about someone who shows no love at all? Jesus went on to assure this woman that her sins were indeed forgiven, not because of her act of worship, but because of her faith (vv. 48, 50); her worship was evidence of her faith and her gratitude over how He had changed her life. In Simon, we see the Pharisee mindset in full bloom. The ancient Pharisees, and their modern-day counterparts, have very little concept, if any, of redemption. From their high horse of self-righteousness, they look down on others perceived to be far worse sinners than they, and to them, once a sinner, always a sinner. Once you've blown it in their eyes, you can never recover. They never let anyone forget what they once were, and they fail to recognize that they too are sinners in need of redemption. The Bible teaches that all of us are sinners, lost in our sins, spiritually dead in our trespasses apart from Christ. One person's sins may be more numerous, more pronounced, and more public than another's, but truly, the only difference between one dead man and another is the rate of decay. All stand in need of new life that only comes through Jesus, Simon the Pharisee no less than this scarlet woman. She had received Jesus' forgiveness. The story is open-ended as to whether Simon ever did.

PRAYER: What about you? Have you received His forgiveness by turning from your sins in repentance and placing your faith in Him as your Lord and Savior? Or are you trusting your religious background, your church membership, or your good works to save you? If you have received His forgiveness, as you think about how much you've been forgiven, express your gratitude to Him. If not, receive Him now! Even if you're trusting in Him and His sacrifice on Calvary alone for salvation, do you still show evidence of a judgmental spirit, looking down in judgment and condemnation, rather than compassion, on those you perceive as more sinful than you? Ask the Lord to show you if there is any Pharisee spirit lurking in you.

FEAR FACTOR
LUKE 8

There are four reactions of fear in this passage. In the first, the disciples are afraid of being, literally, in over their heads as a storm tossed their boat on the Sea of Galilee. Jesus was asleep while all this chaos was unfolding around Him, which indicates two things. Number one, He was fully human, and was apparently absolutely exhausted. If He could feel power going out from Him every time He healed someone (v. 46), how exhausting must it have been to go from village to village teaching and preaching (v. 1) and healing multitudes of their infirmities (6:17-19). Second, Jesus' ability to sleep in the storm showed His absolute confidence. He knew that His life would not end in a boating accident, but on a cross for the redemption of the world, so He could sleep even in the midst of a storm. The disciples, though, conclude in their fear that they are perishing. The second reaction of fear is unusual to be sure. After Jesus' deliverance of Legion from the hive of demons infesting him, the people of the area reacted in fear: *"Then they...found the man from whom the demons had departed sitting at the feet of Jesus, clothed and in his right mind. And they were afraid"* (v. 35). They asked Jesus to leave there area, because *"they were seized with great fear"* (v. 37). I find those verses quite amazing. Apparently, they had gotten used to the naked, demonized wild man running around in the tombs, but seeing him clothed and in his right mind caused not celebration, but great fear! With the destruction of the herd of pigs, the people of the region didn't know what to make of Jesus. Was He a healer, or a destroyer? A third reaction of fear came after the woman touched the hem of Jesus' garment, and came trembling to confess that it was she who had done it (v. 47). Finally, Jairus greatest fear came true when he received the word that his daughter had died (v. 50). What is the cure for fear, whatever may have elicited it? Faith! After Jesus had calmed the sea, *"He said to them, 'Where is your faith?'"* (v. 25). Jesus left the Gadarenes as requested, but He left behind Legion to proclaim to those who were fearful the great things Jesus had done for him. When He returned to this area later, a great crowd came to Him, bringing those who were sick (see Matthew 15:29-31). No longer afraid of Jesus, they demonstrated faith in His ability to heal. Jesus assured the trembling woman, *"your faith has made you well"* (v. 48). Finally, as Jairus reeled from the devastating news of his daughter's death, Jesus told him, *"Do not fear. Only believe, and she will be made well"* (v. 50). When we find ourselves experiencing fear, it is an indicator of lack of faith: lack of faith in His presence (v. 24), His person (v. 37), His power (v. 48), or His promise (v. 50). When we truly believe that He will never leave us nor forsake us, that He always knows what's best and only does what's best for us, that there is no power that can thwart His plans for us, and that He makes all things work together for good for us, what do we have to fear?

PRAYER: Are you dealing with fear today? Pray that He will replace your fear with faith. Take His words to Jairus into your own heart: *"Do not fear. Only believe..."*

WHAT KIND OF SPIRIT ARE YOU OF?
LUKE 9

Having spent most of His ministry successfully convincing His disciples about His identity (v. 20), Jesus now turns His attention to showing them what He had come to do. The reason He forbids them from telling anyone His identity is because both they and the crowds have a faulty understanding of the Messiah's mission. He has not come to set up an earthly kingdom, which was their expectation, but to give His life as a sinless, perfect sacrifice for men's sins, and as He heads to Jerusalem to accomplish that mission, the last thing He needs is a defective form of Messianic fervor getting in the way. Jesus' words about His own impending death were frightening (v. 22), but His words about the cost of discipleship were no doubt even more frightening (vv. 23-26). These are words that we tend to allegorize, but the disciples would have seen them as absolutely literal. They knew that anyone carrying a cross was carrying it to the place of execution to be placed upon it. It is to their credit, in light of such teaching, that only Judas fell away. They stayed with Him, even to the point of misguided defense. First, they forbade a man from casting out demons in Jesus' name because *"he does not follow with us"* (v. 40). I find it amazing that rather than rejoicing that demons were fleeing and people were being set free, their main concern was whether the exorcist was in "their group." In our day, do we rejoice at what God is doing in people's lives through churches or denominations other than our own, or is our rejoicing limited to God's actions through our group? Having rejected a man who was actually a friend, their reaction to those who were genuinely against them was not unexpected. When a Samaritan village refused to welcome Jesus, James and John (the Sons of Thunder - lots of hot air, noise and bluster) offered to call down fire on that village to avenge this insult to Jesus (one wonders what made them think they had such ability!). Such an overkill response to rejection was a far cry from Jesus' instruction on the matter (v. 5). Jesus' reaction to their suggestion was a strong rebuke: *"You do not know what kind of spirit you are of. For the Son of Man did not come to destroy men's lives but to save them."* Rather than taking some measure of revenge upon this Samaritan village, they traveled on to another village, where presumably they were welcomed. The good news would years later return to Samaria (see Acts 8) through the ministry of Philip. We can only wonder if, perhaps, this village that initially rejected Jesus later received Him. I remember vividly hearing a story about a pastor who took a visiting evangelist to see the unsaved husband of one of his church members. The pastor had witnessed to the man often, but with no result, and he hoped that the evangelist would be able to convince him to be saved. After speaking to the man about God's plan of salvation, the evangelist asked if he wanted to be saved, to which the man replied, "I don't think so, not now." He exhorted him further, and asked him again, and again received a no. Finally, in his frustration, the evangelist jumped up and shouted, "Well, go on to hell then!" and stormed out of the house. Because the evangelist "called down fire" upon him, that lost man would never grant the pastor another hearing, and presumably, the evangelist's curse came true. We must always leave the door open, and refuse to burn bridges to those who refuse Jesus, because those who refuse Him today may receive Him tomorrow.

PRAYER: Think of a church in your community that is not in your denomination, but that lifts up the name of Jesus. Pray for that church's members, their ministry and their ministers. Pray that you would always keep the lines of communication open to those who need Jesus, and never do or say anything that would burn those bridges.

PRIDE AND PRIORITY
LUKE 10

As Jesus makes His way to Jerusalem, He sends out 35 two-person "advance teams" to prepare the various villages He would pass through for His coming. These seventy followers of Jesus were told to take no provisions for their journey (v. 4). They were to trust in God alone to provide for them through the kindness of those they ministered to (vv. 5-9), and to trust Him even when people did not receive them kindly (vv. 10-12). When these seventy followers returned to Jesus, they were rejoicing over their ministry successes, in particular that *"even the demons are subject to us through Your name"* (v. 17). Jesus tells them, and by extension, us, that *"I give you authority to trample on serpents and scorpions, and over all the power of the enemy"* (v. 19). In Christ, we have authority over the enemy. Our enemy is powerful, far more powerful than we are, but we have the authority by which Jesus cast Satan out of heaven (v. 18) to overcome his superior force and take people out of his kingdom of darkness. Jesus warned us that our main source of rejoicing should not be our power over the enemy, but our salvation, the fact that we are children of God whose names are written down in heaven. Why this warning? It is very easy, in seasons of ministry success, to start believing that *we* are somehow responsible for the enemy's demise, that it is our work, our effort, our eloquence or our ability that has overcome the power of the enemy. Pride can creep in, oh so subtly, when we forget that it is the Lord's authority, not ours, by which the enemy is defeated. Rejoicing in our salvation, which He accomplished from start to finish, keeps us grounded in the truth that it's not about us, but about Him, that without Him, we can do nothing. In our service to the Lord, we must avoid the trap of misplaced pride. In Martha, we see a second trap, the trap of misguided priorities. While Mary sat at Jesus' feet, just basking in His presence, Martha was distracted from being with Jesus by her efforts to serve Jesus. She was concerned about providing a nice place for Him to sleep and a good meal for Him and His disciples. Think for a moment about the things she was anxious about. Jesus said, *"Foxes have holes and birds of the air have nests. But the Son of Man has no place to lay His head"* (9:58). This was a man who spent many a night outside under the stars. Was He really that concerned about where He would sleep that night? Was a man who had fed multitudes with a few loaves of bread and fish greatly concerned about His next meal? Did Jesus come to Martha's home because of her grand hospitality? Or was it because He loved her and her sister and brother (John 11:5)? When Martha's frustration finally boiled over, she didn't take it out on Mary, but on Jesus (v. 40), but Jesus responded that it was not Mary who was in the wrong, but Martha. Jesus does not condemn Martha's service - after all, it was rendered out of a heart of love - but He does question her priorities. The first task of a disciple is just to spend time with Jesus (note the order in Mark 3:14). Our service will naturally flow out of our devotion to Him, but when we get those priorities out of order, the result will always be frustration - frustration with our service, frustration with our Savior, and frustration with our sisters and brothers.

PRAYER: Take a few moments to rejoice in your salvation today. Pray that the Lord will keep you free from misplaced pride and misguided priorities in your service to Him. Pray also to the Lord of the Harvest, that He will send out more workers into His harvest field (v. 2).

TEACH US TO PRAY
LUKE 11

As far as we know, the only thing the apostles ever specifically asked Jesus to teach them was about prayer.

They saw in His prayer life something that they longed for, an intimacy with God that they did not have. Jesus' teaching here begins with a model (vv. 2-4), proceeds to a parable (vv. 5-8), and ends with encouragement (vv. 9-13). The model prayer focuses on relationship; God is our Heavenly Father. That was a truth not completely absent from first century Judaism, but no one had emphasized it (for obvious reasons) like Jesus did. Everything flows out of those first two words: *"Our Father"* (v.2). Lest we approach that relationship with a kind of flippant familiarity, we are reminded that His name is hallowed - holy. Our desire should be to please our Father, as children want to please their earthly fathers, by seeking His will to be done on Earth, just as His will is done in heaven. As our Father, He is concerned about every aspect of our lives, even such mundane things as the food we eat. He is our redeemer, who has forgiven us, and who expects us to be like Him in forgiving others. He is our protector, leading us not into temptation, but when temptation comes, delivering us from evil. After the model, Jesus tells a parable about a man going to a friend at midnight and asking for bread for another friend just coming in from a journey. Notice the reason the man receives the bread: *"I say to you, though he will not rise and give him anything because he is his friend, yet because of his persistence he will rise and give him as much as he needs"* (v. 8). If a reluctant friend at midnight can be persuaded to accede to a request, how much more should we expect to receive from God, who as our Father is never reluctant to bless? Indeed, when we ask, seek and knock (the tense of the verbs carries the sense of "keep on asking, keep on seeking and keep on knocking"), we are promised that *"it will be given to you...you will find...it will be opened."* It should be noted that what is given to us may not be exactly what we've asked, what we find may not be exactly what we were seeking, and the door that's opened may not be the one we've been pounding on! God doesn't always give us what we ask, but He always gives us what we need when we ask, even if we ask wrongly. This passage teaches us to pursue the P.U.S.H. Principle - Pray Until Something Happens. We are to pray until God answers, or until He shows us we've been praying wrongly. But something *will* happen, and it will be good: *"If a son asks for bread from any of you who is a father, will you give him a stone? Or if he asks for a fish, will you give him a serpent instead of a fish? Or if he asks for an egg, will you offer him a scorpion?"* (vv. 11-12). Only a monster of a man would so treat his children! *"If you then, being evil, know how to give good gifts to your children, how much more will your heavenly Father give the Holy Spirit* (Matthew renders it *"good things"*) *to those who ask Him?"* (v. 13). That should put to rest once and for all the oft-repeated statement, whispered in hushed, conspiratorial tones, "Be careful what you pray for...YOU JUST MIGHT GET IT!" What a horrible disincentive to pray, and what a horrible portrait of God. It pictures Him just waiting for someone to pray foolishly so that He can stick it to them. NO! If our Father will not give us stones for bread or serpents for fish or scorpions for eggs, neither will He give us those things if we are foolish or deceived enough to ask for them. Why not? Because He is OUR FATHER, who always knows what's best and only does what's best for us. We are encouraged to ask, because answers will be forthcoming, and while they may not be the answers we initially hoped for, they will be good answers! Now, *that* is an incentive to pray!

PRAYER: Go through the Lord's model prayer line by line today, personalizing it to your particular situation and needs. Don't pass over verse 13 too quickly. Have you asked the Father for the Holy Spirit lately? True, the Spirit came to personally indwell you when you were saved. But as God, He is infinite. Whatever you have of Him or from Him, whatever you know of Him, to whatever extent He's leading you, guiding you, and speaking to you, there's more...for those who ask. Ask the Father today to fill you to overflow with His Spirit, and then to expand your capacity to receive more of what He wants to give!

THE LINE IS BEING DRAWN
LUKE 12

Jesus has pronounced woes against the scribes and Pharisees, and they are beginning to oppose Him violently (11:37-54). Jesus makes it clear here that a line is being drawn, and that straddling that line is neither acceptable nor ultimately possible. Everyone is either for Him or against Him; there is no gray area and no middle ground. Those who try to avoid controversy by following Him secretly and denying their relationship with Him will eventually be found out (vv. 2-3). We think of Joseph of Arimathea, a member of the Jewish ruling council, the Sanhedrin, who was *"a disciple of Jesus, but secretly for fear of the Jews"* (John 19:38). He managed to keep his faith in Jesus a secret from his fellow Jewish leaders for awhile, but a time came when he had to stand up for his faith in Him, first before the Council in opposing Jesus' death (Luke 23:50-51) and then by boldly going to Pilate to ask for Jesus' body (Mark 15:43), taking the risk of being identified with a man crucified as an enemy of Rome! Fear of human opposition, persecution, or even death can push us toward the hypocrisy of denying Jesus (vv. 4-7), but far better to experience human rejection than to disappoint our Savior (vv. 8-10). When "crunch time" comes in our lives, and we're tempted to deny the Lord under pressure, it is then that we must rely on the supernatural power of the Holy Spirit to make His defense through us (vv. 11-12). What a testimony the martyrs give (both in times past and in our present day) by not denying Jesus even under threat of death. Stephen's eloquent testimony in his dying moments (Acts 7:58-60), not to mention the reactions of dozens of other Christians that he persecuted, played a role in bringing about Paul's conversion. As I am writing this, reports are coming in daily from the Middle East about Christians having their heads cut off, refusing to acknowledge Allah or Mohammed and speaking the name of Jesus right up until their final breaths, sealing their testimony with their own blood (Revelation 12:11). The parable of the rich fool and Jesus' teaching about possessions seem at first to be a new subject, but the two discussions are related. Sometimes, it is not fear of losing our lives that causes us to deny our Lord, but fear of losing our possessions. Again, as I am writing this, various Christian bakers, photographers and florists in the United States are facing the loss of their businesses and ruinous fines over their refusal to lend their talents to so-called "gay weddings." Standing up for Biblical morality has the potential to cost them everything they have worked for. Jesus teaches us here that we can hold onto possessions, hoarding things in an effort to acquire "security" (vv. 16-19), or we can be *rich toward God* (v. 21) by holding things loosely, trusting Him for our security (vv. 22-32) and giving generously to others (v. 33), which not only garners us eternal rewards, but keeps our hearts focused in the right place during our earthly lives (v. 34). Jesus' teaching about His second coming in verses 35-48 certainly suggests that such pressure to deny Jesus will become much more prevalent as we approach the end. The dividing line between those who stand for Christ and those who oppose Him (or deny Him) will become more and more pronounced, even dividing the closest of relationships (vv. 49-53).

PRAYER: Pray for our brothers and sisters who are standing up for the Lord, even in the face of persecution, loss of possessions, and even martyrdom. Pray that you will stand boldly for the Lord, even in the face of rejection, even in the face of persecution, even in the face of loss, and even in the face of death.

WORSE SINNERS?
LUKE 13

There is within all of us a tendency to blame the victim. When some calamity befalls someone, we, like Job's "friends," want to assign blame to that person, to make sense of it by believing that the victim somehow deserved it. Jesus addresses this attitude head on, as He deals with two incidents that people in Israel where apparently talking about at the time. In the first, people came and told Jesus about some Galileans *"whose blood Pilate had mingled with their sacrifices"* (v. 1), apparently putting them to death as they came to the Temple. These men may have been in rebellion against Rome (Galilee was a hotbed of such activity), or just suspected of being rebels, but the horror of their deaths in the context of worship had struck fear in the populace. Jesus Himself brings up another incident, an accident in which a tower had fallen and crushed eighteen people. Jesus makes it clear that the Galileans killed by Pilate were not worse sinners than any other Galileans, nor were the ones who perished when the tower fell worse sinners than others in Jerusalem. All people are sinners, and without repentance, all will likewise perish. We may not die as the Galileans did, as victims of a repressive government, or as the eighteen did, as victims of a tragic accident, but we will all perish, and without repenting of our sins and receiving Christ as Lord and Savior, our fate beyond death makes whatever form our death takes pale into insignificance. There was also a tendency in that time to blame illness on sin (see John 9:1-3), to assume that a person with an ongoing infirmity was being punished by God for some sin in his life. The story of the woman in verses 10-17 shows that this assumption is untrue, not to mention

117

unkind. This woman had been bent over, unable to stand up straight for eighteen years because of back problems. Many would have assumed that she had committed some horrible sin for which God was punishing her, but the text attributes her sickness to *"a spirit of infirmity"* (v. 11), and Jesus stated that she was *"a daughter of Abraham whom Satan has bound these eighteen years"* (v. 16). In calling her a *"daughter of Abraham,"* I suspect that Jesus was doing more than identifying her Jewish heritage; after all, she was in the synagogue, and everyone knew that she was Jewish. He was speaking of her spirituality, commending her as one who carried the faith of Abraham. Far from being punished by God for some sin, she was in fact being oppressed by Satan because of her righteousness! While sickness in general came into the world because of sin in general, and while some sickness can be attributed to specific sin (see I Corinthians 11:30), it is wrong to assume that everyone who takes ill is being punished for sin. Sickness is part and parcel of living in a fallen world and dealing with a hateful enemy. While others were obsessed with pointing fingers and assessing perceived blame, Jesus was interested in setting her free from the devil's painful affliction. May we likewise be people not of condemnation, but of compassion. May we never heap greater hurt upon those who are already hurting by pointing the finger of blame, but work to alleviate their pain through the power and presence of Jesus.

PRAYER: Is there someone you know who is currently struggling with illness? Pray for their comfort during the affliction, and for their healing from the affliction.

INVITATIONS AND EXCUSES
LUKE 14

The Parable of the Great Banquet (vv. 15-24) is a picture of God's great invitation to salvation. In the parable, a man issues an invitation to a great banquet. He was in no way obligated to prepare a supper or to invite these guests to partake of it. They had in no way earned the supper. He was not paying them back for some good work that they had done for him. He just decided out of the goodness of his heart to prepare a feast and invite these people to it. The meal was absolutely free. They didn't have to work for it or pay for it. All the expense had been taken care of, and all the preparations had already been made. All they had to do was come and receive the meal freely. The application is obvious. The rich man in the story represents God. The supper represents all of the glories of salvation: forgiveness of sin, an abundant earthly life in Christ, and eternal life in heaven. God issues His invitation freely through His servants - pastors, evangelists, teachers, witnesses - as a matter of pure grace, and like the rich man's invitation, God's invitation requires nothing of us, other than to respond to the invitation in repentance and faith. We don't have to pay for our salvation, and we don't have to work for our salvation, because Jesus paid the price for it on the cross of Calvary. As the servant in the story came to those invited, they all began to make excuses. One man had bought a piece of land, and was going out to look at it. Another had bought five yoke of oxen, and was going to try them out. The third man had married a wife, and insisted that he couldn't come. At first glance, all of these excuses sound perfectly reasonable, but in truth, they are far from it. What kind of man buys a field without first seeing it? How much surveying could he do at such a late hour, when the sun was going down? And surely he could have gone the next day. The man with the oxen faces the same questions. It is doubtful that he would buy five yoke of oxen without testing them out first, and was he planning to plow by torchlight? Finally, the third man had perhaps the weakest excuse of all. What young wife wouldn't love to be relieved of her cooking duties that night in favor of a nice banquet?

There are many who respond to God's invitation to salvation with excuses. And while their excuses may sound legitimate, particularly to themselves, NO excuses are legitimate for refusing God's invitation. In the light of the refusal of his original guests, the master expanded the invitation to others: *"the poor and the maimed and the lame and the blind"* (v. 21). Jesus here is speaking of His own ministry to the outcasts, those often overlooked and rejected by the polite religious society of the day. The further expansion, to the laborers just getting off of work at sundown (v. 23), is a hint of the fact that the gospel, which for the most part would be rejected by the Jews, would eventually expand to the Gentiles.

PRAYER: Pray for those you may know who are answering God's invitation to salvation with feeble excuses that may ease their minds now, but will never stand before God's judgment seat. It is a tragedy when the invitation is refused, but it is also a tragedy when the invitation is never issued. Who do you know who needs an invitation to God's banquet? Pray for opportunities to witness to the lost, to *"compel them to come in"* (v. 23) to the Master's feast.

REJOICE WITH ME
LUKE 15

The three parables of Luke 15 all deal with something that was lost and then found, but that is not the main theme of the parables. The main theme is the reaction of the person who has found the lost item, and the reaction of those who love that person. The context of the parables in verses 1-2 is the key to their interpretation. Jesus was welcoming gladly tax-collectors and sinners who drew near to hear Him, but the Pharisees and scribes murmured against Him, complaining that *"This Man receives sinners and eats with them."* In response to their grumbling, Jesus tells the parables of the lost sheep, the lost silver, and the lost son. In the first parable, a shepherd, upon counting his sheep, discovers that one of his 100 sheep is missing, so he leaves the 99 and goes looking for the one lost sheep. When he finds it, he rejoices greatly, but not only does he rejoice, his friends and neighbors rejoice with him. The reason, obviously, is not because they love sheep, but because they love the shepherd. The second parable, about the lost silver coin, proceeds in much the same way. A woman, noticing that one of her 10 silver coins is missing, sweeps the house and searches diligently until she finds it. *"And when she has found it, she calls together her friends and neighbors, saying, 'Rejoice with me, for I have found the coin which I had lost.'"* (v. 9). Again, they rejoice because of their love of the woman who has found the coin. In the more elaborate third parable, the parable of the lost son, a man receives his son back safe and sound after the son has gone off to a far country and squandered his inheritance. How does the man react? He throws a party, and he and his whole household rejoice. All, that is, except his older son, who is disgusted by the whole situation. The point of the parables is fairly clear: God rejoices when the lost are found, and so do those who love God. What then does that say about those who don't rejoice when the lost are found? The Pharisees had a high sense of morality and an almost non-existent sense of redemption. To them, once a tax-collector, always a tax-collector. Once a prostitute, always a prostitute. Whereas the Pharisees delighted in their perceived superiority to sinners, Jesus delighted in receiving sinners and changing their lives. Like the older son in the parable, the Pharisees had kept the rules and never wandered off to the far country to indulge in wild living (v. 29), so to speak. But just as the older son's attitude showed how far he was from his father's heart, so too their grumbling over those who were being reclaimed from lives of sin showed just how far they were from the Father's heart. Just as the older son needed to be reconciled to his father, so too they needed to be reconciled to God. The father in the parable made it clear that the party was for everyone, and the older son was welcome to rejoice with the rest, if he so chose. At that point, the parable ends abruptly and in an open-ended manner. We're not told if the older son came into the party, or turned away in disgust. That's because the invitation was still open for those Pharisees who heard it to repent and come into the Kingdom. Sadly, most of them turned away in disgust and refused His invitation.

PRAYER: Some who are in the Kingdom came in from the far country, rescued from lives of great degradation and sin. If that is the case with you, thank the Lord for His delight in redeeming even those who are deeply mired in sin. Others came in from close by - raised in church, saved at a young age, never in too much trouble - but no less lost than the "far country" sinners (Romans 3:23). If that is your testimony, thank the Lord for opening your eyes to the truth of your lost condition before you became mired in self-righteousness. Ask the Lord to point out any tendency in you to look down upon those in sin, rather than looking with compassion upon them.

MONEY, MONEY, MONEY, MONEY
LUKE 16

The Parable of the Unrighteous Steward (vv. 1-8) is one of Jesus' most bizarre parables. In it, a rich man dismisses the chief manager of his assets, apparently giving him some time to prepare a final accounting of his business dealings (vv. 1-2). Before he loses his authority over the man's assets, though, the steward makes some shady deals to ingratiate himself to the rich man's debtors in the hope that they will take care of him after the loss of his position. In the parable, the rich man actually commends his dishonest steward, not for his dishonesty, but for having acted shrewdly. What possible meaning can we derive from this story? Surely, it is not encouraging us to act in a dishonest fashion, and it certainly cannot be telling us that God commends dishonest activity. The key to understanding the parable is in verses 8b-9: *"For the sons of this world are wiser in their own generation than the sons of light. I say to you, make friends for yourself by means of unrighteous wealth, so that when you fall short, they may receive you into eternal dwellings."* Jesus is saying that if an earthly employer can commend an employee for misusing his money in a dishonest but shrewd way, how much more will God commend His stewards for using His money in a righteous and shrewd way? Just as the dishonest steward used his master's money to gain friends and lodging for himself when his job ended, so too we are called to use our Master's money (all that He entrusts to us) to gain friends (converts to the Kingdom) so that we might receive a rich welcome (and the commendation of our Master) when we exit our stewardship here on Earth. Jesus goes on to teach that the money entrusted to us by God is a test designed to show what we can be trusted with in terms of spiritual responsibility (vv. 10-13). No one who is unfaithful in the proper stewardship of money can be trusted to be a proper steward of the glorious riches of the gospel. Isn't it interesting that many of those who most pervert the gospel often do so in a manner that allows them to amass great wealth to themselves? The Pharisees, *"who were lovers of money"* (v. 14), hearing Jesus' teaching, derided Him over it. They tended to see wealth as a sign of God's favor, and poverty as a sign of God's curse. Jesus' next parable, of the Rich Man and Lazarus, completely turns the tables on their thinking. In that parable, the rich man, far from being favored by God, ends up in the eternal torment of hell. Conversely, the poor man Lazarus (not to be confused with Jesus' friend of the same name whom He will soon raise from the dead), far from being rejected by God, ends up in heaven. In eternity, the tables are turned indeed. Now, the rich man who denied Lazarus even the barest of comfort (v. 21) is himself denied the least comfort, and in far worse circumstances (vv. 24-26), while Lazarus is welcomed into paradise. While not the main point of the parable, this parable teaches us that hell is a terrible place indeed, a place of unimaginable suffering, a place of no comfort, a place of no escape, and a place of great regret.

PRAYER: If you're asking the Lord for greater responsibility in His Kingdom, He may be asking you how responsible you've been with the finances He's entrusted to you (vv. 10-12). Ask the Lord to show you how you can be a better steward of all that He has given you, including your finances. Pray for those you know who are on the path to eternity separated from God in hell. Pray for their salvation before it is eternally too late, and pray that the Lord will use you to reach them.

GRATITUDE
LUKE 17

All Christians are well aware that we are in the Kingdom only by the grace of God, and not because of any merit purchased by any good works of our own. But it is important for us to understand that *everything* we receive from God is a matter of grace, not just our salvation. It is very easy to fall into a pattern of believing we've earned some special treatment from God because of our good works or our service to the Kingdom, and then to feel robbed somehow if we don't receive it. In truth, our service to Him, as Jesus' words in verses 7-10 teach us, can never measure up to what we owe Him for saving us. We serve Him out of gratitude for what He has already done, not in the belief that we are somehow earning additional favor from Him. But it should be noted that our Master is not like the human master in the story. A human master would expect his servant to work all day, and then to prepare and serve him dinner before eating his own, and he certainly would not express gratitude to the servant for having faithfully obeyed his commands. Our Master, though, doesn't call us slaves, but friends (John 15:15), and He freely invites us to His table. Because of *His* goodness (not ours!), He lavishes us with blessings far beyond anything we deserve, because we could never deserve even the least of His blessings. The blessings we receive from Him are gifts of His grace, and not rewards for our service. The theme of gratitude continues in the story of the ten cleansed lepers. Leprosy was a horrible disease, a disease that cut its victims off from society as it slowly killed them. These lepers called to Jesus from a distance, asking for His mercy, and He called out to them to go and show themselves to the priest. Under the Mosaic Law, if a leper was cleansed, he was required to present himself to be examined by a priest, who would then declare him healed and allow him back into the community. For these lepers to start out for the priest while still leprous was an act of faith on their part, and that faith was rewarded by their cleansing along the way. Of the ten, though, only one came back to Jesus to thank Him and glorify God for his healing. The contrast of verses 7-10 and 11-19 should not be missed. Far from expecting God to be grateful to us for our service to Him, we should live lives constantly expressing our gratitude (in word and deed) to Him for what He has done for us!

PRAYER: Spend some extended time today expressing your gratitude for the Lord for saving you and for all of His abundant blessings in your life. Ask forgiveness for any time you've felt He "owed" you something because of your service to Him.

PERSISTENCE
LUKE 18

Chapter 18 begins with Jesus' parable about a persistent widow. Widows in that culture, particularly if they had no adult male relative to care for them, had no legal rights, and someone was taking advantage of this woman and her lack of legal standing. She appealed to a judge to avenge her against her adversary, but at first, the judge was reluctant to do anything about her situation. Given that he was a man who *"did not fear God or regard man"* (v. 2), his reluctance to help the widow may have been because she had no money to pay him a bribe. But she had something else with which to persuade him: her persistence. She would not stop coming to him and making her appeal until justice was done. The "bribe" she would pay would be to finally leave him alone! Unfortunately, many people read that parable and totally misunderstand its meaning. To them, God is the judge, the poor widow represents us, and the point of the parable is that our only hope of dragging a blessing out of our reluctant God is by wearing Him out with much praying. Nothing could be further from the truth. The parable is not one of comparison, but of contrast. Jesus is saying that if a crooked judge could be persuaded to answer the request of a widow with no legal standing merely through her persistence, how much more can our loving Father-God, who is always eager to bless, be persuaded to enact justice on behalf of His children when we persist in prayer? Prayers are not always answered immediately, and trials sometimes last for an uncomfortably long time, but in the interim between our seeking God and His rescue, *"it is necessary always to pray and not lose heart"* (v. 1). The answer will come, in His perfect timing. Even when circumstances or other people dissuade us, let is call out to Him all the more. The chapter ends with a perfect example of prayer that will not be deterred. When the blind beggar near

Jericho heard that Jesus was passing by, he cried out in faith, *"Jesus, Son of David* (a Messianic designation), *have mercy on me!"* (v. 38). When those who were leading the processional rebuked him and tried to silence him, he would not keep quiet, but cried out with even greater fervency and volume to Jesus. Because of his persistence and faith, *"he received his sight and followed Him, glorifying God. When all the people saw it, they gave praise to God"* (v. 43). When God reverses long-standing problems that have been matters of long seasons of prayer, great is the glory He receives from us and from those who hear our testimony!

PRAYER: Is there some matter about which you've been praying for a long time with no answer? Have you felt like giving up, or have you given up? Lift up that prayer again! Persist in bringing it before the throne of God, knowing that He is not a reluctant judge, but an all-wise Father, and when the time is right, His perfect will will be manifested fully in your life.

A WEE LITTLE MAN...
LUKE 19

Most of us at some point have sung about him: "Zacchaeus was a wee little man, a wee little man was he. He climbed up in the sycamore tree for the Lord he wanted to see..." In truth, there was far more to Zacchaeus than his stature. We're told that he was *"a chief tax collector, and he was rich"* (v. 2). Tax-collectors were Jews, but they worked for the occupying Roman government in collecting the various taxes and fees that Rome exacted from its conquered subjects. Rome's only concern was getting its taxes in full, and they looked the other way as tax-collectors enriched themselves by collecting more than the allotted tax and keeping the difference for themselves. Tax-collectors, as you can imagine, were highly resented, branded as traitors to their people, and treated as outcasts. The attitude of the Jewish people was, "You want to work for the Gentiles, then we'll treat you like a Gentile." They were generally dismissed from the synagogue and forbidden to go past the Court of the Gentiles at the Temple, and their wives and children would likewise be ostracized. One wonders if, human nature being what it is, Zacchaeus had endured no end of abuse as a child and young man because of his short stature. Already feeling rejected and ostracized, he found a way to turn the tables on his tormentors, and now the victim had become a bully, with the whole force of the Roman army backing him up. Whatever had drawn him into this sordid business, he still possessed a draw toward spiritual things, shown in his desire to see Jesus and his efforts to do so (vv. 3-4). Jesus called him by name, and invited Himself to his home. That was shocking, because, again, tax-collectors were treated like Gentiles, and Jews believed that entering a Gentile's home made them unclean. Many were those who murmured against Jesus for going to Zacchaeus' house (v. 7), but Jesus' loving attention toward Zacchaeus brought about a profound change in the man, highlighted by his repentance, his newfound generosity, and his commitment to make restitution for the wrongs he had committed (v. 8). Jesus declared, *"Today salvation has come into this house, because he also is a son of Abraham"* (v. 9). It is important to note that Zacchaeus was not saved by "turning over a new leaf" and righting his wrongs. Jesus' statement that he was now a *"son of Abraham"* speaks not of his Jewish background, but of the fact that he now possessed the same kind of faith as Abraham. It was his faith in Jesus that brought about the dramatic change in Zacchaeus.

PRAYER: Do you know someone who is an outcast? Pray that you might have an opportunity to show genuine love and compassion to that person, and that you might introduce that outcast to Jesus, who delights in seeking and saving the lost (v. 10).

MARRIAGE AND THE RESURRECTION
LUKE 20

The Pharisees (the party of the scribes who, for the most part, held sway in the synagogues) and the Sadducees (the priestly party who were in control of the Temple and its rituals) were hated enemies with very different views of Biblical interpretation. Indeed, about the only thing they ever agreed upon was their mutual disdain for Jesus! The Sadducees accepted only the five books of Moses as Scripture, and they did not believe in the resurrection of the dead. The Pharisees accepted the entirety of the Old Testament as Scripture, and they did believe in the resurrection of the dead. Their disagreement over these and other points of doctrine was a matter of constant bickering between them. The Sadducees presented a case to Jesus that they had undoubtedly used often in their debates with the Pharisees, a hypothetical situation intended to make belief in an afterlife appear foolish. Under the Jewish Law (Deuteronomy 25:5-6), if a man died without a male heir, leaving behind a widow, his next closest male relative (usually a brother) was required to marry the widow, and the first male child resulting from that union would be considered legally the dead man's son and would inherit his property. This so-called "Levirate Marriage" (from the Latin word *levir*, which means "brother-in-law") was a provision intended to provide for widows and to keep property in families. In the Sadducees' hypothetical scenario, a woman went through this marital arrangement with all seven brothers in a family, all of them dying childless before she too died. Now, they asked Jesus, *"in the resurrection, whose wife will she be? For the seven had her as a wife"* (v. 33). Jesus' answer was that the life to come is not simply a continuation of this life, but is much different in nature and quality, and one of the differences is that there is no marriage or giving in marriage in that future state. That answer is a bit disturbing to us, because we are so tied to this life, and in particular, to our most treasured relationship in this life, to our spouse. It is disturbing to think that our marriage relationship, which is so meaningful to us in this life, would not continue into the next life. I think we should note that Jesus did not say that our relationships will not continue, but He did indicate that they would continue in a much different and much higher form. We should take comfort in knowing that whatever form our current relationships take in heaven, it will be of such magnificent quality that our current earthly relationships, no matter how wonderful they may be, cannot compare, and are but a dim shadow of what is to come. After dismissing the Sadducees' hypothetical situation, Jesus goes on to settle the debate once and for all. He points them back to the words of God spoken from the burning bush to Moses in Exodus 3 (certainly within the Sadducees' five accepted Biblical books). There, God told Moses, *"I am...the God of Abraham, the God of Isaac, and the God of Jacob,"* all of whom had passed from this life long before Moses' time. Jesus, noting the present tense of the verb (He said, "I AM their God" not "I WAS their God"), makes the point that God is not the God of the dead, but of the living. When God spoke to Moses, He was STILL the God of Abraham, Isaac and Jacob, because those three patriarchs were still very much alive! Even the scribes, no friends or fans of Jesus (note verses 45-47), were impressed at how thoroughly He had dismantled the Sadducees' pet argument (v. 39).

PRAYER: For those who have become "one flesh" in marriage (Genesis 2:24), the greatest hurt imaginable is when that one flesh unity is torn asunder by death. Pray for those you may know who have recently experienced the death of their spouses. Pray that God will bring His comfort to their grieving hearts.

WHEN PERSECUTION COMES
LUKE 21

No one in these present days can read Jesus' words in verses 12-19 without a bit of pause. Persecution has been a fact of life for most Christians in most places at most times throughout history, but in our day, there seems to be a definite up-tick of persecution of Christians worldwide, or, at the very least, much more publicity surrounding the issue. The shocking thing is that the publicity is not coming so much from people outraged over these acts of aggression, but from the perpetrators themselves, bragging about them! Almost daily, we hear about the kidnapping and enslavement of Christians in parts of Africa, the forced relocation of Christians in the Middle East from their homes and property, the brutal beheadings of Christians by ISIS and other groups in Muslim countries, and the firebombing of Christian churches in various parts of the world. Even here in the United States of America, which has enjoyed an unprecedented degree of religious liberty throughout its history, there is a growing hostility toward all things Christian, and a growing attempt to force Christians to violate their consciences, particularly in matters surrounding homosexuality. The old saying about "If you were put on trial for being a Christian, would there be enough evidence to convict you?" comes into sharp focus here. If the answer is yes, you may very well be convicted, and you may very well face various forms of punishment, including death, for your Christian faith. Jesus, both here and elsewhere, made it clear that such things would be the case, that it is *lack* of persecution that is unusual, not persecution. He wants us not to be taken by surprise by it, but not to be overly concerned about it either. He tells us that we are to view persecutions as opportunities for testimony (vv. 12-13). What greater testimony can there be than standing firm for our faith under pressure, even under pain of death? He tells us not to practice our defense beforehand (v. 14). On the surface, having some idea of how we would defend ourselves would seem to be a prudent measure. But practicing our defense in advance might make us more likely to live with hesitancy rather than boldness, building "plausible deniability" into our lives rather than an absolute certainty of where we stand. Jesus promises that He Himself will give us wisdom in what to say when the time comes. The betrayal of those closest to us, the irrational hatred of society at large, and even violent death are definite possibilities for those who stand firm in the faith (vv. 15-17), but still, *"not a hair of your head shall perish"* (v. 18). A story is told of an old-time evangelist whose multiple-week crusade was hurting the liquor business in a town. The local liquor distributor stuck a gun in the evangelist's belly and announced, "If you're not out of town by tomorrow, I'm going to kill you." The evangelist looked at the gun in the man's hand and said quietly, "You can't threaten me with eternal life." The liquor distributor was so jarred by the calm response of the evangelist that he himself came to Christ! For the believer, death is just a one-way ticket out of the sufferings of this life and into our heavenly home. That means that the worst thing that can happen to us is the best thing that could happen to anyone!

PRAYER: Pray for your brothers and sisters in Christ who are facing intense persecution in various parts of the world. Pray that religious liberties in America would be strengthened, and not eroded further. Pray that when you face pressure to compromise your commitments, whether light pressure or the heaviest of pressures, you will stand strong and speak boldly for Christ.

SIFTED LIKE WHEAT
LUKE 22

Jesus' words to Peter in verse 31 were frightening indeed, and not just to Peter: *"Satan has demanded to have you to sift you as wheat."* It doesn't come out in our modern English translations, but the "you" pronouns in verse 31 are plural, whereas the "you" pronouns in verse 32 are singular. In other words, Satan had demanded permission to sift all of the disciples like wheat, but Jesus states that He had especially prayed for Peter. Of all of them, none was a bigger target of the enemy. Great potential for leadership and great potential for failure often go hand in hand, and that was certainly the case with Peter. Jesus says that the content of His prayer was that Peter's faith would not fail. He did not pray that Peter himself would not fail; indeed, he prophesies his failure in verse 34. Failure would dog Peter all night long. He failed to pray with Jesus, he failed to protect Jesus, and he failed to proclaim Jesus. First, he failed to stay awake and pray at Jesus' command. Then, when the mob came to arrest Jesus, John, the final gospel writer, tells us that it was Peter who attacked the high priest's servant, whose name was Malchus (John 18:10). His effort was so pitiful, about what you would expect from a fisherman wielding a sword, perhaps for the first time. He was swinging at the man's head, but he missed, and only managed to cut off his ear. It's almost comical, but what's not comical about the situation is that if Jesus hadn't stepped in and healed Malchus, the soldiers would have made quick work of Simon Peter, and that would have been the last we ever heard of him. Interestingly, only the physician Luke chose to tell us about this last healing of Jesus' ministry, and he is also the only gospel writer who mentions Jesus' sweating of blood (v. 44), a medical condition called *hemathydrosis.* This condition results when great stress gives way to great resolve. Under stress, the capillaries in the forehead contract, but when the person comes to a resolution of the stress (*"Nevertheless, not My will, but Yours, be done"* - v. 42), the capillaries open suddenly, and the blood rushing in bursts them, causing blood to drain into the sweat glands. It is interesting that this took place in Gethsemane, which means "olive press." This was the place where the precious oil was squeezed out of the olives grown there on the Mount of Olives. After Jesus' arrest, Peter failed to stand strong for Jesus as he had protested he would in verse 33, denying Him three times while in the courtyard of the high priest. Luke gives us a detail that the others do not, that at the moment of the third denial, the rooster crowed and Jesus made eye contact with Peter across the courtyard. No wonder *"Peter went outside and wept bitterly"* (v. 62). The sifting of wheat involves a violent shaking, and Peter and the others were violently shaken by the events of that horrible night. But the image of "sifting like wheat" speaks to us of more than just shaking; it shows us God's purpose in allowing that shaking. Just as wheat is sifted to remove impurities from it, God allows us to be shaken at times to remove impurities from our lives. Satan shakes us to try to ruin us; God allows it to refine us. What determines the result is not the violence of the shaking, but the strength of our faith (v. 32). Peter's faith would not fail. He would survive this shaking, but he emerged from it with all of his (unfounded) self-confidence shaken away, leaving only die-hard confidence in Christ alone. In that God-confidence, he and the others would shake the entire world!

PRAYER: Do you know someone who is going through a terrible time of shaking right now? Pray that his faith would stand strong and not fail in the time of trial. Are you going through a time of shaking? Consider this great truth: Jesus is praying for you (Hebrews 7:25), just as He prayed for Peter. Pray that all of God's purposes for allowing this shaking would be realized, and that everything not of Him would shake loose from your life.

INJUSTICE
LUKE 23

Have you experienced injustice in your life? Jesus knows how that feels. His trial was an absolute mockery, a miscarriage of justice of the highest order. He was first brought by the Sanhedrin to Pontius Pilate, the Roman governor of Judea. They had already determined that He was worthy of death in a "trial" that violated their own rules of jurisprudence. Under Jewish law, a person in a death penalty case could not be sentenced on the same day as the trial, but they had immediately rushed to the sentence of death. As eager as they were to put Him to death, they had no authority to carry out that sentence; only a Roman official could order an execution. So off to Pilate they went. Knowing that Pilate wouldn't care less about their charge of blasphemy, they came spouting trumped-up charges that would be of concern to a Roman governor, that He was *"perverting our nation, and forbidding us to pay taxes to Caesar, and saying that He Himself is Christ, a King"* (v. 2). Thus, the charges against Him were changed right in the middle of the legal proceedings. Pilate examined Him (John 18:28-38 gives greater detail about this examination than the synoptic gospels do), and declared Him innocent of any violation of Roman law that would deserve the death penalty. When the council members insisted that Pilate do something about this Galilean troublemaker (v. 5), Pilate seized the opportunity to move the problem off of his desk and onto someone else's. Roman law stipulated that a criminal could be tried by the governor over the territory in which he was arrested, or by the governor of his home area. Knowing that Herod, the Roman ruler of Galilee, was in town for the feast, Pilate remanded Jesus to him for his evaluation. Herod was happy about the situation. He had heard about Jesus and hoped to see Him perform some miracle, but Jesus was silent in the face of his questions. Herod and his soldiers mocked Him, dressed Him in a fine robe, and sent Him back to Pilate. In doing so, Herod also declared that he saw no reason for a charge against Jesus. Pilate announced to the council that neither he nor Herod had seen any reason to execute Jesus, and, as the council members stirred up the crowds, he ordered Jesus scourged, hoping that seeing Jesus punished in this manner would satisfy them. Scourging was less severe than crucifixion, but still a horrible punishment. So severe were the wounds from scourging that many of its victims would eventually die from blood loss, shock, or infection. When that still did not satisfy them, Pilate relented and ordered Him crucified. What enormous injustice! Jesus was declared innocent three times by two different governing authorities, was sentenced to a terrible, undeserved punishment, and even after enduring that initial punishment, He was still sentenced to die the most cruel death imaginable! How did Jesus cope with this degree of injustice? He grieved for the hardness of heart of those who had inflicted this injustice on Him, and for the terrible price they would pay as a result (vv. 27-31), He prayed for their forgiveness, even as they "rubbed it in" by mocking Him on the cross (v. 34), and He extended forgiveness freely to one of the criminals who initially abused Him (Matthew 27:44) but then had a change of heart (vv. 40-43). When we experience injustice in this life, we would do well to respond in the same manner.

PRAYER: In our day, we see believers increasingly becoming the victims of unjust treatment at the hands of corrupt court systems: Christian bakers, photographers and florists losing their businesses and being assessed ruinous fines for refusing to lend their talents to gay "weddings," military chaplains losing promotions and being mustered out of the service for standing firm on the Word of God, university faculty members being denied positions or tenure because of their Christian faith, Christian organizations being denied approval on college campuses, and Christian students being denied entry into certain degree programs because of their Christian convictions. Pray for anyone you know who is experiencing such injustice. Have you experienced unjust treatment from some person, some group, or some system? Look again at how Jesus handled the high level of injustice He endured, and pray that you might respond as He did.

BELIEVE WHAT WAS SPOKEN
LUKE 24

The resurrection experiences and appearances in Luke 24 contain an interesting common theme. After the women came to the tomb on the first Easter Sunday and found it open, two angels stood before them, reminding them of what Jesus had said: *"Why do you seek the living among the dead? He is not here, but has risen! Remember how He spoke to you while He was still in Galilee, saying, the Son of Man must be delivered into the hands of sinful men, and be crucified, and on the third day rise again"* (vv. 5-7). The two disciples who were on their way to Emmaus were joined on that journey by Jesus, but were initially prevented from recognizing Him. After hearing their story, Jesus said to them, *"O fools! And slow of heart to believe what the prophets have spoken! Was it not necessary for the Christ to suffer these things and to enter His glory?"* (vv. 25-26). Then He took them through the books of Moses and the prophets and explained to them how all that had happened to Him was prophesied in the Old Testament. When Jesus appeared to the disciples in the Upper Room that evening, after He had showed them His wounds, He took them to the Scriptures: *"He said to them, 'These are the words which I spoke to you while I was still with you, that all things must be fulfilled which were written in the Law of Moses and in the Prophets and in the Psalms concerning Me.' Then He opened their minds to understand the Scriptures. He said to them, 'Thus it is written, and accordingly it was necessary for the Christ to suffer and to rise from the dead the third day'"* (vv. 44-46). Do you see the common theme? First the angels and then Jesus pointed those who witnessed the resurrection to the Word of God: the spoken Word through the Living Word, Jesus, and the written Word of the Old Testament. As miraculous as the events of that day were, those events could only be properly understood and judged in light of the revealed Word of God. Their experiences and their testimonies were important, but standing alone, those experiences and testimonies could be dismissed as lies or delusions (even by those who should have been the first to accept them - v. 11!). But their testimonies, verified by the infallible Word of God and endued with supernatural power by the Spirit of God (v. 49), would bring redemption to all nations (v. 47).

PRAYER: A preacher once told of seeing a notation written in the flyleaf of a parishioner's Bible that said, "I don't care what the Bible says. I've had an experience." It is important for us to know that the Bible is the arbiter by which we determine the validity of our experiences, and no experience is valid that does not line up to the revealed Word of God. But personal testimony that is in harmony with the Word and is empowered by the Spirit is a mighty battering ram that can break through walls of resistance to bring people out of bondage and into God's Kingdom. Pray that the Spirit will lead you to opportunities to share your story and His Story, and to share how they intersect, so that others might be saved.

JOHN

A CREDIBLE WITNESS
JOHN 1

Matthew, Mark and Luke are called the synoptic gospels. "Synoptic" means "seeing together," and they are called by this designation because they follow the same general outline in telling Jesus' story. John, the last gospel writer, apparently decided to go in a different direction, focusing primarily on events and teachings that the others had not been led to record. Thus, John's gospel is often called "the Supplementary Gospel." Taking all four accounts together gives us a much broader understanding of Jesus than any one of them alone does. A good example of how John gives us "the rest of the story" is in the account of Jesus' first meeting with some of the men who would become His apostles. In the synoptics, the first mention of these men has Jesus just showing up one day beside the Sea of Galilee, calling to them to *"Follow Me."* They, seemingly having just met Him, drop their nets to follow Him (see Matthew 4:18-22). John gives us the background behind that call to them and why they were so willing to respond. They knew Jesus already. They had heard John the Baptist testify about Him. They had already spent time with Him. They had already seen Him teaching and healing and performing miracles. They already believed that He was the Messiah, although their understanding of what that meant was limited. The call to them to follow Him that fateful day beside the Sea of Galilee was not their first meeting with Him, but rather a call to leave the lives they were living to travel with Him on a full-time basis. We also discover from John's gospel that these men had been followers of John the Baptist, who had pointed Jesus out to them as *"the Lamb of God, who takes away the sin of the world"* (v. 29) and as the Son of God (v. 34). John had come to that conclusion about Jesus because of the supernatural events surrounding His baptism (vv. 32-33), and it was on the basis of his testimony that Andrew and another unnamed man (the gospel writer John? Philip?) went with Jesus to see where He was staying and to see for themselves if John's testimony about Him was true. Then, Andrew, convinced already that Jesus was the Messiah, went and told his brother Simon, whom Jesus nicknamed Peter (v. 42). Jesus called Philip, who was likewise convinced that Jesus was the Messiah, and he told his friend Nathanael. Thus, John's testimony influenced Andrew. Andrew's influenced Peter. Philip's influenced Nathanael. And the story goes on, as the testimony of these and others has spread throughout the entire world from person to person. It started with one credible, respected, faithful witness telling his friends what he knew about Jesus, and then it spread from person to person like wildfire.

PRAYER: As you think back over your life, who were the "credible witnesses" whose testimonies (both in word and deed) convinced you to consider the claims and the person of Jesus? Thank the Lord for those faithful witnesses, and ask Him to use you as a faithful witness to bring the good news to others.

WATER INTO WINE
JOHN 2

It seems to me that every drunk I've ever encountered in 30 years of ministry knows two things about the Bible: that Paul told Timothy to take a little wine (note, a little) for his stomach ailments, and that Jesus turned water into wine (not whiskey, bourbon, beer or vodka, mind you). It is important to put Jesus' turning water into wine into a proper cultural understanding. Wedding feasts were multiple-day affairs, with meals, and games, and formal and informal socializing, finally culminating in the wedding ceremony itself. It was a community event with many guests, both family and friends. You can imagine what a disaster it would be if everyone got rip-roaring drunk on the first night of the wedding feast! It was the job of the master of the banquet (v. 8) to make sure that didn't happen. Back then, the juice from grapes was stored in wineskins, bags made from animal skin sewn together. Because this was not an airtight seal, over time, the wine would ferment and become alcoholic. The job of the master of the banquet was to taste the wine every time a new wineskin was opened, to determine its degree of fermentation, and to order it watered down appropriately to mute its intoxicating effects. The more potent the wine, the greater amount of water would be used. There is no indication that the wine Jesus created from the water was necessarily alcoholic wine. The master of the banquet's words to the groom simply relate to the wine's quality, not its "kick" (v. 10). And certainly, in turning water into wine, Jesus was not condoning or encouraging drunkenness, which was greatly frowned upon in Jewish society and Jewish Scripture. Looking past the question of alcohol, it is interesting that Jesus' first miracle was performed at a wedding feast, and in response to a potentially embarrassing social situation. For a groom to run out of wine at his wedding would have sullied his reputation, marking him forever in people's minds as a bumbler who couldn't properly plan ahead, hardly a good way to begin his married life in the community. Jesus rescued the groom from his embarrassment, showing that He cares not only about the spiritual aspects of our lives, but also about the social aspects of our lives. Whatever is of concern to us is of concern to Him. It is also to be noted that the expert in such things, the master of the banquet, declared that Jesus' wine was the best of all that was served. Whatever the world may offer, what Jesus offers is always infinitely better. Think about that image of water being turned to wine. Water is necessary for life. Wine is not necessary for life, but in that world with few options for beverages, it certainly added flavor to the proceedings. Jesus gives us freely the water of life (John 4:13-14), but also far more than that. He not only gives us what is necessary for life, but also what leads to joy and celebration (John 10:10b).

PRAYER: Thank Him today that He not only provides for our needs, but blesses us lavishly beyond that. Thank Him not only for giving you eternal life, but also abundant life. Thank Him that the blessings that He gives are the best blessings of all, far superior to anything the world offers. Jesus gave a great blessing to the young couple being married that day in Cana by His presence, and by His miracle of turning the water into wine. Lift up your marriage to Him today, asking that He might be a welcome, honored guest in your married life, and that He might supply all that you and your spouse need, and beyond, in your life together.

FOR GOD SO LOVED
JOHN 3

Perhaps no verse of the Bible is more familiar than John 3:16. It is a powerful verse that speaks to us in one sentence of God's plan of salvation. In that verse we see *the author of salvation* (*"For God..."*). It was God who set in motion this drama of salvation whereby the precious Son of God, the second person of the Trinity, fully and completely and eternally God, would come to Earth as a human being and give Himself as a sacrifice for our sins. And it is appropriate that God would be the author of salvation, for He was the aggrieved party in our sins. We've all known the hurt of being sinned against. It is a hurt that God experiences billions of times every minute of every day. It is a hurt that in any of us would cry out for vengeance and payback, but for God, His love was greater than the wounds we inflicted upon Him. And that leads us to *the affection of salvation* (*"...so loved the world..."*). When we say that God loved the world, we need to understand that it was an individual embrace: "For God so loved YOUR NAME HERE." God not only so loved us all; He so loved each one of us. His love was extended to us not on our best day - not on a day we were worshiping Him, serving Him and loving Him back. The Bible says that *"while we were yet sinners, Christ died for us"* (Romans 5:8). In other words, on our worst day, at our most sinful, at our most rebellious and blasphemous, God loved each one of us enough to save us and Jesus loved each one of us enough to go to the cross for us. And that brings us to *the agony of salvation* (*"...that He gave His only begotten Son..."*). It is difficult to imagine the physical agony of scourging and crucifixion, but the physical aspect of Christ's suffering is only part of the story. The spiritual aspect was even worse, as on the cross, this one who from all eternity had known no sin, took the ugliness, and the shame, and the degradation, and the contamination of every sin of every human being who has ever lived or will live upon Himself. And imagine not just the agony of the Son, but the agony of the Father as He witnessed His beloved Son, in whom He was always well-pleased, sullied by our sins and tortured for them. And what did it accomplish? What was the point of all this physical and spiritual suffering? It purchased for us *the availability of salvation* ("...*that whoever...*"). That word "*whoever*" means that salvation is available for all. Jesus' death on the cross was not just for some people's sins; it was for all people's sins. It was God's final solution to the sin problem, that He would once and for all pay the penalty Himself for the sins of all humanity, and thus He would make forgiveness available to all who will receive it. And that brings us to *the acceptance of salvation* ("...*believes in Him should... have eternal life.*"). Christ's death makes salvation available to all. But He forces it on no one. He will not enter any heart where He is not invited. Each person must make a personal decision to place their faith in Christ to be saved. But we must also note *the alternative to salvation*. It tells us that "*whoever believes in Him will not perish, but have eternal life.*" That indicates that those who don't place their faith in Him will indeed perish. They will not experience eternal life with Him in heaven, but will be forever removed from the presence, power, and praises of God in the eternal prison of God called hell. Because He is an eternal being, Jesus could pay for all of our sins in a finite period of time. But because we are finite beings, if we refuse what He has done for us and choose to pay for our sins ourselves, we must pay for them for eternity.

PRAYER: Today, let the grand truths of John 3:16 lead you into prayers of thanksgiving. Thank Him for authoring the plan of salvation. Thank Him for His affection for you even at your worst. Thank Him for the agony He endured to make salvation available to you. Thank Him for the conviction of sin that led you to accept His free gift of forgiveness and eternal life. Pray for those you know who are still on the path that leads to hell, and pray for God to use you to bring them to salvation.

JESUS AMONG THE SAMARITANS
JOHN 4

Jesus' encounter with the woman at the well shows that He refused to be limited by many of the social constraints of His time. Verse 4 says that *"it was necessary that He go through Samaria."* While going through Samaria was the most direct route between Judea and Galilee, it was not a geographical necessity. Most Jews of the time would have taken the longer route through Perea and Decapolis in order to avoid going through Samaria. When John says in verse 9 that *"Jews have no dealings with Samaritans,"* he is a master of understatement. Jews absolutely hated Samaritans, even more than they hated Gentiles, and the feeling was mutual. The Samaritans were the descendants of Israelites who had been left behind during the Exile and had intermarried with other nationalities that had been resettled in the area, and the animosity between them and the Jews was hundreds of years in duration, stretching back to the time of the Jews' return from Exile. The necessity of going through Samaria was a spiritual necessity. There were people there who, despite their limited understanding of spiritual things (v. 22), were still looking ahead to the coming of the Messiah (v. 25). Jesus sat down by Jacob's well, exhausted from the journey (a testament to His full humanity; in becoming human, He became susceptible to hunger, thirst, fatigue, pain and ultimately, death). It was about the sixth hour, or noon, when an outcast woman came to the well to draw water. The normal time to draw water was in the morning or in the evening when it was cooler, and women would come to the well together in order to socialize. This woman came in the heat of the day when no one else would be there, probably because of her bad reputation in the city (v. 18). She was shocked when Jesus spoke to her and asked her for a drink. Jewish men did not speak to women in public (note v. 27), and certainly not to Samaritan women. And asking her for a drink? Most Jews would have believed that the mere act of drinking from her water jar would have made them unclean. What kind of Man was this? Jesus reached across that cultural divide, treated her with dignity, engaged her in spiritual conversation, showed her love and compassion in spite of her sins, revealed Himself to her as the Messiah (it is notable that Jesus rarely came right out and said that He was the Messiah, and here He does so to a lonely, rejected, sinful Samaritan woman) and brought about a dramatic change in her (vv. 28-29). This change was so profound that it brought others to Him, and they likewise came to believe in Him (vv. 30, 39). Jesus stayed there in this Samaritan village for two more days. Again, for most Jews of the time, lodging with and eating with Samaritans would have been taboo, but Jesus, as He has shown throughout this account, did not play by those cultural rules. His allegiance was to a higher standard: the law of love.

PRAYER: Pray for those you know who are outcasts, either because of social reasons or sinful reasons. Pray for opportunities to reach across cultural barriers to show the love of Christ. Pray that the love of Christ in you would be greater than any prejudices that may have been ingrained in you by parents or others, whether those prejudices are social, racial, economic, denominational, etc.

DO YOU WANT TO BE HEALED?
JOHN 5

The Pool of Bethesda in Jerusalem had colonnades on each of its four sides and one down the middle. People with various diseases and ailments waited by the pool for the stirring of the waters, for when an angel stirred the waters, the first one who got into the water was healed (vv. 3-4). One man had been there for 38 years, being brought regularly if not daily by family or friends in the hope that he would be healed. He had seen the water stirred in the past, but his condition kept him from getting into the water before someone else did. He was obviously not completely paralyzed, because he indicates that he could move toward the water, but he was sufficiently crippled that he was unable to get there first. What an exercise in hope and frustration. Every time he saw someone else healed, it raised hope that he likewise would be healed if he could just get to the water first, but every time, time after frustrating time, it was always someone else. Jesus asked him in verse 6 what on the surface seemed to be a silly question: *"Do you want to be healed?"* Our first thought upon reading that is probably "Of course he wants to be healed! Why else would he be there?" But let us not be so hasty in our assessment. Not everyone wants to be healed. There are many who suffer from long-standing ailments - physical, mental, emotional and spiritual - who, if the truth were known, really don't want to be well. For some, their malady has become the sum total of their identity. Others have become addicted to sympathy. Others have an addiction that is pleasurable even as it destroys, and while they don't relish the destruction, they are unwilling to let go of the pleasure. Still others are afraid to do whatever it might take to be made well; it's just easier to wallow in their negative situation than put forth the effort to change it. In answer to Jesus' question, the man poured out his frustrations and limitations: *"Sir, I have no one to put me into the pool when the water is stirred. But while I am coming, another steps down before me"* (v. 7). It is obvious from his statement that he wanted to be healed. He had not given up, despite the many disappointments he had endured; indeed, he had been thinking about employing a new and different strategy, saying to himself, "If only I had someone to *help* me into the water..." Perhaps he hoped that Jesus would be that person, that He would camp out there with him beside the water to help him get in first the next time the water was stirred. But Jesus had a much better solution for him: *"Rise, take up your bed and walk"* (v. 8). The man could have responded, "What are you talking about? Look at me! I've been lying here for 38 years and I can't get into the water!" but instead, Jesus' word of command stirred the waters of his faith, and he jumped right in! He was healed instantly, took up his bed and walked. Sometimes the Lord waits an uncomfortably long time, at least from our perspective, to change everything about our situation in an instant. This man had endured bitter disappointment at every stirring of the water, but he never gave up hope. His faith, though tried and tested by many disappointments, was now being rewarded.

PRAYER: Is there an area of your life where you long for change, but change does not seem to be forthcoming? Does it seem that others are receiving the blessing you seek, while you continue on in frustration? Ask yourself the question, "Do I want to be healed?" and then seek the Lord in prayer for the true answer. Renew your faith, and express to Him in prayer your faith that He can change everything in an instant. Then commit yourself to doing whatever He commands you to do to see your situation change.

IMPROPER MOTIVES
JOHN 6

Other than the resurrection, the only miracle recorded in all four of the gospels is the feeding of the five thousand. John, as we have seen, tends to focus his attention on aspects of Jesus' teaching and ministry not found in the synoptics, and even here, he shows us some aspects of the miraculous feeding that the other gospel writers did not record. First of all, he shows us in verse 2 why such a large crowd had gathered: *"And a great crowd followed Him, because they saw His signs which He did for the sick."* Why did Jesus heal the sick? Some think that His healings were for the purpose of drawing crowds that He might teach them, but that does not seem to be His motivation. He healed the sick because He had compassion for them (Matthew 14:14), not to draw crowds. Indeed, the numerous times He tells people not to speak of their healings shows that He did not want to be known primarily as a healer. To Jesus, the healings were always secondary to the message of the Kingdom that He was proclaiming. Likewise, His miraculous feeding of the crowd was motivated by His concern for their welfare. Matthew and Mark tell us that after the feeding of the five thousand, *"Jesus commanded His disciples to get into the boat and go ahead of Him to the other side, while He sent the crowds away"* (Matthew 14:22, see also Mark 6:45, where the verb is even stronger - *"He <u>compelled</u> His disciples to get into the boat..."*). John tells us why Jesus was so adamant about getting His disciples out of this situation: *"Jesus, knowing that they intended to come and make him king by force..."* (v. 15, NIV 84). The crowd that had followed Him to see His healings, and had marveled at His miracle of multiplying the loaves and fish, was aflame with Messianic fervor. The common expectation of the Jews at this time was that when the Messiah came, He would raise an army, overthrow the hated Roman occupation army and re-establish a Jewish Kingdom. They were not intending to force Jesus to be king, but they were plotting to storm the nearest Roman army garrison in His name to begin the rebellion! The disciples had been steeped in such teaching their whole lives, and Jesus did not want them caught up in this misdirected zeal. The next day, after Jesus had walked across the lake and stilled the storm, the crowd He had fed found Him there, amazed at how He had arrived there without a boat. Jesus cut through to their illegitimate motives for following Him in verse 26: *"Truly,*

truly I say to you, you seek Me not because you saw signs, but because you ate of the loaves and were filled." He tried to redirect their attention to spiritual matters (vv. 27-40), but they were more focused on literal bread than spiritual truth. Indeed, their perspective seems to be that if He wouldn't be their military leader, He could at least be their meals on wheels every day (v. 34)! Further teachings (that were admittedly difficult - just imagine how His teachings on eating His flesh and drinking His blood must have sounded to those who first heard them) drove away most of His followers (v. 66). As the crowd dwindled, Jesus turned to the twelve and asked them, *"Do you also want to go away?"* (v. 67). Simon Peter, speaking for them all, answered, *"Lord, to whom shall we go? You have the words of eternal life. We have believed and have come to know that you are the Christ, the Son of the living God"* (v. 68). In that answer, Peter showed that the apostles' motives for following Jesus were the right ones - not for the healing "show," not for the miraculous feedings, and not out of patriotic fervor. They were following Him because they recognized Him as the only source of eternal life, the true Son of God, the only one worthy of their allegiance. Yet, even among this inner circle of Jesus' followers, there was one with false motives, the one who would ultimately betray Him, Judas Iscariot (vv. 70-71).

PRAYER: There are many who follow Jesus today out of faulty motives. Some follow Him out of a mistaken belief that He has promised those who serve Him comfort, ease, material prosperity and happiness. When such earthly rewards are not immediately forthcoming, when the cost of following Him becomes steep, and when His teachings become impossible to reconcile with their selfish and/or sinful desires, such "followers" tend to become angry with Him or even fall away. Others name the name of Christ out of social considerations, but if the truth were told, they are far more attached to a church they enjoy than to Him. This faulty motivation is revealed when someone has his feelings hurt at a church and drops out, not just out of that church, but out of church altogether. Still others have a form of civil religion, identifying Christianity with being an American (this is surely why surveys show so many Americans professing to be Christians, but with so little positive impact in the culture). In truth, our motive for following Him and serving Him must be who He is and what He has done in saving us from our sins (vv. 68-69). He is our Savior, if we have received Him as such, and even if He never did anything else for us beyond that, the fact that He has rescued us from eternity in hell deserves every last ounce of our allegiance for this short lifetime. He is Lord of all, and thus worthy of all of our heart, soul, mind and strength. Thank Him for saving you, and for all the many blessings He bestows upon you beyond salvation. Ask Him to point out any faulty expectations or motivations you may have in your service to Him.

REACTIONS
JOHN 7

John 7 shows a number of different reactions to Jesus, all occurring in the context of the Feast of Tabernacles. The first reaction, recorded in verses 3-5, was the reaction of His own brothers (Joseph and Mary had at least four sons and at least two daughters after Jesus was born - see Mark 6:5). Given that Jesus was ministering in Galilee because the Jewish authorities were seeking to kill Him in Judea, the brothers' insistence that He go to Jerusalem for the feast seems strange. At best, they seem to be mocking Him and His ministry. The sense seems to be, "Why are you here in backwoods Galilee? If you want to be a big shot, you need to go where the action is in Jerusalem and do your thing there!" At worst, they seem to be egging Him on to go to Judea in the hope that something bad will happen to Him!

Verse five tells us that their reaction was a reaction of unbelief. We know that none of Jesus' brothers believed in Him until after the resurrection, but at least two of them, James and Jude, became believers and leaders in the early church. Many a believer in an unbelieving home has had to deal with such mockery and resentment. Knowing that Jesus Himself dealt with such treatment should be a comfort and an encouragement. Jesus was a common topic of conversation in Jerusalem even before he revealed Himself at the feast. Some said that He was a good man, while others insisted that He was a deceiver (v. 12). Still others accused Him to His face of being demonized (v. 20). As C.S. Lewis famously said, it is impossible to dismiss Jesus as merely a good man and a moral teacher, as many in our culture attempt to do. He claimed to be God, and in doing so, He limited the options of what we can logically believe about Him. If He was not God, then our only options are to believe that He was either a liar or a lunatic. In our day of radical, aggressive atheism, many are quite willing to do just that, to condemn Him as a liar or a lunatic. Others in the crowds at the feast suspected that Jesus might be the Messiah, but their preconceived notions about the Messiah and their lack of understanding of Jesus' history (vv. 26-27, 41-42) kept them from believing. The Pharisees and chief priests were concerned about the murmuring of the crowds, and sent officers to arrest Jesus. Sent on a mission to arrest Jesus, after they heard Him speak, the officers returned without Him, proclaiming *"No man has ever spoken like this Man"* (v. 46). The Pharisees reacted with frustration and anger, but Nicodemus, who had spoken to Jesus privately in chapter 3 and would later assist in His burial, tried to calm the situation by reminding them of the requirements of the Law (v. 50). The extent of their hatred is revealed as Nicodemus is shouted down with insults, a foreshadowing of how they would eventually ignore the Law altogether in condemning Him. Some people, though, did believe in Him

(v. 41a). To them, and to all who would believe thereafter, Jesus made a wonderful promise: *"'If anyone is thirsty, let him come to Me and drink. He who believes in Me, as the Scripture has said, out of his heart will flow rivers of living water.' By this He spoke of the Spirit, whom those who believe in Him would receive."* (v. 38). Those to react to Jesus by placing their faith in Him receive the gift of the indwelling Holy Spirit, and they become conduits of living water flowing out of their lives and into the lives of others.

PRAYER: Who do you know who may be reacting to Jesus with indifference, hostility, confusion or ignorance? Pray that their spiritual thirst might become so intense that it would drive them to Jesus to have that thirst satisfied. Pray that you might be filled with the Spirit to overflow, that rivers of the water of life might flow out of you into the lives of every unbeliever around you. Pray that your life might be a witness, and pray for opportunities and boldness to speak a word of witness to them.

WORDS IN THE DIRT
JOHN 8

The story of the woman caught in adultery in verses 1-11 is not found in some of the early manuscripts of John, so some have questioned its legitimacy. I cannot fathom why. It is classic Jesus, thwarting the murderous intentions of His enemies, and showing forth grace to a sinner without excusing her sin. The woman in question had been caught in the very act of committing adultery, and the Pharisees were no doubt delighted, seeing in her sin a perfect opportunity to trap Jesus. Bringing her to Him at the Temple, they said to Him, *"Teacher, this woman was caught in the act of adultery. In the Law, Moses commanded us to stone such women. Now what do you say?"* (vv. 4-5, NIV 84). They thought they had placed Jesus in a hopeless situation. If He agreed that the woman should be stoned, they could accuse Him before the Romans of disregarding Roman law, and urging others to do the same, because the Roman authorities reserved the right of execution to themselves. If He declined to call for her stoning, they could accuse Him before the crowds of disregarding the Old Testament Law given through Moses. The fact that they were not nearly as concerned about the Law of Moses as they claimed is evident from the fact that the woman alone was brought to Jesus. She couldn't very well have been caught in the act of adultery unless a man had been caught in the act also, but apparently, they had let the man go. The Law commanded the stoning of both guilty parties, not just the woman. Jesus bent down and started writing on the ground with His finger, in essence, ignoring them. When they continued to press Him, He arose and proclaimed, *"Let him who is without sin among you be the first to throw a stone at her"* (v. 7). Then, He stooped down and began writing again on the ground. We're not told what He wrote either time, but it is fascinating to speculate what it may have been. My personal speculation is that whatever He wrote, each of her accusers saw something different, something intensely personal, some sin he thought was completely hidden. Imagine the sudden horror of realizing that Jesus knew! One by one, they turned and left, the older men first and then the younger, until only Jesus and the woman were left. Jesus then asked her, *"Woman, where are your accusers? Did no one condemn you?"* and she replied *"No one, Lord"* (vv. 10-11). Under the Law, if there were no witnesses to the crime, the case was summarily dismissed, so Jesus was justified in declaring *"Neither do I condemn you."* But note that though He dismissed the case, He did not excuse her sin. Just as He was well aware of the sins of her accusers, He was well aware of hers, and He warned her to *"Go and sin no more"* (v. 11). It is interesting that the Bible records three times when the hand of God wrote. The first was the writing of the Ten

Commandments on tablets of stone. The second was in Daniel 5, the famous "handwriting on the wall" as the hand of God wrote the words, "MENE, MENE, TEKEL, UPHARSIN," the interpretation of which meant, among other things, *"you have been weighed in the balance and are found wanting"* (Daniel 5:27). And then there is this unknown writing that effected the release of a guilty party. All of us have been weighed in the balance of God's commandments and found wanting in our obedience. We have all sinned and fallen short of God's righteous standards. But just as Jesus' writing in the dirt set this woman free from her condemnation, He has written for each of us a pardon, printed in His own blood, at Calvary. He offers to free us from our condemnation and from our lives of sin, if we will receive by faith His grace purchased for us through His death on the cross.

PRAYER: Jesus always walked the perfect line between not ignoring sin and yet always offering grace. Pray that in your interactions with those lost in sin, you might have the wisdom to do likewise. Thank Him today that though you were weighed in the balance and found wanting, He took your sentence upon Himself, and His grace has set you free.

WHO SINNED?
JOHN 9

There is within all of us a desire for the universe to "make sense," to "be fair," at least as we understand such things. We want to sort out the reason behind things, particularly bad things, the cause and effect relationship, probably out of a desire to gain some measure of understanding over things that are beyond our control. It is that desire that lies behind the disciples' question in verse 2 about the man born blind: *"Rabbi, who sinned, this man or his parents, that he was born blind?"* Notice that there was no question in their minds that this man's blindness was somebody's fault. Somebody *had* to have sinned. His blindness was obviously God's punishment. They had adopted the theology of Job's friends, who insisted that Job *must* have sinned to be suffering so, or else the universe makes no sense at all. In defense of the disciples, the rabbis of their day taught this very idea, even going so far as to posit the possibility of a person sinning before birth to explain congenital defects such as this one. Jesus eliminates the premise of the question altogether, declaring that the man's blindness had nothing to do with his sins or with the sins of his parents, but instead *"it happened so that the works of God might be displayed in him"* (v. 3). The Bible does teach that sickness in general came into the world because of the sin of our first ancestors, Adam and Eve, and it also teaches that a particular sickness may be the result of a particular sin (I Corinthians 11:30). Beyond that, we're told that some sickness is the result of demonic attack. But it is wrong for us to assume that every sickness, every accident, or every natural disaster is God's direct response to some sin of a person or a region. I was appalled years ago by the number of Christians who were quick to attribute Hurricane Katrina's destruction of New Orleans to voodoo practices there or to their Mardi Gras celebrations. If God sent Hurricane Katrina to punish New Orleans, why was so much of the rest of the Gulf region (one of the most Christian areas of the country) likewise devastated? There seems to have been an awful amount of collateral damage just to punish one city. We need to understand that we live in a fallen world (see Romans 8:20-22), a world marred by sin and its consequences, and in such a world, bad things happen. Illnesses, injuries, and disasters (both natural and man-made) are part and parcel of living in this world, and believers are not exempt from such things (Romans 8:23). The groaning of this world, and the groaning of our own bodies, just make us long for the afterlife, and for the day when God redeems this fallen world. It also gives us opportunities to display the works of God as we minister to the hurting. To the disciples, this man's blindness was an opportunity for theological speculation; to Jesus, his blindness was an opportunity to minister to his needs and glorify God. While they looked upon him with curiosity and condemnation, Jesus looked upon him with concern and compassion. As a result of Jesus' ministering to his physical need, this man not only received physical sight, but also profound spiritual insight (vv. 30-33) resulting in his salvation (v. 38).

PRAYER: A story is told of a pastor who was always full of thanksgiving in his pastoral prayers. As he stood to pray one particularly nasty, snowy, icy Sunday morning, one of his parishioners thought, "Surely, he will find nothing to be thankful for on such a dreadful day as this." He was surprised to hear the pastor pray, "We thank Thee, O God...that it is not always like this." As we look at the world around us, with its disasters, its illnesses, its injuries and its evil, we can give in to despair, or we can look up with thanksgiving, recognizing that it will not always be this way. Praise Him today for the world to come, a world where *"There shall be no more death. Neither shall there be any more sorrow nor crying nor pain, for the former things have passed away"* (Revelation 21:4). In the meantime, ask the Lord to give you opportunities to minister with His compassion to the hurting, that they might come to know Him and thus be a part of that world to come.

THE GOOD SHEPHERD
JOHN 10

In much of John 10, Jesus speaks of His relationship to His followers using the image of Himself as a The Good Shepherd and His followers as sheep. The sheepfold (vv. 1-6) was an enclosed walled or fenced space where several shepherds would take their sheep at night. Because the sheep were so familiar with their own shepherd and his distinctive voice, the shepherd could stand at the door of the sheepfold and call out, and all of the sheep belonging to him would separate from the larger group and come to him to go forth to pasture. Jesus has called us as believers out of the larger population of the world. We hear His voice, He goes before us, and we follow Him (v. 4). When we are intimately familiar with His voice through His Word, the voice of strangers (i.e., false teachers) will be foreign to us, and we will run away from their destructive doctrine (v. 5). Jesus then speaks of Himself as *"the door of the sheep"* (v. 7). The sheepfold only had one way in or out, and the shepherd, once he had herded his flock into it, would bed down across that entryway to protect them from anything that might try to come in to do them harm. In identifying Himself as the door of the sheep, Jesus was saying that He is the only way of salvation. All others claiming to offer salvation are thieves and robbers (v. 8). He alone offers eternal life and abundant life (vv. 9-10), and once we are in His sheepfold, we are secure in that salvation (a truth made even more explicit in verses 27-29). The switch to the singular *"thief"* in verse 10 is likely a reference to the evil one, Satan, who only comes *"to steal, kill and destroy,"* in contast with Jesus, who gives life and life more abundantly (v. 10). That new life, both abundant and eternal, comes about through The Good Shepherd's own death (vv. 11, 15, 17-18), but the Shepherd is no victim of the thief of verse 10. He willingly lays down His life, only to take it up again (vv. 17-18), a reference to His coming death for the sins of the world and His subsequent resurrection. Jesus' statement that *"I have other sheep who are not of this fold"* (v. 16) is a foreshadowing of the fact that after the resurrection, the gospel would go to the Gentiles as well as the Jews. Verses 28-29 comprise one of the clearest affirmations of the doctrine of eternal security in the Bible. Eternal life is not something that is (maybe) given at death, but is a present possession of every believer in the here and now (see John 6:47, and note the present tense). Jesus said, *"I give them eternal life* (in the present)*, and they shall never perish* (in the future)" (v. 28, NIV 84). Eternal life by its very definition must be, well, eternal. It's not revocable life or probationary life that He promises, but eternal life, and if even one person who has ever had eternal life perishes, then that would make the Son of God a liar. Jesus goes on to speak of the secure position of the believer as being in the hand of Jesus, with the hand of the Father wrapped around His (vv. 28b-29). An old insurance commercial once intoned, "You're in good hands with Allstate." If you are a believer in Jesus, you're in far better hands than that!

PRAYER: Praise the Lord today that He is The Good Shepherd. Thank Him for rescuing you from the malicious intentions of the thief, for His loving care, for His daily leading and for His gift of abundant life. Thank Him for the gift of eternal life, and for the high cost of His own life by which He purchased it. Thank Him that you are secure in His hand and in the Father's hand, and that nothing can remove you from the realm of salvation (see also Romans 8:35-39).

MISUNDERSTANDINGS
JOHN 11

The raising of Lazarus from the dead in John 11 shows Jesus' power over life and death, a power that would be even more miraculously displayed shortly in His own resurrection. When Jesus announced that He was going to Bethany, His disciples tried to talk Him out of it (v. 8). There had been an attempt on His life in Jerusalem not too long previously (10:39), and Bethany, at only two miles from Jerusalem, was uncomfortably close to that raging inferno of hostility. Jesus, using symbolism (which often went right over the heads of

His disciples), stated that Lazarus had fallen asleep, and that He was going to wake him up. The disciples, not understanding the symbol, insisted that Jesus need not go, that if Lazarus was sleeping, surely he would recover. I am often amazed in the gospels at how dull the disciples frequently come across. It is one of many reasons I believe in the truthfulness of the gospel narratives; surely, if they had made up the story, they would have made themselves look better! The disciples were not the only ones who misunderstood Jesus' words and actions. When Lazarus took seriously ill, his sisters Mary and Martha sent word to Jesus. From other accounts, we know that Jesus was particularly close to this family, and often stayed in their home in Bethany whenever He visited Jerusalem. The fact that they knew where He was (10:40) and could send a messenger to Him indicates that they were special friends who were kept apprised of His whereabouts. Mary and Martha no doubt expected Him to drop everything and come immediately, but they were shocked when He stayed where He was for two more days, during which time Lazarus died. Beyond that, they may very well have known that Jesus had healed others from a distance without even having to be there (such as in Matthew 8:5-13 and 15:21-28), but in this case, He chose not to. They were confused (which seems to be Martha's primary reaction) and angry (which seems to be Mary's primary reaction), wondering why Jesus would extend His hand of healing to complete strangers, but not to a close personal friend. The fact that they said the exact same words to Jesus upon meeting Him (vv. 21, 32) shows that they had been talking to one another about their disappointment with Jesus' delay. Yet, in spite of their confusion and bitter disappointment, the sisters still held on to their faith in Jesus (vv. 21-27). John 11:35's statement that *"Jesus wept,"* beyond being the shortest verse in our English Bibles (I Thessalonians 5:16 is actually shorter in Greek), shows His marvelous compassion. He was not weeping over Lazarus, for He knew that He was going to raise Lazarus from the grave (v. 11); He was weeping for Mary and Martha, and the trauma they had endured in their brother's death, a trauma that was necessary that both He and His Father might be glorified (v. 4). Never forget that when we weep and grieve and struggle, our Great High Priest is touched with the feeling of our infirmities (Hebrews 4:15). After Jesus raised Lazarus from the dead in front of many witnesses, many of them believed in Him (v. 45), but others reported what happened to members of the Sanhedrin, who were not at all pleased. They could not deny the miracle, but their concern was that *"This Man is performing many signs. If we leave Him alone like this, everyone will believe in Him, and the Romans will come and take away both our temple and our nation"* (vv. 47-48). Interestingly enough, it was precisely because of their rejection of Him that those very fears were realized (Luke 19:41-44). The high priest Caiaphas spoke words of prophecy that he himself did not understand (v. 50): *"it is better for you that one man die for the people than that the whole nation perish"* (NIV 84). Indeed. As verses 51-52 point out, that was exactly Jesus' purpose in dying, not only for the nation of Israel, but for all who would believe in Him (John 3:16). They were plotting to kill Him to "save" the nation from the Romans; He was planning to give His life to save all who would believe in Him from death and hell.

PRAYER: Have you ever struggled to understand, or even completely misunderstood, God's Word? Pray for the Spirit's illumination as you study the Bible. Have you ever misunderstood God's actions, such as why someone had to die or a prayer was not answered as you'd hoped? Even in your disappointment and confusion, respond as Mary and Martha did. Don't be afraid to express your feelings, but hold onto your faith in Him. As the great preacher Charles Spurgeon (1834-1892) famously said, "God is too good to be unkind. He is too wise to be confused. If I cannot trace His hand, I can always trust His heart." He is working all things together for our good and His glory (Romans 8:28). He turned the plotting words of a fake high priest into a prophecy of His salvation, and He turned their plan of murder into a plan of salvation for us!

MARY'S GIFT
JOHN 12

The last time she was at Jesus' feet, (11:32), she was pouring out her frustration, her grief and her anger at Jesus. Now, Mary is at His feet again, this time pouring out her love and gratitude to Him with a precious gift. She didn't give something cheap to Jesus to express her thanksgiving for Lazarus' being raised from the dead; she gave something precious, something costly, and she gave it all. She was completely sold out in her thanksgiving and adoration. Once the box was broken, there was no turning back, no way to stop, no way to take it back, no way to keep from pouring it all on Jesus. True worship always demands a sacrifice - a sacrifice of praise from our lips, a sacrifice of time, a sacrifice of resources. Mary had the attitude that was expressed by David in the last chapter of II Samuel. There, he went to buy a threshing floor to build an altar for sacrifice to God, and the owner told him that he would give it to him free of charge, along with the wood and the oxen for the sacrifice. David replied, *"No, I insist on paying you for it. I will not sacrifice to the LORD my God burnt offerings that cost me nothing"* (II Samuel 24:24, NIV 84). Would that more Christians understood that principle, that God does not deserve the leftovers and the cheap but the very best we have. He deserves the firstfruits of our finances, but how often he gets only whatever, if anything, is left over after everything else has taken its cut. He deserves our best effort, but how often is it that the effort we give to the work of the Lord would be insufficient to keep us in our jobs, on a ball team, or in a social club? He is worthy of all of our praise, but how often is it that other things receive praise far more readily than He does? Mary's lavish praise resulted in a loud protest, led initially by Judas, but, according to the other gospels, quickly joined by the other disciples. There are always those who think they know better than you do how you should express your gratitude to the Lord, how you should worship Him, what you should give to Him, and how you should serve Him. Don't listen to the critics or let them intimidate you, because the motives of critical hearts are seldom centered on the things of God. Judas and the others disguised their true motives in high-sounding religious talk about helping the poor, but in truth, they were motivated by greed and selfishness. Judas wanted the money so that he could steal it; indeed, considering that he betrayed Jesus for less than half that amount, if he had gotten his hands on Mary's perfume, that would have likely been the last they ever saw of him. Note that Mary's was not the only extravagant gift Jesus received that night. The large banquet in Jesus' honor no doubt entailed a sizeable expenditure, but nobody complained that the money spent on the banquet should have been given to the poor, because they were sitting there enjoying the meal also. Mary's gift, though, was just between her and Jesus, and although the fragrance of it filled the room, when they left that room, only Mary and Jesus smelled of it, a fragrance that may have lingered in His hair and His clothes right up until His death six days later. Their loud protest resulted in Jesus' loving protection. Jesus rebuked the disciples for their scolding of Mary. He told them to leave her alone, that Mary's act of worship, that they had criticized, had an unintended prophetic significance as it showed forth His death and burial less than a week later. Be careful of criticizing someone else's expression of worship and praise to God.

There may be far more going on in their lives, and in their relationship with the Lord, than you could possibly know.

PRAYER: All three times Mary appears in the Scripture, she is at Jesus' feet. In Luke 10, she is at His feet enjoying His company and listening to His teaching. In John 11, she is at His feet weeping and crying out in grief and anger. In John 12, she is at His feet in extravagant worship. As you come into His presence today, where are you? Are you enraptured by His teachings, confused by His dealings, or grateful for His blessings? Whatever you're going through right now, hold nothing back. Pour out your heart to Him today.

WASHING THE DISCIPLES' FEET
JOHN 13

In keeping with his supplementary approach, John records an aspect of the Last Supper that the other gospel writers skipped over: Jesus washing the feet of the disciples. As part of their preparation for the Passover feast, Jesus and His disciples would have bathed, probably at an outdoor cistern or other body of water. Walking to the upper room along dusty roads either barefoot or in sandals, their feet would have gotten dirty. It was normally the job of the lowest servant in the household to wash the feet of those who entered the home, but there was no one among them willing to assume this role. Could this be the source of the argument that arose among them during the meal about which of them was the greatest (Luke 22:24)? Can't you just hear them? "I'm not washing anybody's feet; why, I've done thus-and-so!" "I don't know who should be the foot-washer of our group, but I know it's not me!" In their pride, none of them was willing to wash the others' feet; indeed, they were unwilling to wash their own feet! How humbling and embarrassing it must have been when Jesus, saying nothing, began going from man to man washing their dirty feet. It was so embarrassing in fact that Peter protested that he would not allow Jesus to wash his feet. When Jesus replied, *"If I do not wash you, you have no part with Me!"* (v. 8), Peter dove in completely, *"Lord, not my feet only, by also my hands and my head!"* (v. 9). Jesus then responded, *"He who is bathed needs only to wash his feet, but is completely clean. You are clean, but not all of you"* (v. 10). Beyond the lesson about humility and servanthood (vv. 12-17), there is also a picture here of our cleansing through Christ and our ongoing confession of sin. We are bathed, washed clean of our sins and their eternal penalty, when we come to Jesus in repentance and faith, but as we walk around in the world, our feet, so to speak, get dirty. All of us as Christians, in spite our best efforts to live each day for Christ, will sin (I John 1:8). When that happens, we do not need a whole new bath. We have not lost our cleansing, our salvation; we just need the Master to cleanse us from the defilement that our brush with the world has brought. That cleansing comes when we confess our sins to Him, agreeing with Him that we have indeed sinned, and we receive His cleansing and restoration (I John 1:9).

PRAYER: Is there some unconfessed, unforsaken sin festering in your life? Confess it to Jesus today, and receive His cleansing and restoration to fellowship. Pray for opportunities (and willingness) today to follow His example of humble service to others.

GOINGS AND COMINGS
JOHN 14

Jesus has made it clear that He will be leaving the disciples (John 13:36), and they are understandably filled with grief at the prospect. He was their best friend, their Lord and Master, the one they had left everything to follow, and now

He was going away, and to a place they could not follow, at least not immediately. How could this be? And how could they possibly go on without Him? Jesus speaks words of comfort to them in John 14. He is going, but He is going with a purpose: to make things ready for their coming to Him (vv. 1-3). Because of their relationship to Him as *"the way, the truth, and the life,"* the only way to the Father (v. 6), they could rest assured that they would eventually be with Him in the Father's house. In the interim, however, they would not be left bereft, like fatherless orphans (v. 18), for He would send them the Holy Spirit. They had experienced the Holy Spirit being with them, but now He would come to actually indwell them (v. 17). Yes, Jesus was going away, but the Holy Spirit was coming to them, and as Jesus hints here and makes explicit in 16:7, it is to the disciples' advantage that He go away and the Spirit come. Only then could they do even greater works than He had done (v. 12) and have a much greater understanding of the things He had said (vv. 20, 26). After following Jesus for three years, their understanding of Him and His teachings was still remarkably limited (vv. 5-9), but when the Spirit of truth came to indwell them, things would become clear to them, and though they were in turmoil now, His peace would soon be theirs (vv. 26-27). But before this could happen, Jesus ominously tells them, *"the ruler of this world is coming"* (v. 30). Lest they believe that Jesus is frightened by this prospect, or that He is anticipating defeat at the hands of this usurper, He emphasizes that *"He has no power over Me. But I do as the Father has commanded Me"* (vv. 30-31). The devil would indeed come with great wrath against Jesus, and he might believe that he was winning over Jesus, but Jesus would be the ultimate victor, because He was doing the will of the Father in dying for the redemption of the world. In that confidence, Jesus declared, *"Rise, let us go from here"* (v. 31), not shrinking back in fear, but moving forward, determined to do the will of the Father, defeat the schemes of the devil, and secure salvation for all who will believe.

PRAYER: Jesus has left planet Earth, but He has sent His Holy Spirit to be our source of truth as He illumines the written Word, our source of power as we serve the risen Lord, and our source of peace as we navigate life in this hostile world. The Spirit came to indwell you at the moment you received Jesus as your Lord and Savior. Are you experiencing His illumination, His power and His peace? It is only as we are filled with the Spirit (rather than being filled with other things) that we experience Him in this way. Pray today for a fresh infilling of the Spirit, for fresh insight into His Word, for fresh anointing in His work, and for fresh joy in the journey.

THE VINE AND THE BRANCHES
JOHN 15

John 15 is a chapter about the believer's relationships: our relationship with our Lord, our relationship with each other, our relationship with the world, our relationship with the Word, and our relationship with the Spirit. The dominant image in the chapter is the image of the vine and the branches. Grapevines were a common sight in Jesus' time, and the keeping of them would have been quite familiar to His disciples. In His illustration, He is the vine, we are the branches, and the Father is the vinedresser. The fruit can be seen as Christian character (Galatians 5:22-23), praise (Hebrews 13:15), converts to Christ (Romans 1:13), and good works (Matthew 3:8). The vinedresser's desire is to bring each branch to maximum fruitfulness, moving it from no fruit (v. 2a) to fruit (v. 2b) to more fruit (v. 2c) to much fruit (v. 5), because the Father is glorified when we bear much fruit (v. 8). How does He bring us along that process? Jesus says that the branch that bears no fruit, *"He takes away"* (v. 2).

There are two ways to understand that statement. It may be referring to "dead wood," branches that are attached to the vine but actually have no life. Such dead wood must be broken off of the vine because it can harbor disease and decay. This would be a picture of those who have attached themselves, in a sense, to Christ, but have not been truly born again to new life in Christ (Judas Iscariot would be an example. See also Matthew 13:20-21). This would certainly correspond with Jesus' later statements in verse 6. Some interpreters, such as Bruce Wilkinson in his book *The Secrets of the Vine* (highly recommended), believe the term *"takes away"* (the Greek word is *aero,* from which we get "aeronautics") would be better translated as "lifts up." They point out that sometimes a branch of a grapevine can run along the ground, where moisture, mud and mildew will make it fruitless. A good vinedresser will lift up those branches, clean them off, and tie them to the trellis so that they can begin producing fruit. Both interpretations have their application. Moving from fruitlessness to fruit-bearing requires both vital relationship with the vine and separation from the world. Obviously, no one who is not vitally connected to the life of the vine (Jesus) in a true relationship can produce any kind of spiritual fruit, and even a true believer who is wallowing in the muck and mire of the world will find himself sorely lacking in spiritual fruit until he is lifted up from that situation and cleansed from it. Moving from fruit-bearing to greater fruit-bearing requires pruning. Sometimes God must cut unproductive things out of our lives to bring us to greater usefulness in His Kingdom, and it can be a painful process. We tend to believe that everything painful in our lives is the result of discipline over sin. While it may be so, it may also be that the divine vinedresser is pruning us so that we might produce more fruit. Moving from more fruit to much fruit requires remaining, or abiding, in Him (v. 5), a relationship of absolute dependence and ever-deepening friendship (vv.

13-16) over a long period of time. As we grow older in Christ, we should be growing ever more fruitful in Him, not looking back to the "good old days" of fruit-bearing (Psalm 92:14). We abide in Him by keeping His commandments (v. 10), being rightly related in love with our fellow believers (vv. 12, 17), enduring persecution faithfully (vv. 18-25), and bearing witness of Him in the power and under the leadership of the Spirit (vv. 26-27).

PRAYER: As you look at your life right now, where do you see yourself? Are you fruitless? Bearing some fruit? Bearing more fruit? Bearing much fruit? Ask the divine vinedresser to do whatever is necessary to take you to the next level, and ultimately, to the level of much fruit, that He might be glorified.

TRIBULATION
JOHN 16

John 16 begins and ends with teaching on the trials and tribulations that Jesus' disciples, both His first disciples and all those after, would face. The word "tribulation" in Greek is *thlipsis*, and it refers to "pressure": the pressure to compromise, the pressure to back down from one's convictions, the pressure to "go along to get along," the pressure to allow the world to squeeze us into its mold. That is a pressure that is becoming more pronounced in our culture every day. In our day, good is often called evil and evil is called good. The sword that the government wields to punish evildoers and reward righteousness (Romans 13:1-5) is often wielded to do the opposite. For example, those Christians who believe, teach, and live by what the Bible says about sexual immorality, particularly homosexuality, are often ridiculed or vilified, while those who compromise are celebrated as "good Christians." Sometimes that pressure comes even from within the professing church (v.

2). Verse 1 begins with *"I have spoken these things to you so that you will not fall away."* That raises the question for us of "what things?" Looking back to the end of chapter 15, Jesus has made it clear that the world hates Him, and that their hatred of Him would be extended to His followers. It is precisely because we know Him and know the Father (v. 3) that we become subject to such ill-treatment by those who don't. A famous quarterback was once asked, "What are the worst hits in football?" His response was, "The ones you don't see coming." As Christians, we should never be blind-sided by persecution. Jesus warned us it was coming, and here He gives some details of what the disciples would soon face: expulsion from the synagogues and even death at the hands of people thinking they were serving God in killing them (the Apostle Paul, prior to his conversion, comes to mind). Knowing it is coming in advance should give us courage to stand strong and not fall away in compromise or in despair. At the end of the chapter (v. 33), Jesus says something similar: *"I have told you these things so that in Me you may have peace."* That tells us that Jesus' desire is not just that we grit our teeth and endure the tribulations of living in this hostile, enemy-held environment, but that we experience internal peace even in the midst of those external trials. Again, the question arises as to what He has told us that would lead to that kind of supernatural peace. Throughout chapter 16, Jesus shows us invaluable resources for living in this hostile world, resources that bring us peace. There is the resource of the Holy Spirit, who energizes our message (and often converts our enemies) through His convicting power (vv. 8-11). He also guides us into all truth, certainly through the Word, but not exclusively through the Word. He also *"will tell you things that are to come"* (v. 13), giving us warning and guidance as we navigate the minefield of this world. He has also given us the resource of prayer. Our relationship with Him is the key that unlocks access to the Father in prayer (vv. 23-27). Beyond those two resources, we have Jesus' own example of overcoming the world, including death itself (vv. 16-22). Unable to squeeze Him into its mold, the world opposed Him, even to the point of killing Him, but even in the face of pressure and opposition, He stood strong, and even after they put Him to death, He arose victoriously! Even if worse comes to worst, and our lives are taken as a result of standing for the truth, how bad is that? That's just a one-way ticket into the eternal joy of heaven, and a final, powerful testimony of our faith in Him! So, even in a world filled with tribulation, we can still be of good cheer, knowing that He has overcome the world, and through Him, we can overcome it also!

PRAYER: Where are you facing pressure today to compromise your faith? Where do you see pressure on the horizon? Pray for strength to stand strong no matter how strong the pressure or the opposition becomes. Pray for those fellow believers in other nations and in our own who are experiencing the fires of persecution, that they might stand strong and know supernatural peace in the midst of whatever storm they may face.

JESUS' DESIRES
JOHN 17

Having taught His disciples many things on that final evening before His betrayal and arrest, Jesus now proceeds into prayer. In the first part of the prayer, Jesus prays *about* His disciples (vv. 1-12); in the latter part, He prays *for* His disciples (vv. 13-26). It is fascinating to read His prayer and to see what was most on His heart for His people as He faced His impending death. First, He prays that His joy might be fulfilled in us (v. 13). Given all of the teaching on tribulation He had done that evening, this joy must be a supernatural manifestation (Galatians 5:22) and not based on external circumstances. Even facing the cross, Jesus was filled with joy (Hebrews 12:2), and even in the midst of the hardships of the world, we can have joy: the joy of knowing Him, the joy of forgiveness, the joy of the prospect of eternity in heaven with Him, and the joy of seeing others come to salvation. Second, Jesus prays for our protection from the evil one (vv. 14-15), that although our enemy will bring all manner of trials and tribulations against us, his plans and strategies in our lives will fail to deter us from living and witnessing for Christ. Third, Jesus prays for our sanctification (v. 17). Sanctification is the process of growing in holiness and righteousness, becoming less sinful and less worldly and more Christlike over time. That sanctification, Jesus says, comes by being constantly immersed in the truth that is found in His Word. Fourth, Jesus prays for our mission (vv. 18-20), that we will be faithful to go into the world and speak the Word of truth to others, that they might also believe. Verse 20 also clues us in that Jesus' desires here were not just focused on His disciples in that upper room; these are His desires for all who would believe in Him. Fifth, Jesus prays for unity among His people (vv. 21-23). One of the enemy's greatest strategies is division, but when we stand strong together, the world sees the truth of the gospel. Sixth, Jesus expresses His desire that we would be with Him in glory (v. 24); indeed, I am convinced that the joy of having us spend eternity with Him was the joy set before Him that gave Him the strength to endure the cross (Hebrews 12:2). Finally, Jesus prays we might display the supernatural love of God (v. 26), that supernatural *agape'* love that always wants the best for the other person, and only does the best for the other person, even at great personal cost, and even for those who are the least loveable.

PRAYER: Pray today that Jesus' desires expressed in this prayer might be fulfilled (or fulfilled more fully) in you and in your church.

I AM!
JOHN 18

When John records material already covered by the other three gospels, he tends to give us details not found in the others. That is certainly the case as the scene of Jesus' arrest unfolds in the Garden of Gethsemane. When the mob approached Him with their lanterns, torches and weapons, Jesus asked *"Whom do you seek?"* When they answered that they were looking for Jesus of Nazareth, He responded, *"I am He"* (vv. 4-5). Note that the pronoun "He" is not found in the original manuscripts; it has been added by translators in an attempt to clarify the meaning. It may very well have done the opposite, obscuring the meaning rather than clarifying it. Jesus was doing more than simply admitting His identity as Jesus of Nazareth; He was proclaiming His identity as God incarnate, the Great I Am! They thought they were coming to arrest an itinerant rabbi who had run afoul of the Sanhedrin; in truth, they were attempting to arrest the Sovereign Lord of the Universe! To show the folly of it all, just those two words spoken from His mouth had enough force to knock the whole crowd to the ground. Obviously, Jesus was planning to go with them (v. 11), so why this demonstration of power? Jesus was accomplishing two things here. First, He was demonstrating that He was a willing participant in this drama of redemption. He was not dragged to the cross against His will; indeed, if He had not chosen to go to the cross, the entire Roman army could not have put Him there. If two words were sufficient to knock them to the ground, what might three words have done? Or four? Jesus was also negotiating the release of His disciples. The mob had no doubt surrounded the small group that was there in the Garden, intending to arrest them all. Jesus' words in verse 8 constitute a demand on His part. He would agree to go with them (and He had shown beyond a doubt that He didn't have to go with them), but only if they let the disciples go. Peter interrupted the negotiations by his rash action of attacking the high priest's servant, but Jesus stepped in quickly stop Peter and heal Malchus (see Luke 22:51), and the disciples were released.

PRAYER: Praise the Lord today that He was not some good man who found Himself caught up in religious and political intrigues beyond His control and got Himself crucified; He was (and is) the Great I Am, the Sovereign Lord of the Universe, completely in control of the situation, and He freely chose to die that horrible death as a substitute and sacrifice for us.

PILATE'S DILEMMA
JOHN 19

Pontius Pilate's relationship with the Jews had been a contentious one throughout his time as governor of Judea. He had nothing but contempt for them, and the feeling was mutual. When the Sanhedrin brought Jesus before him in the early morning hours, insisting that He be executed, Pilate was suspicious of their motives (Matthew 27:18) and not at all convinced of the charges (Luke 23:2). His interview with Jesus (18:33-38) convinced him that whatever Jesus was, He was most certainly not a revolutionary seeking the overthrow of the Roman government. Pilate had several reasons for wanting to release Jesus. First, while the Romans ruled with an iron fist over conquered people, there was a highly developed sense of justice among them. They had no reservations about issuing brutal punishments to the guilty, but they did not administer such punishments arbitrarily against the innocent. Second, Pilate's wife had had a bad dream about Jesus, and had warned him that He was innocent and not to have anything to do with Him (Matthew 27:19). Third, given Pilate's strained relationship with the Jewish authorities (note both how they insulted him in 18:28 by refusing to come into the Praetorium, lest they be defiled and unable to eat the Passover, and their sneering response to his question in 18:30), he did not want to crucify Jesus precisely because they wanted Him crucified so badly. But Pilate was on shaky political footing with Rome. Several uprisings in his territory had drawn the ire of the emperor, and the man who had appointed Pilate to his position had been found disloyal to the emperor and executed just a year before, casting suspicion on Pilate as well. He could not afford any more uprisings in his territory or any bad reports getting back to the emperor. The Jewish authorities took advantage of Pilate's situation to pressure him into doing their will. They stirred the crowds into a frenzy to demand Jesus' crucifixion, and Pilate quickly realized that there was real potential for a riot (Matthew 27:24), a riot that could quickly explode into a mass uprising with the city swelled with Passover pilgrims from all over Judea and beyond. Then, they issued a not-so-veiled threat: *"If you let this man go, you are no friend of Caesar. Anyone who claims to be a king opposes Caesar"* (v. 12, NIV 84). "Friend of Caesar" was a technical term for someone loyal to Caesar. They were threatening to report him to Caesar if he dared to let the "insurrectionist" Jesus go (interestingly enough, he ended up letting a real insurrectionist, Barabbas, go in His stead). Under this political pressure, Pilate did the "politically correct" thing and gave in to their request, but he had one more insult up his sleeve for the Jewish authorities. When it came time to write the charges against Jesus that would be affixed to the cross, he declared Him *"JESUS OF NAZARETH, THE KING OF THE JEWS,"* and refused to alter it, even under their protests (vv. 19-22). This was mockery on his part, not so much of Jesus, but of the Jews in general, but it told the truth about His identity.

PRAYER: Have you ever felt pressured by outside circumstances or threats to do what you knew to be the wrong thing? Jesus said that those who put the pressure on Pilate were guilty of *"the greater sin"* (v. 11), but that did not excuse Pilate from his own guilt in the matter. Pray for those you may know who find themselves in situations where they are pressured to do the wrong thing by outside forces, whether elected officials, Christians standing up for the truth, teenagers dealing with peer pressure, or businessmen tempted to cut corners ethically to turn a profit. Pray that you will have the strength to do right even when pressured to do wrong.

LOVE AND DOUBT
JOHN 20

Mary Magdalene's intense love for Jesus, even when she believed He was dead, is on full display in this account. She had come to the tomb early in the morning, hoping to do a better job of the burial rituals than Joseph of Arimathea and Nicodemus had been able to do on Friday with the Sabbath rapidly approaching. Finding the tomb open, she ran to get Peter and John, and they found the body missing, with only the linen graveclothes left behind. When the two of them left, Mary was left outside the tomb, weeping inconsolably. It is not difficult to understand the intensity of her love. Jesus had delivered her from a horrible life, casting out of her seven demons (Mark 16:9). Afterward, she had traveled extensively with Jesus (Luke 8:1-3). Now, she was left to wonder, what now? What would her life be like now that He was gone? What would she do without Him? Where would she go? Would the demons return to haunt her now that her deliverer was gone? She had so wanted to perform one last act of service for this one who meant so much to her, but now even that had been denied to her. When she looked into the tomb, she saw an amazing sight - two angels, one at the head and the other at the foot of the blood-stained platform where Jesus' body had rested. This was a picture of the mercy seat of the Ark of the Covenant, where the blood from the Day of Atonement sacrifice was sprinkled between the two golden cherubim. After she had a brief conversation with the angels, and after a brief moment when, through the haze of her tears, she thought the risen Christ was a gardener, He spoke her name, and she knew from just that one word that He was alive. All her fears about the future melted in that moment. He gave her a short-term assignment (v. 17), and that evening, He would give to her and to all of His disciples a long-term assignment that would occupy them for the rest of their lives (v. 21). Although He would not be with them as He had in the past, He would be with them through the Holy Spirit, who would empower them for this task of ministry and evangelism (v. 22). Thomas, for whatever reason, was not there on that first Easter Sunday evening when Jesus appeared to the disciples, and thus he could be thought of as "The Patron Saint of Those Who Skip Church." Someone might argue that he had no way of knowing that Jesus was going to show up that night, but we don't have that excuse, for He has promised to show up whenever two or three of us gather together in His name (Matthew 18:20). When the others informed Thomas about what he'd missed, he refused to believe it until he had seen it himself, and because of this incident, he has gone down in history as "Doubting Thomas." In Thomas' defense, I think it's only fair to note that he was merely seeking and insisting on the same degree of proof that the others had already experienced. Before Jesus appeared to them again eight days later, we can only imagine what went through Thomas' mind: Why would these friends of mine lie? Did He really show up alive? Did I miss it? Is He going to come back? What if I never get to see Him like the others did? But then, when Jesus returned, He made His way right to Thomas to give him the level of proof he had insisted upon. Thomas had refused to believe merely on the testimony of his fellow disciples, but Jesus said that *"Blessed are those who have not seen, and have yet believed"* (v. 29). That blessing echoes down through the centuries to us who have believed because of the disciples' testimony, empowered by the Holy Spirit and recorded in His Holy Word (vv. 30-31).

PRAYER: Are you struggling with an uncertain future? Express your love to Him, insist upon serving Him in spite of any obstacles (v. 15), and you may be surprised how quickly one word from Him can clarify your future. Do you struggle with doubts? Ask Him to show Himself to you powerfully, and watch your doubts dissipate.

RESTORATION
JOHN 21

Simon Peter had not been the only one of the apostles to insist that he would not fall away, but he had been the most vocal (Mark 14:27-31). His had also been the most prominent of their failures. They had all run away as predicted, but Peter actually denied even knowing Jesus three times while in the courtyard of the high priest (see John 18). He was thrilled that Jesus was alive, but understandably embarrassed about his failure, and perhaps unsure if Jesus' assignment given in chapter 20 applied to him. After all, having failed to stand strong for Jesus before, how could the Lord trust him with this assignment now? Three times, the same number as his denials, Jesus asked Peter if he loved Him, and three times, Peter assured Him that he did. Three times, in response to Peter's profession of love, Jesus gave him the assignment, expressed the first time as *"Feed my lambs"* and the last two times as *"Tend my sheep"* and *"Feed my sheep"* (vv. 15-17). Then Jesus prophesied about Peter and his future in verses 18-19, a barely veiled reference to the fact that when he was old, he would glorify God by dying the death of crucifixion. Peter had recoiled in fear from such a possibility earlier, but now he embraced it, and he would indeed follow Jesus throughout the rest of his life and even to his martyr's death as an older man. The knowledge of how he would die, and when, no doubt gave him tremendous confidence in days to come. Picture him standing before the crowds in Jerusalem, a mere 50 days after the crucifixion, proclaiming that *"God has made this Jesus, whom you have crucified, both Lord and Christ"* (Acts 2:36). Picture him standing boldly before the Sanhedrin, the Jewish council that had handed Jesus over to Pilate, proclaiming the name of Jesus as the only way of salvation (Acts 4:10-12) and refusing their orders to stop preaching in His name (Acts 4:19-20). Picture him sleeping soundly while facing the next-day threat of execution (Acts 12:6-7). He could speak boldly and sleep soundly in the knowledge that he was not old yet, and Jesus had said he would only die when he was old! From that day beside the Sea of Galilee on, Peter knew that he was immortal until God's purposes had been fulfilled in him. Let me let you in on a secret: so are we all! John, who by all early historical accounts was the last of the apostles to die and the only one not to die a martyr, addresses in the last verses of his gospel a rumor that had arisen that he would not die (the fact that he lived to a very old age, some believe over 100, no doubt lent credence to this rumor). Jesus was obviously not saying that John would never die, but He was emphasizing to Peter that John's future was not Peter's business; each of us must follow Him on the path He lays out for us. Our earthly path (and how that earthly path comes to its end) may be different than others', but all of us have His calling on our lives to *"Follow Me!"* (v. 22).

PRAYER: Are you dealing with embarrassment over failing the Lord in some way? He longs to restore you to His service and use you again. Confess that failure to Him (I John 1:9), and get back on the path of following Him!

ACTS

THE ASCENSION
ACTS 1

After the resurrection, Jesus spent forty days with His disciples, teaching them, proving to them that He was truly alive and not simply a vision, and bringing them instruction about the Kingdom of God (vv. 2-3). He gave them strict orders not to depart from Jerusalem until *"the promise of the Father,"* the Holy Spirit, had come upon them to give them power for the mission to come, the mission of local, area, and world evangelization (vv. 4-5, 8). Amazingly, despite having been instructed by the risen Lord about the true nature of His Kingdom as spiritual (see John 18:36 and Luke 17:20-21), they were still fixated on the idea of Jesus establishing an immediate, earthly Israelite kingdom (v. 6). Truly, spiritual things are spiritually discerned (I Corinthians 2:14), and until the Spirit came upon them, they could not fully grasp what Jesus had taught them, both in the forty days after the resurrection and in the 3½ years prior. Neither can we grasp the meaning of the Word without the Spirit's ministry of illumination, as the one who inspired the Scriptures and indwells our spirits speaks to our hearts as we read and study, giving us understanding and personal application of the Scriptures. Jesus told these first disciples in verse 7, *"It is not for you to know the times or the dates, which the Father has fixed by His own authority,"* and the same is true for His disciples in every time. In spite of this authoritative word from Jesus (along with Matthew 24:36) about the timing of His coming and the setting up of His future earthly Kingdom, people down through the centuries have nevertheless engaged in speculation and date-setting about the Lord's coming, and all of them have one thing in common: they have all been 100% dead wrong! The timing of the Lord's coming is not our concern; our concern is to be His witnesses in our Jerusalem, Judea, Samaria and throughout all the earth (v. 8, see also Matthew 24:14). As someone well put it, it is not our job to determine the date of the wedding, but to get the bride ready! Jesus will come again (v. 11), but in the meantime, there's much work to be done. Out of the more than 500 who had seen Jesus alive after the resurrection (I Corinthians 15:6), about 120 were gathered in the upper room for the ten days from His ascension until the coming of the Spirit at Pentecost, waiting, praying, attending to the business of replacing Judas (vv. 14-26), and holding on to the Lord's promise of verse 5. The stage was now set for the dramatic birthday of the church in Acts 2.

PRAYER: Pray today for the Spirit to teach you through His Word and His illuminating power. As a believer, you are indwelt by the Holy Spirit. Are you experiencing His power to be His witness? Pray that His fullness, presence and power might fill you to overflowing (John 7:37-39) such that others might be brought into His Kingdom. Thank Him for the promise of His future coming, and pray that you might accomplish every purpose He has for your life in the meantime.

WHERE THE SPIRIT OF THE LORD IS
ACTS 2

In Acts 2, on the Day of Pentecost, the Holy Spirit came in power to baptize the waiting 120. In past times, the Spirit had come upon certain people for certain tasks at certain times, but from this point on, He would permanently indwell all believers. As signs and symbols of this new epoch in His dealings with humanity, there was the sound of a rushing, mighty wind, tongues of fire rested upon each of their heads, and they spilled out of the upper room speaking in tongues they had never learned, such that those from many countries who were in Jerusalem for Pentecost heard them praising God in their own languages. When a crowd formed, Peter stood up to preach, proclaiming that what they were witnessing was a fulfillment of Old Testament prophecy (vv. 16-21). Launching from the last verse of that prophecy, *"And whoever calls on the name of the Lord shall be saved,"* Peter then preached to them about Jesus, reminding them of what they personally knew about Him (vv. 22-24), showing that His death and resurrection had likewise been prophesied (vv. 25-32), proclaiming Him as both Lord and Christ (vv. 33-36), and calling them to repentance and salvation through Him (vv. 38-40). The same Spirit who had filled the 120 now brought conviction to the crowds, and about 3000 of them repented and were saved, signaling their newfound faith by baptism (v. 41). While the early part of the chapter presents the birthday of the church, the latter part of the chapter, verses 42-47, present a snapshot of everyday life in the early church. While Pentecost, with its mighty, rushing wind and tongues of fire, was a one-time inaugural event, the attitudes and activities recorded in verses 42-47 should be normative for all churches of all time. One of the key words in this passage is the Greek word *koinonia*, translated as *"fellowship"* in verse 42. John R.W. Stott has pointed out that this word never appears in the

Bible until it appears here, because it couldn't exist until the coming of the Holy Spirit. Only the Holy Spirit indwelling them could take a large, diverse group of people from many different backgrounds (see vv. 9-11) and turn them into a family. When the Holy Spirit is in control of a church, there will be a commitment to the apostles' teaching (as recorded for us in the Word of God) and prayer (v. 42), a sense of awe and reverence as God is at work (v. 43), the meeting of needs through sacrificial giving (vv. 44-45), true unity and friendship (v. 46), a desire for worship (v. 47) and people being born again on a regular basis (v. 47).

PRAYER: Pray for your church today, that it will be more closely conformed to the "prototype" church of the first church at Jerusalem. Pray that you will always do your part to *"keep the unity of the Spirit in the bond of peace"* (Ephesians 4:3) in your church family.

THE CRIPPLED MAN HEALED
ACTS 3

One of the aspects of this account that always strikes me is the fact that this lame man, crippled since birth, had been laid daily at the Beautiful Gate of the Temple by family or friends to beg for alms (v. 2). Given that he was over forty years of age (4:22), that means that Jesus had no doubt seen him in His visits to the Temple, and had evidently walked right by him, probably more than once. Jesus had healed many others at the Temple during His sojourn on Earth. Why not this man? There is a mystery about healing, actually several: why some are healed and others are not, why some go for years without being healed and then suddenly are healed, and why some are healed suddenly and others only through painful procedures or treatments. The best explanation for why this man had not been healed earlier is surely that the timing wasn't right. Like the man born blind in John 9, we can attribute the delay of this man's healing to a desire on God's part that *"the works of God might by displayed in him"* (John 9:3) on this particular day. This man's miraculous healing at the hands of Peter and John (the first such miraculous healing recorded in Acts) caused a great crowd to form at Solomon's Porch, all of them greatly amazed that this familiar beggar was now walking and leaping about, praising the Lord. Never let it be said that Peter didn't know what to do when a crowd formed! Just as he had done on the day of Pentecost, he used the amazement and attention of the crowd as a launching pad to preach Jesus and call for repentance. Of particular note in Peter's message is its beginning: notice that he refuses to take any personal credit for the man's miraculous healing, attributing it instead to *"The God of Abraham and Isaac and Jacob"* (vv. 12-13). What a change from their pre-Holy Spirit days when the apostles often bickered among themselves about which one was the greatest, no doubt listing and comparing and boasting of "their" accomplishments. Let us never allow ourselves to horn in on even the smallest part of God's glory, for that is a sure way to lose it. It is our job to shine the spotlight on Him, not share the spotlight with Him, and when we are truly filled with the Spirit, seeing His name exalted rather than our own will be our delight. In his message to the crowd, Peter lifts up the name of Jesus, speaking of Him as God's Son (v. 13), and speaking of His rejection by Israel (vv. 13-14) and His death and resurrection (vv. 15-16). He speaks of Jesus as the one predicted by the Old Testament prophets (vv. 17-18), and he issues a call for repentance and conversion (v. 19). This message is very similar to the one he preached at Pentecost, with similar results: another mass conversion through which the church grew to about 5000 men (4:4). It is also a concrete example of Paul's words in II Corinthians 4:5: *"...we do not preach ourselves, but Christ Jesus the Lord."*

PRAYER: Notice verse 19: *"Therefore, repent and be converted, that your sins may be wiped away, that times of refreshing may come from the presence of the Lord."* When we are saved, we repent (a word that means "a change of mind" - a change of mind about ourselves, our sin, and our Savior) and we turn to God in faith (the meaning of *"be converted"*), trusting Him alone to save us. When we respond to the gospel message and the conviction of the Holy Spirit in that way, our sins are forever wiped away. But that is not the end of our journey with the Lord; it is just the beginning. Regular time spent in the presence of the Lord brings refreshing and renewal. Are you in need of a refreshing today? Ask Him to fill you anew and afresh with His Spirit.

FULLNESS AND BOLDNESS
ACTS 4

The large crowd that gathered and the commotion that resulted over the miraculous healing attracted the attention of the priests and the Sadducees, who were in charge of the Temple. Upon hearing Peter's message about Jesus (whom they had not long ago condemned to die) and the resurrection of the dead (a doctrine which this particular sect of Judaism rejected), they ordered Peter and John arrested to put a stop to their preaching. Even still, a great number believed and were saved (v. 4). The next day, Peter and John were brought before the Sanhedrin, the same group led by the same men that had conspired to crucify Jesus (vv. 5-6). These men asked them, *"By what power or by what name have you done this?"* which gave Peter all the opening he needed. Filled with the Holy Spirit, he let them know immediately that the man's healing had come about in the name and through the power of Jesus Christ of Nazareth! As if that were not enough, he added the accusation *"whom you crucified"* and the declaration *"whom God raised from the dead"* (v. 10), a truth that this same body had gone to great pains to deny and cover up (Matthew 28:11-15). The Sanhedrin members were amazed at their boldness (v. 13), a boldness that only grew in the face of their intimidation tactics and demands to speak of Jesus no more (vv. 17-18). Peter and John refused to agree to such terms, proclaiming that *"Whether it is right in the sight of God to listen to you more than to God, you judge. For we cannot help but declare what we have seen and heard"* (vv. 19-20). When the two were released, they returned to the other church members and told about their experiences at the Temple and with the Sanhedrin, which sent the church into a season of prayer, amazingly, not for protection, but for greater boldness (v. 29)! They knew that persecution was a given, that it had been both prophesied (vv. 25-26) and fulfilled in Jesus' earthly life (v. 27), and that it was continuing in His ongoing life through His body, the church (v. 29). God answered their prayers by filling them with the Holy Spirit such that they were not intimidated, but continued to testify of Jesus with boldness (v. 31). Notice that both the boldness of Peter and John and of the church is connected to the fullness of the Holy Spirit (vv. 8, 31). There is one baptism of the Holy Spirit (it occurred at Pentecost for them; at conversion for us - see I Corinthians 12:13), but many fillings or refreshings which come in time of need (see Luke 12:11-12) and in answer to prayer (see Luke 11:13). Those who believe in a "second blessing" are too limited; God wants to send a second blessing, and a third, and a fourth, and a ten-thousandth blessing of His Spirit upon those who ask!

PRAYER: Pray for the fullness of the Holy Spirit today, that you might be bold to speak of Jesus in every opportunity that presents itself, no matter how intimidating it may be. In a world of increasing aggression and persecution of believers, pray for those who are most in the line of fire, that they would stand strong for the faith and not back down in the face of threats and intimidation, but continue as faithful, bold witnesses of the name, power and salvation of Jesus.

DISCIPLINE
ACTS 5

The story of Ananias and Sapphira is a difficult one in many ways. It certainly serves as a severe example of God's discipline, and it reminds us that God is not to be trifled with, that He and His commands are to be taken seriously. After Barnabas had sold a field and given the money to the apostles for distribution (4:36-37), this couple apparently decided to do the same, the difference being that they gave only part of the money from the sale of the land, keeping the rest for themselves. They desired to receive the acclaim that had apparently come to Barnabas, but without the same degree of sacrifice. According to Peter's statement of verse 4, it was certainly within their rights to have kept the field or to have kept the proceeds after selling it. The sin in question was that they had lied about it, attempting to make the others in the church believe that they had given the entire amount of the proceeds. They may have fooled their fellow believers, but they could not fool God. The Holy Spirit apparently revealed this conspiracy to Peter, who then confronted the two of them individually about it. Note the correlation between verse 3, where Peter asks, *"Why has Satan filled your heart to deceive the Holy Spirit...?"* and verse 4, where he states, *"You have not lied to men, but to God."* The Holy Spirit, far from being the impersonal "force" He is sometimes made out to be, is shown here to be fully and completely God, one of the members of the divine Trinity. In verse 3, Peter presents this conspiracy on their part as a Satanic attack, a dangerous incursion of the evil one into the fellowship of the church. Dishonesty is serious business in the eyes of God, and a deadly weapon in the hand of the devil. It can destroy friendships, businesses, marriages and churches. Jesus said, *"I am the...truth"* (John 14:6), and the

187

Bible says that God cannot lie (Titus 1:2). On the other hand, Satan is *"a liar and the father of lies"* (John 8:44). Therefore, we are never more godly than when telling the truth, and never more devilish than when telling a lie. God dealt with this Satanic invasion of His church severely, putting Ananias to death first and then his wife as well. God's discipline is not always as drastic, and is usually deployed for the purpose of restoration rather than retribution (Hebrews 12:5-11), but in some extreme cases, God may take a person home to be with Him prematurely (I Corinthians 11:30). There is no indication that Ananias and Sapphira were not genuine believers, so they were taken to heaven, but their sin in this instance was such that their lives, and therefore their opportunities to serve the Lord and earn eternal rewards, were cut short. Thus, they not only lost the earthly acclaim they had hoped for, but they also lost heavenly rewards as well. The result of God's discipline of them was that *"Great fear came on the entire church, and on all those who heard these things"* (v. 11).

PRAYER: Have you ever allowed deception to color your interactions with fellow believers, particularly the deception of trying to make others think you are better than you are? Pray that you might never become an agent of Satan and his deceptive plots in your life and in the life of your church. Thank the Lord for the times He has disciplined you to bring you back into a proper walk with Him.

THE FIRST DEACONS
ACTS 6

Having failed in his attack of deception against the church, the evil one now injected a virus of discord into the fellowship. The Hellenistic Jews in the church were those from other parts of the Roman Empire who had been converted on the day of Pentecost and who spoke Greek as their native language. The Hebrews were those from Israel whose native language was Aramaic. While not as culturally divided as Jews and Gentiles would be, there were still significant cultural differences between the two groups, and Satan sought to drive a wedge between the two groups to widen that divide to the point of fracture. The issue in question was that the widows of the Hellenistic group were being overlooked in the daily distribution of food. This seems to have been merely an oversight on the part of the apostles and not an intentional slight, but the devil is the master of putting a sinister spin on the most innocent of actions. The apostles saw the growing strife in the church and called a meeting of the body. Knowing that they could not adequately administer the food program and still maintain their primary ministries of prayer and the Word, they asked the church to choose seven men to whom they could entrust the widow ministry. Note the priorities of the apostles, priorities that should mark all those who are in ministry: prayer and the ministry of the Word, in that order. The devil has no fear of prayerless ministry of the Word, but the Word empowered by prayer is a battering ram to his kingdom. Unfortunately, in many churches, the ministerial staff is tasked with so much administrative minutiae that these primary callings become secondary, if not further down the list, to the detriment of both the ministers and the ministry. Note also the qualifications for the men chosen, whom most people consider the first deacons. They were not to be chosen for their wealth or their contributions or their popularity or even their business acumen; they were to be known for being *"full of the Holy Spirit and of wisdom"* (v. 3). They were not called to be a "board of directors," as deacons in many churches have become, but servants of the church (a much higher calling than a board of directors could ever be - see Matthew 20:25-28), ministering to the needs of the body and freeing up the apostles to focus on their primary calling. With these wise and Spirit-filled men managing the ministry arm of the church, and the apostles once more able to concentrate on their principal tasks, the result was dramatic: *"the word of God spread, and the number of the disciples grew rapidly in Jerusalem, and a great number of the priests were obedient to the faith"* (v. 7).

PRAYER: Pray for the deacons of your church, that they might always be full of wisdom and the Holy Spirit, and that they might serve in harmony with the ministerial staff. Pray that they might have servant hearts, and that your ministers might keep the ministries of prayer and the Word primary in their lives.

THE FIRST CHRISTIAN MARTYR
ACTS 7

The story of Stephen's martyrdom actually begins in the latter part of chapter 6. There, we see how this deacon (v. 5), full of the Spirit and wisdom, *"did great wonders and miracles among the people"* (6:8), which led some of the Synagogue of the Freedmen to dispute with him. *"But they were not able to withstand the wisdom and the Spirit by which he spoke"* (6:10). Oh, the irony! These "Freedmen" were actually in bondage, and Stephen only desired to show them how they could truly be free! How like so many in our world today, who, instead of receiving the message of liberty, seek to silence it by any means possible. Unable to answer Stephen in debate, they told lies about him in order to have him arrested and brought before the Sanhedrin. There, they accused him of speaking blasphemy against the Temple and the Law (6:13), and in his defense, Stephen took the Sanhedrin on a journey they knew well, a journey through Hebrew history going all the way back to Abraham. His conclusion, though, was totally unexpected. Rather than refuting the charges or pleading for mercy, Stephen turned the charges upon his inquisitors, showing that they were following in the path of their ancestors, but not in a good way: *"You stiff-necked people, uncircumcised in heart and ears! You always resist the Holy Spirit. As your fathers did, so do you. Which of the prophets have your fathers not persecuted? They have even killed those who foretold the coming of the Righteous One, of whom you have now become the betrayers and murderers"* (vv. 51-52). Upon hearing this accusation, *"they were cut to the heart"* (v. 54), a phrase indicating conviction (see 2:37), but rather than repenting of their sins and placing their faith in Jesus for salvation, they gnashed their teeth at him in anger. When Stephen reported that he was seeing a vision of Jesus standing at the right hand of God (vv. 55-56), it was too much for them; the seventy members of the Sanhedrin, plus the high priest and the false witnesses, *"rushed at him in unison,"* dragging him outside the city and stoning him to death. Their anger was so intense that they had completely lost all reason. The Roman government reserved the right of execution to itself; the Sanhedrin had no authority to execute anyone, and by doing so, they were risking Roman retaliation (no doubt why they dragged him outside the city to a secluded location to do their dirty deed). In our time, when many Christians worldwide are facing the prospect of martyrdom, Stephen's example shows us how we should face such a death, should it come to that. First, we should face martyrdom in the full knowledge that we will see the glory of God (v. 55). There is a dying grace that comes upon those who die for the Lord. Rather than begging for our lives, we should continue to proclaim our Savior and call upon Him, even to our dying breath (v. 59), and rather than cursing our tormentors, we should pray for their forgiveness (v. 60). The last sentence of the chapter, *"Having said this, he fell asleep,"* seems strangely serene in a scene of such vicious brutality, but it reflects the supernatural peace that Stephen had even as his life ebbed away, a peace that is available to us all (Philippians 4:7). Saul, at this time a young rabbi, watched the coats of those who stoned Stephen (v. 58), and consented to his death (8:1), but the way Stephen faced death no doubt played into Saul's later conversion. Stephen's dying grace was a testimony of Christ that defied refutation.

PRAYER: Pray for those facing martyrdom around the world. Pray that should they be put to death, they will stand strong and give a powerful final witness for Him in how they face their final moments. Pray that should that day come for you, you will do likewise. Stephen is not just an example to us of how to die; he is also an example of how to live. If Stephen could pray for the forgiveness of those who were bludgeoning him to death, is there someone you need to forgive today?

SCATTERED...LIKE SEED
ACTS 8

The martyrdom of Stephen set off a great persecution against the Christians in Jerusalem, which caused the early church to be scattered. This is a powerful example of Romans 8:28 in action. Clearly, the persecution that arose was not a good thing (v. 2), but God used it to move the church into the next phase of its mission (see Acts 1:8). Up until this chapter, everything that has happened in the book of Acts has taken place within the confines of Jerusalem. Now, the church would spread out into Judea and Samaria (v. 1) and beyond (v. 4). Chapter 8 records the adventures of just one of those scattered church members, Philip, another of the first deacons. Philip first took the gospel to Samaria, and a great number there believed. This is significant in that it is the first time the gospel had spread outside of Jewish culture. The Samaritans were the descendants of Israelites left behind during the Exile who had intermarried with Gentiles. The Jews and Samaritans absolutely hated each other, but the gospel overcame that cultural barrier. Then, at the height of his success in Samaria, Philip received a message from an angel to *"Rise up and go toward the south on the way that goes down from Jerusalem to Gaza"* (v. 26). Luke goes on to tell us that *"This is desert."* Indeed, the road in question went through the desert, and it led to Gaza, a town that had been destroyed and uninhabited for 100 years. That doesn't seem to make sense at all. Philip was in a major population area in Samaria, winning multitudes to Christ, and suddenly the Lord was telling him to leave there, go out to the middle of nowhere, and travel down a road leading to a ghost town. No wonder the Lord sent an angel to give him the message! He would never have believed it otherwise! It seemed absolutely crazy to abandon a productive work for a desert road. And beyond that, who wants to go to a desert? It's hot and uncomfortable in the desert, and it's dangerous to travel alone, especially in the desert. But sometimes God leads us in ways that we don't immediately understand in order to use us in ways we could never imagine. When a chariot came along carrying an Ethiopian court official, the Spirit ordered Philip to run up to the chariot. There he heard the Ethiopian reading from Isaiah 53, a powerful Messianic prophecy about Jesus' death and resurrection. Philip offered to explain it to him, and showed him how Jesus fulfilled that prophecy. The man believed, and Philip baptized him before being caught away and transported miraculously to Azotus. Philip never knew what became of the Ethiopian he had witnessed to, but the church in Ethiopia traces its beginnings back to this royal official won to the Lord by Philip. It was this man who first carried the gospel into Africa. Truly, we will never know on this side of heaven the far-reaching impact that one moment of obedience, one kind act, or one word of witness can have.

PRAYER: When the Jerusalem church was dispersed by persecution, they did not run and hide; they went forth *"preaching the word"* (v. 4). Pray that whatever adverse circumstances may arise in your life today and in days to come, you will be willing to find ways to turn it to the advantage of the gospel. Pray for willingness and opportunities to reach across racial or cultural lines for the sake of Christ. Commit yourself to the Lord to obey whatever He commands, no matter how crazy it may seem at first, and no matter how far outside your comfort zone it may take you.

TURNAROUND
ACTS 9

Saul begins this chapter *"breathing out threats and murder against the disciples of the Lord"* (v. 1), but before it ends, he is having threats and murder breathed out against him as a disciple of the Lord (vv. 23, 29). He starts for Damascus with the intent of rooting Christianity out of the synagogues there (v. 2), but he winds up proclaiming Christianity in those very synagogues (v. 20)! What an incredible change, a total reversal, took place in this man after this Damascus Road experience where Jesus Himself appeared to him and called him to salvation and service. Notice Jesus' initial words to Saul: *"why do you persecute Me?"* (v. 4). In persecuting His followers, His body, Saul was attacking the Lord Jesus Himself, and either through his conversion or his being struck blind, the Lord was intent on putting an end to his brutality. As significant as this powerful resurrection appearance of Jesus was in Saul's total turnaround, there were two others whose courage and obedience played a part in Saul's shift from persecutor of the church to missionary evangelist. Ananias, in spite of his fears (v. 13-14), was obedient to the Lord's words to him in a vision, going to minister healing to Saul and to confirm what had happened to him on the road. Having been converted, healed and baptized, Saul wasted no time (note the word *"Immediately"* in verse 20), and began proclaiming the gospel in Damascus with such effectiveness (v. 22) that he had to be smuggled out of town because of the threats arising against him (vv. 23-25). When he went to Jerusalem to meet with the original apostles, they at first refused to see him. After all, this man's persecution had succeeded in scattering the church from Jerusalem (8:1) and condemning many of the believers to prison (8:3). Not content with what he had done in Jerusalem, he was intent upon hunting down the dispersed believers wherever they had gone (9:2). The apostles obviously suspected that the story of his newfound faith was just a ruse to launch further attacks against them (v. 26). One man, though, Barnabas, took a chance on Saul. He listened to his story, and brought him to the apostles (v. 27). Having been accepted by the church in Jerusalem, Saul ministered with such power there that he again was threatened with death (no doubt by his former Pharisee colleagues), and once again, he had to leave town, going for a time back to his hometown of Tarsus. In converting Saul, God took the spearhead of persecution and would use him to spearhead the spread of the gospel to the Gentiles. The result was that, at least for a time, *"the churches throughout all Judea and Galilee and Samaria had peace and were built up. And walking in the fear of the Lord and in the comfort of the Holy Spirit, they were multiplied"* (v. 31).

PRAYER: The conversion of Saul shows that even the most virulent enemy of the gospel can become its greatest champion. When you think of modern-day enemies of the church, who immediately comes to mind? Take a few minutes today to pray for that person's salvation.

PETER AND CORNELIUS
ACTS 10

Most of what has occurred thus far in the book of Acts has happened in Jewish circles, but the gospel is showing signs of expanding beyond its Jewish roots. The first tentative steps were when the gospel went to the Samaritans, who were of mixed Jewish and Gentile blood, and then to the Ethiopian eunuch, who had come to Jerusalem to worship (see chapter 8). Now, the gospel will take another step forward, this time to the home of a God-fearing Roman soldier named Cornelius. "God-fearer" was a technical term for Gentiles who believed in the God of Israel as the one true God, but who had not gone through the prescribed rituals to officially convert to Judaism. Not only would Cornelius and his household be converted, but Peter would be transformed by these events as well. As a devout Jew, he had lived his life under the Jewish dietary requirements (v. 14) and rules about entering Gentile homes or eating with Gentiles (v. 28), despite Jesus' teachings and examples to the contrary (see Mark 7:14-23 and Matthew 8:5-13, particularly vv. 7-8). It is notable that even years after this incident, Peter still struggled with hypocritical actions in this area, and was confronted about it by the Apostle Paul (Galatians 2:11-14), showing the strength of this ingrained prejudice in him. Because of the vision he had on the rooftop, Peter was willing to go with the Gentile messengers to a Gentile's home and preach the gospel to the Gentiles gathered there. The result was that the whole household believed in Jesus, and the Holy Spirit fell upon them powerfully, leaving no doubt about the genuineness of their conversions (vv. 44-46). Peter's divinely arranged experience with these Gentile believers would help prepare him, and the church, for the time when Gentiles with no previous connection with Judaism would accept Christ as their Lord and Savior, and this experience would teach him that the Gentiles need not first convert to Judaism to be saved by the Jewish Messiah. Indeed, it was his testimony about this experience that would carry the day at the Jerusalem Conference in Acts 15.

PRAYER: Prejudices ingrained in childhood can be difficult attitudes to kill. It took Jesus' teaching and example, this divine vision and experience, and Paul's later confrontation to fully eliminate Peter's prejudice against non-Jews. Are there any prejudices - racial, religious, social or otherwise - still lurking in your heart? Ask the Lord to make you fully aware of any area of prejudice, and any time it comes to the surface, repent of it and reject it immediately.

THE STAGE IS SET
ACTS 11

Visiting a Gentile home and eating with Gentiles was taboo among the Jews, and when Peter returned to Jerusalem after the dramatic events of the previous chapter, the critics were waiting for him: *"You went in and ate with uncircumcised men!"* (v. 3). Peter explained the situation, telling them the supernatural events that had transpired to bring about his visit to the Gentiles at Caesarea, how God had changed his own mind in the matter, and how the Holy Spirit had fallen on the Gentiles when they believed. After that explanation, in verse 18 we read that *"When they heard these things, they were silent. And they glorified God, saying, 'Then God has granted to the Gentiles also repentance unto life.'"* I suspect that the subjects of the two sentences do not completely refer to the same people. The critics were put to silence for the moment, but later events show that at least some of them remained unconvinced (see Acts 15:5 and Galatians 2:12). What was first in the early church at Jerusalem a question and a source of confusion over the nature of the gospel and its relation to Gentiles (the question being, could Gentiles be saved by the Jewish Messiah without first becoming converts to Judaism), would eventually grow into the full-blown heresy of the Judaizers that Paul addressed forcefully in Galatians. Others, though, glorified God, recognizing that He had granted salvation to the Gentiles directly through their faith in Christ, and not through the agency of Judaism. The remainder of the chapter tells about the rise of the church at Antioch of Syria, founded by those who were scattered by the persecution arising after Stephen's martyrdom. At first, these scattered believers preached the gospel only to Jews (v. 19), but eventually began speaking the gospel to *"Hellenists"* (v. 20) or *"Greeks"* (NIV 84). The church at Antioch would launch the first major outreach to the Gentile world, preaching the gospel to Gentiles and seeing great numbers of them receive Jesus as Lord and Savior (v. 21). The church at Jerusalem, hearing about this successful outreach, sent Barnabas to them. Barnabas then went to Tarsus and brought Saul to Antioch, where they spent an entire year teaching considerable crowds. Given that many of the converts at Antioch had no Jewish background whatsoever, who better than a converted former Pharisee to ground them in the Old Testament roots of the faith? The stage is now set, in both Jerusalem and in Antioch, for the dramatic breakout of the gospel from its Jewish roots into all the world.

PRAYER: Peter responded to the accusations leveled against him not with defensiveness, argument or anger, but with a straightforward explanation of how God had worked in his and other people's lives. Pray that when you are criticized, you might respond with the same degree of grace. Romans 8:28 is on full display in this chapter as well. Obviously, persecution is not a good thing, but what Satan meant for evil, God allowed for good. As the believers were scattered from Jerusalem, the gospel spread to new locations and across racial and ethnic divides. Pray that whatever adverse circumstances you may face, you may cling to God's promise of Romans 8:28, and that He might show you how to turn those circumstances to the advantage of the gospel.

JAILBREAK!
ACTS 12

The Herod in question here is Herod Agrippa I, not to be confused with his grandfather Herod the Great (Matthew 2) or his uncle Herod Antipas (Luke 23:6-12). Herod Agrippa, under the Romans, ruled over the whole territory that had once been controlled by his grandfather, but as a member of the Herod family, he was hated by his subjects. Trying to ingratiate himself to the Jewish leadership, he launched an attack against the church. He put James, called here *"the brother of John"* to distinguish him from Jesus' brother James (mentioned in verse 17), to death by sword, and imprisoned Peter. He did not immediately put Peter to death, apparently because of the Passover (v. 4), and probably because he wanted to mount a "show trial" against him, putting the whole Christian movement on trial and condemning it along with Peter. On the night before his scheduled trial, Peter was sleeping soundly, so much so that the appearance of an angel in his cell did not awaken him (vv. 6-7)! Notice the instructions of the angel to him. First, he told him to *"Rise up, quickly"* (v. 7), and it was only when he did so that *"the chains fell off of his hands."* Then he told him to dress himself and follow him, and when he obeyed, they walked right past the guards, right out of the prison, and right up to the iron gate leading to the city, which opened by itself to let them pass. What is significant in this passage is that the angel did nothing for Peter than he could do for himself, but when Peter was obedient, the angel did for Peter what Peter couldn't do for himself. What if, when the angel had told him to rise, Peter had said, "What's the use? I've got chains on my hands"? What if, when the angel had told him to get dressed and follow him, Peter had said, "Why bother? There's four squads of soldiers guarding me"? What if Peter had looked at the gate and said, "There's no way out; I might as well go back to my cell"? God doesn't always show us the full plan in the beginning. If He did, our faith would be in the plan, and not in Him. Instead, He calls us to follow Him, one step at a time, one instruction at a time, even when we can see the obstacles looming ahead of us. After leading Peter one street away from the prison, the angel disappeared, and Peter realized that this was no vision, that he had been miraculously rescued. The scene at the door of John Mark's mother's house is almost comical. They were gathered there to pray for God to intervene in Peter's situation (vv. 5, 12). When Peter arrived and knocked on the door, the servant girl Rhoda was so excited she didn't open the door; she just went into the prayer meeting and announced that he was there. Their response? *"You are insane,"* followed by *"It is his angel"* (v. 15). The answer to their prayers was at the door, but they didn't believe it! At first, they thought she was out of her mind, and then, when she insisted, they thought surely Peter had died already. I wonder if, perhaps, they didn't believe her because God had answered their prayers differently than they expected. Could it be that they were praying about the impending trial, praying that Peter would be exonerated and released? When God chose a much more miraculous and dramatic rescue for Peter, it didn't register immediately. When we pray, God may choose to answer our prayers exactly as we've prayed them...or not. He always reserves the right to do *"exceedingly abundantly beyond all that we ask or imagine"* (Ephesians 3:20).

PRAYER: Pray for faith to follow Him, one step at a time, even in the face of impending obstacles. Pray for God to keep your eyes open to unexpected answers to prayer.

THE EMERGENCE OF PAUL
ACTS 13

The church at Antioch is a prime example of a Kingdom-minded church. Things were going well at Antioch. They were being successful in winning the lost, both Jew and Gentile, in their area (11:20-21). They were blessed with five prominent teachers who were grounding those converts in the Word. But as they were worshiping and fasting, the Holy Spirit instructed them to *"Set apart for Me Barnabas and Saul for the work to which I have called them."* It would seem that Barnabas and Saul had already felt the missionary urge to take the gospel where it had not yet gone, and the church now recognized that this impulse was from God, so they commissioned them and sent them forth. They could have made the argument that "There are so many lost people needing to be evangelized right here in Antioch, and so many new converts needing to be discipled; how can we afford to send Barnabas and Saul away?" but they didn't. Instead, they were willing to give up 40% of their staff, so to speak, to see the gospel spread to *"the ends of the earth"* (1:8). Too many churches act as if the Kingdom begins and ends at the edge of their property. Any endeavor that is not designed to bring more bodies, bucks and buildings onto that campus is deemed unworthy of time, effort, money and attention. God blesses churches that are willing to look to the fields beyond their own and share their financial, physical or human resources to take the gospel to those fields. Notice in verse 1 the listing of the teachers at Antioch: *"Barnabas, Simeon who was called Niger, Lucius of Cyrene, Manaen who had been brought up with Herod the tetrarch, and Saul."* Saul is listed last among the five, and it seems as if he is almost an afterthought. Then, in verse 2, we read where the missionary assignment was given to *"Barnabas and Saul."* As the team goes forth, again we read *"Barnabas and Saul"* in verse 7. Then suddenly, in verse 9, *"Saul, who is also called Paul, filled with the Holy Spirit"* confronts Elymas the sorcerer, and from that point on, everything seems to change. In verse 13, the team is now referenced as *"Paul and his companions."* It is Paul who brings the message in the synagogue at "the other Antioch," Antioch of Pisidia. and from that point on, the missionary duo is almost always referenced as *"Paul and Barnabas"* (vv. 42, 46). I think Luke, very subtly, is showing us that Paul really came into his own when he hit the mission field. That was his calling, God's purpose for him, to take the gospel where it had not gone before, to be the apostle to the Gentiles. He may have been number five of five in the church at Antioch, but on the mission field, he was second to none! In the Old Testament, God would sometimes mark a dramatic change in a person's life by changing his name. The change in Paul was so dramatic that Luke no longer calls him by his Jewish name, Saul, but by his Greek name, Paul.

PRAYER: God calls and equips different people in different ways for different tasks. Pray for the Holy Spirit to show you how He has wired you with your unique mix of gifts, talents, abilities, and interests. Pray that you might follow His will into a situation of maximum effectiveness in His Kingdom. Pray for your church, that it might always be generous with its resources to reach beyond its local field to the world beyond.

TRUE GRIT
ACTS 14

The opposition that began in Antioch of Pisidia (13:45-51) would grow in intensity as Paul and Barnabas moved on to other cities. A conspiracy to murder them drove them from Iconium. In Lystra, they were first honored as gods (vv. 11-18), only to have public opinion turn against them so dramatically that Paul was stoned and left for dead (vv. 19-20). The next day, they departed from Lystra for Derbe, where apparently, they were received without significant opposition, at least not any noted in the Scripture. Notice verse 21: *"When they had preached the gospel to that city and had made many disciples, they returned to Lystra and to Iconium and to Antioch."* You would think, given the treatment they had received in those cities, that they would have never returned there, but return they did, and their reason for returning is given in verse 22: *"strengthening the minds of the disciples and exhorting them to continue in the faith, to go through many afflictions and thus enter the kingdom of God."* There was still work to be done in those cities. Those fledgling churches made up of new believers needed to be discipled, the oft-neglected third part of the Great Commission (Matthew 28:20), and despite the danger, Paul and Barnabas would not leave that task undone. Paul and Barnabas knew that the believers would not have an easy time in those cities that had so opposed and persecuted them. How could they expect those new Christians to stand strong in the fire of affliction if they were unwilling to model that courage? They stayed in each of those cities until they had grown mature disciples who could take over the leadership of the churches (v. 23), then took the gospel to Perga on their way back to their home base at the church at Antioch, where they reported on their mission.

PRAYER: Pray about how you can be involved in the Great Commission of making disciples through the gospel, marking them through baptism, and maturing them through discipleship. Pray for believers and missionaries who are living and ministering the gospel in difficult and dangerous locations. Pray for their courage to fulfill the Great Commission in spite of all opposition and obstacles.

HARMONY...AND DISHARMONY
ACTS 15

The Jerusalem Council brought the issue of the Jewish Law and its relation to the gospel of grace to a head. It was precipitated when *"Some men came down from Judea and were teaching the brethren, 'Unless you are circumcised in the tradition of Moses, you cannot be saved'"* (v. 1). These were Jews who believed that Jesus was the Messiah, probably converted Pharisees like Paul, but who misunderstood the nature of grace and had not been commissioned by the church at Jerusalem (v. 24). Paul and Barnabas disputed their claim, and the Antioch church decided to send Paul and Barnabas to Jerusalem to consult with the apostles and elders there about the situation. Even though some in Jerusalem still insisted on a grace plus works theology (v. 5), Peter's testimony about his experiences in the home of Cornelius (recorded in chapter 10), Paul and Barnabas' testimony about their work among the Gentiles, and James' exposition of the Scriptures made it clear to most of them that God was indeed pouring out His Spirit among the Gentiles without reference to circumcision and the Jewish Law. Their judgment was that they *"should not trouble those of the Gentiles who are turning to God, but that we write to them to abstain from food offered to idols, from sexual immorality, from strangled animals, and from blood"* (vv. 19-20). The reason for these prohibitions was so that Jews living in those Gentile cities would not be so offended by such conduct among the Gentile believers that they would be unwilling to hear the gospel (v. 21). Thus, there was harmony between the church at Jerusalem and the church at Antioch, and between Jewish and Gentile believers in Christ. It is interesting that in the wake of this affirmation of harmony and unity, the rest of the chapter deals with the breakup of Paul and Barnabas. The issue that brought them into *"sharp contention, so that they separated from each other,"* was John Mark, Barnabas' cousin (Colossians 4:10) who had initially accompanied them on their first missionary journey, but had turned back and returned home (13:13). Barnabas wanted to take him along as they returned to the churches they had started, but Paul refused. Looking at the two men's personalities gives us a clue as to why this dispute arose. Paul was the more task-oriented of the two. He was a visionary, a strategist, a big picture thinker whose heart was set on world evangelization. He was looking at the mission and the importance of that mission; in his mind, he couldn't allow anyone on his team who wasn't fully committed, anyone that he couldn't trust for the long haul. Barnabas, *"the son of encouragement"* (Acts 4:36), was more people-oriented. He was looking at a young man with a world of potential who had failed once and needed someone to give him another chance. He was willing to take a risk on John Mark (just as he had been willing to take an even greater risk on Paul - 9:27), but Paul was unwilling. It is not that one of their perspectives was wrong and the other was right. The church needs both perspectives. God gives different gifts to different members of the body, and with those different gifts oftentimes come different perspectives on what is most important, which, if we're not careful, can lead to conflict. Whether the two men parted in anger, or by mutual agreement, is unclear, but what is clear is that what Satan designed for evil, God allowed for good. Now, there would be two mission teams out preaching the gospel (vv. 39-40), and whatever rift existed between the men, it would eventually be healed (I Corinthians 9:6, Colossians 4:10, II Timothy 4:11 and Philemon 24).

PRAYER: Most of the conflicts in most churches are not fundamental questions of doctrine and practice such as the issue settled by the Jerusalem Council, but personality clashes such as the one that occurred between Paul and Barnabas. Pray that when such clashes arise, each person would be willing to see the other's perspective, and if the situation cannot be compromised (after all, they couldn't both take and not take John Mark with them), that they will agree to disagree and disagree agreeably, going on faithfully in the work of the Lord.

JAILHOUSE ROCKED
ACTS 16

Paul had been on an absolute roll. He and Barnabas had gone on the first missionary journey, in which they saw the gospel spread out of its Jewish roots and into the Gentile world. **And Paul worshiped God.** It's easy to worship God when He is doing powerful things through you and you can actually see the growth of the Kingdom of God through your efforts. In Acts 15, the original apostles had upheld Paul's position on the gospel and the Gentiles and had extended to him both their friendship and their approval of his ministry. **And Paul worshiped God.** It's easy to worship God when your opposition has been defeated, and when you and your ministry have been affirmed and celebrated by those you respect. After his separation from Barnabas, Paul had found a new partner in Silas. **And Paul worshiped God.** It's easy to worship God when you have companions you're in harmony with, people you can trust on the journey of life. As Paul visited the churches he had founded, he found them doing well, strengthened in the faith and increasing in number daily. **And Paul worshiped God.** It's easy to worship God when you see a work that you started that is still going forward even in your absence. After visiting the previously founded churches, Paul determined to take the gospel where it had not gone before. In a vision, Paul saw a Macedonian pleading with him to preach the gospel in Macedonia. **And Paul worshiped God.** It's easy to worship God when He's guiding your journey and promising you success. At Philippi, Paul shared the gospel with some women praying by the river, and a wealthy merchant named Lydia opened her heart and received Christ as her Lord and Savior, along with her whole household. **And Paul worshiped God.** It's easy to worship God when you see people being saved, and influential people are on your side. But the devil wasn't going to give up Philippi without a fight. He dispatched a demonized slave-girl fortune-teller to follow Paul around, declaring that *"These men are servants of the Most High God, who proclaim to us the way of salvation"* (v. 17). Even though what she said was true, Paul neither needed nor wanted the endorsement of a demon, and he did not want their message confused with the occult practices of the slave-girl and her masters. Finally, Paul wheeled around and cast the demon out of her. **And Paul worshiped God.** It's easy to worship God when you see those who have been enslaved by the devil to all kinds of degrading lifestyles being set free. But when people are being set free from his grasp and taken out of his kingdom, the devil will increase his attacks every time. Her masters, seeing their income evaporate, dragged Paul and Silas before the authorities and told lies about them. The magistrates, without even asking for their side of the story or giving them a trial, ordered them stripped of their clothing and beaten. Then they were dragged to the town jail, and put in the inner prison, the worst part of the jail, the part with no windows and no ventilation. It was smelly, hot, damp, moldy, vermin infested, filthy and completely dark. And to add further insult to injury, their feet were fastened in the stocks, which forced them into a seated position with their legs at an awkward angle such that they couldn't even lie down. **And Paul worshiped God.** It's *not* easy to worship God when clear skies and smooth sailing erupt into a storm. It's not easy to worship God when you've been accused, lied about and treated unfairly. It's not easy to worship God when your body is wracked with pain. **But still Paul worshiped God.** It looked like their ministry at Philippi was over; maybe their ministry *anywhere* was over. Would they be executed in the morning? Would they be left in that jail to rot? The future looked bleak. But when midnight came, there were no cries of anger from the inner jail, no moans and groans of pain, no curses against those who had mistreated them; instead, there were prayers and songs of praise. In the bleakest hour, after a horrible day, **Paul worshiped God**. And God drew near. And when God drew near, powerful things began to happen. A great earthquake shook the prison, the chains fell off of the prisoners, and the prison gates fell open. Amazingly, the prisoners were so enthralled by the presence of God in that prison that they didn't even think of trying to escape. Praise, particularly praise through pain, attracts the lost and wins us a hearing for the gospel, and God uses our praise to break chains in our own and in others' lives. Before the night was over, the jailer, his whole family, and undoubtedly some of the prisoners had been changed forever by the power of the gospel.

PRAYER: Whatever you're going through today, good or bad, worship! Praise Him, if for nothing else, that it is not always like this! Praise Him for who He is. Praise Him for His salvation. Praise Him, and watch things begin to change!

REVIVALS AND RIOTS
ACTS 17

Whenever Paul entered into a town, the result was usually revival or riot or both, but certainly not indifference! In Thessalonica, he spent three Sabbaths at the synagogue, reasoning from the Scriptures that the Messiah had to die and rise from the dead, and proclaiming to them that Jesus had fulfilled these ancient prophecies. A number of Jews and devout Greeks believed, but some who did not believe stirred up trouble, which fell upon the missionaries' host, Jason, and some of the other believers. Of note is one of the accusations leveled against them: *"These men who have turned the world upside down have come here also"* (v. 6). In a very short time, even the enemies of the gospel had to admit its incredible impact on the Roman world. Would that we might have such an effect on the world around us! Because of this uprising, the missionaries left Thessalonica and went to Berea. The Bereans *"were more noble than those in Thessalonica, for they received the word with all eagerness, daily examining the Scriptures, to find out if these things were so"* (v. 11). The Berean reaction is one that all of us as believers should emulate. We must be eager to receive the Word, but not so gullible that we believe immediately anything and everything a teacher is telling us. The Scriptures are our final arbiter of truth and falsehood, and we must verify what we are being taught by the Word of God. Many of the Bereans, both Jews and Gentiles, believed, but the hostile Jews of Thessalonica, not content with having run the missionaries out of their town, arrived in Berea to cause trouble for them there. Paul was forced to leave, but Silas and Timothy stayed to strengthen the new believers. Meanwhile, Paul made his way alone to Athens, a center of Greek philosophy. His message to the Areopagus is a lesson in contextualization. In his earlier sermons in Acts, we see him in the synagogues, using the Old Testament Scriptures as a launching pad to preach Christ. At the Areopagus, speaking to the philosophers, Paul began where they were, using their altar to an unknown god to preach the one true God. He speaks of God as Creator, and calls them to repent of their idolatry. He speaks of the coming judgment, and of Jesus' resurrection from the dead. They had originally pegged him as *"a babbler"* (v. 18), and seem to have brought him to their meeting out of curiosity and for entertainment (vv. 19-21). While some scoffed at the idea of the resurrection, others wanted to hear more (v. 32) and some of them believed (v. 34).

PRAYER: No matter where he was or the reaction he received, Paul never hesitated to proclaim the gospel. Pray that you might have that same courage to speak of Jesus boldly.

UNEXPECTED
ACTS 18

Paul's willingness to go anywhere for the sake of the gospel is on full display in this chapter. Corinth was an extraordinarily wicked city, even by notoriously lax Roman standards. Indeed, in the Roman world, "to Corinthianize" was a slang term for committing sexual immorality. Given the riots that his teaching had engendered in less evil cities, what could Paul expect in a wicked city like Corinth? He might have been tempted to think that going there would be at best a waste of time, but what happened there was quite unexpected. First, he found some new friends in Aquila and Priscilla. Aquila is described as *"a Jew"* in verse 2; it is unclear whether he and his wife were already believers, or whether they came to know the Lord through Paul's ministry. Paul worked with them in their mutual trade as tentmakers, and they would eventually travel with him to Ephesus. Unlike other places where Paul was run out of town in a matter of weeks, he stayed at Corinth for over a year and a half (vv. 11, 18). He began his ministry, as was his normal pattern, in the synagogue (vv. 4-5), and while some of the Jews there believed (v. 8), the majority rejected his message of Jesus as Messiah (v. 6). This rejection on the part of the Jews might have persuaded Paul to leave the city, fearing the kind of violent reactions he had seen before, but *"The Lord spoke to Paul in the night, through a vision, 'Do not be afraid, but speak and do not be silent. For I am with you, and no one shall attack you and hurt you, for I have many people in this city'"* (v. 9). Who would have believed that in spite of the reputation of Corinth, God had many people there? Some of those people had perhaps not come to know the Lord yet, but they would through Paul's ministry there. After a year and a half, it appeared that an attack was coming against Paul, as he was hauled into court by a unified effort of the Jews. Before Paul could even speak in his defense, however, the proconsul Gallio dismissed the case, refusing to be a judge in religious matters (vv. 14-15). Not only did he drive Paul's accusers out of the court, he turned a blind eye when the Greeks seized the ruler of the synagogue, Sosthenes, and beat him in the courtroom (vv. 16-17), which put an end to any thoughts of the Jews using the Roman courts in Corinth against the Christians.

PRAYER: Often, our fears and expectations are unfounded. Had Paul let the reputation of Corinth or the response of the Jews there intimidate him, he would have missed out on meeting valuable comrades in Priscilla and Aquila, he would have missed the opportunity of being God's instrument in calling out His many people there, and he would have missed seeing God's miraculous protection through a Roman proconsul. Pray today for eyes that look beyond the surface to see God's higher purposes. Pray for faith that never considers anyone too far gone to be saved. Think today about the person who, in your mind, would be the last person to receive the gospel. Pray that their eyes might be opened, and that they might receive Jesus today!

DEFICIENT "DISCIPLES"
ACTS 19

Like Apollos (18:25), there were at least twelve other men at Ephesus who had heard and believed the message of John the Baptist that the Messiah was coming, but for some reason did not know that the Messiah had come. Paul recognized that there was something lacking in these disciples, and so he made inquiry of them to find out what it was. Discovering that they knew only the baptism of John, and that they had not even heard of the Holy Spirit (which means that their knowledge of John and his baptism must have been at least second-hand - see Matthew 3:11), Paul preached Jesus to them as the fulfillment of John's prophecies, just as Aquila and Priscilla had done with Apollos (18:26), and the Holy Spirit fell upon them. Unfortunately, there are many today like these men, believing a truncated gospel, trusting in baptism (whether as an infant or later) to save them rather than truly trusting in the Lord Jesus Christ and His sacrifice on Calvary. Such people are both bereft of the Spirit and bereft of the eternal life He brings. Once again, as was his normal pattern, Paul began his ministry in the synagogue in Ephesus, but when his message was rejected there, he took his teaching to a local lecture hall for some two years. During that time, significant miracles were performed by him (vv. 11-12), enough to gain the attention and admiration of unbelieving Jewish exorcists (v. 13). It is amazing that Paul's miracles in the name of Jesus influenced them to use the name of Jesus as an exorcism tool, but did not lead them to place their faith in Him! The seven sons of Sceva learned the hard way that invoking Jesus' name is not some magic formula; the power of His name over demonic forces is given only to those in relationship to Him. When they confronted the demonized man with the command, *"We command you to come out in the name of the Jesus whom Paul preaches"* (v. 13), the demon knew immediately that they themselves did not know Jesus, and therefore did not possess His authority or His Spirit. He answered them, *"I know Jesus, and I know Paul, but who are you?"* (v. 15). Without the authority of the Lord Jesus and the empowerment of the Holy Spirit, even seven of these men were no match for the one demonized man. In a burst of supernatural strength, he assaulted and overpowered them, sending them fleeing from the house wounded and naked (v. 16). Because of this incident, many people became believers and abandoned their occult practices (vv. 17-20). Shortly before Paul planned to leave Ephesus, trouble arose when Demetrius and other silversmiths, seeing their income from the sale of silver shrines to Artemis evaporating, caused a riot. Paul was protected from the mob by wise friends (v. 30) and by the city clerk who calmed the crowd (vv. 35-41). Once again, God used a Roman official and Roman law to protect Paul and the Christian movement from their adversaries.

PRAYER: The invoking of Jesus' name and the ordinances of baptism and the Lord's Supper are meaningless without a personal relationship with Him (Matthew 7:21-23). Are you trusting in Christ and Christ alone, based on His sacrifice on the cross, for your salvation, and not good works, religious ritual, church membership, or family relationship to save? If the Lord has revealed that your faith is not truly in Christ, call upon Him to save you, repenting of your sins and placing your faith in Him now, surrendering to Him as Lord of your life. Pray for those whose faith is misplaced and not in Jesus, that their eyes might be opened before it is eternally too late. Pray that your life and ministry might be such that demons know your name and your relationship to Jesus. Pray that you might have wise friends and divine protection when the winds of persecution arise.

DEATH AND LIFE
ACTS 20

It has been said that preaching is the art of talking in other people's sleep. Such was the case with Eutychus, a disciple at Troas who was listening *"as Paul talked on and on"* (v. 9, NIV 84). Falling into a deep sleep during the sermon, he fell out of the third floor window in which he was sitting and died from the fall, only to be brought back to life through the ministry of Paul (compare v. 10 with I Kings 17:31). After this unscheduled "intermission," the service still went on until morning! In Eutychus' defense, Sunday back then was a work day like any other, thus the need for the church to meet at night. He had probably put in a full day's labor before coming to church that night, and the sermon, in a warm, crowded upper room with many lamps, went on until midnight (vv. 7-8). Before we condemn him too harshly for falling asleep and falling out the window, let's give him credit for being there in the first place, and let's admit that all of us have probably taken (or induced) a "Eutychus Nap" under far less conducive circumstances! Paul's words to the Ephesian elders in the latter part of the chapter are a portrait of a man who is heading toward possible death (vv. 22-24), but with no regrets about how he has lived his life. As he looks back over his ministry, he can say that he is *"innocent of the blood of all men"* (v. 26) because he had proclaimed the whole counsel of God to them (v. 27). He had warned all people with tears about the impending judgment (v. 31) while calling them to *"repentance toward God and faith in our Lord Jesus Christ"* (v. 21). He had conducted his ministry not only with theological integrity, but with financial integrity as well (vv. 33-35), and he urged the Ephesian elders to follow his example, to shepherd their flocks faithfully and to protect them from false teachers. To do so, they would have to continue in *"the word of his grace, which is able to build you up and give you an inheritance among all who are sanctified"* (v. 32), an echo of Jesus' words in John 17:17.

PRAYER: In our day, at least in America, Christians allow any excuse (or no excuse at all) to keep them from church attendance, especially on Sunday evenings. Consider the example of the early Christians, who put in a full day's work and then went to church on Sundays. Pray that you might be faithful in your attendance in the Lord's services (Hebrews 10:25), and that you might be awake, alert, and fully engaged when you're there. If you knew that your death was possibly coming up soon, would you be able to say that you've lived such that you could die with no regrets? If not, pray about what you need to do to remedy that situation.

PAUL'S ARREST
ACTS 21

Paul's determination to go to Jerusalem, despite all the warnings given to him about what would happen to him there, parallels Jesus' final journey to Jerusalem, the difference being that Jesus told His disciples along the way what was going to happen to Him there, whereas in Paul's case, disciples were telling him along the way what would happen when he arrived in Jerusalem. Paul visited with the Jerusalem church there, and met particularly with James, a brother of Jesus who was a leader in that early church. Despite the Jerusalem Council of Acts 15, there was still a great deal of Jewish-Gentile tension in the air. James and the Jerusalem church had previously affirmed Paul's mission to the Gentiles, and they rejoiced to hear of the success of that ongoing mission (v. 20), but it had apparently impacted their own ability to reach Jews with the gospel. A rumor had spread that Paul was urging *Jews* to reject circumcision and other customs of the Law, and not just that he was not requiring such things from Gentile believers (v. 21). James' solution was for Paul to go through a purification rite at the Temple, and that he pay for the sacrifices of four Jewish Christians who had taken a Nazirite vow (vv. 23-24). Surely, he thought, Paul's personal and financial participation in these Jewish rituals would be enough to put the rumor about him and his teaching to rest among the Jews. Paul agreed to this plan, but it didn't work. Indeed, as he was at the Temple for the ceremony, some Jews from Asia, spotting him there, accused him of bringing a Gentile named Trophimus into the Temple, beyond the Court of the Gentiles, which was a capital offense. Enough people believed the lie that a riot started, with Paul being savagely beaten by the mob before being rescued by the Roman soldiers. Once again, the Roman penchant for law and order came to Paul's rescue. Doing the right thing will always bring good results in the long run, but those good results may come through much difficulty. Affirming and supporting the preaching of the gospel to the Gentiles was the right thing for the Jerusalem church to do, but it resulted in difficulty for them in spreading the gospel among the Jews. Attempting to assuage the situation by taking part in the Jewish rituals was the right thing for Paul to do, but it backfired as it exposed Paul to his enemies and their lies. Ultimately, though, all these things would work out for good, as many Gentiles received the Lord, and as Paul would be taken to Rome to proclaim the gospel before Caesar's court.

PRAYER: Have you had the experience of doing the right thing, only to have negative consequences rain down upon you as a result? Rejoice! Romans 8:28 is still in the book: *"For we know that all things work together for good to those who love God, to those who are called according to His purpose."* God is working in your situation both for your good and for His glory!

DUAL CITIZENSHIP
ACTS 22

After removing Paul from the riot (21:33-34), the Roman commander amazingly allowed him to address the crowd. Despite their violence and loud cries (21:35), the crowd was brought to *"great silence"* (21:40) by the wave of Paul's hand, and *"they became even more quiet"* (v. 2) when he began to address them. I don't know how you can become even more quiet than great silence, but those verses seem to indicate a supernatural calm coming over the crowd so that they might hear Paul's words. Paul recounted the testimony of his background and his conversion to the crowd, but when he told them how God had sent him to the Gentiles (v. 21), they flew into an even greater frenzy than before (vv. 21-23), reminiscent of the reaction to Jesus at the synagogue at Nazareth when He taught that God's concern extended beyond the Jews to the Gentiles (Luke 4:16-30). Neither Jesus' claim of Messiahship at Nazareth nor Paul's recounting of his vision and conversion drew the ire of the crowds, but the idea that God loved Gentiles, well, that was too much for them to take! After removing Paul from the murderous mob, the Roman commander *"ordered him to be brought into the barracks and examined with scourging"* (v. 24). As they were preparing him for this interrogation by torture, Paul exerted his rights as a Roman citizen. Roman citizens (as opposed to members of a conquered people) could not be scourged unless they had been tried and found guilty of a crime. After discovering that Paul was a citizen, indeed, that he had been born a citizen, the interrogators backed away, and the commander was afraid of how he had previously treated Paul (v. 29). While Paul was certainly willing to endure any punishment that came to him for his belief in Christ (II Corinthians 11:24-25), he was not willing to surrender his rights as a Roman citizen and allow himself to be beaten unnecessarily. As citizens of the Kingdom of God, we serve a higher kingdom, but despite what some would say, we do not surrender our rights and privileges as citizens of the United States. We too should avail ourselves of all legal recourse when the enemies of the faith come against us.

PRAYER: Do you know someone so blinded by their prejudices (such as the growing cultural prejudice against Christianity and Christians) that they refuse to see the truth of the gospel? Pray for that person today, asking that the veil over their eyes might be lifted by the Holy Spirit, and that they might see the light. Pray for anyone you know (either personally or otherwise) who is under fire for his Christian convictions.

A POWERFUL PROMISE AND A RASH OATH
ACTS 23

Paul's appearance before the Sanhedrin and the high priest in verses 1-5 parallel Jesus' treatment by the same assembly recorded in John 18:19-23. Both Paul and Jesus were struck by bystanders for making fairly innocuous opening statements, which showed that the trials were fixed from the beginning, and both of them reacted by pointing out that striking them was illegal (v. 3, cp. John 18:23). Unlike Jesus, however, Paul, in a flash of anger, actually hurled an insult at the high priest (v. 3), an insult for which he quickly apologized (v. 5). After the appearance before the Sanhedrin erupted into a debate between the rival Pharisees and Sadducees, the Roman commander once again was forced to rescue Paul by removing him from their midst (v. 10). In verse 11, God makes a special promise to Paul, the promise that *"as you have testified about Me in Jerusalem, so you must also testify at Rome."* This appearance of the Lord and promise from Him would sustain Paul through years of imprisonment, threats to his life, legal wrangling, and dangerous travel; if God had promised him that he would testify in Rome, then nothing could possibly keep him from arriving safely in Rome, not even forty men who were conspiring to murder him. These forty men had sworn an oath neither to eat or drink until they had killed Paul, thinking they would have their chance the next day. Somehow, Paul's nephew heard about the plot and reported it to Paul and to the Roman commander, and Paul was taken quickly from Jerusalem to Caesarea under guard to be tried before the Roman governor of Judea, Felix. We can only imagine how hungry and thirsty Paul's enemies got before they were forced to break their oath!

PRAYER: All of us, under severe and unjust provocation, have responded in anger. Pray that when you find yourself in such a tense situation, you will respond with calm, and not insults, and if anger does get the best of you, that you will be quick to apologize. What promises has God given to you that have sustained you through difficult days? Thank Him for those precious promises, those that have come true and those that have yet to be fulfilled.

OUR DIVINE DEFENSE ATTORNEY
ACTS 24

Paul's trial before Felix has more fascinating parallels with Jesus' trial before Pontius Pilate. As was the case with Jesus, the Sanhedrin's problems with Paul were purely religious in nature. Knowing that religious disputes held no interest to Roman officials, both Jesus and Paul were presented to the respective governors with the implication that they were troublemakers and political revolutionaries. The lawyer Tertullus, under the employ of the Sanhedrin, began his accusation dripping with insincere compliments to Felix, a governor who was certainly not the object of Jewish gratitude for peace and reforms, but was rather hated among the Jews for his violence and corruption (vv. 2-3). The three accusations leveled against Paul were that he was a troublemaker throughout the Roman Empire, he was a ringleader in the sect of the Nazarenes, and that he had attempted to profane the Temple. In his defense, Paul, though not a trained attorney like Tertullus, was given wisdom by the Holy Spirit to completely destroy the accusations against him (Luke 12:11-12). In terms of the first accusation, he pointed out that he had only been in Jerusalem for twelve days (hardly time to start a revolution), and that during that time, he had not so much as engaged in debate in the Temple or in the synagogues, much less stirred up the crowds (vv. 11-12). Whatever they might have heard of his activities elsewhere in the Empire was pure hearsay; they had no firsthand evidence of Paul's alleged troublemaking from his twelve days in Jerusalem. As for the accusation of being a ringleader of the Christians, Paul freely admitted to the charge, but then argued that it was not illegal, that Christianity was not some new sect, but rather an offshoot of Judaism and thus protected under Roman law (vv. 13-16). As for the accusation of profaning the Temple, Paul pointed out that even if it were true, the charge must be dismissed under Roman law because the eyewitnesses making the accusation had failed to appear in court (vv. 17-19). Felix, showing both his corruption and his cowardice, put off making a decision indefinitely, keeping Paul under guard (and thus protection) in Caesarea but with considerable freedom (v. 23). According to verses 26-27, Felix often sent for Paul and listened to him, hoping that Paul would bribe him to effect his release, but with no bribe forthcoming, he kept Paul imprisoned as a favor to the Jews.

PRAYER: On the day I am writing this devotion (April 28, 2015), attorneys are arguing before the Supreme Court the case against homosexual "marriage." No matter what decision those justices render, religious liberty cases surrounding this subject will no doubt proliferate in coming years. Pray for those attorneys who argue such cases, that they might have the same kind of supernatural wisdom as Paul, and pray for the judges who will hear such cases, that they might, unlike Felix, have courage and honor in deciding those cases.

APPEARING BEFORE KINGS
ACTS 25

For two years, Paul had been in legal limbo (24:27), but with the appointment of a new governor of Judea, Festus, it appeared that his case might finally be resolved. Festus inherited a tense situation in the province. Relations between the Jews and their Roman conquerors had always been tense, but that tension had been greatly exacerbated by Felix's corrupt and violent administration. Festus, after only three days on the job, went to Jerusalem to meet with the Jewish leaders. Amazingly, even after two years, their first priority was Paul! Having him imprisoned had not been good enough for them; they wanted him dead, even if they had to risk the new governor's wrath by ambushing him on his way to Jerusalem (vv. 2-3). This plan was foiled when the governor declined to transfer Paul to Jerusalem, preferring to hear the case in Caesarea. The trial is covered in just a few verses (vv. 6-8), and apparently was just a rehash of the same charges brought against Paul in the previous chapter. Once again, Paul proclaimed his innocence, and once again, the Jewish leaders could muster no evidence to prove his guilt. The dilemma for Festus was that Paul, as a Roman citizen, held all the cards legally, while the Jewish leaders, in the tense environment of Judea, held all the cards politically. The Romans had a high standard of justice, particularly for Roman citizens (v. 16), but Festus had no desire to antagonize the Jews so early in his tenure as governor. In an effort to appease them, he considered transferring the case to Jerusalem (v. 9), but Paul, knowing the murderous intent of his enemies, appealed his case to Caesar, which was the right of every Roman citizen (vv. 10-11). This appeal would serve the dual purpose of removing him from the hostile realm of the Jewish leadership and taking him to Rome, where God had promised he would testify of Him (23:11). Several days later, King Agrippa and his sister Bernice arrived to greet the new governor. This was Herod Agrippa II, ruler of an area north of Judea, the son of Herod Agrippa I, who had put James the apostle to death (12:2). Although he did not rule over Judea, he had nevertheless been given authority by the emperor to appoint or depose the high priest and to oversee the Temple in Jerusalem. Because of that responsibility, he had great interest in the Jewish faith, and was looked to by the Romans as an authority on Jewish religious matters (see 26:3). Before he could send Paul to Rome, Festus needed to write up the particulars of the case and the charges against him, and he hoped that Agrippa could help him in that task for which he felt unqualified (vv. 18-20a, 26). Once again, Paul would have the opportunity to testify of the Christian faith before yet another influential Roman official.

PRAYER: As Christians, nothing comes into our lives except what is sent or allowed by God for His purposes (Romans 8:28). As someone once put it, everything that happens to us has been "Father-filtered." Paul's long imprisonment and ongoing legal proceedings were certainly not pleasant, but they fulfilled God's purposes for his life, as stated in 9:15-16: *"For this man is a chosen vessel of Mine, to bear My name before the Gentiles and their kings, and before the sons of Israel. For I will show him how much he must suffer for My name's sake."* Paul was willing to suffer in order to fulfill God's plans for his life. Pray that you will likewise be willing to endure any difficulties to fulfill His plans for your life. Pray that in every circumstance of life, you will look for how God is using it to fulfill His purposes for you and through you.

THE POWER OF TESTIMONY
ACTS 26

Paul's speech to King Agrippa is a classic example of how to give a good testimony of one's faith. Paul begins by telling about his life before he came to know Christ (vv. 4-11). Then he tells of the circumstances by which he was converted (vv. 12-18), before concluding with details about his life and how it has changed since his encounter with Christ (vv. 19-23). Finally, he calls upon his hearers to likewise be saved (v. 29). The Roman governor Festus, upon hearing Paul's story of visions of Jesus and His resurrection from the dead, believed him to be insane (v. 24), but King Agrippa, with greater familiarity with Old Testament Messianic prophecies (v. 27) declared, *"You almost persuade me to be a Christian"* (v. 28). Paul's response is a classic insight into the heart of the apostle, whose desire was for everyone, both Jew and Gentile, to come to know the Lord Jesus Christ: *"I pray to God that not only you, but all who hear me this day, might become not only almost, but thoroughly and altogether, what I am, except for these chains"* (v. 29). Agrippa was so shaken by Paul's testimony and his urging him to salvation that he arose and left the room, followed by Festus and Bernice. Paul's testimony had not persuaded them to become Christians, but it had planted a seed, and it had persuaded them of his innocence of the charges leveled against him (v. 31).

PRAYER: Today, take a few moments to think about how you would tell your own story: your life before Christ, how you came to know Him, and your life since you became a believer. Thank God today for the wonderful change in your life since Jesus came into your heart. Pray for opportunities to share your testimony with others. Pray for those you know who are *"almost persuaded"* to receive Christ, that they *"might become not only almost, but thoroughly and altogether"* converted.

GETTING FROM HERE TO THERE
ACTS 27

It had been God's stated desire for Paul to go to Rome for some time (23:11), but he had been "stuck" in Caesarea in legal limbo for over two years. Finally, the delay was over and he was on his way, albeit as a Roman prisoner under the guard of a centurion named Julius. But the journey would not be without its difficulties. In verses 3-8, we are struck by the hazards of normal sea travel in the first century. Luke speaks of how *"the winds were against us"* (v. 4), how they *"arrived with difficulty"* (v. 7), how *"the wind did not allow us to proceed"* (v. 7) and how they sailed *"with difficulty"* (v. 8). After all that, he then says that with the approach of winter *"the voyage was now dangerous"* (v. 9)! Paul urged those in charge of the ship not to proceed until the stormy winter season had passed, but the captain and the owner of the ship persuaded the centurion to continue. They sailed right into a furious storm which buffeted them for many days. Paul, though, was reassured by an angelic visitation, promising him again that he would stand before Caesar, and giving him the additional promise that none of the 276 passengers would perish. Paul proclaimed to his fellow passengers that though the ship would be lost, they themselves would be saved, and he urged them to eat their fill, no doubt to gain strength for the coming shipwreck, before they threw the wheat cargo overboard to lighten the ship. When the ship ran aground on Malta and was destroyed, all of the passengers, as Paul had predicted, *"escaped safely to land"* (v. 44). It is not unusual for there to be a delay between the announcement of God's will and the fulfillment of it. What starts as delay often gives way to difficulty, which then gives way to danger. Your faith in the promise may be tested by adverse circumstances (note Paul's words of doubt in verse 10). You may find that some "cargo" in your life needs to be thrown overboard in order to get you there (vv. 18, 38), that the vehicle that you expected to take you there might be destroyed (v. 41), and that the people you trusted to take you there might prove untrustworthy (v. 30). But take courage! God's plans, purpose and promises will always stand, no matter the delay, the difficulty, or the danger.

PRAYER: Where are you today in God's process? Are you experiencing delay, difficulty or danger as you move toward the fulfillment of His will? Pray for faith to believe that, come what may, God's will for you will be fulfilled. Pray that you will have patience in every delay, wisdom in every difficulty, and courage in every danger that you may face.

SNAKEBITE!
ACTS 28

The natives of Malta kindled a fire for the shipwrecked passengers and crew, who were shivering in the rain and cold as they escaped onto the beach. Paul went and gathered a bundle of sticks to feed the fire, and a poisonous snake, driven out of the bundle by the heat of the flame, attached itself to his hand. Paul shook it off into the fire, and suffered no ill effects. That viper had been in the bundle the whole time, but as long as Paul was in the cold and dark, it was content to stay there. It was only when Paul got close to the fire that it struck. Likewise, our enemy, that old serpent Satan, is always lurking around, but as long as we're in the cold and dark in our Christian lives, he stays quiet. We're no threat to him as long as we're there. It's when we get close to the fire of God that he is threatened, and it's then that he strikes! And where does he strike? In the hand, symbolic of our service. The attacks of the enemy are designed to take our focus off of what the Lord has called us to do. The good news is that though the serpent can wound us, he can't kill us, and when the Lord's fire is fully kindled, his plans and purposes will burn up in it! Don't get distracted by the snakebite; keep kindling the fire! Whatever trouble he's trying to inject into your life to keep you from doing God's will, shake it off! When we're going through the trial, some will misunderstand, thinking that it is the judgment of God rather than an attack of Satan (v. 4), but when we successfully navigate the trial, it will open up opportunities for greater influence (vv. 6-9).

PRAYER: Jesus said, *"I have given you authority to trample on snakes and scorpions and to overcome all the power of the enemy; nothing will harm you"* (Luke 10:19). Pray that you will stand firm in that authority when the enemy strikes, not distracted by his attacks, but aggressively taking the fight to him.

ROMANS

WHEN GOD GIVES UP
ROMANS 1

In Romans, Paul establishes clearly the bad news of human sin before moving on to the good news of the gospel. Verses 18-32 are an indictment of all humanity, and those verses read like a description of our times. Paul begins by speaking of the wrath of God falling on humanity because of our rejection of Him (v. 18). Keep in mind that the wrath of God is not some divine temper-tantrum; it is rather God's settled opposition to sin, His utter unwillingness to tolerate it, and His absolute commitment to punish it. All of us abide under His wrath apart from Christ because we have all sinned. The question that is often asked about the fate of those who have never heard the gospel is answered here. They are *"without excuse"* (v. 20), and therefore lost. Many respond to that truth by proclaiming, "That's not fair!" but keep two things in mind. Number one, it *would* be unfair if they were lost for rejecting a message they had not heard, but they are not lost for rejecting the gospel. They are lost because they have rejected what may be known of God through nature and the conscience, which is available to all (v. 19). Number two, if ignorance of the gospel could get people into heaven, then the worst thing we could do is preach the gospel! If

Jesus wants all people to be saved, and ignorance of the gospel would accomplish that, He would have been better served to rise from the dead and not tell anybody! But it is precisely because ignorance of the gospel cannot save (and indeed, the gospel is the only thing that can save - v. 16), that He has commissioned and sent His servants into the world to proclaim the gospel (vv. 1, 5). That rejection of God, whether active or passive, invariably leads to some form of idolatry. Human beings are by nature religious, and in the absence of the worship of God, they will worship something or other (vv. 21-23). Idolatry is not limited to primitive civilizations with their gods of stone, wood and metal (v. 23). Modern man worships himself (the created rather than the Creator - v. 25) and his "wisdom" in rejecting God (v. 22, see also Psalm 14:1). Idolatry then naturally leads to a downward spiral of sin, both in the individual and in society. Three times Paul says here that God gives sinful humans up to ever-increasing sin against themselves and against others. What does it mean that *"God gave them up"* or *"God gave them over"* (vv. 24, 26, 28)? It means that God allowed the natural downward progression of sin to go forward unabated. The characteristics Paul describes here that marked the pagan Roman Empire also mark our day: sexual immorality (v. 24), including homosexuality (vv. 26-27), along with all of the various other forms of social pathology listed in rapid succession in verses 28-31. Not only do sinful people do such things, but *"they give hearty approval to those who practice them"* (v. 32). God has given sinful man up to the consequences of his sin, but He has not given up on us completely! He has also given us His Son as the atoning sacrifice for our sins (vv. 3-4).

PRAYER: Pray today for those who have never heard the gospel, and for those who are taking the gospel where it has not gone before. Pray for those who are trapped in the downward spiral of sin, that they might turn to Christ before it is too late. Pray for revival to come to our depraved society (II Chronicles 7:14).

YOU TOO!
ROMANS 2

Imagine Paul preaching Romans 1 as a sermon in a Jewish synagogue. As he looks out into the congregation, his stinging indictment of the Gentile Roman world is hitting home. Heads are nodding in agreement. Shouts of "Amen!" arise at key moments. "You tell it, Paul, tell about those depraved pagans who have not the Law!" Paul has drawn his prey into a trap by using the enticing bait of Gentile condemnation (vv. 1-3). Now, he shows that those who have the Law are no less under God's condemnation than those who do not have it, because they don't obey it, at least not perfectly. He states clearly that hearing the Law, studying the Law, knowing the Law and even teaching the Law cannot save (vv. 13, 18, 20); only those who actually *obey* the Law could be saved by it (v. 13), and no one obeys it perfectly (vv. 21-24). Therefore, Jews who have the Law are under God's judgment no less than Gentiles who have never heard the Law (v. 12). Jews often disdainfully referred to Gentiles as the "uncircumcised," but Paul shows that the Jewish ritual of circumcision likewise cannot save; indeed, an uncircumcised man might be more righteous than a circumcised Jew (vv. 25-27). In verses 28-29, Paul hints at a truth that will become more and more clear as he expounds his argument: salvation cannot be found in good works or religious ritual. Something deeper must take place, something of the heart, something that can only be brought about by the Spirit of God. As Christians, when we read Paul's words in Romans 1 and see their application in our own society, we might likewise be tempted to view ourselves as superior. Let us never forget that, except for the grace of God that came into our lives through Christ, we could be trapped in that downward spiral of sin, guilty of any, or all, of the litany of sins he lists there.

PRAYER: Just as hearing the Law, studying the Law, knowing the Law, teaching the Law and performing the rituals of the Law could not save, neither can hearing the gospel, studying the gospel, knowing the gospel, teaching the gospel, or participating in the rituals of the gospel (baptism and the Lord's Supper) save. It is only by repenting of our sins and placing our faith in Christ alone, apart from good works or religious ritual, that we can be saved. Pray for those who have been blinded by religious knowledge and religious practice to the true gospel, the grand truth that "nothing in my hand I bring, only to the cross I cling," because "Jesus paid it all, all to Him I owe!"

NO, NOT ONE, BUT ALL
ROMANS 3

Paul continues pressing his argument home in the first part of chapter three. He has established in chapter 1 the guilt of the Gentile world, and in chapter 2 the guilt of the Jewish world. He continues to hammer home the sinfulness of both Jew and Gentile in chapter 3. In verses 10-18, he presents Scripture after Scripture from the Old Testament in rapid-fire testimony to the universal sinfulness of humanity. The Jews have a distinct advantage over the Gentiles in that they have the Law, the very oracles of God (v. 2), but that advantage in and of itself is not sufficient to save them, for *"by the works of the law no flesh will be justified in His sight, for through the law comes the knowledge of sin"* (v. 20). Paul here speaks briefly of what he teaches in greater detail later in the letter, that the Law was not given to give us a roadmap to follow to save ourselves through our good works; rather, the Law was given to show us clearly that we are lost, that we cannot live up to God's standards. The Law shows us clearly our sin, and it drives us to appeal to God's mercy. Justification does not come through law-keeping, but only *"through faith in Jesus Christ to all and upon all who believe"* (v. 22). Just as *"all have sinned and come short of the glory of God"* (v. 23), God's solution for sin, the sacrificial death of Jesus (v. 25), is available to all. Both Jew and Gentile alike (vv. 29-30) are subject to *"being justified freely by His grace through the redemption that is in Christ Jesus"* (v. 24). Paul has established the bad news that *"There is none righteous, no, not one"* (v. 10), but he has also established the good news that all may be saved by grace through faith in Christ.

PRAYER: Thank God today for the availability of the salvation purchased by Christ. If it were a matter of good works, we might come up one good deed short. If it were a matter of payment, we might come up one dollar short. If it were a matter of making a pilgrimage to a holy site, we might come up one mile short. But faith is within the grasp of all of us. Thank Him today that He has made the way for us, and that He has made that way simple and accessible to all.

FATHER ABRAHAM
ROMANS 4

Paul's teaching that salvation from sin comes by faith and not by works of the Law was in direct contradiction to the common Jewish teaching of the time, and he recognized that some would accuse him of propagating a new and different teaching unheard of previously. On the contrary, Paul asserts, the teaching of justification by faith is found in the Old Testament Scriptures, and can be traced all the way back to Abraham, the father of the Jewish nation. Quoting Genesis 15:6, Paul establishes in verse 3 that Abraham was not saved by his good works, but rather *"Abraham believed God, and it was credited to him as righteousness."* Then, to drive home his point still further to those Jews who were relying upon the Law, and perhaps also to those Jewish believers who insisted that Gentiles must be circumcised in order to be saved, Paul points out that Abraham's justification by faith came about before he was circumcised (vv. 9-12). He was not circumcised in order to be justified, but was circumcised in recognition of his justification and in obedience to the one who had justified him (v. 11). Thus, Abraham is not only physically the father of the circumcised (Jews), he is also the spiritual father of all who believe, both Jew and Gentle, circumcised or not (v. 12). What is most important is the faith he displayed, not the ritual that testified of that faith. We can make a similar application to the New Testament ordinance of baptism. While some insist that baptism saves, or that a person cannot be saved without being baptized, the truth is that a person is saved by grace through faith in Christ apart from baptism. Baptism is a recognition of that salvation, and a proclamation of that salvation, and certainly, a convert should be baptized as an act of obedience to the one who has brought about his salvation. But to insist that baptism is necessary for salvation is to add works to faith as a prerequisite for salvation.

PRAYER: Do you know of anyone who has placed their faith in Christ but has never taken that next step of obedience in being baptized? Could that person be you? While baptism is not necessary for salvation, you cannot be an obedient, faithful, growing disciple without it. You will never grow past your last "no." At whatever point you say "no" to the Lord, your spiritual growth will stall out right there. If you have refused His first command, to be baptized as an outward sign of your inward commitment to Him, you are walking in continual disobedience to Him. Pray for anyone you know who is in that disobedient state, and if that person is you, confess that sin to the Lord and make arrangements to be baptized as soon as possible.

THE BENEFITS PACKAGE
ROMANS 5

Paul begins chapter five with the word *"Therefore."* Anytime you see a "therefore" in the Scriptures, you should ask yourself what it's there for! A "therefore" means that what the writer is about to say flows naturally from what he has just said. Paul has already established in previous chapters that *"we have been justified by faith"* (v. 1); now he shows us some of the wonderful benefits that come to us because of that justification. First, *"we have peace with God"* (v. 1). We were once His enemies, abiding under His wrath, but through Christ's sacrifice, we have been saved from His wrath and reconciled to Him (v. 9). Second, *"we also have access by faith into this grace by which we stand"* (v. 2). Two warring countries can sign a peace treaty to stop active hostilities against each other, but still live in deep animosity and distrust of one another. Not so with our peace with God. It goes beyond a mere "cease-fire" to an actual relationship as we are adopted into His family as His children. Just as the children of an earthly king would have access to him that others would not, so too we as His children have anytime, anywhere access to our Father-King through prayer. Verse 2 echoes Hebrews 4:16, which says *"Let us then come with confidence to the throne of grace, that we may obtain mercy and find grace to help in time of need."* God's grace is not a one-time gift that we receive at salvation; it is an ongoing, continual process of God extending His unmerited favor toward us throughout our lives. Third, *"we rejoice in hope of the glory of God"* (v. 2b). One day, we will be glorified. We will spend eternity in His presence, removed from the presence of sin in us and around us forever. Fourth, *"we rejoice in our sufferings"* (v. 3, NIV 84). We look forward to the time we will be in heaven with Him, but that time is not yet. In this life, we will have tribulation (John 16:33), but we can rejoice in the midst of those sufferings because we realize they serve a positive purpose. Suffering is not pleasant, but it does produce in us patience (or perseverance), which then produces godly character, which in turn produces hope (v. 4). If this life were always perfect, we would have no longing for heaven, but the sufferings of this life create in us a greater hope and desire for our heavenly home. Fifth, *the love of God is shed abroad in our hearts by the Holy Spirit who has been given to us* (v. 5). As children, whenever we were hurt, our first instinct was to run to our parents. As they comforted us, we experienced the depth of their love for us. The same is true of our Heavenly Father. It is often during our darkest times that we experience His love most powerfully in His divine comfort. In the darkness of the cross, God proved His love for us once and for all. Let us never doubt His love in our darkest hours. Let us never allow suffering to drive us from Him, but to drive us toward Him. All of these wonderful benefits, both in life and in death, come to us not because we have earned them or are deserving of them, but because *while we were yet sinners, Christ died for us* (v. 8). We were sinners by our nature inherited from Adam (vv. 12-21) and by our own personal choice (v. 12b), but in Christ, we have become God's own dear children.

PRAYER: If God merely removed us from the penalty of hell and did nothing else for us in Christ, we would still have reason to praise Him throughout our lives. But He has done so much more! Thank Him and praise Him today for the abundance, the sheer lavishness, of His blessings in Christ.

OUR NEW MASTER
ROMANS 6

Having established the truth of justification by faith, Paul moves on in the next few chapters to discuss sanctification. Justification takes place in an instant, at the moment of receiving Christ, but sanctification is a life-long process of becoming less sinful and more Christlike daily. Paul uses the image of baptism to speak of what has happened to us in placing our faith in Christ: we have died to the old life of sin, and we have been resurrected to walk in a new and different kind of life. God did not save us for our lives to be no different than before, for us to be merely forgiven, but not changed (vv. 1-2). He saved us to transform us, to conform us more and more over time into the image of His own dear Son. This is an ongoing process that continues throughout our lives, and one that requires our cooperation. Part of our cooperation is realizing our new status in Christ. Paul speaks of two slave masters in the chapter, the master of sin, and the master of righteousness. Prior to being saved, we were the slaves of sin (v. 6), but no longer (v. 7). Now, we are slaves to righteousness (v. 18). Imagine a person who is a slave to a horrible master named Mr. Sin. Mr. Sin is a vicious, cruel, hateful master, who drives his slaves mercilessly with no regard for their welfare. But one day, another man, Mr. Righteousness, comes along and has compassion on the slave. He purchases him from Mr. Sin at an exorbitant price (note how many times this chapter alone talks about the death of Christ as the payment for our freedom from sin). Mr. Righteousness is a kind master, who only wants what's best for the slave. One day, this slave is in town on an errand for his new master, and he spots his old master, Mr. Sin, who calls out to him, "Slave, load my wagon!" Can that slave choose to load Mr. Sin's wagon? Yes. It would be an insult to his new master who has been so kind to him and has paid such a price for him, and it would take away from the energy that he rightly owes his new master, but he can choose to load the old master's wagon. Does he *have* to load that wagon? No. That old master no longer has any authority over him. It may be difficult for him to refuse that order, because he has been conditioned for years to respond to that cruel voice, but he can walk right by, never even acknowledging the command given to him. After all, why would he choose to obey this man who has been so cruel to him if he doesn't have to? Paul is calling upon us to reject the commands of our old master, sin, and to follow the commands of our new master, righteousness. Or, as we could also understand it, we are not to respond to the tempting voice of Satan, but to the loving commands of God. Can we yield to the old master of sin? Yes. Note the "do nots" in verses 12-13. If we are commanded not to do something, it's because we can choose to do it. We can choose to obey the old master, but we don't have to; we can instead choose to refuse those commands and obey the commands of our new master. It will be hard, particularly at first, to refuse those commands of our old master, because we have a long history of obeying that voice, but every time we refuse to obey, and every time we instead obey the voice of righteousness, the stronger we'll grow in our resistance to the old voice and the more conditioned we'll be to obey that new voice. Our old master does not deserve our obedience, because he never did us anything but harm (v. 21). Our new master, on the other hand, deserves our obedience, because he has never done us anything but good (v. 22).

PRAYER: Ask the Lord for strength today to refuse the voice of your old master, and to walk in obedience to your new master. If you have not already, confess and ask His forgiveness for any time that you listened to the voice of the old master.

THE STRUGGLE
ROMANS 7

Romans 7 is one of the most hotly debated sections of the book of Romans. Of particular concern to interpreters are verses 14-25. Is Paul there speaking of his experience before he became a Christian, or of his struggle for sanctification since becoming a Christian? There are good arguments on both sides, and I think that most of us can see elements in the passage from both our pre-Christian and post-Christian experiences. Paul begins the chapter with another analogy. Having used a slavery illustration to speak of our freedom from sin, he now uses a marriage image to speak of our freedom from the Law. Just as a woman's legal union with her husband lasts only until death parts them, so too our dying with Christ in salvation breaks our obligation to the Law, which had no ability to save, only to condemn. The key to understanding the rest of the chapter is verse 6: *"But now we are delivered from the law, having died to things in which we were bound, so that we may serve in newness of Spirit, and not in the oldness of the law."* Paul is saying that our new life in Christ is governed by the indwelling Holy Spirit, and not by the external sanctions of the Law. Having said that, Paul is aware that his critics often accuse him of speaking against the Law, so he pauses to state categorically that the Law is not sin (v. 7a), and to illustrate both the purpose and the shortcomings of the Law. The Law's purpose is to reveal to us both God's holiness and our sin (through our failure to live up to His holiness) (v. 7b). The problem with trying to be saved by following the Law is that our sinful nature tends to react to the Law with characteristic rebellion; the very prohibition of something makes us want it more (vv. 8-11)! It's not that the Law is bad, but it reveals the evil that is in us all (vv. 12-13). Paul, as a pious Pharisee, had gone down that path of trying to achieve salvation by keeping the Law, and it had brought him up empty. With that background, verses 14-25 begin to make better sense. If it were not for the fact that Paul switches to the present tense here, there would be little doubt in anyone's mind that he was continuing to talk about his experience with the Law before Christ, continuing to talk about how he struggled with all his willpower to obey the Law, only to be stymied by his sinful flesh over and over (vv. 14-23). Only Jesus could deliver him from that frustration and failure (v. 24-25) and save him from his sinful flesh. That was no doubt Paul's true testimony of his pre-Christian failure to live according to the Law and his freedom that came only through faith in Christ. But could this passage not also be the testimony of a Christian trying to live for Christ in the power of the flesh? All of us face the daily internal struggle of the flesh warring against the Spirit and the Spirit against the flesh (Galatians 5:17, also v. 25b), and the answer to that struggle is not to be found in a more stringent set of rules or in a greater exercise of willpower. The answer, as Paul will expound upon more fully in chapter 8, is to *"walk in the Spirit, and you shall not fulfill the desire of the flesh"* (Galatians 5:16).

PRAYER: Thank Him today that though the struggle within is very real and ongoing, we can have victory over the flesh in Christ. Pray about any area where you particularly struggle with the flesh and its sinful desires. Your victory will not come from resisting the flesh in your own power, but from yielding to the Spirit and depending upon His power. Ask Him to fill you, lead you, guide you, and fight for you today.

IN THE MEANTIME...
ROMANS 8

The constant struggle with the flesh is a wearisome thing, so much so that Paul cries out in 7:24, *"O wretched man that I am! Who will deliver me from the body of this death?"* Paul longs for the day when he will be released from his earthly body and its fleshly impulses, the day when he will be glorified, removed from sin forever. That time will come, but it is not yet. For now, we must remember the truths he has already taught us about justification and sanctification as we look forward to our glorification. He deals again with justification in verses 1-4. In our struggles with the flesh, temptation and sin, and particularly in our failures, we might give way to self-loathing and condemnation. The evil one accuses us, often with the stinging accusation of "You're worthless! A *real* Christian wouldn't act that way!" While God through His Spirit will convict us when we sin, He attacks the sin, putting His finger on the specific action, attitude, thought pattern or motivation and saying, "*That's not pleasing to me.*" Satan's accusations are always attacks against us personally. He cries out, "*You're* not pleasing to God! He couldn't possibly love you! You're a failure!" Verses 33-34 tell us that that kind of condemnation does not come from God; it can only come from the enemy. Let us always remember that "*There is therefore now no condemnation to those who are in Christ Jesus*" (v. 1). Verses 5-17 summarize the previous teachings on sanctification, expressing again the necessity of being led by the Spirit and not the flesh. We are no longer slaves to sin, but children of God (v. 14), and therefore our obligation is to obey Him, not sin (v. 12). Even though we groan within ourselves in the midst of the struggle (v. 23), and even though we live in a fallen world full of calamities and natural disasters that is likewise groaning from the damage done to it by sin (vv. 19-22), we have the hope that this life and its struggles (both internal and external) are temporary, and the struggles of this life will fade into insignificance when we enter our glorified state (v. 18). It is a difficult journey from justification to glorification, but we are not alone in the journey. The Holy Spirit, who indwells all believers (v. 9), bears witness of our status as God's children (v. 16), which gives us hope for our future glorification (vv. 23-25). He also helps us in our weakness, interceding for us even when we don't know what to pray (vv. 26-27). Don't ever be afraid of praying wrongly; even if you do, the Holy Spirit will translate it into a prayer in accord with God's will! We have the assurance that whatever may befall us in this life, *all things work together for good to those who love God, to those who are called according to His purpose"* (v. 28). We have the assurance that no matter how many starts and stops and slips and falls we may experience on the path of sanctification, those who have been justified will ultimately be glorified, fully conformed to the image of Christ (vv. 29-30). We have the assurance that nothing in this life, not *"tribulation, or distress, or persecution, or famine, or nakedness, or peril, or sword"* (v. 35), and *"neither death nor life, neither angels nor principalities nor powers, neither things present nor things to come, neither height nor depth, nor any other created thing, shall be able to separate us from the love of God, which is in Christ Jesus our Lord"* (vv. 38-39).

PRAYER: Is the Holy Spirit pointing out some sin in your life? Do not allow the conviction of the Spirit to be transformed into the condemnation of the enemy. Reject the feelings of condemnation, thank the Holy Spirit for His conviction, confess the sin and thank Him for His forgiveness and cleansing (I John 1:9). Whatever difficult situation you may be dealing with today, thank Him for the wonderful provisions and wonderful assurances He gives in this difficult journey of life.

ADVANTAGE SQUANDERED
ROMANS 9

In light of his embrace of Christianity and his ministry among the Gentiles, Paul is well aware that many would accuse him (and no doubt had accused him) of rejecting his own people Israel, of despising his own race. Nothing could be further from the truth. In verses 1-5, he expresses his *"great sorrow and continual anguish"* (v. 2) over Israel's rejection of her Messiah. He even goes on to say that if he could, he would himself choose to be accursed from Christ if by doing so his kinsmen would be saved! He goes on to speak of the many advantages that Israel had: *"to whom belong the adoption, the glory, the covenants, the giving of the law, the service of God, and the promises, to whom belong the patriarchs, and from whom, according to the flesh, is Christ"* (vv. 4-5). They were God's chosen people. How could those with such incredible advantages fail to embrace the Savior, while Gentiles with no such background were embracing Him gladly? Paul explains this phenomenon in verses 30-32: *"The Gentiles, who did not pursue righteousness, have attained righteousness, even the righteousness which is by faith, but Israel, pursuing the law of righteousness, did not attain the law of righteousness. Why not? Because they did not seek it by faith, but by the works of the law."* Seeking to be righteous by keeping the Law, the Israelites fell short of it, because no one can keep the Law perfectly, and God is so absolute in His holiness that even one sin committed one time brings us up short of His glory (3:23). The Gentiles, though, recognizing their sinful status and inability to live up to God's standards, attained the righteousness of God through faith in Christ. Many are those in the modern church who likewise have amazing advantages. Their parents and even grandparents may have been Christians. They have been raised in a Christian home, regular in Sunday School and worship from childhood. They have been taught the Bible both at home and at church. They know the path of Biblical morality and walk in it, far exceeding the morality of most. They're good people, good neighbors, good workers, and good parents. They give of their time and finances to the church. But they're lost, because they're relying upon their good works, their family background, their morality, their church membership and attendance, their baptism, and/or their participation in the Lord's Supper to save them, rather than recognizing their sin and trusting in Christ and Christ alone, based on His sacrifice on the cross, to save them. To them, Jesus will speak the most chilling words of the Bible: *"I never knew you. Depart from Me, you who practice evil"* (Matthew 7:21-23).

PRAYER: Billy Graham was once asked about the greatest mission field in America. The reporter who asked the question expected an answer like "the inner cities" or "the Indian reservations" or "the prison system." Billy Graham's answer? "The professing church." What are you trusting to take you to heaven? If you were standing before God right now and He asked you, "Why should I let you into my heaven?" what would you say? If your answer is anything you've done, any good works you've performed, or any religious ritual you've gone through; indeed, if your answer is anything other than Christ's sacrifice on the cross and your receiving it by repentant faith in Him, you're lost. Call upon Him right now for salvation, trusting Him alone to save you. If you are saved, and you grew up with the great advantages of a Christian home and upbringing, thank Him for those wonderful advantages, and thank Him that they did not blind you to the truth of salvation by grace through faith. If you are saved, but did not grow up with such advantages, thank Him that He found you anyway, showing you the truth of your lost condition and saving you by His grace.

HOW SHALL THEY?
ROMANS 10

Paul has established clearly that all are under sin and condemnation; now he establishes clearly that all can be saved through Christ, *"For there is no distinction between Jew and Greek, for the same Lord over all is generous toward all who call upon Him. For, 'Everyone who calls on the name of the Lord shall be saved'"* (vv. 12-13). A person calling upon the Lord for salvation is the end result of a process that Paul delineates (in reverse order) in verses 14-15: *"How shall they call on Him in whom they have not believed? And how shall they believe in Him of whom they have not heard? And how shall they hear without a preacher? And how shall they preach unless they are sent?"* The process is that those who have been born again through Christ are sent out by God into the world to preach and otherwise communicate the gospel to the lost. Those who hear that message then can believe it and call upon the Lord for salvation. Paul's repeated "how shall they" questions are haunting, because the answers are obvious and disturbing. *"How shall they call on Him in whom they have not believed?"* They can't. *"And how shall they believe in Him of whom they have not heard?"* They can't. *"And how shall they hear without a preacher?"* They can't. *"And how shall they preach unless they are sent?"* They can't. And people that Jesus died for stay lost. God is sending. Are we willing to go?

PRAYER: Pray for those missionaries, evangelists, pastors and teachers, especially those you know personally, who have been called and commissioned to go forth and proclaim the gospel to the lost. Pray that many will believe and call upon the Lord because of their work. But recognize that this passage is not just about ordained ministers. It's about all of God's people. Pray for opportunities and willingness to share the gospel with someone today.

THE REMNANT REMAINS
ROMANS 11

Have you ever felt like you were the only one still standing, the only one in your circle still committed to the things of God as those around you compromise and fall away? Elijah felt that way when he was sitting in the cave on Mount Sinai, bemoaning his fate. He believed that all of Israel had bowed down to Baal, that he was the last faithful one left and the last of the prophets, and that he would soon be killed as well (I Kings 19:10). God assured him that he was far from alone in his faithfulness, that there were 7000 others in Israel who had never bowed down to Baal and who were standing strong against Ahab and Jezebel and their false religion. Paul uses that Old Testament narrative as an illustration of the fact that there was still *"at this present time...a remnant according to the election of grace"* (v. 5) from Israel. It might look like all of Israel had rejected the way of grace in favor of trying to achieve righteousness by works. Gentile believers, who had received salvation by grace as they responded to the gospel, might even be tempted to think that God had completely rejected Israel (v. 1), cutting them off completely. But that was not true at all (v. 2). Paul himself was part of the remnant of Israel that had come into the Kingdom by grace, and there were others as well from Israel who had received Jesus as their Messiah, Savior and Lord. In this church age, Israelite believers in Jesus will always be a minority, both in the church and in Israel, a mere remnant of the total. In Paul's illustration, the natural branches of the olive tree (unbelieving Israel) have been broken off because of their unbelief, making room for the wild olive branches (believing Gentiles) to be grafted into the tree, but he looks forward to the time when *"the fullness of the Gentiles has come in. And so all Israel will be saved"* (vv. 25-26). After Christ returns for His church (made up of Gentiles and the current remnant of Israel), the Bible teaches that there will be a great turning of the Jewish people to Christ in faith (Zechariah 12:10 - 13:2).

PRAYER: If you're feeling like "the last man standing" for the Lord in your circle, ask the Lord to show you other members of the remnant, other faithful followers that you can encourage and who can encourage you. Pray for any Jewish people you know personally, that they might come to know Christ and become part of the remnant according to grace. Pray for opportunities to share the gospel with them.

A LIVING SACRIFICE LIFESTYLE
ROMANS 12

As Paul begins winding down his letter to the Roman church, he moves from deep theology to practical guidance for living the Christian life. The overall theme of this section is stated right off the bat: *"I urge you therefore, brothers, by the mercies of God, that you present your bodies as a living sacrifice, holy, and acceptable to God, which is your reasonable service of worship. Do not be conformed to this world, but be transformed by the renewing of your mind"* (vv. 1-2). He urges us to live as *"living sacrifices"* (v. 1), not squeezed into the world's mold (the meaning of the word *"conformed"* in verse 2) but transformed by having a renewed mind. In light of what Christ has done (*"the mercies of God"*), living as living sacrifices is our only reasonable response to Him, but as someone has well put it, the problem with living sacrifices is their tendency to climb off the altar and right back onto the throne! To battle against this fleshly tendency, we must constantly be in a process of renewing our minds, washing our thinking clean from the world's influence through constant exposure to the Word of God. What will that "living sacrifice lifestyle" look like? The rest of the chapter shows us in a series of rapid-fire exhortations. It is a lifestyle of humility (vv. 3, 16), service empowered by spiritual gifts (vv. 4-8), love (v. 9a), goodness (v. 9b), fellowship in good times and bad (vv. 10, 15), fervency in service (v. 11), rejoicing, perseverance and prayer in time of difficulty (v. 12), generosity and hospitality (v. 13), and love and grace for enemies (vv. 14, 17-20). By living in this way, we will *"not be overcome by evil, but overcome evil with good"* (v. 21).

PRAYER: As you look over Paul's list here, can you honestly say you are living a living sacrifice lifestyle? If not, pray a prayer of rededication, relinquishing anew the throne of your life to Him and placing yourself once again on the altar. If you find that you're wandering far from where you should be, a good strategy would be to cut off the bombardment of the world's input for a time and diligently seek the Lord in His Word and in extended times of prayer (v. 2).

CHRISTIANS AND THE STATE
ROMANS 13

If we were to take Romans 13 in isolation, it would seem to teach that Christians are to obey without question any decree, no matter how ungodly, from any government, no matter how tyrannical. In truth, Romans 13 is not only spelling out the duty of the believer to government, but the duty of governments before God. In God's system of authority, human governments exist to punish evil and reward good (vv. 1-4). Such governments are to be supported with taxes and respect (vv. 6-7), and submission to such governments is part of our submission to God (vv. 1-2, 5). But what about a government that does the opposite, that rewards evil and punishes good, that becomes itself an instrument of evil? Are Christians to blindly follow such governments? Should the Israelites have blindly followed King Ahab and Queen Jezebel into the worship of Baal, and was Elijah wrong to oppose them? Should Christians have participated in herding Jews into concentration camps and gas chambers because of the edicts of the Nazi regime, "just following orders" in obedience to Romans 13? Of course not. As someone put it, Romans 13 must be balanced by Revelation 13, the ultimate picture of government run amuck. Those governments that step out of their God-given authority as instruments of righteousness to become instruments of evil opposing God are to be resisted, that resistance coming in proportion to the degree of their deviation. That resistance might come through civil disobedience, through peaceful protest, through prayerful entreaty, through the voting booth and, on rare occasions with absolutely evil governments, through forceful overthrow. Christians are to obey the edicts of government until and unless that government tries to require of them what God has forbidden or forbid to them what God has required. In such instances, God's commands trump human edicts, and the believer must respectfully, but firmly, refuse to obey any law that contradicts God's higher law. It is important to note that every instance of government wrongdoing should not elicit complete rebellion against the state. There may be some laws that we cannot in good conscience obey, but that is not a warrant for disobeying other laws that do not contradict God's Word. In all of our dealings with government, we must keep in mind the principle that Jesus gave: *"Render therefore to Caesar the things that are Caesar's, and to God the things that are God's"* (Matthew 22:21). The things that are Caesar's are delineated in verse 7. The things that are God's are absolute loyalty and complete obedience (vv. 11-14).

PRAYER: Pray today for your mayor, your governor, your state and federal representatives, the President and the courts (I Timothy 2:2). Pray for them that they might have God's wisdom, that they might govern according to that wisdom, and that if at any point they refuse to walk in God's wisdom, their plans and purposes might be defeated.

JUDGMENT IN THE CHURCH
ROMANS 14

Romans 14 deals with a common issue in the churches of the first century: the issue of eating meat. Those who came out of a Jewish background often continued to hold to the Jewish dietary laws, which declared some meat unclean, while those who came from a Gentile background struggled with the fact that meat sold in the marketplaces was usually from sacrifices to pagan gods. Was it right or wrong to eat meat in those cases? Paul states categorically here that *"I know and am persuaded by the Lord Jesus that nothing is unclean in itself"* (v. 14), and elsewhere he declares that meat sold in the marketplace, even if it had been sacrificed to a pagan god, was in no way spiritually contaminated (I Corinthians 10:25-26). Paul is dealing with a bigger issue here than meat, specifically, the issue of how believers in the church related to one another over the issue. Paul gives three principles on how to deal with "disputable matters" in the church. First, he urges us to hold to our own convictions strongly (vv. 22-23). It is important to note that the "to eat or not to eat meat" controversy was a matter of personal conviction and personal preference, not a matter of heresy or a matter of sin. On clear doctrinal or moral issues, there should be no disagreement. Second, he urges us not to judge those who feel differently about the issue. His specific concern was that the person who had faith to eat all things might look down on the person who could not bring himself to do so, and vice-versa (v. 3). Whatever side one's preference brought him down on, he must not judge his brother in the matter, for *"Who are you to judge another man's servant? To his own master he stands or falls"* (v. 4). Paul also alludes to another issue with the potential to divide: holy days carried over from Judaism (v. 5) that Gentiles might or might not feel led to observe. The third principle Paul gives is to do nothing that would cause a brother to stumble, but instead to pursue loving interactions that lead to peace and to the edification of our fellow believers. *"If your brother is grieved because of your food, you are no longer walking in love. Do not destroy with your food one for whom Christ died...For the kingdom of God does not mean eating and drinking, but righteousness and peace and joy in the Holy Spirit"* (vv. 15, 17). *"Therefore let us pursue the things which produce peace and the things that build up one another"* (v. 19). It is better to suspend one's freedom in the presence of a weaker brother than to bring offense to him and cause him to stumble or be made weak (v. 21).

PRAYER: What are some disputable matters you can think of in the modern church? Pray that the Lord might show you how to apply the principles here to those situations.

PAUL'S HEART
ROMANS 15

It is important to remember that Paul had never visited the church at Rome at the time he wrote this letter. His letter to them was an introduction of himself and his teaching in anticipation of his impending visit to them. As Paul speaks of his upcoming plans here, his apostle's heart comes through clearly. What was it that drove this man of God? He felt a call from God to be *"a minister of Jesus Christ to the Gentiles"* (v. 16), a call made all the more remarkable given his background as a Gentile-despising Pharisee. He felt an obligation to defend the mission of taking of the gospel to the Gentiles (vv. 15-16). It would seem that the church at Rome was still largely Jewish, and Paul could only imagine what would happen if this church, in the capital city of the Roman Empire, became fully committed to Gentile outreach. Paul desired to boast in the Lord about what He had done among the Gentiles (vv. 17-19), bringing praise, honor and glory to Him and inspiring the Romans and others to be a part of what God was doing through the Gentile mission. He was driven by a missionary impulse to take the gospel where it had never gone before rather than pastoring a church founded by another (v. 20). He makes it clear that his coming to Rome was not out of any desire to stay and "take over" the church, but out of a desire to stop and minister there, and hopefully to receive some help, on his way to take the gospel to Spain (vv. 22-24). Before he would come there, though, he first had to go to Jerusalem to take the offering that the Gentile churches had gathered for the famine-stricken Jewish believers there (v. 25). Paul's desire in doing so was that the unity of Jewish believers and Gentile believers in Christ might be strengthened (vv. 26-27). Paul knew that the age-old prejudices between Jews and Gentiles could cause the Christian movement to split into Jewish and Gentile expressions of Christianity rather than coming together to form a united church. His request for prayers that he might be *delivered from the unbelievers in Judea and that my ministry for Jerusalem may be acceptable to the saints"* (v. 31) shows how seriously he took this possibility. He was willing to put himself at risk to carry this love gift, and he desperately hoped it would have the desired effect of endearing the Gentile churches to the Jerusalem church. As we know from Acts, his concerns for his safety were well-founded. Indeed, he would eventually come to Rome, but not as he hoped for here; rather, he would come as a prisoner to be tried before Caesar's court.

PRAYER: Paul understood his mission and calling, his place in God's Kingdom, God's desire for his life and work. Do you understand yours? If not, pray that God might make clear His desire for you. If so, pray that you might be faithful in carrying out His will for your life.

A VIOLENT PEACE
ROMANS 16

In chapter 16, Paul concludes his letter to Rome with some personal greetings to people he knows who are in Rome (vv. 1-16) and from those who are with him (vv. 21-23), a final warning about false teachers (vv. 17-19), and a final doxology of praise to the Lord (vv. 25-27) - all fairly "routine" stuff (at least as routine as any part of the Word of God can be). Nestled in the midst of all that, though, is an interesting verse: *"The God of peace will soon crush Satan under your feet"* (v. 20). I'm struck by the contrast in that verse between God as the God of peace and the violent image of crushing Satan (an image borrowed, no doubt, from Genesis 3:15), and I'm also struck by the fact that Paul says God will do it, but He will do it with our feet! Meditate on that awhile. Paul has earlier spoken of the importance of maintaining unity in the church (chapter 14) and of the essential need of unity in the church between Jews and Gentiles (chapter 15). In the immediately preceding verses, he has spoken of *"those who cause divisions and offenses, contrary to the teaching which you have learned"* (v. 17), knowing full well that such false teachers come from the devil himself. Paul has faith that the devil's schemes will not ultimately succeed. As believers unite and stand together against false teaching and other Satanic schemes to divide the church, God will empower them to crush the devil's plans and plots. Verse 20 teaches us that peace does not come through the absence of conflict, but in the midst of the conflict and through victory in our battles with the forces of evil. Peace, in ourselves and in the church, is not to be found in passive pacifism; it is won through aggressive, God-ordained, and God-empowered action as the church marches out in unity and harmony against the devil's kingdom (Matthew 16:18).

PRAYER: Pray about any issues of disunity affecting the "fighting readiness" in churches or among churches of your community. Pray that believers will come together in unified action, so that through them, God might crush Satan and his nefarious schemes underneath their feet as they march forward in obedience.

I CORINTHIANS

I AM OF...
I CORINTHIANS 1

Of all the churches he had founded, none gave Paul more heartache than the church at Corinth; indeed, that one church may have caused him more sleepless nights than all the rest combined. There were a number of issues he needed to address in his letter to them, so after his normal greetings, he dives right into one of the main problems facing the church: a crippling lack of unity as the church had divided up into "fan clubs" around their favorite preachers: *"Every one of you is saying, 'I am of Paul,' or 'I am of Apollos,' or 'I am of Cephas,' or 'I am of Christ'"* (v. 12). What's interesting about the situation is that there was no division or rivalry between Peter, Paul and Apollos, and all three of them were preaching Christ. What was the source of the controversy then? It would seem to be a controversy based primarily on style. All three men were faithful ministers, powerful preachers, and fully committed to Christ, but their styles differed dramatically. Peter was more homespun, as one would expect of a Galilean fisherman, punctuating his preaching with personal accounts of his time with Jesus. Paul was a theologian of the first rank, a deep thinker, but one whose critics at Corinth alleged that *"his letters...are weighty and powerful, but his bodily presence is weak, and his speech contemptible"* (II Corinthians 10:10). Apollos was *"an eloquent man and powerful in the Scriptures,"* according to Acts 18:24, a golden-voiced orator whose applications of the Old Testament were eye-opening and thrilling. The Corinthians had been blessed to experience the ministry of these great preachers, but sadly, rather than appreciating all of them and the unique gifts each one brought to the table, they compared them, contrasted them, and divided in their preferences over them. In our day, with the availability of different preachers and different styles on TV, radio and the Internet, there may be some of that Corinthian spirit of division out there as it relates to different preachers, but my experience has been that it is music style that causes most of the division in churches today. Are not the so-called "worship wars" merely expressions of personal preference, as modern disciples declare, "I am of Chris Tomlin" or "I am of Bill Gaither" or "I am of Fanny Crosby" or "I am of Isaac Watts"?

PRAYER: Ask the Lord to reveal to you today any area of your life where you have allowed personal preferences to divide you from other believers.

THE HEART OF AN EVANGELIST
I CORINTHIANS 2

Sharing the gospel is a human undertaking with a divine empowerment. Paul speaks of how he had brought the gospel to Corinth, a notoriously wicked city in the ancient world, during his second missionary journey (Acts 18:1-17). Although he certainly could have come into that city *"with superiority of speech or wisdom"* (v. 1), impressing his hearers with his extensive knowledge and superior education, he chose instead *"not to know anything among <them> except Jesus*

Christ and Him crucified" (v. 2). He proclaimed the simple yet profound message of the atoning death of Christ for sin. Paul understood that no matter how skilled his presentation, how persuasive his arguments, or how airtight his logic might be (v. 4), it would all be for naught, because *"the natural* (unsaved) *man does not receive the things of the Spirit of God...because they are spiritually discerned"* (v. 14). It is only through the convicting power of the Spirit of God that men are brought to repentance and salvation (vv. 4-5), not by our eloquence or persuasiveness, and He works through that simple call to faith in Christ as our sacrifice for sin. Once a person is saved, and has the mind of Christ (v. 16), then he can discern spiritual things, and can learn and understand the deeper things of God as he grows in the Word and in maturity (vv. 6-13).

PRAYER: Pray that as you study the Word, your eyes might be opened by the Holy Spirit to know the fullness of God's riches in Christ (v. 9-10, 12).

THE CURSE OF CARNALITY
I CORINTHIANS 3

In chapter 2, Paul had spoken of the normal course of the Christian life: salvation through faith in Christ, followed by spiritual growth as the believer matures in Christ. He had spoken of how he delights in leading new believers along that path of greater maturity (2:6-7). Now, in chapter 3, he speaks of his frustration with the Corinthians over the fact that they have derailed on that path. Rather than moving on into maturity, they have settled into a mind-numbing immaturity which is rendered in various translations as "carnality," "fleshliness" or "worldliness." Whatever title we place on it, it is the tragic state of a person who has grown older in Christ but not up in Christ. Paul here gives five characteristics of such a life. The first characteristic is *a genuine spiritual experience*. The carnal Christian is in fact a Christian; he is not like the natural man spoken of in chapter 2, although in many ways, unfortunately, he resembles him. Notice that in verse one, Paul calls them *"brothers"* and he says specifically that they are *"in Christ"* albeit *"babes in Christ."* They were believers, but they were sorely lacking in spiritual growth. The second characteristic of carnality is *a depressed spiritual appetite* (v. 2). Just as babies do not feed themselves and must be bottle-fed by others, so too carnal believers trust others to feed them the Word of God, and like babies, they are totally disinterested in meat. Many Christians don't want in-depth Bible teaching or preaching. They want to be entertained but never challenged, encouraged but never exhorted, and comforted but never convicted. A third characteristic of carnality is *a jealous spiritual attitude* (v. 3). Children are notoriously jealous. When one child in the family gets something and the others don't, jealousy almost invariably erupts. The same thing often happens in the church. Jealousy over attention. Jealousy over recognition. Jealousy over position. Jealousy over perceived power. Fourth, carnality is marked by *the lack of a spiritual outlook*. In verse 4, Paul accuses them of *"behaving as mere men."* The carnal believer's basic outlook on life, his basic worldview, is still in accord with the ways of the world, rather than the ways of the Word. The fifth characteristic of carnality is *a horizontal spiritual focus* (v. 4). As we have seen, the Corinthians were focused on men, not God, and as a result, they had broken off into factions clustered around their personal preferences and favorite preachers.

PRAYER: As you read through the above checklist, do you detect any pockets of carnality in your life? Pray for the Spirit to invade those areas and bring you to maturity in Christ.

RESPONDING TO REJECTION
I CORINTHIANS 4

The extent and seriousness of the division at Corinth becomes more evident as the book progresses. It was not just a matter of some in the church having a preference for one preacher over another, but a matter of some in the church actually *rejecting* these men of God in favor of their favorites. That some in the church were rejecting Paul was especially painful to him, as he was the founder of the church. As he says in verses 15-16, *"For if you were to have ten thousand instructors in Christ, yet you do not have many fathers. In Christ Jesus I have become a father to you through the gospel. So I implore you, be followers of me."* It was a personal wound to Paul to be so rejected, but his concern was deeper than the personal affront. In rejecting him personally, they were in danger of rejecting his apostolic authority, and that left them open to the very real possibility that they might be led astray in their immaturity by false teachers (v. 14). It was for that reason that he determined to send Timothy to them, to *"remind you of my ways which are in Christ, as I teach everywhere in every church"* (v. 17), until he himself could get there to straighten out the mess and re-establish his authority (vv. 18-21). All of us will experience some degree of rejection in our lives, both of a personal and professional nature, and it is always heartbreaking. Paul here gives us a good pattern to follow in dealing with rejection: *"Being reviled, we bless. Being persecuted, we endure. Being slandered, we encourage"* (v. 12). A difficult path, to be sure, but a blessed one that brings healing.

PRAYER: Are you experiencing rejection in your life now? Pray that you would respond to that rejection in a godly manner, and pray for God's healing of your heartbreak.

PURGE THE OLD YEAST
I CORINTHIANS 5

Paul is appalled by reports coming out of the church at Corinth regarding an ongoing situation of immorality, that a church member was openly carrying on an adulterous affair with his father's wife. The wording of verse 1 indicates that this woman was not his mother, but rather his stepmother, but still, it was a violation of such magnitude that it was a scandal even among the Gentiles, and you had to go some to scandalize the Gentiles in Corinth. Corinth was known throughout the Roman Empire for shocking sexual license. It is a fascinating phenomenon that the world often holds Christians to a higher standard than the Christians hold themselves. Even the world understands that Christians are called to a higher standard. If a professing Christian is caught in a sin, in the minds of the lost, it legitimizes their own sin and de-legitimizes the faith, giving them "permission" to carry on in their sin. But Paul's biggest concern was not for the sensibilities of the pagans in Corinth, but for the apparent lack of sensibility among the Christians in Corinth. Rather than mourning over this man's sin and addressing it through appropriate confrontation and church discipline, he says that they were instead *"arrogant"* about it. Like many churches today, they celebrated what they saw as love and open-mindedness: "Oh, how loving and accepting we are at the church of Corinth! Oh, what an understanding of grace we have!" On the contrary, what a perversion of grace they were practicing! Grace is not license to continue in sin, but the power to overcome sin (Romans 6:1-2)! It was imperative that they remove this evil from among them, both for the sake of their testimony (v. 1) and because such evil, if not addressed, had the capacity to spread throughout the whole body like yeast in dough (v. 6). Paul's words in verses 9-13 are an important corrective to the oftentimes too lenient, too harsh, or wrongly directed judgments in the church. We should not be surprised when lost people act like lost people, and rather than rejecting them (vv. 9-10), we should make all efforts to love them into the Kingdom by demonstrating our own changed lives and showing them a better way (the *"sincerity and truth"* of v. 8b). Those who claim salvation, though, need to be held to a Biblical standard of appropriate behavior, not harsh, self-righteous condemnation over every slip-up or indiscretion, but certainly loving, firm intervention in the case of flagrant ongoing sin (vv. 11-12). Such intervention involves confrontation about the sin in the hope of bringing the offender to repentance, and, in the case of lack of repentance, removal from the body (Matthew 18:15-17). This is both for the protection of the body (v. 6) and in the hope that such an extreme measure will bring the offender to repentance (v. 5).

PRAYER: Pray that your life might be an example to unbelievers of the change that comes through a personal relationship with Christ. Pray for any professing Christians you know whose walk is not as it should be. Ask the Lord to show you how you might be used to bring that believer back to where he or she needs to be.

FLEE SEXUAL IMMORALITY
I CORINTHIANS 6

As aforementioned, Corinth was an exceedingly wicked city, noted throughout the ancient world for its sexual license. The temple of Aphrodite, the goddess of love, was a prominent feature of Corinth, employing over 1000 women as priestesses, or better, as "sacred" prostitutes. The worship of Aphrodite involved sexual intercourse with one of these temple prostitutes, and that "worship" was an ingrained part of Corinthian culture. The Christians in the church there had been saved out of that social and religious background (vv. 9-11), but the draw of it was still strong, and apparently, at least some of them were going back into that lifestyle and attempting to justify it with a mishmash of faulty Christian theology and Greek philosophy. They argued first that, because we are under grace and not law, and all of our sins have been forgiven, *"All things are lawful to me"* (v. 12). Paul does not refute their premise that we are under grace and that our sins have been forgiven, but he does challenge their conclusion that all things are lawful. Even if all things were lawful for the Christian, God would certainly not have us engage in that which is not helpful; indeed, in that which would bring us again into slavery to sin (v. 12). Their second argument seems to be related to the issue of food, and the fact that in Christ, all foods had been declared clean. "Eating is a natural function," they argued (v. 13a), "and it doesn't affect us spiritually. Sex is also a natural function, and likewise, it doesn't affect us spiritually." Paul responds to that argument by pointing out that food is necessary for life, but sexual immorality most certainly is not (v. 13b). He goes on to show that all sex outside of marriage, including fornication, prostitution, adultery and homosexuality (v. 9) does indeed affect our spiritual lives. Unlike Greek philosophy, which made a radical break between body and spirit, Jesus is Lord (and Savior) over all of us, not just our immaterial spirits, but our bodies as well. Our bodies are so important that God will one day raise them from the dead (v. 14). For now, our *"bodies are the parts of Christ"* (v. 15) and *"the temple of the Holy Spirit"* (v. 19), not our own to do with what we will, but bought with a price and therefore the property of the one who purchased us (vv. 19-20). Therefore, we must not *"take the parts of Christ and make them the parts of a harlot"* (v. 15), but instead, we must flee from sexual immorality (v. 18) and glorify God not just in spirit, but with our bodies as well (v. 20).

PRAYER: Pray for anyone you know (even if it is yourself) who is caught up in the web of sexual sin, or any of the other sins listed in verses 9-10. Note the encouragement of the past tense of verse 11: *"Such were some of you..."* Remember, in Christ, you are not defined by what tempts you. For example, you are not by nature a homosexual, denying who you are, as the world would have you believe. You are a child of God who is tempted by same-sex attractions, who will choose either to act on those temptations or to glorify God by refusing to do so. Old habits and old patterns from the old life may have a strong hold on us, but in Christ, we can have victory even over such strong temptations and life-dominating sins.

MARRIAGE AND SINGLENESS
I CORINTHIANS 7

Having dealt with the subject of sexual immorality (sex outside of marriage), Paul now turns his attention to the subject of sex in marriage, and marriage in general. The Corinthians had written Paul, asking a number of questions about these subjects, and, in the absence of the questions, we're left to try to reconstruct their concerns from his answers. In the process of answering their questions, Paul affirms both marriage and singleness as appropriate life choices for believers. The primary advantage of marriage that Paul speaks of here (though the Bible certainly speaks of other benefits elsewhere) is that it provides an appropriate sexual outlet, which reduces temptations toward sexual sin (vv. 2-5). It has been suggested that some in the Corinthian church, reacting against the sexual immorality all around them, were rejecting sex altogether, even sex in marriage. Paul dismisses such a teaching, showing that sex in marriage is moral, honorable and right. Husbands and wives are to engage in an active sex life that is mutually satisfying, not denying one another the sexual benefits of marriage. Paul is not commanding believers to marry (v. 6), but is commanding those who do marry to commit themselves fully to the marriage, including sexually. When he says in verse seven, *"I would that all men were even as I myself,"* he is not saying, as some have suggested, that he wishes that everyone were single! How then would the world be populated? What he is saying is that he is not frustrated in his singleness, nor overly tempted to sexual immorality, but he recognizes that others are not so gifted (see vv. 8-9). Paul goes on to encourage Christian spouses to stay together and not divorce (vv. 10-11), and for believers married to unbelievers to remain in their marriages (if possible - v. 15) in the hope of influencing their spouses and children to Christ (vv. 12-14). Paul also speaks of the advantages of singleness in this chapter. Those believers who are single are able to commit themselves more fully to the work of the Lord, unhindered by obligations to a spouse and children (v. 34). They also have less concern during times of persecution, for they only have themselves to worry about (vv. 26, 28).

PRAYER: If you are single, pray that you might take full advantage of your singleness in serving the Lord, and that you might be content in your singleness until the Lord brings the right person into your life. Just a thought: what if God is waiting until you accomplish all you can for Him as a single disciple before He brings that person into your life? If you are married, pray that your marriage might be used to honor God, and that you might serve Him faithfully side-by-side with your spouse.

FREEDOM AND RESPONSIBILITY
I CORINTHIANS 8

The issue of eating meat was a huge issue in the early church, particularly in those churches located in pagan cities.

Animals would be sacrificed to various pagan gods, and then the meat consumed as part of the worship of that god. Any leftover meat was then sold in the marketplace. The issue in many believers' minds, particularly those who came out of that kind of pagan background, was whether eating meat purchased in the marketplace involved the believer in the worship of a false god. Paul makes it clear that *"an idol is nothing"* (v. 4), that there is *"but one God, the Father...And there is one Lord Jesus Christ"* (v. 6). In other words, the idol was fake, the sacrifice was meaningless, and the meat was therefore undefiled. However, Paul recognizes that some, having come out of that background, would have difficulty separating the consumption of the meat from the false worship they had come out of, and he urges those who had no compunctions about eating to be considerate of those whose consciences would be defiled through its consumption. They were to *"take heed, lest by any means this liberty of yours becomes a stumbling block to those who are weak"* (v. 9). Our freedom is not as important as the spiritual well-being of our brothers and sisters in Christ; indeed, *"When you thus sin against the brothers, wounding their weak conscience, you sin against Christ"* (v. 12). Paul concludes with a principle we should all remember: *"if food causes my brother to stumble, I will never eat meat, lest I cause my brother to stumble."* Obviously, the issue of meat offered to idols is not an issue today, but consider this scenario. A mature believer might feel that he is free to listen to any kind of music, secular or Christian, provided the lyrics are not obscene. A younger believer, just coming out of the world, might reject listening to secular music, because it reminds him of the bar scene and sinful activities he has left behind. If the two are going on a road trip together, would the more mature Christian, knowing the younger Christian's hesitation, be justified in saying, "Your attitude is silly. There's nothing wrong with the music I listen to. My car, my radio!" and listening to secular music on the journey, or would the loving thing be to listen to only Christian music?

PRAYER: Can you think of any other matters where these principles might apply? Pray that you would never insist on your freedom in an unloving manner toward another believer.

THE RIGHTS OF AN APOSTLE
I CORINTHIANS 9

Paul illustrates the principle of freedom and responsibility he has taught in chapter nine from his own life. As an apostle, he had certain rights by virtue of his calling. He was certainly within his rights to marry and to take a wife with him on his missionary journeys, if he so chose. The brothers of the Lord (which would include James and Jude) did so, and other apostles did so, including Cephas (Peter) (v. 5). There was nothing inappropriate or unseemly about their doing so. As an apostle, Paul also had the right to receive his living from the gospel (v. 14) rather than by working in his trade as tentmaker (v. 6). Again, there would have been nothing wrong whatsoever with receiving material support from those he was ministering to spiritually (v. 11). Even though he was well within his rights to do these things, he did not, because he did not want the gospel hindered (v. 12). As Paul had earlier taught in chapter 7, he believed that he could accomplish more for the Kingdom without the responsibilities of a wife. In terms of receiving material support, Paul's ministry was to take the gospel to places it had not gone before, Gentile locations with very little Jewish background. In Judaism, the principle of supporting ministers financially was well-established, and not an issue (v. 13). In ministering to Gentiles, Paul was concerned lest they think the gospel was for sale (v. 18). Paul's overarching desire was not to express his freedoms and claim his rights, but to win people to the Lord: *"For though I am free from all men, I have made myself a servant to all, that I might win even more. To the Jews, I became as a Jew, that I might win the Jews; to those who are under the law, as under the law, that I might win those who are under the law; to those who are outside the law, as outside the law...that I might win those who are outside the law. To the weak, I became as weak, that I might win the weak. I have become all things to all men, that I might by all means save some"* (vv. 19-23). While setting aside his freedom and rights was at times a hardship, Paul viewed doing so as the equivalent of an athlete in training (vv. 24-27). The training might be difficult, but the reward was well worth it!

PRAYER: What rights might the Lord be calling you to give up for the sake of the gospel? Pray that you would always be willing to sacrifice that others might be saved.

TEMPTATIONS AND TRIUMPHS
I CORINTHIANS 10

As Paul continues his discussion of the common temptations of Corinth, he goes back into Old Testament history to use the example of the Exodus generation, showing that the things that happened to them were written as examples to us. Details change, but the same temptations that descended upon the Israelites in the wilderness were manifesting in first century Corinth, and those same temptations are alive and well in 21st century America: temptations to sexual immorality, temptations to idolatry, and temptations to murmuring against God-called leadership (vv. 7-10). The temptations the Corinthians faced, living in the wicked environment they did, were difficult temptations to be sure, but Paul assures them, and us, that *"No temptation has taken you except what is common to man. God is faithful, and He will not permit you to be tempted above what you can endure, but will with the temptation also make a way of escape, that you will be able to bear it"* (v. 13). Paul then returns to his earlier treatment of eating meat, clarifying his position so that there is no misunderstanding. In 8:4, he had said that *"an idol is nothing"* in teaching that meat that had been offered to an idol was not defiled and could not defile a Christian who consumed it. He fears that some might read that and conclude that it was therefore permissible to participate in the feasts held in pagan temples. While the meat itself was not defiled and could be freely purchased from the market and eaten with no spiritual ill effects (vv. 25-26), participating in the pagan feasts at the temples of false gods would indeed bring spiritual defilement. Just as the Lord's Table was a communion with the Lord (vv. 15-17), so too participating in pagan temple feasts was a communion with demons (vv. 19-21), and therefore to be avoided at all costs.

PRAYER: What temptations are especially difficult for you to resist? Pray that with every temptation, you might claim the promise of verse 13, and that you might always have eyes to see the escape route provided.

TABLE MANNERS
I CORINTHIANS 11

In understanding Paul's teaching on the Lord's Supper here, it is important to understand some aspects of first century church life that differ from our meetings today. The early churches met on Sundays, but in the evening. Sunday was a work day like any other day back then, and the believers would come to church in the evening after they had put in a full day's labor. The churches usually began their time together with what was called a "love feast," basically a potluck dinner. Richer members of the congregation at Corinth, who did not have to work as day laborers until sunset, were bringing most of the food, but they were also arriving first and eating up all the food, leaving little or nothing for the poorer members coming in directly from their jobs. It was this abuse that Paul was speaking of in verses 21-22 and 33-34. They may have even eaten up the elements of the Lord's Supper before the others got there (v. 20)! Thus, they were dishonoring their fellow church members and dishonoring the Lord. Paul takes them back to the original establishment and intent of the Lord's Supper in verses 23-26, showing them that the purpose of the memorial meal is to remember Christ, meditating upon His sacrifice and proclaiming the Lord's death until His return. All of the blood-bought church *"are one bread and one body, for we are all partakers of that one bread"* (10:17). The Lord's Table should be a celebration of our unity in Christ, but in their inconsiderate actions, they had made it a point of division along social and economic lines. Far from being a small matter, it was a big deal to God, so much so that Paul declares that *"whosoever eats this bread and drinks this cup of the Lord unworthily will be guilty of the body and blood of the Lord...for he who eats and drinks unworthily, eats and drinks damnation* (better *"judgment"* - NIV 84) *to himself"* (vv. 27, 29), the judgment being in the form of God's discipline: *"For this reason many are weak and unhealthy among you, and many die."* Oh, how much unnecessary fear and sorrow has been created by a misunderstanding of that word *"unworthily."* I have heard sad tales of Christians being denied the Lord's Supper because someone deemed them unworthy, or of people who went for years without partaking because they felt themselves unworthy. I even knew of one church where the pastor refused to serve the Lord's Supper, because he felt that no one in the church was worthy! I would point out that the word is an adverb, describing actions, not an adjective describing people. It says not one word about the worthiness or unworthiness of the person partaking of the Supper, just of the worthiness or unworthiness of the *way* they were partaking of the Supper. The NIV 84 brings this out admirably as it translates verse 27 *"whoever eats the bread or drinks the cup of the Lord in an unworthy manner..."* If you are a child of God, born again by faith in Christ, you are always welcome at your Father's table. But you are to observe proper table manners, toward your fellow believers and toward the meal itself, coming to the table in a spirit of self-examination. If in that time of self-examination the Spirit points out some deficiency in your walk with Christ or some unconfessed sin, it is not for the purpose of excluding you from the Table, but for the purpose of drawing you back to the Father's heart and fellowship with Him.

PRAYER: The early church applied the Greek word *eucharisto* to the Lord's Supper, a word that means "thanksgiving." Spend some time in thanksgiving about all that the Lord's Supper symbolizes: the broken body and shed blood of our Lord on the cross, the common experience of salvation that brings believers together as God's family, and the promise of Jesus' future coming.

Q & A ON SPIRITUAL GIFTS
I CORINTHIANS 12

Apparently, one of the reasons the Corinthians were divided was a lack of understanding of spiritual gifts. Rather that honoring Paul, Peter and Apollos for the different gifts that they brought to the church, some wanted Apollos to be more like Peter, Peter to be more like Paul, Paul to be more like Apollos, etc. That same division seems to have been present among the members of the church, as those who had certain gifts looked down on those who had other gifts, rather than honoring all of the gifts as being from God. Let's look at some questions and answers about spiritual gifts in this passage.

WHO RECEIVES SPIRITUAL GIFTS? All of God's children receive spiritual gifts. Verse 7 (NIV 84) says that *"to each one* *the manifestation of the Spirit is given."* Some of God's children may have gifts that seem to be more prominent, or that get more attention or praise, but all of God's children are gifted, and all of those gifts are needed and important to the functioning of the body of Christ.

WHAT ARE SPIRITUAL GIFTS? Spiritual gifts are supernatural empowerments given to Christians to enable them to minister effectively in edifying believers and evangelizing the lost. Spiritual gifts are the means by which believers grow, worship, witness and serve.

WHEN DO WE RECEIVE SPIRITUAL GIFTS? The Holy Spirit enters a Christian's life at the moment he receives Christ as his Lord and Savior, and He brings with Him all of the gifts that He knows that new Christian is going to need for a lifetime of service to Him. It may take years for that believer to discover and completely unwrap those gifts, but as he walks with the Holy Spirit and serves the Lord, he will become more and more aware that there are areas where God especially blesses his service with both effectiveness and delight.

WHERE DO WE EXERCISE SPIRITUAL GIFTS? Verse 14 and the verses that follow tell us: we exercise those gifts in the body of Christ. Verse 7 says that whatever gift we have, it is to be used for the common good of the whole body. Just as it takes all of our body parts working together for our bodies to function to their full potential, so too it takes all of the members of the church, functioning in accord with their spiritual gifts, for the church to function to its potential.

HOW DO WE DISCOVER OUR SPIRITUAL GIFTS? 1) Learn about the gifts. 2) Reflect on what kinds of service create maximum joy in you, and result in maximum effectiveness through you. 3) Pray for God to reveal to you what your gifts might be. 4) Spiritual gifts inventories can be helpful in discovering one's gifts. CHURCHGROWTH.ORG offers an excellent and free spiritual gifts analysis.

PRAYER: Pray that God would help you to discover your gifts and how you can be more diligent in using them for the edification of believers and the evangelization of the lost.

A MORE EXCELLENT WAY
I CORINTHIANS 13

Right in the midst of Paul's discussion of spiritual gifts, he stops to show the Corinthians *"a more excellent way"* (12:31), far more excellent than bickering over favorite preachers, or walking in sexual immorality, or taking one another to court, or being prideful over spiritual gifts. That more excellent way is the way of *agape'* love, God's supernatural love that flows into us and out of us through the ministry of the Holy Spirit. *Agape'* love is deeper than the love between friends, family or romantic interests. It is a selfless love that always wants and only does the best for the other person, even at great personal sacrifice, and it is absolutely necessary in the practice of spiritual gifts, which become useless (and sometimes even dangerous) without it (vv. 1-3). What are the characteristics of this love? It is patient and kind, not envious, prideful, rude, self-seeking, easily provoked or obsessed with holding grudges. Its delight is not in evil, but in truth. It is a love that protects, trusts, hopes and perseveres. Obviously, then, lack of love is marked by just the opposite: impatience, harshness, envy, pride, rudeness, selfishness, short temperedness, unforgiveness, and a delight over evil rather than truth (the driving force of gossip). If love protects, lack of love rejects. If love trusts, lack of love is suspicious. If love hopes for the best in others, lack of love expects and suspects the worst in others. If love perseveres, lack of love gives up. Our spiritual gifts may fail (v. 8), because our knowledge is partial and limited (v. 9), but love doesn't fail. The Corinthians were bickering, boasting and seeking pleasure like immature children. They would know they had come to maturity when they were walking in God's *agape'* love (v. 11).

PRAYER: As you examine your life in light of the characteristics of love (and lack of love) illustrated in this chapter, are you walking in maturity or immaturity? Pray that you might *"put away childish things"* (v. 11) and walk in the way of love.

DECENTLY AND IN ORDER
I CORINTHIANS 14

Not only was the Corinthian church confused about doctrinal and ethical matters, their corporate meetings had degenerated into chaos: *"When you come together, every one of you has a psalm, a teaching, a tongue, a revelation and an interpretation"* (v. 26), apparently each one trying to top the others in their zeal to display their spiritual gifts (v. 12). Paul calls them to a different motivation: not self-exaltation, but the edification (building up) of the body as a whole. Of particular concern to Paul was the indiscriminate use of the gift of tongues. Again, apparently each of them was trying to outdo the others (we can imagine in both length and volume) in displaying "their" tongue, and the result was a cacophony of noise in which believers were not edified (vv. 5, 11-12, 17) and unbelievers who happened into the meeting would think the Christians insane (v. 23). In order to correct the abuse of tongues in the church, Paul does not throw the baby out with the bathwater and forbid tongues-speaking altogether (v. 39). He states that he speaks in tongues more than any of them (v. 18), and shows that while tongues has benefit for personal edification (v. 4) and personal worship

(v. 15), it is of limited usefulness in the public gathering of the church (v. 19). Therefore, he places several limits on its use in the public assembly. First, he insists that prophecy, the proclamation of a word from God in the vernacular of the congregation, should take precedence over tongues-speaking (vv. 1-4). Such proclamation both edifies the saints (v. 4) and brings conviction to the lost (vv. 24-25). Second, he insists that any public display of tongues must be accompanied by interpretation, in which case it functions as a prophecy and brings edification (v. 5). Third, he says that tongues-speaking is not a necessary part of the service, but if it does take place, there should be no more than three instances of it, one at a time, with each message in tongues interpreted (v. 27). If at any point, there is no interpretation, public tongues-speaking should cease (v. 28). While tongues-speaking is seen as optional (v. 27a - *"If anyone speaks in a tongue..."*), prophecy is not (v. 29 - *"Let two or three prophets speak..."*). Following these guidelines would allow all things to be done decently and in order (v. 40).

PRAYER: In what ways might a desire for self-exaltation ("Look at me! Look at me!" - a sign of immaturity) manifest in the modern church? In what ways can believers seek to build up others? There's certainly nothing wrong with building yourself up; after all, you're reading this devotional out of just that desire, but pray for a heart that seeks not only your own edification, but the building up of others as well.

RESURRECTIONS
I CORINTHIANS 15

In chapter 15, Paul reiterates the gospel message: *"that Christ died for our sins according to the Scriptures, was buried, rose again the third day according to the Scriptures, and was seen..."* (vv. 3-5a). The fact of Christ's resurrection is an essential part of the gospel in that it guarantees our own future resurrection, but some in Corinth, perhaps influenced by Greek philosophy (v. 33), were denying any resurrection of the dead (v. 12). Paul argues that such a teaching would not only deny any future resurrection, but would also deny Christ's resurrection as well (v. 13). If Christ has not risen, Paul says, the result would be that the gospel was false (v. 14), Paul and other preachers of the gospel were false witnesses (v. 15), believers were clinging to a false hope of salvation when in fact they were still lost in their sins (v. 17), those who had died in Christ had perished (v. 18), and our labors for the Lord are a waste of our short lives (v. 32). What a miserable state of affairs that would be (v. 19)! We might as well *"eat and drink, for tomorrow we die"* (v. 32). But, Paul insists, Christ *has* risen from the dead, and the result of that is that we can have faith in our own coming resurrection (v. 20) and our salvation from sin (vv. 21-22). Death will be conquered in our own lives (v. 23), and eventually done away with altogether (vv. 24-26). All of this happens at Christ's coming, when we will be either resurrected (if we have died) or gloriously changed (if we are living) (vv. 50-52). This will be Christ's final triumph and ultimate victory over the last enemy, death (vv. 26, 54-57). In light of that coming victory, we should be *"steadfast, unmovable, always abounding in the work of the Lord, knowing that <our> labor in the Lord is not in vain"* (v. 58).

PRAYER: Thank the Lord today for the assurance of the resurrection, the hope of Christ's coming, and the encouragement that future hope gives for holy living in the here and now.

FINAL MATTERS
I CORINTHIANS 16

It is interesting that after his most lofty theological chapter of the letter, in which he has soared to realms of Christ's (and our) future glory, Paul comes back down to Earth, so to speak, with this final chapter, dealing with mundane issues like organizing an offering (vv. 1-4), travel agendas (vv. 5-9), uncertain plans (v. 10), and scheduling conflicts (v. 12). That is the stuff of life on planet Earth, the sometimes aggravating and frustrating process of getting things done, but we can glean from this chapter some words of wisdom for navigating life on this fallen planet. 1) Be generous (v. 2), but give where there is accountability (vv. 3-4). Paul was organizing an offering for the famine-stricken saints in Jerusalem, but he would not take it to Jerusalem himself, at least not alone, lest anyone accuse him of stealing it. Those who gave the money would choose their own trusted representatives to take it to Jerusalem. Be wise in how you give. 2) Look for open doors of opportunity, and do not be discouraged by adversaries (v. 9). Adversaries are sure to come. Satan only sends his soldiers where his kingdom is being threatened. Their very presence is a sign that great and effective doors are opening. 3) Don't let disagreements destroy relationships (v. 12). Paul says that he greatly wanted Apollos to come to them, but Apollos was unwilling to go at that time. Despite this disagreement, Paul still speaks of him lovingly as *"our brother."* 4) Be steadfast, bold and strong in the Lord and in the hope of His coming (v. 13). Yes, this life can be frustrating and difficult. But this life is not all there is! And God promises that *"according to your days, so shall be your strength"* (Deuteronomy 33:25). He gives us strength adequate for whatever the day holds. 5) Do all things out of a heart of love (v. 15). 6) Express gratitude freely (vv. 15-18). 7) Stay in contact with and fellowship with other believers in the body of Christ (vv. 19-20).

PRAYER: Use the seven points above as a checklist to examine your "navigational skills." Pray about any areas of weakness you see.

II CORINTHIANS

COMFORTED TO COMFORT
II CORINTHIANS 1

Most scholars agree that II Corinthians was written about a year after I Corinthians. While I Corinthians no doubt cleared up many of the difficulties at Corinth, it by no means completely solved the problems there. There were some in the church who completely rejected Paul's authority as an apostle and thus rejected his letter, false apostles who were undermining the faith of the saints there. Those false apostles were continuing to undermine Paul's authority, using something as innocent as a change in his travel plans to proclaim him untrustworthy, someone who spoke out of both sides of his mouth, saying one thing and doing another (vv. 15-20). In the year between the two letters, Paul himself had made a visit to the church, a visit he describes as *"painful"* (2:1, NIV 84), he had written a severe letter (7:8) that has not been preserved as Scripture, and he had sent Titus as his envoy to the church. Titus had reported to him that the situation was improving at the church at Corinth, although there were still adversaries and difficulties to be addressed. Before addressing those issues, Paul expresses his thanksgiving and relief over the good news he had received from Corinth. In doing so, he leaves us with a powerful principle: that we are comforted in order that we might become comforters. God *"comforts us in all our tribulation, that we may be able to comfort those who are in any trouble by the comfort with which we ourselves are comforted by God"* (v. 4). Whatever difficulties, heartaches and opposition we may face, God is using them to mold us into instruments he can use to guide others through the same kinds of heartaches and hurts. Once we have received His healing, we become conduits of His healing in the lives of others, particularly in the areas of our hurt. It is a great comfort when someone can truthfully say, "I know how it feels. I've been there." I saw this play out years ago when a friend of my son, then 14, had died suddenly and unexpectedly of a heart ailment. While I was able to offer some comfort to the grieving mother as a pastor, her greatest comfort came from another mother who had earlier lost a child unexpectedly. They shared a bond of shared hurt and shared suffering, but the testimony and example of that first mother was that healing was possible, and healing would come.

PRAYER: In what areas of your life has God brought you through difficulty, suffering, pain and heartache? Pray that you and your story might be used as a healing balm in the lives of others.

FORGIVENESS AND RESTORATION
II CORINTHIANS 2

In chapter two, Paul explains the reason for his change of travel plans. His earlier sorrowful visit had crushed him (vv. 1-2). He was heartbroken over the unresolved situation at Corinth, and he did not want to make another difficult visit there. He sent a letter instead, carried by Titus (vv. 3-4). Paul goes on to address the situation of a man in the church who had been disciplined by the church, apparently at

Paul's insistence. While some scholars believe this offender was the man mentioned in I Corinthians 5:1 who was sexually involved with his father's wife, others believe that this was a different person altogether, someone who had opposed Paul during his visit there, perhaps the person primarily responsible for making the visit so painful. The speculation is that Paul's severe letter had been a demand for the church to deal with this person for his attack on Paul and his apostolic authority, a demand that would reveal whether they were standing with Paul or with his adversaries (v. 9). While we have no way of knowing for sure, the state of affairs that Paul addresses here does seem to be something more personal than the situation addressed in I Corinthians 5, something requiring personal forgiveness on his part. The church had stood with Paul and had disciplined the offender, and the discipline had done its work and had brought the offender to repentance. Now, Paul tells them, they *"ought to forgive him and comfort him, lest perhaps he might be swallowed up with excessive sorrow"* (v. 7). Perhaps they were being overly harsh with the man, refusing to lift his discipline even in the face of repentance, out of concern that Paul would not be satisfied with how they had handled the situation. Paul assures them that what they had done was sufficient (v. 6), that his desire had been for the man's repentance, not for ongoing punishment, and that he had already forgiven the offense (vv. 10-11). Note carefully verses 10b-11: *"...for your sakes I forgave it in Christ, lest Satan take advantage of us. For we are not ignorant of his devices."* One of Satan's *"devices"* (a word that means "schemes, plots, battle plans or strategies") against us is to sow lack of forgiveness in our midst. Had Paul refused to forgive this offense, it would have given Satan a foothold of bitterness in Paul's life, which would have then impacted all those he was called to minister to (see Hebrews 12:15). Paul *"forgave it in Christ,"* and in the same way we must forgive. In light of how much Christ has forgiven us, how can we refuse to forgive others? We must recognize that every sin against us was also a sin against Him. If we forgive, we bring joy to His heart that has been grieved by the sin. If we carry a grudge, we heap yet another hurt, and an ongoing one at that, upon Him.

PRAYER: Is there any person in your life you are refusing to forgive, or perhaps someone who, despite their repentance, you're refusing to be reconciled to? Ask forgiveness for holding that grudge, and for thus grieving your Father's heart.

LETTERS
II CORINTHIANS 3

Reading Paul's letters is often like listening to one end of a telephone conversation and trying to reconstruct from it what the other person is saying. In the case of chapter 3, we can extrapolate from Paul's words some of the accusations being leveled against him by those who opposed him at Corinth. His first question in verse 1, *"Do we begin again to commend ourselves?"* probably indicates that some were accusing him of arrogance, of shameless self-promotion in exercising his office of apostle. The second question, *"Or do we need, as some others, letters of commendation to you, or letters of commendation from you?"* suggests that the false teachers who had infiltrated the church had come carrying letters of recommendation, perhaps forgeries claiming to be from the apostles in Jerusalem, or, as other scholars suggest, unauthorized letters from the Pharisaic, legalistic segment of the church at Jerusalem. "Where are Paul's letters of recommendation?" they may have sneered. Paul's response was that he needed no such letters, certainly not among the Corinthians. How could they require such a letter when *they* were his letter, written through his ministry among them by the Spirit of God (v. 3)? It was he who had brought the gospel to Corinth and founded the church, he who had led many of them to the Lord personally, he whose ministry had been approved by God's working through him among them (vv. 4-6). Was that not sufficient to establish his credentials as an apostle? The fact that he moves from there to discussing the old covenant and the new covenant suggests that at least some of his opponents at Corinth were legalists, those who insisted upon continued adherence to the Old Testament Law in such matters as dietary choices and circumcision. Paul does not deny the glory of the old covenant, but he insists that its glory was temporary, like the glow that came to Moses' face when he had been in the presence of the Lord that then faded over time. Paul gives an interesting application to Moses' veiling of his face after he had been in the Lord's presence. It was not only to keep the dazzling nature of the glow from frightening the Israelites, but also to spare them the disappointment of seeing it fade (v. 13). That same veil, he says, was over the faces of those who were clinging to the old covenant, preventing them from seeing that its glory had faded (vv. 14-15), replaced by a new and more glorious covenant (vv. 7-11). The glory of the new covenant will never fade (v. 11); indeed, it continues on to greater and greater levels of glory in our lives (v. 18). It is a covenant not of condemnation (v. 9), but of salvation, a covenant not of bondage to rules and regulations (v. 6), but of life and freedom in the Spirit (v. 17).

PRAYER: Pray that your life might be a living letter, written by the Spirit of God in your heart, a letter that commends Christ to others.

TREASURES IN EARTHEN VESSELS
II CORINTHIANS 4

Far from being the arrogant self-promoter his opponents accused him of being, Paul insists that *"We do not preach ourselves, but Christ Jesus the Lord, and ourselves as servants for Jesus' sake"* (v. 5). There was nothing about Paul that brought people into the Kingdom; it was, rather, that *"God, who commanded the light to shine out of darkness, has shone in our hearts to give the light of the knowledge of the glory of God in the face of Jesus Christ"* (v. 6). Paul was a carrier of the glorious message of the gospel, but the glory was in the gospel, not in the carrier. The image he uses to illustrate this truth is of a treasure being carried in old clay pots (v. 7). The value is in what is contained in the pots, not in the pots themselves. No matter how battered, weathered, and worn the clay pots might get, the treasure inside of them loses none of its value (vv. 8-15). Paul has endured many hardships in carrying that treasure, but he recognizes that he has a supernatural empowerment for doing so (v. 16), and he knows that there is great reward in eternity for his sufferings for the gospel in the here and now (v. 17). By keeping his eyes on the eternal, rather than the temporal, he is able to testify that *"We are troubled on every side, yet not distressed; we are perplexed, but not in despair; persecuted, but not forsaken; cast down, but not destroyed"* (vv. 8-9).

PRAYER: Do you feel like a worn-out clay pot today? Are you troubled, perplexed, persecuted or cast down? You need not be distressed, despairing or destroyed, for in Christ, you will never be forsaken! Pray today for His supernatural empowerment to bring renewal to your spirit, and fix your eyes upon the life and the reward to come.

TAKING DOWN THE TENT, AND GOING HOME
II CORINTHIANS 5

The Bible tells us that Paul supported himself and his ministry through the trade of tent-making, so he knew some things about tents. Here in II Corinthians 5, he speaks of our bodies as tents, using that image to teach us about life and about the life to come. What is it about tents that make them an appropriate metaphor for these earthly bodies of ours? First, tents are usually temporary lodging. Very few are those who live out their entire lives in a tent, and most of those who live in tents are certainly desirous of better, more permanent lodging. Second, no matter how well-made a tent might be, it will eventually wear out. It can be patched for awhile, but eventually it will become so threadbare that it can no longer serve as adequate protection against the elements. Third, tents are easily damaged, far more easily than a house would be. Finally, tents are uncomfortable. Even the most luxurious of tents is still a tent, and even the most modest of houses affords greater protection from the elements than the most expensive of tents. So it is with our bodies. Our earthly bodies are but temporary lodging for our souls. They are fragile. They are easily injured. They wear out. And the longer we remain in them, the more uncomfortable they become. Thankfully, we have the assurance that this life is not all there is. Verse 1 promises us that *"if our earthly house, this tent, were to be destroyed, we have an eternal building of God in the heavens, a house not made with hands."* What is our guarantee of this great promise? How do we know that this life is not all there is, and that when it ends, our souls go on to a much better existence? We know because of the guarantee of the Holy Spirit (v. 5). Paul tells us that God has given us the Spirit as a guarantee, a pledge, a down-payment, of our final inheritance. The presence of the Holy Spirit in our lives, leading us, guiding us, empowering us, and cultivating in us the fruit of Christian character, assures us of our final redemption. It is He who assures us, even when facing our own death or the death of a loved one, that to be absent from the body is to be present with the Lord (v. 8). In the meantime, we who have the hope of eternal life through Christ have the assignment of bringing others into that same hope: God *"has reconciled us to Himself through Jesus Christ and has given us the ministry of reconciliation"* (v. 18). That ministry of reconciliation is to announce that because of Christ's sacrifice for our sins (v. 21), nothing prevents God from being reconciled to us except our unwillingness to be reconciled to Him (vv. 19-20). Therefore, we urge the lost to receive Him, to receive His gift of forgiveness and eternal life, knowing that when this life is done, we will give an account to our Lord for how well we've fulfilled this ministry (v. 10).

PRAYER: Can you feel the sides of your tent growing thin? Thank the Lord that you have an eternal life with Him when this life is done. When you stand before Him, will you be rewarded or ashamed at how you have discharged the ministry of reconciliation entrusted to you? Pray that you might be diligent in bringing others to Him.

THE UNEQUAL YOKE
II CORINTHIANS 6

"Do not be unequally yoked together with unbelievers" (v. 14) - an image thoroughly familiar to Paul's first readers, but to us, not so much. Yoking refers to attaching two animals, usually two oxen, together to pull a plow or wagon. The two animals would be joined by a wooden yoke that went around their necks and across their shoulders, and they needed to be roughly the same size, because if there was a great disparity in their sizes, the yoke would fit crooked, and it would chafe the shoulder bone of one of the animals, eventually crippling it. Similarly, in a yoking of a believer and an unbeliever, one of them will be "crippled," and it will invariably be the Christian. This passage is often applied to the situation of a believer knowingly marrying an unbeliever, and while that is an appropriate application, this principle is not limited to marriage. It has reference to any close, equal partnership between a believer and an unbeliever, such as two people going into business together.

The great historian Arnold Toynbee once spoke about the relationship of a man and a dog. A man and a dog, he said, can have a good relationship. They can have true affection for one another. They can genuinely enjoy each other's company and have fun together. But, he said, the relationship will always take place on the level of the dog, because that's the best the dog can do. While the dog is capable of chasing a ball or other such games, he is hardly capable of giving the man advice, engaging him in deep philosophical discussions, or speaking words of encouragement to him. The same principle is at play in a relationship between a believer and an unbeliever. (Please do NOT think I am comparing unbelievers to dogs! It is a *principle* we're speaking of, not a direct correlation!) A believer and an unbeliever can have a good relationship, but it will always take place on the level of the unbeliever, and thus when a believer is yoked together with an unbeliever, there will be a crippling effect on him. In a marriage, the believer will be limited, to a lesser or greater extent, in his ability to serve the Lord and raise the children in the nurture and admonition of the Lord. He will be partnered with a spouse who cannot share or even fully understand his interest in spiritual things. In a business situation, the believer will be hindered from running the business according to Christian standards and as a Christian witness to employees, vendors and customers. Does this mean that Christians must break off all relationships with unbelievers? No, it just means that we are to avoid "yoking" ourselves knowingly with unbelievers. Biblical separation is an often misunderstood concept. *"Come out from among them and be separate, says the Lord"* (v. 17) does not call us to *isolation* from the world, but *insulation* from the world. If we isolate ourselves from the world, cutting ourselves off from all unbelievers, we won't be able to influence them toward Christ. But we must make sure that the influence only flows one way, that we don't allow unbelievers to take us away from our commitment to Christ. As Christians, we are called to a high standard, and we must not link ourselves to anything or anyone who would pull us away from that high standard.

PRAYER: If you are in an unequally yoked situation of any kind, pray for wisdom to know how to influence the unbelieving partner, and for how to keep their influence on you to a minimum. Pray for wisdom today in how to remain insulated from the world while not being isolated from the world.

GODLY SORROW
II CORINTHIANS 7

To understand chapter 7, we must again remind ourselves of the interactions between Paul and the church at Corinth. After his first letter (I Corinthians) had failed to straighten out all of the problems there, Paul had gone to Corinth personally, hoping to put things in order. A vicious attack against him had made that visit a painful one, and he had left Corinth with things still unresolved. His next interaction with them was by letter, a letter that has not been preserved, apparently calling for the church to deal with the person who had so attacked him. It would seem to have been an ultimatum demanding this person be appropriately disciplined. Paul's purpose in writing that letter was not out of a desire for vengeance on his adversary or to receive personal vindication from seeing him punished, but out of love for the Corinthian church (v. 12). If the church chose to follow this person who had so brashly attacked him, they would be rejecting Paul and his apostolic authority and following this person into apostasy. After Titus took the letter, Paul was waiting anxiously to hear about their response (v. 5), and he was comforted when Titus brought the news that the Corinthians had made the right choice and sided with Paul. Paul had regretted sending the letter, not wanting to cause them sorrow (it must have been some letter!), but he no longer regretted sending it, because it had led the Corinthians to repentance (vv. 8-9). Paul goes on to contrast *"godly sorrow"* with *"the sorrow of the world"* (v. 10). Godly sorrow leads to true repentance, marked by *"what earnestness, what eagerness to clear yourselves, what indignation, what alarm, what longing, what concern, what readiness to see justice done"* (v. 11, NIV 84). True repentance results in a fervent desire to make things right at all costs. Worldly sorrow, Paul says, leads to death (v. 10), but he gives no further details. However, we can extrapolate from godly sorrow the contrast of worldly sorrow. Worldly sorrow is not regret for the wrong itself, but merely regret over its consequences. Rather than leading to repentance, it leads to resentment and rejection of the one who has pointed out the sin (which was Paul's fear in confronting the Corinthians with his letter). For from creating a desire to make things right and be reconciled, it leads to a stubborn refusal to admit wrongdoing, and thus to the death of fellowship with God and with others.

PRAYER: Pray that whenever you're confronted with sin, whether through the ministry of the Word, the Spirit or a Christian brother or sister, you might respond with godly sorrow leading to true repentance. Pray that pride would never lead you to defensiveness and rebellion. Is there any area of wrongdoing in your life that still remains unsettled? Confess that sin to God (I John 1:9) and pray about what steps you can take to make things right.

GIVE LIKE A MACEDONIAN
II CORINTHIANS 8

Paul commends the churches in Macedonia in chapter 8 for their amazing generosity in giving to the relief of the famine-stricken believers in and around Jerusalem. In verses 2-4, Paul says that the Macedonian churches were mired in deep poverty, yet their circumstances did not hinder them from giving. Indeed, they gave joyfully, generously and enthusiastically, above and beyond what anyone would have expected. The Corinthians had originally pledged to give, but then they had allowed circumstances to distract them from their commitment to give. The Bible teaches that the bare minimum that a Christian should be giving to the work of the Lord is the tithe, or 10% of his income. That's the beginning point, not the ending point, but most American Christians are totally ignoring that Biblical mandate. It has been estimated that if every American Christian were reduced to the poverty level, and then tithed on that, overall giving to the Lord's work would more than double. Tithing is never spoken of in the Bible as a request; it is always a command. God does not say to give when it is convenient, or when the mood strikes us, or when the economy is strong; He says to give, period. Make giving an absolute commitment, something you're determined to stick with no matter what happens. The Macedonians also gave in the context of their overall commitment to the Lord (vv. 5-7). They gave their money, but first they gave themselves to God. They surrendered their lives to Christ and were living daily under the Lordship of Christ, seeking to know and do the will of God in all things. Their giving wasn't separate from that commitment; rather, it just flowed naturally as one part of that overall commitment. It is also important to note that they gave with an attitude of gratitude (v. 9). Verse 9 speaks of how Jesus gave up the glories of heaven, taking on humanity and going to the cross for us, that through His poverty and affliction, we might be made spiritually rich - saved by His blood, blessed by God and eventually elevated to the glories of heaven. In light of what Christ has done for us, how could we fail to give cheerfully and generously to His work?

PRAYER: Are you giving generously to the work of the Lord as one part of your overall commitment to Him and as an expression of your thanksgiving to Him for all of His blessings? Pray that your giving might be acceptable to Him, and that you might grow in your generosity.

SOWING AND REAPING
II CORINTHIANS 9

It is a universal law that planting small amounts of seed leads to small harvests, whereas planting large amounts of seed leads to large harvests (v. 6). Paul encourages the Corinthians to sow generously, to give not grudgingly but cheerfully to the offering whatever the Lord had placed on their hearts to give (v. 7). We can give generously and cheerfully to the Lord's work, knowing that our giving to Him always brings harvests. In the Father's economy, there are no crop failures. We've all heard the charlatans who preach on giving as if it were an automatic financial investment, a windfall just waiting to happen: "Give $50 today, and God will give you $5000 tomorrow!" Paul is not teaching that giving is a "get rich quick" strategy, but he is promising that God will both meet our needs (not our greeds) and give us the ability to give: *"so that you, always having enough of everything, may abound to every good work"* (v. 9). The harvest we receive may come in the form of financial blessings so that we can give even more (v. 10a), but the specific harvests promised are that He will multiply our seed, empowering our gifts to accomplish much more than we could imagine (v. 10b); He will *"increase the fruits of <our> righteousness"* (v. 10c); and He will inspire prayers from others for us and thanksgiving and praise for Himself (vv. 12-14). Increasing His worship through our giving and through the thanksgiving of others blessed through our giving should be of far greater importance to us than the bottom line of our bank balances. God is worthy of all praise, glory and honor for His *"indescribable gift"* of Jesus (v. 15). How can we give grudgingly when He freely gave His very best for us?

PRAYER: Pray in thanksgiving today for God's supplying of your needs, and also for His supply of seed for you to sow in generous giving. Pray that you might never be disobedient in the matter of giving, and that you might give cheerfully and not grudgingly. Thank Him for all the ways you can think of that others' giving has blessed you, and thank Him especially for those who gave so that you might hear the gospel.

PAUL AND THE FALSE APOSTLES
II CORINTHIANS 10

Among the accusations hurled at Paul by his critics at Corinth was that he was bold when writing letters, but weak and unimpressive in person. In this chapter, he turns the tables. He appeals to them here (as opposed to his earlier painful letter) *"by the meekness and gentleness of Christ"* (v. 1), calmly urging them to do the right thing by ridding themselves once and for all of the false teachers among them. But, he threatens, if they do not rectify the problems at Corinth, when he comes to them again, his opponents will see the boldness displayed in his letters live and in person (vv. 2, 11)! His opponents had leveled all kinds of scandalous, unfair, and hurtful criticisms and accusations against him. They had attacked his character, accusing him of walking according to the flesh (v. 2). They had accused him of arrogance in his assertion of apostolic authority (v. 8), and had even insulted his appearance and his preaching, declaring that *"his bodily presence is weak, and his speech contemptible"* (v. 10). Paul will not stoop to such carnal insults and scandalous accusations. He does not wage war in the fleshly manner of his opponents, but recognizes that *"the weapons of our warfare are not carnal, but mighty through God to the pulling down of strongholds, casting down imaginations and every high thing that exalts itself against the knowledge of God, bringing every thought into captivity to the obedience of Christ"* (vv. 3-4). What are Paul's weapons? While his opponents relied upon lies, innuendos, false boasting and insults, Paul's weapons were the Word of God, prayer, the power of the Holy Spirit, the truth, and God-given authority. Even if they accuse him of arrogance in his claim to be an apostle, the truth is he *is* an apostle (v. 8), with a God-given assignment (v. 13) to take the gospel to new places (v. 16), just as he had brought the gospel to them (v. 14). Standing in that authority to defend them against those who would pervert the gospel is not arrogance, because he is not boasting in himself, but in what God has done (v. 17). With these divinely inspired weapons, and in his divinely appointed authority, Paul is confident he will win the battle for the hearts and minds of the Corinthians.

PRAYER: Are you facing unfair criticisms, unjust accusations, and/or personal insults today? Pray that you might not respond in a fleshly manner, returning insult for insult and unkindness for unkindness, but instead with the mighty weapons available from God. Pray not simply that your opponent may be defeated, but that he may be won to the truth.

THE OPPOSITION
II CORINTHIANS 11

More clues emerge in chapter 11 concerning the criticisms aimed at Paul and his ministry. Apparently, his opponents criticized his speaking ability, dismissing him as *"unpolished in speech"* (v. 6). In the ancient Roman world, trained speakers would travel from place to place, giving speeches and taking offerings afterward. Obviously, the better speakers would receive the bigger offerings. Paul had received no offerings from the Corinthians. His normal pattern was to receive offerings from established churches to take the gospel to places it had not gone before, lest some misunderstand and think that the gospel was for sale (vv. 7-9). His opponents turned even that against him, sneering that Paul took no offerings because he knew his speaking was worthless. Paul might not have been a trained rhetorician, skilled in oratory, but his preaching was according to knowledge (v. 6), proclaiming the true gospel of the true Christ in the power of the Holy Spirit (v. 4). His opponents, on the other hand, were *"false apostles and deceitful workers, disguising themselves as apostles of Christ"* (v. 13) in the manner of their master, Satan himself, who *"disguises himself as an angel of light"* (v. 14). Whereas Paul came to them in gentleness, these false apostles were abusive in their teaching and in their actions, and Paul is amazed that the Corinthians would choose to accept such treatment from them (v. 20) while rejecting him. Whereas the false apostles abused the Corinthians in the name of their false gospel, Paul was willing to be abused for the sake of the true gospel. The litany of suffering Paul catalogues in verses 23-33 makes us marvel at Paul's tenacity. A lesser man would have long since quit, but Paul was still going forward to proclaim the name of Christ despite all of the physical and emotional traumas he had endured. Could any of the false apostles lay claim to such sacrifices for Christ? Verses 28-29 are especially poignant: *"Beside the external things, the care of all the churches pressures me daily. Who is weak, and I am not weak? Who is led into sin, and I am not distressed?"* That is the heart of a true pastor, willing to endure all of the external hardships out of love of Christ and love for His people.

PRAYER: Pray that you might have the tenacity of Paul, willing to endure any hardship, any opposition, and any criticism to fulfill God's call on your life. How has Satan come to you as an angel of light in your life? Pray for discernment always to be able to see through his clever disguises.

VISIONS AND THORNS
II CORINTHIANS 12

In chapter 12, Paul determines to *"move on to visions and revelations of the Lord"* (v. 1). Apparently, the false apostles at Corinth claimed such experiences, whether they had actually had them or not, in order to bolster their authority. Paul had actually experienced visions and revelations from God, but had remained silent about them. His silence on the subject gave his detractors one more point of ammunition against him to claim their superiority: "Paul never spoke about the kind of visions and revelations we've had, did he?" Why had Paul not spoken of this experience for 14 years, and why is he so reluctant and embarrassed to do so now, even to the point of referencing himself in the third person? Undoubtedly, this vision had been for him alone, and what he heard in the third heaven consisted of *"inexpressible words not permitted for a man to say"* (v. 4, see also Revelation 10:4). To speak of this vision, then, would have done nothing to edify the church; it would have served only to exalt Paul and stroke his ego. He is reluctant to speak of it even now (v. 6), but feels compelled to do so in order to protect the Corinthians from the false apostles (vv. 11-12). Paul had apparently been tempted toward pride because of the revelations given to him, but, he says, *"a thorn was given me in the flesh, a messenger of Satan, to torment me, lest I be exalted above measure"* (v. 7). We don't know what Paul's thorn was, and any number of speculative theories have been set forth about it. It really doesn't matter. What's important is the result of the thorn. Three times, Paul begged the Lord to take this painful affliction away, and three times He refused. Finally, He said to Paul, *"My grace is sufficient for you, for My strength is made perfect in weakness"* (v. 9). Paul's true strength was not to be found in incredible visions or in the abundance of the revelations he had been given. His true strength was found in total dependence on Christ and His grace. That grace would be his lifelong message, not boasting about his spiritual experiences, but boasting in the saving and sustaining power of Christ (vv. 9-10).

PRAYER: Have you ever been tempted to become prideful in your service for the Lord? Pray that you might never succumb to that kind of pride. Are you suffering some affliction? Ask that Christ's strength might be made perfect in your weakness.

EXAMINE YOURSELVES!
II CORINTHIANS 13

It's time for the Corinthians to make up their minds once and for all and stop wavering between Paul and the false apostles. When he comes to Corinth, he hopes that they will have completely disposed of the false apostles, and that they will be living in the harmony and joy described in verses 11-14. Such peace would never be possible until they completely rejected the falsehood and wholeheartedly embraced the truth. To reject Paul would be to reject the gospel he had preached to them. To embrace the false gospel of the false apostles would indicate that they had never truly embraced the true gospel, and therefore, he encourages them to *"Examine yourselves, seeing whether you are in the faith; test yourselves"* (v. 5). It's a good assignment for all of us. Many who are church members, claiming to be born again, are in fact lost, trusting in all of the wrong things to get them to heaven (Matthew 7:21-23). Imagine you were standing before God right now, and He asked you, "Why should I let you into heaven?" What would you say? If your answer concerns your family background, your church membership, your baptism, your partaking of the Lord's Supper, or some good works done in His name, friend, you're lost. Entry into heaven is not about what we've done for Him, but about what He has done for us in Christ. Christ's death on the cross, and our reception of that sacrifice by repentant faith in Him as our Lord and Savior - that's what gets us into heaven, not anything we've done. Examine yourself. Is your faith in Christ and Christ alone for salvation?

PRAYER: Which set of verses best describes your church: 12:20-21, or 13:11-14? Pray that your church might never be marked by the former, but would be a shining example of the latter.

GALATIANS

DISTURBING THE PEACE
GALATIANS 1

"Grace to you and peace from God our Father and the Lord Jesus Christ" (v. 3). Peace - both peace with God and peace from God - comes through grace, saving grace and sustaining grace. But there were those in the churches of Galatia who were disturbing the peace by preaching a gospel not of grace, but a gospel perverted by law. These so-called Judaizers were Jews who believed in Jesus as the Messiah, but who insisted that Gentiles coming into the faith were required to abide by certain Old Testament ceremonies and rites, in particular the rite of circumcision. Their argument was that since Jesus was the Jewish Messiah, Gentiles essentially had to become converts to Judaism in order to become Christians. These false teachers tended to follow Paul around, going into the churches he founded after his departure and confusing the young Christians' understanding of the gospel with their false gospel. Paul's argument, both here and elsewhere, was that Gentiles could come to Christ directly through repentance and faith in Him; Jewish law and rituals were not required. The Judaizers (falsely) claimed that they came as representatives of the

true faith, that their message had been taught to them by the original apostles of Jesus in Jerusalem, and that Paul was a false apostle whose message of grace was a perversion. Paul maintains that he was an apostle not because of any human appointment, but by God's divine call (v. 1), and the gospel he had preached to them had not been taught to him by any human teacher, but by divine revelation (vv. 11-12). It *must* have been a divine message, because it was so radically different from what we would expect from Paul, given his background. Before his conversion, Paul had, according to his testimony, *"progressed in Judaism above many of my equals in my own heritage, being more exceedingly zealous for the traditions of my fathers"* (v. 14), so zealous in fact that he *"persecuted the church of God beyond measure and tried to destroy it"* (v. 13). We would expect him, with that history, to have been a leader among the Judaizers, not opposing them, but the divine revelation of the true gospel had delivered him from the bondage of trying to achieve salvation by works. Furthermore, if Paul's gospel were contrary to that preached by the Jerusalem apostles, then surely Peter and James would have corrected him during his time in Jerusalem (vv. 18-19), and the churches in Judea would not have glorified God that Paul was preaching the faith he once tried to destroy (vv. 23-24), but would have rejected him as preaching another faith entirely. It was the Judaizers, not Paul, who were preaching a perverted gospel (v. 7), and Paul proclaims in verses 8-9 that such men are *"accursed,"* or *"eternally condemned"* (NIV 84).

PRAYER: There are those even today who seek to add ritual or good works, like baptism or the Lord's Supper or church membership, to the simple gospel of salvation by grace through faith. Pray for those who are preaching the true gospel of salvation by grace alone through faith alone in Christ alone, that many would be saved through their proclamation. Pray that those preaching a false gospel would see the light and be converted. Pray that those exposed to a false gospel would reject it, and embrace the truth instead.

HYPOCRISY AND CONFRONTATION
GALATIANS 2

Paul continues his argument from the previous chapter, showing that a second trip to Jerusalem 14 years after his initial visit with the apostles had included Titus, a Greek convert to Christ. Titus had not been circumcised, but the apostles at Jerusalem did not require it of him in order to receive him as a brother (v. 3). Furthermore, the pillars of the Jerusalem church, Peter, James and John, hearing the message that Paul preached (v. 2), affirmed him and recognized his special calling to take the gospel to the Gentiles (vv. 7-10). Far from having his message corrected by Peter, Paul had been used by God on at least one occasion to correct Peter! The situation was that Peter had come to Antioch, a church composed of both Jews and Gentiles, and he had joined in freely with the Gentiles, eating with them as brethren without any reservations. But when other Jewish believers came from Jerusalem, men who were still caught up in the old Jewish taboos against eating with Gentiles, Peter *"withdrew and separated himself, fearing those who were of the circumcision"* (v. 12), refusing to eat with the Gentiles. Given Peter's exposure to Christ's example of ministering among the Gentiles, His teaching about all foods being clean, and the vision he had received reiterating that fact and its implications for Jew-Gentile relations (Acts 10:1-28), this was an especially egregious act of hypocrisy on Peter's part. Because of his influential status in the church, the other Jews in Antioch followed his example, distancing themselves from the Gentiles. Even Barnabas, Paul's partner on the first missionary journey, was led astray. Paul recognized the potential this hypocrisy had to split the church, both the church at Antioch and the church at large, along old dividing lines of Jew and Gentile, and so he confronted Peter about it. The implication is that Peter, thus rebuked, had recognized that Paul was right and had repented of this hypocrisy. Those who claimed that Peter would support their assertion that Gentiles must live like Jews would be surprised to know that in many ways, Peter, though Jewish, lived like a Gentile (v. 14)!

PRAYER: Confrontation is an uncomfortable but necessary act of love when brothers and sisters are *"not acting in line with the truth of the gospel"* (v. 14, NIV 84), because others might also be led astray if they are not corrected. If the Lord brings someone in that situation to your mind, ask Him how He might want to use you to confront their wrongdoing and lead them to repentance.

FAITH OR WORKS?
GALATIANS 3

The false teachers who had invaded the churches of Galatia had been successful in confusing the Galatians on the issue of salvation. These Judaizers were insisting on salvation by faith plus works, that Gentile believers in Christ must live according to the Old Testament Law. Paul's message of faith in Christ, according to them, was inadequate and incomplete, only part of the equation. In answering this accusation, Paul appeals first to the Galatians' own personal experience. He invites them to think back in their lives to before the false teachers had come in and muddied the waters of their thinking. They had received the Holy Spirit merely by faith in the message of Christ crucified (vv. 1-2). If that message were in fact inadequate to save, how could they explain the coming of the Spirit into their lives on the basis of that incomplete message? They had begun growing in Christ prior to the coming of the false teachers (v. 3), and they had been willing to suffer persecution for His name's sake prior to their coming (v. 4). Did they really believe that the dramatic changes and supernatural courage in their lives had come about through an incomplete gospel? Beyond that, miracles had been performed among them, presumably by Paul and then by others in the congregation, prior to the coming of the false teachers with their so-called "complete" gospel (v. 5). Why was God doing miracles among them before the false teachers came with their supposed "true gospel" of salvation by faith plus works? Not only does Paul appeal to their experience, he appeals to the Scripture (which is always the judge of our experiences, not the other way around). He shows that Abraham was justified not by the works of the Law (which would not even come until 430 years later - v. 17), but by faith (v. 6). The Law was not given to annul this covenant given to Abraham (v. 17) and available to all people who would have his kind of faith (vv. 7-9); it was given *"because of transgressions"* (v. 19) and as a *"tutor to bring us to Christ"* (v. 24). One purpose of the Law was to curb man's sinfulness by putting legal sanctions on it. Obviously, there is less murder, for example, when there is a law against murder and a penalty for murder. The other purpose of the Law was to show us our need of a Savior. The Law reveals God's standard of acceptance, which is absolute, impeccable, sinless perfection, not even one sin committed one time: *"Cursed is everyone who does not continue in all things which are written in the Book of the Law, to do them"* (v. 10). Attempting to be saved by good works is a fruitless endeavor. Doing more good than bad, turning over a new leaf, doing better than most people - none of that will suffice. Only if a person could live in sinless perfection, never sinning even once in word, deed, motivation or attitude, could he be saved by his good works (v. 12). Because none of us can live up to that standard, we are under a curse, but Christ came to redeem us from the curse of the Law by becoming a curse for us, taking our penalty upon Himself on the cross (vv. 13-14). His payment on our behalf is not received by good works, but only by faith in Him (v. 22). The Law was not given to show us how to save ourselves, but to show us that we can't save ourselves; we must embrace Christ!

PRAYER: Thank Him today that though you fell woefully short of His standard, He was willing to take your curse upon Himself on the cross.

EXCHANGES
GALATIANS 4

Paul continues his appeal to the Galatians by speaking of several exchanges. He speaks of how Jesus, the Son of God, came, born under the Law, to redeem those under the Law so that they might become sons of God (vv. 4-5). We were like slaves trying to obey the master's rules and failing miserably; Jesus came and obeyed the Law perfectly. Now, through our faith in Him, we are no longer slaves under the Law and its penalties, but we have been adopted as sons and heirs (v. 7), our hearts crying out *"Abba, Father!"* *"Abba"* is the Jewish equivalent of "Daddy." It is a term of love and endearment. The word translated *"Father"* is the Greek word *pater,* which spoke of the absolute, unquestioned authority of the father as head of the household in ancient homes. I think it is important to hold those two aspects of our relationship with God in balance. He is our King, our Master, our Lord, our absolute authority, but He is also our beloved "Daddy." Those who lean too far toward the "Father axis" tend to view God as a stern taskmaster who is never satisfied, hard to please and eager to punish (it doesn't help that many had earthly fathers who were just that way), and they spend their lives trying to gain the love and approval of a Father who already loves them unconditionally. Others lean too far toward the "Abba axis," and they view God as an indulgent father, winking at sin and unwilling to discipline it. They tend to spend their lives wallowing in sin that breaks fellowship with their Father, wounds His heart, and invites His discipline. Both extremes are a perversion of who God truly is and of the relationship He wants to have with His children. The second great exchange Paul speaks of concerns himself and the Galatians. Just as the Son of God became as one under the Law so that those under the Law might become sons, so too Paul became as the Galatians so that the Galatians might become as he is (v. 12). When Paul came to them, he was not living under the Jewish Law, but living in the manner of the Gentiles so that he might introduce them to Christ (see I Corinthians 9:19-21). Now, he pleads with them not to become as he once was by adopting the very aspects of the Jewish Ceremonial Law that he had jettisoned, but to become as he is now: free in Christ, living according to the Spirit, and not in bondage to the Law. He is grieved that they seemingly had exchanged their allegiance to him, whose only desire was to set them free, for allegiance to the Judaizers, whose great desire was to bring them into bondage (vv. 14, 17).

PRAYER: How balanced are you in your understanding of God as *"Abba, Father"*? Do you tend to lean more toward one of these aspects of God's nature than the other? Today, approach God first as Abba, expressing your love and adoration of Him, and receiving His love and affection for you. Then, approach Him as Father, expressing your total submission to His will.

WALK BY THE SPIRIT
GALATIANS 5

Paul is aware that his opponents will attack his message on salvation by grace through faith, proclaiming that it would inevitably lead toward sin and license on the part of believers. If all of our sins are already forgiven, what incentive is there for holiness? Paul addresses that objection in verse 13: *"You, brothers, have been called to liberty. Only do not use liberty to give an opportunity to the flesh."* Paul's critics maintained that there were only two options. A person would either live by the Law with its rules and regulations, or else be totally immersed in sin, completely out of control. Paul shows here that there is a third option: not *out* of control, but *under* control, the control of the Spirit: *"walk in the Spirit, and you shall not fulfill the lust of the flesh."* All of us have a battle going on inside of us, a war that rages between the flesh (the old sin nature we were born with, inherited from our parents and their parents going back to our first parents, Adam and Eve) and the Holy Spirit, who invaded our lives the day we were saved and who is moving out into all parts of our lives, bringing more and more of our lives under the Lordship of Christ (v. 17). The flesh tempts us toward sin, while the Spirit urges us toward righteousness. How do we win this battle? Think of the images Paul employs here. The flesh has been crucified (note the past tense of v. 24). A person who has been crucified is absolutely helpless, completely powerless, totally immobile and dying a slow death. That is the state of our flesh, nailed to the cross the day we received Christ. It's not dead yet, but it is growing weaker by the day, and it is utterly helpless and powerless. Its hands and feet are nailed to the cross. It cannot force us to do anything. Ultimately, all it can do is shout suggestions. The Spirit, on the other hand, is walking (vv. 16, 25). He brought us to the place of crucifying the flesh by convicting us of our sins and drawing us to Christ, but there's more to this life in Christ that just being born again. Now He is moving on from the place of crucifixion, and we are free to walk with Him into the full life Christ desires for us. When we move on with the Spirit, the flesh cannot follow, because it's been crucified, and the longer we go on with the Spirit and the farther we go from the flesh, the less audible the voice of the flesh grows over time and distance. That voice will never be completely silenced on this side of the grave, and as long as we can hear it, we can make the choice to obey it. But the longer we walk in the Spirit, the more His voice becomes the one we're most used to hearing and obeying, and our lives will be marked less and less by the works of the flesh in verses 19-21, and more and more by the fruit of the Spirit in verses 22-23. All too often, though, Christians reverse the order of verse 16. Their thinking is along these lines: "If I can just deal with the flesh, then I'll be spiritual." They identify certain fleshly habits, actions or attitudes in their lives, and throw the full weight of their willpower toward conquering them. Such a mindset leaves us at the foot of the cross, focused on the flesh, and subject to its ear-piercing shrieks of temptation. We must instead put our focus on the Spirit, moving on with Him through prayer, through the Word, through spiritual disciplines, through service and through obedience, and when we do, we'll find the flesh's influence and allure diminishing in our lives.

PRAYER: Is your life marked more by the fruit of the Spirit or by the deeds of the flesh? Are you reversing the order of verse 16? Pray a prayer of focus today, not focusing on fighting your fleshly impulses, but on obeying the Spirit's guidance.

BEARING LOADS
GALATIANS 6

At first glance, there seems to be a contradiction between verse 2 (*"Bear one another's burdens"*) and verse 5 (*"For each one shall bear his own burden"*). The seeming contradiction clears up when we look at the original language. Although translated the same, the words referencing the burdens are dramatically different. The word used in verse 2 refers to a crushing load, a load too much for any one person to carry alone. As it is used here, it refers to an overwhelming difficulty, a problem that would be impossible to cope with on one's own. In the context of verse 1, it also speaks of a persistent temptation, a besetting sin in a person's life. When a church member is staggering under such a load, those who are spiritual in the church body are called to step in and *"restore"* him, a word used elsewhere in Greek literature for setting a broken bone. That restoration comes through warning, comforting, support and patience (I Thessalonians 5:14), always with a sense of gentleness and an understanding of our own capacity to be tempted (v. 1). It is sad but true that many in the church never receive such ministry until they have been completely crushed under the burden of trying to go it alone and then *"caught in <a> transgression"* (v. 1). It is equally sad but true that the "ministry" the crushed often receive from the church has less to do with restoration and more to do with piling on! James 5:16 has a far better option: *"Confess your faults to one another and pray for one another, that you may be healed."* When we are being crushed by temptation, bringing a spiritual brother into our confidence to support us, hold us accountable, and pray for us and with us is often the difference between being victorious and being crushed. By contrast, the word in verse 6 refers not to a crushing load, but to a load that a person should be expected to carry on his own. It is a word that was often used to refer to a soldier's backpack. Obviously, each soldier should be expected to carry his own gear, and not expect someone else to carry it for him. This is a command for each of us to take personal responsibility for our lives. In terms of ministry, there are times when we must step in to rescue a believer from overwhelming difficulties, but we are under no obligation to relieve someone of the normal burdens of life or to rescue him from his own irresponsibility.

PRAYER: Do you know someone today who is struggling with an overwhelming load? Pray for that person, and pray for how you might be used to help him bear that heavy burden. If you are staggering under a heavy load, particularly a load of sin and temptation that is "eating your lunch," ask the Lord to show you another believer you might bring into your confidence to fight that battle with you.

EPHESIANS

PREDESTINED
EPHESIANS 1

The issue of predestination is a controversial one that has confused and divided believers for centuries. First Augustine, and then later the Protestant Reformer John Calvin, taught a doctrine of unconditional election that eliminated completely any concept of free will. Calvin taught that God, in eternity past, before He ever created anything, looked forward in time and decided that certain individuals He would create would be saved and others would be lost. God's choice of those individuals was completely arbitrary, based on nothing except His own sovereign decision. In other words, if you are saved, it is because God decided before the foundation of the world that you would be saved and then caused you to believe at the time He decided you would believe. If you die lost and go to hell, it is because God has decided to leave you in your sins, without any hope or chance of salvation, and nothing you can do can change that destiny. Most people, when they hear the Calvinistic doctrine of election, immediately respond, "That's not fair!" but when you consider that God is under no obligation to save even one soul from hell, then God is to be praised even if He only chooses to save one soul from hell. My problem with Calvinism is not that it seems unfair; I just don't think it's Biblical. The Bible says in II Peter 3:9 that God *"does not want any to perish, but all to come to repentance."* I Timothy 2:4 echoes that same sentiment when it says that God *"desires all men to be saved and to come to the knowledge of the truth."* The Biblical invitations to repent and believe, such as Isaiah 45:22, Romans 10:13 and Revelation 22:17, are always universal in scope, limited only by the response of those who hear. So what do we do with Ephesians 1? Verse 4 says *"He chose us...before the foundation of the world,"* and verse 5 says that *"He predestined us."* The key to understanding those verses is a little prepositional phrase repeated over and over, the phrase *"in Him"* and other phrases similar to it (vv. 3, 4, 5, 6, 7, 9). Verse four doesn't say that He chose us arbitrarily, but that *"He chose us in Him."* Verse 5 doesn't just say that He simply predestined us according to His Sovereign choice, but that *"He predestined us...through Jesus Christ."* (v. 5). The Greek word for "predestine" is *pro-horidzo*. It does not mean to determine someone's destiny beforehand; it means to set the horizons, or boundaries, of something. These verses teach that before the foundation of the world, God set the boundary of salvation, and that boundary is *"in Christ."* All those who are *"in Christ"* will be saved; all those who are not *"in Christ"* will be lost. That brings up the question then of how we get in Christ. Verse 13 tells us. First we must hear the gospel message, then we must believe, turning from our sins in repentance and turning to Christ in faith. And when we do that, we are from that time on *"in Christ,"* and therefore within the predestined realm of salvation.

PRAYER: Note the calls to praise in this passage: *"to the praise of the glory of His grace"* (v. 6), *"for the praise of His glory"* (v. 12), and *"to the praise of His glory"* (v. 14). This is a Trinitarian call to praise, as the first one speaks of praise for the Father's role in our salvation, the second of praise for the Son's role in our salvation, and the third of praise for the Spirit's role in our salvation. God's plan of salvation - His determination to save those who are in Christ, His making a way for their salvation through Christ and His administering the sacrifice of Christ to our hearts by the Spirit - deserves our highest praise. Praise Him today for His marvelous gift of salvation!

B.C. AND A.D.
EPHESIANS 2

As Christians, we believe that Jesus Christ is the center of all history. For proof of that, we need only look at the calendar. Time itself is divided into designations of B.C. ("Before Christ") and A.D. ("Anno Domini," Latin for "in the year of our Lord"). But not only is history divided into categories of before Christ and after Christ, for us as Christians, our very lives are divided into those categories. Before Christ, we were *"dead in <our> trespasses and sins"* (v. 1). Obviously, a person without Christ walks, talks, thinks, breathes, eats, and otherwise functions as a physically alive person, but spiritually, he is dead. In physical death, the soul is separated from the body. In spiritual death, the soul is separated from God. The reason for our dead state outside of Christ is our trespasses and sins. All human beings, the Bible says, have overstepped the boundaries established by God. All of us have broken the commandments of God, and as a result, we are *"by nature children of wrath"* (v. 3), condemned, abiding under the just sentence of God, and destined for hell. It is a grim picture to be sure. But verse 4 opens with two blessed words of transition: *"But God."* Our situation was totally hopeless - we were spiritually dead, and a dead man cannot do anything for himself or anyone else for that matter. BUT GOD intervened in that hopeless situation to give us life. We couldn't get to God, so He came to us in Christ. A price had to be paid for sin. God's justice demanded it. But God could not stand to have us pay that awful price ourselves, so in Christ, He paid that price for us through His atoning death on the cross. Why did God the Father go through the agony of giving His Son? Why did the Son go through the agony of the cross? One reason: love. God loved us so much, even in our sins, even at our worst, that He was willing to pay that awful price and extend His mercy and grace to us freely. Verse 6 describes the present aspect of salvation. Our names are already inscribed in heaven's register, and our interests are being promoted there by our great Advocate, the Lord Jesus Christ. The blessings of heaven are already descending upon us, and we are already enjoying the power and position of being children of God. Verse 7 speaks of the future aspect of salvation. We will spend eternity in heaven with Christ. In heaven, we will stand as trophies to the marvelous grace of God, and we will sing of His amazing grace for all eternity. How do we receive this great salvation purchased for us on the cross? Is it by some religious ritual, or by good works? No, for verse 9 says that salvation is not as a result of works. Salvation is a gift, according to verse 8, and by definition a gift is not worked for or paid for, or else it is no longer a gift. We must make the decision to receive that gift by placing our absolute faith in Christ, turning to Him in repentance, trusting Him alone to save us, surrendering our lives to His Lordship. When we do that, we become His *"workmanship"* (v. 10), the Greek word from which we get our English word "poem." He makes us into His work of art, His masterwork, His unique and personal expression of Himself, as we walk with Him.

PRAYER: Thank Him today for His rescue of you through the blood of Jesus. Thank Him for the ways you see Him molding and making you into His special work of art.

THE PRISONER OF JESUS CHRIST
EPHESIANS 3

When Paul wrote this letter, he was under house arrest in Rome awaiting trial before Caesar's court because of trumped-up charges lodged against him by the Jews in Jerusalem. But notice in verse 1 that he doesn't describe himself as a prisoner of the Jews, or as a prisoner of Rome, or as a prisoner of Caesar. He describes himself as *"the prisoner of Jesus Christ."* Paul understood that his circumstances had come about because of his commitment to Christ, and that nothing about his situation had taken the Lord by surprise. Whatever he did, wherever he went, and whatever happened to him was completely under Christ's control. He would never have been made subject to the power, the plans, the punishments or the prison of any man or government without the Lord's consent. He was in prison because the Lord had allowed it for some higher purpose, and whether he understood that higher purpose or not, he was completely submitted to God's will. Nothing would affect or alter that commitment. Perspective is everything when it comes to dealing with life's hardships and difficulties. Paul's perspective was that God is sovereign; He is in control, and He sends nothing and allows nothing into our lives except for our ultimate good. Paul could have reacted differently to his situation. He could have shaken his fist at God and said, "God, here I've given my life to serving you and proclaiming your Word and planting churches, and how do you repay me? You let me end up as a prisoner, deprived of my freedom!" He could have concluded that since his circumstances were currently unpleasant, that God either didn't love him, or that the devil had put one over on God somehow and defeated God's purposes. He could have just curled up in a corner, gotten depressed and given up. Or he could have denied the faith in order to be set free, and said to himself, "When all this is over, I'm going back to making tents and I'm never saying another word about Jesus!" But that would not be the case. Paul was unwilling to compromise the message of the gospel for the sake of comfort and convenience. Even if it meant hardship, persecution, imprisonment, or even death, he would not back down, but would remain strong in his commitment to Christ. He was willing to sacrifice for what he believed. I fear in this modern age we live in that we have lost that element of die-hard submission and sacrifice, that absolute commitment that says, "No matter what the circumstances or the consequences, I will serve the Lord!" Compromise is the order of the day. At crunch time, rather than doing what is right, all too often people today choose to do what is popular. Rather than being moved by conviction, all too often believers today yield to the lure of convenience.

PRAYER: Pray that come what may, in any circumstance of life, you will trust the Lord in it and with it. Pray that pressure from the world will not back you off from your convictions, but that you will stand firm for Christ and His truth regardless of the cost.

AND HE GAVE SOME...
EPHESIANS 4

Some ministers think they're God's gift to the church...and they're right! Verse 11 says that *"God gave some to be apostles, prophets, evangelists, pastors and teachers."* God raises up and equips certain members of the body of Christ for leadership in the body. The job of those called into that leadership role is *"for the equipping of the saints, for the work of service, and for the building up of the body of Christ"* (v. 12). Unfortunately, the

Modern English Version follows the King James Version in what has been called "the heresy of the comma." As the passage above reads, with the commas intact, it would appear that those called to church leadership have three functions: equipping the saints, doing the work of the ministry, and building up the body of Christ. Such an understanding down through the centuries has often created a situation where the clergy tries to do it all, and the laity is content to let them, resulting in inadequate ministry (after all, how can one man or a small staff do it all?), ministry burnout, weak churches and immature believers. In fact, verse 12 does not contain a list of three clergy responsibilities, but is rather a sequence of events that continues on into verses 13-16. There is only ONE function given in verse 12 to those who are called as apostles, prophets, evangelists, and pastor-teachers: equipping the saints for the work of the ministry! That is the first domino that sets off a chain reaction delineated in the following verses. When the saints are thus equipped, and are actively engaged in doing the work of the ministry, then the body of Christ is built up, unified, mature (both individually and corporately), able to discern between true and false teaching, and functioning as a body, with each one doing his designated part.

PRAYER: Have you thanked God lately for those He has put into your life for your equipping? Thank Him today. Have you succumbed to a "we pay the preacher to do that" attitude? Repent of it, and ask the Lord what ministry He would have you to do.

BE FILLED WITH THE SPIRIT
EPHESIANS 5

Paul says in verse 18 that we are not to be drunk with wine, but rather to be filled with the Spirit. What does it mean to

be filled with the Spirit? It means to be under His control.
Whatever a person is filled with, that is what controls him.
If a man is full of anger, anger controls him. If he is full of
love, love controls him. If he is full of alcohol, alcohol
controls him. Likewise, to be full of the Spirit is to be
controlled by the Spirit. When you were saved, the Holy
Spirit came to indwell you. At that point, you received all of
the Spirit you'll ever have. The question is not how much of
the Spirit you have, but how much of you He has. To the
extent that we are allowing Him to control each aspect of our
lives, to that extent we are filled. The Greek verb translated
"Be filled" has four elements to it. It is in the imperative
mood, which indicates that it is a command. As Christians,
we are commanded to be filled with the Spirit, and therefore
not to be filled with the Spirit is sin. It is in the plural form,
which indicates that it is addressed to all Christians. Being
filled with the Spirit is not just for some kind of super-saints;
all Christians are commanded to be filled. It is in the passive
voice, which indicates that it is not something we do for
ourselves, but something that we allow to be done to us. We
do not somehow appropriate more of the Spirit; we allow
Him to appropriate more of us. Finally, it is in the present
tense, which indicates that it is not a one-time experience,
but an ongoing, continual experience. We are not filled
once, and that's it, but we are to be continually filled with
the Spirit. Indeed, that command could be literally
translated, "Keep on being continually being filled with the
Spirit." Paul gives us three practical evidences of being
filled with the Spirit. First, when a believer is filled with the
Spirit, he has a heart for worship (v. 19). Verse 19 speaks of
corporate worship - speaking and singing to each other - and
also of private worship - singing and making melody in your
heart. Do you know why so many Christians are spotty in
their church attendance, and can't find time to study the
Word and pray each day? It's because they aren't filled with
the Spirit; they're filled with all kinds of other things. When

the Spirit is in control, worship becomes a priority. The second evidence of the Spirit's control is a heart of thanksgiving (v. 20). What marks your prayers? Are your prayers marked more by thanksgiving, or by complaints and requests? The Spirit-filled believer has a heart that cries out in praise and thanksgiving to God for all things. The third evidence of the Spirit's control is a heart of submission (v. 21). Submission is an attitude by which we move self from the center of our lives, and put others there. As a result, we don't insist on our own rights, but we submit to others, putting their needs above our own.

PRAYER: Submit yourself to the Holy Spirit today, and ask Him to fill you anew and afresh. Repent of anything that is filling you and controlling you other than Him.

PUT ON THE FULL ARMOR OF GOD
EPHESIANS 6

Paul, writing this letter under house arrest in Rome while chained to a Roman soldier, saw in that soldier's battle gear parallels to our divinely issued provisions as we do battle with our enemy, the devil and all his minions (v. 12). Note the items of the Christian's armor:

The Belt of Truth: An essential preparation for spiritual warfare is a firm grasp of the truth, because our enemy is a master of deception; indeed, he is called a liar and the father of all lies. Deception is one of his greatest weapons, and we must be prepared to recognize and deal with his untruths by having a firm grasp of the truth that comes only from the Word of God.

The Breastplate of Righteousness: The Roman soldier's breastplate protected the vital organs - the heart, kidneys, liver, lungs and intestines - from arrows, swords and spears.

The breastplate of righteousness refers first of all to Christ's righteousness. When we were saved, the righteousness of Christ was imputed to our accounts. We are saved not because of our righteousness and our good works, but because of the good work of the righteous, holy, sinless Son of God on the cross. At the moment we placed our faith in Christ, all of our sins - past, present and future - were covered by Christ's sacrifice on the cross. Try as he might, the devil can strike no blow against us that would return us to our lost condition. But does that mean that we continue in sin? No, because that breastplate of righteousness also refers to personal righteousness. Those who have truly been covered with the imputed righteousness of Christ will grow in actual, personal holiness. The more we grow in personal holiness, the more we take away the enemy's weapon of accusation against us.

The Shoes of Readiness: The Roman soldier's footwear was imbedded on the bottom with small spikes which helped him to stand his ground in hand-to-hand combat. Paul says that the preparation of the gospel of peace gives us that same kind of stability. There is nothing that makes a Christian stronger than sharing his faith through personal witnessing.

The Shield of Faith: We are called to trust God. No matter how bad it looks, no matter if everything around us spells defeat, we are called to continue to stand strong in faith, doing the right thing and trusting Him with the consequences. That kind of faith extinguishes the fiery arrows of doubt that the evil one fires our way.

The Helmet of Salvation: The mind is where our battles with temptation are won and lost. That is where the ultimate decision is made to obey or disobey. Just as the helmet protected the head of the solider, so too does our salvation protect our minds, giving us the ability to say no to sin and yes to God. But just as the helmet needed to be on the head to protect the soldier, so too we must put on the helmet of salvation by renewing our minds through the Word of God (see Romans 12:1-2 and Philippians 4:8).

The Sword of the Spirit: The sword of the Spirit is not the Bible sitting on a shelf, but rather that specific word of Scripture that answers the specific point of temptation or falsehood that we're facing. If we are going to be successful in our battles, we must wield the sword of the Spirit with great precision. You can wave your Bible at the devil all day, and it doesn't bother him in the least, but if you can recall and hit him with the specific Scripture that deals with your specific situation, you can put him to flight and emerge victorious.

PRAYER: Take inventory of your spiritual armor today. Are there pieces missing? Pray for the recovery of those lost items so that *"you may be able to resist in the evil day, and having done all, to stand"* (v. 13).

PHILIPPIANS

ENCOURAGEMENT
PHILIPPIANS 1

As he encourages the Philippians here in chapter 1, Paul demonstrates four methods by which we can encourage one another. Notice first, *he articulates his appreciation* (v. 3). Many people get discouraged because they don't believe they are making a difference, that if they left the church tomorrow, or quit their job, or disappeared altogether, nobody would notice or care. They need a word of appreciation, a word that says, "You're doing a good job. I thank God for what you're doing." The Philippians were special to Paul. Some of the other churches had fallen into doctrinal error, questioned his authority, and even turned against him, but the Philippian church was his pride and joy, and Paul articulates his appreciation for what they meant to him. He says that every time he thinks of them, he thanks God for them. That begs two questions for us. Number one, are we living a Christian life such that when fellow believers think of us, it elicits thanksgiving to God? And number two, are we thanking God for and expressing appreciation for those that God uses to bring blessing into our lives? Second, notice that *he promises his prayers* (v. 4). Paul assures them that he is praying for them. Don't ever tell someone you'll pray for him and then neglect to do it, but if you are praying for someone, let him know it. To someone who believes in the power of prayer, that can be one of the biggest encouragements of all. Third, notice that *he surveys their successes* (v. 5). It's unfortunate but true that many times, no one remembers our successes, but they never seem to forget our failures. A good way to encourage someone, especially someone reeling from current failure, is to remind him of all the times and ways God has used him mightily in the past. Paul praises them for the good work that they've done in the past, and encourages them to keep up the good work in the future. He praises them for their *"fellowship in the gospel,"* or as it can also be understood, their *"partnership in the gospel"* (NIV 84). How had they partnered with Paul in the gospel? First, they had been active in spreading the gospel, both in their verbal witness and in their unified spirit. True fellowship in the church revolves around a common Lord and a common goal: the spreading of the gospel to the lost. Second, they had supported Paul's preaching of the gospel, both through their prayers and their financial contributions. Even though they were among the poorest of the churches, the Philippians excelled in giving because of their desire to see the gospel go out into all the world. Paul reminds them of their past successes in order to encourage them toward future faithfulness to God. Finally, notice that *he details their destiny* (v. 6). He tells them, "Look, your past is great, but the future is brighter than you can imagine. God's still at work in you, and He will bring you to perfection." It's good to be reminded in the midst of all the hardships of life and failures of the flesh that God's not finished with us yet. He will continue His work in us, for us and through us until the day of Christ.

PRAYER: Who do you know who needs encouragement today? Look for ways to use these four methods of encouragement in that person's life. Pray for him, and then let him know you are praying for him with a phone call, a text message, an email, or a card.

WORKING OUT
PHILIPPIANS 2

In our day, working out for physical fitness has become a national obsession, but in verse 12, Paul speaks to us about another kind of workout when he commands us to *"work out your own salvation with fear and trembling."* When Paul tells us to "work out" our salvation, understand he did not mean that we work *up* our salvation or work *for* our salvation. Salvation is not based on our effort or good works; it is a gift of God based on the sacrifice of Christ on the cross. We don't work for salvation or pay for it; we merely receive it by repenting of our sins and placing our faith in Christ. The Greek word translated *"work out"* here was used of "working out" a mine, getting all the precious metals out of it so that it would yield maximum profit. Paul is telling us not to be satisfied with a surface Christian faith, but to mine out all of the spiritual treasures God has for us, to live in such a way that we become all we can be in Christ. Reaching our potential as Christians does not come automatically; it must be a priority. It cannot be a hit-or-miss thing, a once-a-week or twice-a-month-on-Sunday thing. No one ever got in top physical shape working out sporadically. Likewise, if we're going to be in a proper spiritual condition, we must work out our salvation on a daily basis, daily yielding our wills to His will, daily communing with Him in the Word and in prayer, daily rejecting the ungodly standards and values of the world, and daily serving Him alongside others in His church. The phrase *"fear and trembling"* shows the utmost seriousness of the task of spiritual fitness. It doesn't speak of fear and trembling of God. Although we are to fear God in the sense of having a proper reverence for Him, we are not called to live in cringing fear of Him. No, the fear and trembling here is over what will happen if we're not in proper spiritual condition. The hostility of our environment in this fallen world, the animosity of our enemy the devil, the iniquity of our old sin nature, and the gravity of our endeavor to win the lost for Christ all require us to be in top shape spiritually, lest we be conformed to the world, overcome by Satan, controlled by our flesh, and failures in carrying out the Great Commission. Notice that we are to work out *our own* salvation. That doesn't mean that we grow spiritually alone; indeed, apart from the fellowship of the local church, a believer will be in sorry spiritual shape indeed. But it does mean that nobody can get you in spiritual shape but you. You can join the finest health club in your town, and hire a personal trainer to design a program for you, but nobody can run those miles or lift those weights for you. Likewise, you can join a great church, and you can listen to the preacher talk about these things, but no one can exercise spiritual disciplines in your life for you; you must become a doer of the Word, and not a hearer only, if you're going to be a spiritually fit believer.

PRAYER: How are your spiritual workouts going? Pray for greater consistency in doing the will of your "Divine Trainer," that you might be all you can be in Him.

SIX R'S OF CHRISTIAN LIVING
PHILIPPIANS 3

Most of us are familiar with the so-called three "R's of education," which of course are reading, writing and 'rithmetic. For generations those three R's served as a basic code for the rudiments of education. In the first three verses of Philippians 3, we can see six R's of Christian living. First, we are called to *rejoice in the Lord* (v. la). Those four words comprise the overall theme of the book of Philippians: the joy that comes from knowing Christ. This joy is more than happiness which comes and goes and depends on circumstances; this is a constant joy that is the birthright of every person who has been born again. But it does not come automatically. There are two very important prerequisites if the joy of the Lord is going to be present in our lives. First, if we're going to rejoice in the Lord, we must be *in* the Lord, in other words, born again. Second, if we are to rejoice in the Lord, we must be submitted to the Lord. It is no accident that Paul says *"rejoice in the Lord"* rather than "rejoice in Christ." He is emphasizing the importance of the Lordship of Christ in our lives. There are many Christians who are not experiencing the joy of the Lord because they have wandered away from His Lordship. They have drifted away from Christ, His Word, and His church, and have fallen into various kinds of sin, and the joy of the Lord is the first thing to go in such backslidden lives. The second R is ***remember the Word*** (v. 1b). Repetition is important for memory. When you had a test in school, I'm sure that you didn't just glance at your notes a few minutes before the test. You pored over those notes numerous times in the days leading up to the test, because that repeated reading of the notes helped the information to lodge in your mind. If the Word of God is going to lodge in our minds so that we can recall it when we need it, we've got to study it, memorize it, read it daily, and most importantly practice it. A third R we see in this passage is ***resist the enemy*** (v. 2). As Christians, we have a powerful, angry, vicious enemy called the devil who resists all that we do for Christ. He is a persecutor, an opposer, a tempter, and a liar, who spreads opposition to the church, dissension in the church, and false doctrine among the churches. He comes against us in the form of *"dogs,"* vicious persecutors from without, and *"evil workers"* working within the church. Fourth, we are to ***rely upon the Spirit*** (v. 3a). Paul here says that we worship in the Spirit of

God. It is the indwelling Holy Spirit who gives us the strength and ability to worship Him through our daily service, who guides us to live righteous lives before the world and to do God's will as a church, who illumines the Word to us, and who energizes our public worship. Fifth, we are called to **revel in the Savior** (v. 3b). To *"glory in Christ Jesus"* is to be proud of Him, to boast of Him, to give credit to Him, and to delight in Him. The final R is to **reject the flesh** (v. 3c). Our only hope of dealing with the flesh (our old sin nature) is to keep it weak by starving it of attention, centering our attention not on the things of the world but on the things of God (Philippians 4:8).

PRAYER: Pray through each of these six R's as a checklist, asking the Lord to show you any deficiency in your Christian life. Pray for the shoring up of any weak areas that He reveals.

WHEN CHRISTIANS CLASH
PHILIPPIANS 4

In verses 2-3, Paul mentions two women, Euodia and Syntyche, who weren't getting along. We don't know what the controversy was in Philippi, but we can draw some conclusions from the information we have. First, for Paul to call these two women out by name in a letter to be read to the entire church indicates that it was a serious matter, and a public one. Paul doesn't describe the dispute, because everyone in the church was already well aware of it. Second, these two women, despite their disagreement, were both committed Christians. Paul says that their names were written in the Book of Life, and he speaks of how they had labored with him in the cause of the gospel. Third, whatever their dispute was, it was not doctrinal in nature, because if it had been, Paul would have surely stepped in with an authoritative apostolic word to put an end to the controversy. It was likely not even a question of how to best proceed in doing the work of the Lord, because Paul never hesitated to give instructions on that score, either. Fourth, the way verse 2 is worded in Greek indicates that both women were at fault. All that taken together leads me to believe that this was just a good old-fashioned personality clash. Something about the two women's makeups just didn't mesh, and the rift between them was big enough that it threatened to engulf the whole church. Most church controversies at their core boil down to just such issues: not great theological issues or fundamental issues of right and wrong, but personality clashes, personal preferences, and lack of communication. Paul calls these two women, and by extension the rest of us, to live in harmony in the Lord. The key to doing that is in that phrase, *"in the Lord."* If I'm in the Lord and you're in the Lord, we are bound together by that common relationship, no matter what our differences may be. We're called to love each other with divine *agape'* love that always wants the best and always does the best for the other person, even if it's someone who's not particularly loveable. That kind of love is not warm fuzzy feelings; it's a decision of the will that we make. Let's be honest: some people just rub us the wrong way. I can't say with Will Rogers that I've never met a man I didn't like. But I've never met anyone that I couldn't want the best and do the best for. I've never met anyone that I couldn't be cordial and friendly to. I've never met anyone I couldn't pray for. And I've found that two things generally happen when I begin to pray for someone and show forth a loving attitude and actions toward someone. Number one, my feelings tend to follow my actions, and I start to feel more loving toward that person; and number two, I find that most people respond favorably to loving actions, and they tend to become more loveable.

PRAYER: Is there someone in your life who just rubs you the wrong way? Pray for that person today, and ask the Lord for opportunities to show forth *agape'* love whenever you may encounter him.

COLOSSIANS

PRAYING FOR FELLOW BELIEVERS
COLOSSIANS 1

In verse 3, Paul declares that he prays always for the Colossians. A little later in the chapter, he details the content of his prayers for them, and his prayers for the Colossians are a good example of how we can pray for our fellow believers. First, we should pray for them to be *"filled with the knowledge of His will in all wisdom and spiritual understanding"* (v. 9). Knowing God's will is a powerful force in our lives, especially when it is combined with the wisdom to carry out His will and the spiritual understanding of God's larger working in the world and our part in it. Second, we should pray for fellow believers that they *"may walk in a manner worthy of the Lord, pleasing to all"* (v. 10a). Walking in such a way as to have favor with both God and man is a high goal indeed, and a difficult one, but one that indicates true Christlikeness (Luke 2:52). Third, we should pray for our fellow Christians to be *"fruitful in every good work, and increasing in the knowledge of God."* The word for *"knowledge"* there is a Greek word that speaks of personal knowledge, knowledge that comes by personal experience. It speaks of knowing someone personally rather than just knowing about him. When we are fruitful in doing the good work of the Kingdom, we will have a deeper, richer and more intimate knowledge of God. When God placed Adam in the Garden to tend it, was it because God was desperately in need of a gardener? No. The Garden was the arena of God's interaction with Adam as He taught Him about Himself through His creation. Likewise, whatever tasks God calls us to, His purpose in doing so is to teach us through it about Himself. Fourth, we should pray for fellow believers to be *"strengthened with all might according to His glorious power, enduring everything with perseverance and patience joyfully"* (v. 11). Notice that Paul does not pray for the relief of their burdens, but for strength to endure and joy in the struggle. Finally, let us pray for our fellow believers to have thankful hearts (v. 12). As Paul writes in I Thessalonians 4:18, *"In everything give thanks, for this is the will of God in Christ Jesus concerning you."* No matter what earthly struggle we may be facing, there is something that would be far worse: going through it as a lost person! We can always give thanks that He *"has enabled us to be partakers in the inheritance of the saints in light. He has delivered us from the power of darkness and has transferred us into the kingdom of His dear Son, in whom we have redemption through His blood, the forgiveness of sins"* (vv. 12-14).

PRAYER: Has God laid someone on your heart to pray these petitions over? Go through each of these five prayer points, praying them for that fellow believer...and for yourself.

CHRIST IS ENOUGH
COLOSSIANS 2

Paul rejoiced over what Epaphras (1:7) had told him about the Colossians. Their fellowship was orderly, not divided and chaotic like the church at Corinth, and not beset by interpersonal squabbles such as at Philippi. Beyond that, they were standing steadfastly in their faith in Christ (v. 5). He is concerned though, lest false teachers come in and *"captivate <them>,"* either through Jewish legalism or Greek philosophy. Having received Jesus as Lord, they needed to be *"rooted and built up in Him and established in the faith"* (v. 7), not led astray *"through philosophy and vain deceit, in the tradition of men and the elementary principles of the world, and not after Christ"* (v. 8). To combat this possibility, Paul fortifies them by demonstrating that Jesus is everything. The false teachers could not possibly promise more than the Colossians already had, because they were *"complete in Him"* (v. 10) and *"In Him lives all the fullness of the Godhead bodily"* (v. 9). There is no higher authority than His authority (v. 10b), and no greater forgiveness than what He offers (v. 13). He has fulfilled all that was just types and shadows in the ceremonies and holy days of the Old Covenant (v. 12). Why would they want to be circumcised when they had already experienced what circumcision symbolized (v. 11)? Why would they want to live under the Law regarding such matters as food and drink, holy days, new moons or Sabbath days (v. 16), when Christ's death had freed them from the Law and its penalties (vv. 13-14)? Why would they want to be led astray into the worship of angels (v. 18) or other supernatural beings when Christ had disarmed them all and triumphed over them in the cross (v. 15)? To do so would cause them to be cheated out of their reward of freedom in Christ (v. 18). While legalism seems to promise greater spirituality, it is in fact *"worthless against the indulgence of the flesh"* (v. 23) and leads to an *"unspiritual mind"* (v. 18).

PRAYER: In our day, Mormons offer "another testament of Jesus Christ" and New Age gurus claim to take their disciples to "deeper levels of the Christ-consciousness within." Pray for those caught up in such false gospels, that they might come to the truth that Christ, the true Lord Jesus

Christ of the New Testament, is all they need. Pray for yourself, that you might be *"rooted and built up in Him and established in the faith"* (v. 7).

REJECTING AND EMBRACING
COLOSSIANS 3

In speaking of the new life in Christ and what it should look like, Paul calls us to put off certain attitudes, actions and motivations of the old nature, and to embrace the attitudes, actions and motivations that mark the new nature. Whenever the old nature rears its head, we must reject it utterly, embracing (think hugging) the new nature. What are the signs of the old nature being dominant in our lives? There are obvious ones like *"sexual immorality, uncleanness"* and *"inordinate affection"* (v. 5a), all of which have to do with uncontrolled and improperly expressed sexual urges. There are sins of the mind and heart, like *"evil desire, and covetousness, which is idolatry"* (v. 5b). There are sins of temperament, like *"anger, wrath"* and *"malice"* (v. 8a), and sins of the tongue like *"blasphemy, and filthy language out of your mouth"* (v. 8b). There are sins against others, like lying to one another (v. 9). Paul speaks of rejecting such things as taking off a soiled garment and throwing it away, and then putting on the clean garments of Christ. When we're walking in those garments, there will be no prejudice among us (v. 11), and we will be marked by *mercy, kindness, humbleness of mind, meekness and longsuffering"* (v. 12). Forgiveness, love, peace, and thankfulness dominate a heart filled with the Spirit (vv. 13-15). In such a heart, there will also be a hunger for the Word of God (v. 16a) and the worship of God (v. 16b), and a desire to serve Christ in all things (v. 17).

PRAYER: Pray today that your life might always be marked by the clean garments of the new life, not by the filthy, tattered rags of the old nature.

HIGH PRAISE
COLOSSIANS 4

Can you imagine what it must have been like to get a compliment from the Apostle Paul? In the last chapter of Colossians, Paul compliments several of his fellow workers. He calls Tychicus *"a beloved brother and a faithful minister and fellow servant in the Lord."* Obviously, we are to love all of our brothers and sisters in Christ, but some of them become especially dear to us. Tychicus had become near and dear to Paul, who recognized him as faithful to his call to minister in the name of Christ and possessing a servant's heart of the same caliber as Paul himself. Apparently, Tychicus, along with Onesimus, also called *"a faithful and beloved brother,"* would be carrying the letter to the Colossians on Paul's behalf (vv. 7, 9). Aristarchus is called Paul's *"fellow prisoner"* (v. 10). Like Paul, he had apparently been willing to put his very freedom on the line for the cause of Christ. That Paul mentions both Mark and Barnabas, and commends them to the Colossians (it's unclear which of them was planning to go to Colossae), is interesting in light of the sharp disagreement over Mark that divided Paul and Barnabas in their younger years (Acts 15:36-41). The rift between them had evidently been healed by this time as both of them practiced what Paul preached in 3:13. Jesus, also called Justus, is included in that group as being of the circumcision, in other words, fellow Jews with Paul. Paul says of this whole group that *"They have been a comfort to me"* in his time of imprisonment (v. 11). Epaphras receives much high praise from Paul as *"a servant of Christ,"* and a prayer warrior who had great zeal for the people of his home area, desiring that they might *"stand mature and complete in the entire will of*

God" (vv. 12-13). Luke is called *"the beloved physician"* (v. 14). He no doubt used his medical skills to minister to Paul and to others as well. And then there is Demas. Of all of Paul's fellow workers, he is only mentioned, and there is no commendation given of him. Perhaps he was already showing signs of what would happen to him later (II Timothy 4:10).

PRAYER: Think of some people in your circle, perhaps members of your church or small group, or fellow workers in a ministry you're involved with. What words would you use to describe them? Beloved? A comfort? Servant? Faithful? Hard-working? Pray for each of them today, thanking God for these characteristics you see in them.

I THESSALONIANS

SO HEAVENLY MINDED...?
I THESSALONIANS 1

I'm sure most of us have heard someone described as "so heavenly minded they're no earthly good." The Thessalonians were certainly waiting for Jesus to come from heaven (v. 10), and they were intensely interested in the events of the end times (4:13-18), but they also understood that there's more to the Christian life than waiting around to die and go to heaven or be raptured at the coming of Christ. They understood that God has left us here for a purpose, and they were serious about fulfilling their earthly responsibilities. They were *an energetic church*, marked by their *"work produced by faith"* and *"labor prompted by love"* (v. 3, NIV 84). The word translated *"labor"* refers to back-breaking, bone-wearying, difficult work. They worked hard in the cause of Christ because of their love of the Lord. There are all kind of motivations for serving the Lord, but our primary motivation should be out of love and gratitude to God for who He is and what He has done for us. They were also *an enduring church* (v. 3). Paul also speaks of their *"endurance inspired by hope"* (NIV 84). The word translated *"endurance"* speaks of a quality in which a person does not surrender to circumstances or collapse under trials. Thessalonica was an especially difficult place to be a Christian. Paul was run out of town there after just a few weeks, and his opponents even followed him to the next town to stir up trouble there. You can imagine how they treated those left behind. Yet, the believers there refused to succumb to the pressure of the society around them, and continued to serve the Lord. Paul further presents them as *an exemplary church* (v. 7). Paul says that they were an example to the other churches in Macedonia and Achaia, two provinces covering several hundred miles, which shows the extent of their influence. Finally, they were *an evangelistic church* (v. 8). The Thessalonians understood that the main task of the church is to win the lost, and God had placed them in a strategic location to do it. Thessalonica was a major trading city on a major highway. People from all over the Empire passed through there, and many of them were won to Christ. Those converts then took the gospel with them as they traveled on.

PRAYER: How would you rate your church on the "Thessalonian Scale"? Keep in mind that the church is just the sum total of its members. An old gospel song asked a pertinent question: what kind of church would my church be, if everybody in it were just like me? Spend some time in prayer today, asking the Lord to evaluate your Christian walk. Are you willing to labor for Him in sometimes arduous tasks? Do you endure under trial? Is your example one that others could follow? Are you seeking to win the lost?

A MINISTRY NOT IN VAIN
I THESSALONIANS 2

Ministry, whether vocational ministry or lay ministry, can be tough. As Paul looks back over his time at Thessalonica, he concludes that his time there was *"not in vain"* (v. 1); in other words, his ministry there had not been a waste of time. What were the characteristics of his ministry at Thessalonica that we should emulate in whatever ministry God has called us to? First, it was *a ministry of boldness* (v. 2). After the painful and shameful way he was treated at Philippi (Acts 16), many people would have given up on the missionary business and gone home. But not Paul. He pressed on to the next city, Thessalonica, where, despite great opposition there, he proclaimed the message of Christ boldly. Second, it was *a ministry of purity*. Paul says in verse 3 (NIV 84) that his proclamation *"does not spring from error or impure motives, nor are we trying to trick you."* It was pure in message, pure in motive, and pure in method. We keep our message pure by staying close to the Word of God and the message of the gospel found in it. In terms of motive, it is possible to preach the true Word out of impure motives - a desire for money, prestige, power, or praise - but the ultimate motivation for preaching the gospel should be love for God and love of the lost. It is also possible to preach the truth using impure methods. Paul didn't use any trickery in his preaching. He did not attempt to cover up the cost of discipleship, nor did he promise fraudulent blessings. He used no high pressure tactics or emotional manipulation. He just preached the gospel, the bad news of human sin and the good news of Christ's sacrifice for sin, and left the results in God's hands. Third, Paul's ministry was *a ministry divinely ordered* (v. 4). What kept Paul going in the face of hardship, difficulty, opposition, persecution and slander? It was the fact that he knew God had called him to his ministry. Why was he so concerned to speak the gospel with accuracy, boldness, clarity and purity? Because he saw himself as a divinely appointed steward, entrusted with the precious treasure of the gospel, and commissioned to pass it on to others. Never forget, if God has called you to it, He will see you through it!

PRAYER: Pray for your pastor today, that he might always speak the Word boldly, even in the face of opposition, that He might minister the Word in purity of message, motive and method, and that he might have the assurance of His call from God in difficult times.

CHRISTIANS ON TRIAL
I THESSALONIANS 3

Trials are a double-edged sword. They can either make us bitter, or they can make us better. They can either weaken our faith, or they can strengthen our faith, and what determines that is how we respond to them. Paul was concerned because he knew that after all of the troubles he'd experienced in Thessalonica, the church there was surely facing a multitude of problems and opposition. Paul expected that, but his concern was that they respond correctly to the trials and not be shaken by them (v. 3). To respond correctly in the midst of trials, we must first recognize that trials are inevitable. The Bible teaches that not only will Christians not be shielded from the normal hardships and difficulties of life, they will many times experience special hardships that come because they are Christians. Paul never preached to anyone that the Christian life was supposed to be free from trials, hardships, problems, opposition or afflictions; indeed, it would seem from verse 4 that he let people know up front, just as Jesus did, that discipleship is costly, and that all who live godly lives in a godless world will be persecuted. If we recognize the inevitability of trials, it will keep us from being blind-sided by them. If we are to respond correctly in the midst of trials, we must also recognize the benefits of trials. As Christians, nothing comes into our lives that does not first pass by the throne of God. Whatever we're going through, *"we were appointed to this"* (v. 3), and He allows nothing into our lives except that which is in our best interests. God may not have directly caused it, but He allowed it for a higher purpose. Trials have the benefit of driving us to the Word and to the Lord. Psalm 119:67 says, *"Before I was afflicted, I wandered, but now I keep your word."* James 1:3-4 speaks of how trials lead us to maturity. He says there, *"the trying of your faith develops patience. But let patience perfect its work, that you may be perfect and complete, lacking nothing."* When we recognize that God only sends or allows trials into our lives for our best interest, to mold us and make us more Christlike, our reaction must not be to become shaken, or to cry out to God "Why are you doing this to me?" Instead, we should humbly bow before God with but one question on our lips: "Lord, what are you trying to teach me in all this?"

PRAYER: If you are experiencing some trial or know of someone else who is, pray that the trial might not be wasted, and that in responding to it appropriately, you or the other person will receive the full benefit God intends from it.

THE LORD'S RETURN
I THESSALONIANS 4

Throughout history, Christians have looked ahead to the climax of human history, the glorious return of our Lord to planet Earth. What a magnificent portrait of victory Paul paints in verses 14-18 as he addresses concerns expressed to him by the Thessalonians. Paul had evidently taught them about the Lord's coming, but since that time, some of their number had passed away, leaving them to wonder whether those departed saints would miss His coming and His

Millennial reign. Paul comforts them with the truth that those loved ones are currently with Christ (if God will bring them with Him, as verse 14 states, then it stands to reason that they're with Him now; see also II Corinthians 5:8), and far from being disadvantaged in any way at the Lord's coming, they will have a front row seat, coming with Him in spirit form, and then having their bodies instantly resurrected, transformed, and rejoined together with their spirits. Then, after the dead in Christ have risen, those believers who are alive at the coming of Christ will be transformed instantly from mortal to immortal (I Corinthians 15:50-53), and caught up in the clouds to meet the Lord in the air (v.17). Note that this event is announced with a loud shout, an angelic cry, and a trumpet call. I disagree with those who proclaim the idea of a "secret rapture," that everything happens so quickly that the unbelieving world will have no idea what has happened until they notice all the Christians gone. In truth, the only thing said to happen *"in the twinkling of an eye"* in I Corinthians 15:54-55 is the change of living saints from mortal to immortal. This is a highly public (and intensely loud!) event, a vindication of Christ and His people in front of the entire unbelieving world, which *"will mourn, and they will see the Son of Man coming on the clouds with power and great glory"* (Matthew 25:30). Revelation 1:7 says, *"Look! He is coming with clouds, and every eye will see Him, even those who pierced Him, and all the tribes of the earth will mourn because of Him."* Why will they mourn? Because *"the great day of His wrath has come. Who is able to withstand it?"* (Revelation 6:17). In ancient Israel, the sounding of a trumpet signaled the gathering of the people for a feast or for worship, or the gathering of the people for war. The sounding of this last trumpet represents both. It calls God's people to the ultimate worship service and the ultimate feast, the Marriage Supper of the Lamb described in Revelation 19. For the lost, that trumpet is a declaration of war, as God's wrath is about to be poured out in the form of the devastating judgments portrayed in Revelation.

PRAYER: Do you know someone who is grieving the loss of a loved one? It is important to note that Paul did not say that believers do not grieve, only that we do not grieve as those who have no hope (v. 13). Pray for those grieving that they will find comfort in the living hope of a living Lord, the living hope of eternal life, and the living hope of His future coming (v. 17).

CHURCHES AND PASTORS
I THESSALONIANS 5

In verses 12-13, Paul speaks of the reciprocal relationship between pastors and churches. As far as the duties of the pastor, he is called first to *diligent labor* in the cause of Christ. Ministry, if done right, is hard work. Conscientious pastors find themselves every Monday morning facing a mountain of responsibilities and demands that no one could ever fully fulfill to everyone's satisfaction. Pastors are also called to a ministry of *derived authority*. They are *"appointed over you in the Lord"* (v. 12). In that phrase, we can see the delicate balance that exists: the pastor is both servant of the church and leader of the church. He is given authority by Christ to lead the church in the accomplishment of its mission, but that authority is not absolute; it is derived from Christ. Christ is the Chief Shepherd, and the pastor is merely the under-shepherd of that Chief Shepherd. Because his is a derived authority, and not an absolute authority, the pastor must never set himself up as a dictator to be served, but must use his authority to serve others and to lead them in serving Christ. Third, pastors are called to *devoted care* of the congregation. The word for *"appointed over you"* not only carries the idea of authority and leadership, but of tender affection and care, like a shepherd caring for sheep. Finally, the pastor is called to give *divine instruction* to the congregation. It is the pastor who is the primary, though not sole, teacher and preacher in the congregation. He has been called and equipped with gifts for understanding, communicating and applying God's Word under the anointing of the Holy Spirit. That's the pastor's responsibility to the congregation. What about the congregation's responsibility to the pastor? First, Paul calls the church to *appreciate* its pastor. The word translated *"acknowledge"* in Greek carries the idea of taking notice of someone and what they do. As such, it is the exact opposite of taking someone for granted. Second, the congregation is called to *highly esteem* their pastor. The word for *"esteem"* carries the idea of recognizing the pastor's God-given position and authority, understanding that he is not a hireling of the congregation, but a herald of the King! Finally, Paul calls upon the congregation to *love* its pastor with *agape'* love, the supernatural love that always wants the best and does the best for the other person, even at great personal sacrifice. That doesn't mean you'll always agree with him, or that he'll always look, act, react or speak in a manner you find pleasing; but even in your disagreements and your disappointments, love him anyway because of the work he's called to do.

PRAYER: Pray for your pastor and other church staff today. Pray that they might fulfill their duties with diligence, and that their ministry might be well-received and greatly appreciated by the congregation.

II THESSALONIANS

THE GREAT TURNAROUND
II THESSALONIANS 1

As mentioned previously, Thessalonica was not an easy place to be a Christian. Persecution abounded there. Pressure to conform to the pagan culture was strong. The Christians there experienced tribulation on a daily basis. But Paul is encouraged by what he hears about the Thessalonian church, that despite its fiery trials, their faith was growing, their love for one another was abundant, and they were standing up to their trials with patience, endurance and faith (vv. 3-4). As an encouragement to them, Paul details a great turnaround to come. Because of their citizenship in the Kingdom of God, they were experiencing tribulation from the kingdom of this world, but one day, in the not-so-distant future, the tables would be turned. And "payback" would be heavy for those doing the persecuting. They would be repaid with tribulation for the tribulation they had inflicted, whereas those who were troubled in this life would be given rest (vv. 6-7). This great separation and ultimate turnaround happens at the coming of Christ, after which the righteous will be taken to heaven for the Marriage Supper of the Lamb, while those who don't know Christ will be left on Earth to experience the horrors of the Day of the Lord judgments. And that's not even the worst of it. Those who do not know Christ, both those alive at His coming and those who've died prior to His coming, will be *"punished with eternal destruction, isolated from the presence of God and from the glory of His power"* (v. 9), while believers will experience His glory with Him forever (v. 10).

PRAYER: The fact that there will be a great turnaround should encourage us and fill us with joy over our future prospects, but the knowledge of the future judgment of the lost should never fill us with a sense of angry triumphalism: "Yeah, those evil people are going to get theirs!" Instead, it should fill us with grief over their lost condition, and with renewed determination to reach them with the gospel. Pray today in thanksgiving for your salvation, and for the salvation of lost people you know.

THE ANTICHRIST
II THESSALONIANS 2

The Thessalonians had apparently been shaken and troubled by some word of prophecy or a fake letter from Paul to the effect that the Day of the Lord (the time of God's judgment on Earth, equivalent to the trumpet and bowl judgments of Revelation, referenced here as the *"day of Christ"* in verse 2) had already begun. Paul sets their minds at ease by informing them that *"that Day will not come unless a falling away comes first, and the man of sin is revealed"* (v. 3). The "falling away" may refer to an end-time apostasy from the truth of God (certainly spoken of elsewhere, such as I Timothy 4:1), but the word could also have another meaning altogether. Many scholars point out that the word translated *"falling away"* can also have the meaning of a departure, or even a disappearance. If that is the meaning intended here, it may be a reference to the rapture of the church as recorded in I Thessalonians 4:13-18. That would certainly fit with the rest of the passage, which says that something is restraining the rise of the man of sin (understood by most to be the final, end-time Antichrist), and that he will not arise until *"He who is now restraining him ...is taken out of the way"* (v. 7). Many scholars believe that the restrainer is the Holy Spirit, resident on Earth in Christ's church, and that the "taking out of the way" will happen when the church is caught up to be with the Lord. Imagine the chaos that will ensue planet-wide when all the Christians are raptured. Imagine a devil-empowered, charismatic leader coming on the scene who brings order out of that chaos (vv. 9-10), as people come under a *"strong delusion"* (v. 11), believing this Antichrist to be God Himself (v. 4). Imagine the judgment that will rain down on this blasphemous figure and upon all who follow him (vv. 8, 12).

PRAYER: No one knows the day or the hour of Christ's coming, but two things are for sure: He *is* coming, and His coming is closer now than it's ever been. Pray that if the Lord returns in your lifetime, He will find you faithful. Pray that His coming will not leave you embarrassed about things you meant to do for Him but never got around to. Pray for the salvation of anyone you know who would be left behind if His coming were today.

IDLE HANDS...
II THESSALONIANS 3

It is an old adage that "idle hands are the devil's workshop." Apparently, there were some among the Thessalonian Christians who were walking in idleness, not gainfully employed, but living off of the good graces of those who were. Paul reminds them that he had set a better example for them than that, laboring tirelessly in ministry and employment so that he might not be a burden to them (vv. 7-

9). Without anything to occupy their attention, these idle Christians had become *"mere busybodies, not working at all"* (v. 11). To those lazy believers, he both commands and exhorts them *"by our Lord Jesus Christ that they quietly work and eat their own bread"* (v. 12). In other words, they are to silence their busybody, talebearing, gossipy tendencies, labor for their own needs, and quit sponging off of others. Good advice, indeed, in Paul's time and in ours. What if they didn't take that advice? His policy was that *"if any will not work, neither shall he eat"* (v. 10). He encourages the church to *"withdraw yourselves from every brother who walks in idleness"* (v. 6), to note those who did not obey Paul's word in this matter and not to socialize with them, so that they might be ashamed (v. 14). He makes it clear that he is not calling for a complete expulsion of such members (v. 15), but he is calling on the other members of the church to adopt a "tough love" approach to stop enabling their idleness. Truly, there are few things that create more weariness in doing good (v. 13) than being taken advantage of by the indolent.

PRAYER: Note that there is a huge difference between those who *will* not work and those who *cannot* work, and thus the response of believers should be much different. Pray for those you know whose lives seem to have little direction, that they might find the right path in Christ.

I TIMOTHY

HANG IN THERE!
I TIMOTHY 1

Paul himself founded the church at Ephesus on his second missionary journey, and then returned later and spent three years there. Paul had warned the Ephesian elders in Acts 20:29 that a time would come when savage wolves would come in among them to destroy the flock. That time had now come, as false teachers had infiltrated the church at Ephesus. Paul had sent Timothy to Ephesus to straighten out the serious doctrinal and leadership problems there and to do battle with the false teachers. It was not an easy task, and Timothy was apparently struggling and ready to quit. Some in the church were looking down on him because of his young age (4:12). Even though he was likely in his thirties, his opponents were much older, and in some people's eyes seemed much wiser. That, plus the fact that Timothy was timid and soft-spoken while his opponents, according to verse 9, confidently asserted even what they didn't understand, left Timothy at a distinct disadvantage in dealing with them. Paul gives his struggling protege' three words of advice that we would do well to heed in all of our ministries. First, he tells Timothy to *resist fleeing*. In verse

3, Paul tells him *"continue to remain at Ephesus."* I like the NIV 84's translation better: *"stay there!"* You'll never have any kind of ministry if you run away in time of trouble. If the devil ever figures out how to run you off from a productive area of ministry, he'll run that same play against you everywhere you go. Second, Paul tells Timothy to ***refute falsehood***. Given Timothy's natural timidity, confrontation wasn't something he enjoyed, but confrontation is sometimes necessary if the purity of the church and its message is to be preserved. Finally, Paul tells him to ***remember his function***. Someone once said that when you're up to your neck in alligators, it's hard to remember that your purpose was to drain the swamp. In the midst of false teaching and personal attacks and accusations, it would be very easy to lose sight of his primary assignment. Even though Timothy was there to confront false teachers, that wasn't his primary task. His primary task, as is the case with all disciples, was to bring the lost to faith in Christ and the saved to maturity in Christ (vv. 4-5). History shows that Timothy was successful in his assignment at Ephesus. He would eliminate the false teaching from the church and establish the truth so thoroughly there that fully 30 years later, in Revelation, Jesus commended the Ephesian church for how well they were still testing false teachers and finding them false (Revelation 2:2).

PRAYER: Is there an area of assignment as a believer where you're tempted to quit? What part of Paul's advice most resonates with you? Pray for the perseverance to *"stay there"* until the task is fully accomplished.

YOU'VE COME A LONG WAY, BABY (BUT THAT'S FAR ENOUGH)
I TIMOTHY 2

Those who still uphold gender distinctives in the church are viewed by the world, and even by some segments of the church, as hopelessly behind the times, still holding to an unfair and outdated standard. In dealing with the issue, the church has usually gone to one of two extremes, either drawing lines far beyond where the Bible draws them, or else erasing lines that the Bible has clearly drawn. Verse 11's admonition that *"a woman should learn in quietness and full submission"* (NIV 84) should be read in light of just how radical it was in the ancient world for women to receive instruction at all. Paul does not forbid women to receive instruction (*"a woman should learn"*), but he insists that she is to receive that instruction in quietness and submission. That does not mean that women are forbidden to speak in church. The quietness Paul enjoins here is a quietness of spirit, an openness to spiritual instruction. Some receive instruction with a critical spirit, others with a closed spirit, and others with a restless spirit, waiting for their chance to speak. Apparently, some women in Ephesus were like that, but both women and men for that matter should receive instruction in quietness, and in full submission to the instruction given from God's Word. Verse 12 says that Paul did not *"permit a woman to teach or to usurp authority over a man."* Both verbs are Greek present infinitives, which indicate an ongoing condition; therefore the verse might be better translated "I do not allow a woman to be a teacher or to hold a position of authority over a man." It is clear elsewhere that women are not absolutely forbidden to teach, or even to teach men, in every situation. In Acts, Aquila and his wife Priscilla both instructed Apollos (Acts 18:26). The deacon Philip had four daughters who prophesied (Acts 21:9). In the Old Testament, the judge Deborah spoke God's word to Barak (Judges 4:6-7), and the prophetess Huldah instructed King Josiah and the religious leaders of his court (II Kings 22:14-20). In I Corinthians 11:3-16, Paul tells women how to dress when they pray or prophesy in the assembly, which would include both men and women. What is forbidden here is for a woman to hold the church office that combines both teaching the church and having authority over the church, and that is the office of pastor. That's why he says in 3:1 *"...if a _man_ desires the office of an overseer..."*; he's just established that it's inappropriate for a woman to aspire to that office. So is it wrong for a woman to teach men in a Sunday School class? No, because she would be teaching under the pastor's authority. What about women in church staff positions? I see no reason to bar women from serving in children's ministry, youth ministry, educational ministry or music ministry, as long as the senior pastor is a man. Why is the pastorate limited to men? Paul gives two reasons. First is the order of creation. Eve was not created first but Adam. They were created for partnership, but within that partnership, Adam had the leadership role. Second, Paul says it was not Adam who was deceived by Satan, but Eve. Paul is *not* saying that women are more gullible than men, nor is he placing the blame for what happened in the Garden solely on Eve. In Romans, most of the blame is placed squarely on Adam, and in Genesis, it was only when Adam ate the fruit that they realized they were naked. Why does Adam get the lion's share of the blame? Because he was in charge! Verse 12 speaks of a woman usurping authority, taking authority that is not rightly hers. That is precisely what happened in the Garden. Eve, rather than receiving Adam's instruction about the fruit in quietness of mind and submissiveness to God's Word, became disturbed in mind by devil's arguments and rejected God's prohibition not to eat of the fruit. Then, rather than being led by her husband, she led him into sin. For women today to insist on the office of pastor and to usurp the pastoral authority that God has limited to men is to repeat the sin of Eve in the Garden, grasping for what is forbidden, rejecting God's Word and leading others into error.

PRAYER: While the Bible calls for the pastor to be male, most churches could not function without faithful women serving in a variety of roles. Think about some of the women who are most necessary to the ministry of your church, and lift them up in prayer today.

REQUIREMENTS OF LEADERS
I TIMOTHY 3

One of the assignments Paul had given to Timothy was to appoint godly leaders in the church at Ephesus as overseers (pastors) and deacons. The qualifications of those men (and both offices were limited to men) were similar. Notice that the qualifications of both offices have far more to do with the man's character and home life than with his business acumen, popularity, talents or financial gifts. Unfortunately, down through history, churches have often erred by appointing men to the ministry and the diaconate who were "the best qualified in the room" in terms of worldly qualifications, but woefully lacking in what God says is most important. Both offices are to be occupied by those who have demonstrated both Christian character (vv. 2-3, 7-8) and spiritual maturity (vv. 6, 10). Note especially how much attention Paul gives to the home life of overseers and deacons. Both the pastor and the deacon are to be *"husbands of one wife"* (vv. 2, 12), a phrase that could be literally translated as "one-woman men." There has been much discussion about what this phrase means in regard to divorce and remarriage, but it should be noted that a man may have only been married once, and yet still be anything but a one-woman man! A one-woman man's mental, emotional, financial and sexual attention is on his wife, not on some other woman, or on some physical or mental image of another woman. Those considered for deacons or pastors are also to be spiritual leaders in their homes, leading their wives to be *"serious, not slanderers, sober, and faithful in all things"* (v. 11). The pastor is to be *"one who manages his own house well, having his children in submission with all reverence"* (v. 4). Those appointed to the task of deacon are likewise to be those who are *"managing their children and their own houses well"* (v. 12). Why this emphasis on the home life of church leaders? Because *"if a man does not know how to manage his own house, how will he take care of the church of God"* (v. 5) which is *"God's household"* (v. 15, NIV 84)? The church is not a business; it is a family. As Jack Taylor once put it, "If God had desired something other than a family, He would have revealed Himself as something other than a Father." The church does not need a CEO and a board of directors; it needs leaders after the Father's heart.

PRAYER: Pray today for your pastor and deacons. Pray for their character, and pray that they will be able managers both of their own households and of God's household, the church.

LET NO ONE DESPISE YOUR YOUTH
I TIMOTHY 4

Timothy was a younger man, and the false teachers at Ephesus were apparently older. In a culture that valued age and experience, that put him at a disadvantage. But Timothy had something those false teachers did not. They were being driven by seducing spirits (v. 1), but he was indwelt by the Holy Spirit, and as he yielded himself to the Holy Spirit, the Holy Spirit would cultivate in him the fruit of the Spirit, which would make him a shining example of what a believer should be *"in speech, in conduct, in love, in spirit, in faith, and in purity"* (v. 12). *"Speech"* and *"conduct"* are fairly self-explanatory words, but let me say a few words about the other four. *"Love"* here is the Greek word *agape'*, which is a sacrificial love that puts the other person's needs first. It's a love that always wants and only does the best for the other person, even at great personal sacrifice. *"Spirit"* refers to living in accord with the Spirit rather than the old sin nature, the flesh. *"Faith"* as it is used here refers primarily to faithfulness, that stick-to-it spirit that lives up to its commitments and stays with the task until it is finished. Finally, *"purity"* as it is used here is a reference primarily to sexual purity, living without even a hint of sexual impropriety, which was certainly needful in the sex-charged culture of Ephesus, where young believers almost invariably came out of pagan religions that practiced sexual immorality as a sacrament, and it is certainly needed today in our own sex-charged culture. Purity is more than simply not having sex outside of marriage; it also refers to the careful disciplining of our eyes, our ears and our thoughts as well. There is, even in the church today, a natural suspicion of the young, a natural tendency to look down upon those who are younger. And that suspicion of the young is often fueled by the deficiencies of so many young people in just these six areas. Many young people today are marked by foul speech rather than wholesome speech, unholy conduct rather than holy conduct, a selfish attitude rather than sacrificial *agape'*, fleshliness rather than spirituality, flippancy rather than faithfulness and sexual promiscuity rather than sexual purity. Any young person who cultivates the sterling character traits of wholesome speech, holy conduct, *agape'* love, a spiritual walk, faithfulness to one's word, and purity of sexuality will stand out in the crowd, and will gain the respect of the godly, the blessing of God, and the influence to make a difference. While people may reject our arguments, they cannot deny the testimony of a truly righteous life being lived out before them daily.

PRAYER: If you are young, pray that you might walk before your peers and your elders in the powerful pattern enjoined here. If you are "not so young," think of several young people, either in your family or in your church. Pray for them, that they might walk according to this prescription for excellence.

FELLOWSHIP IN A FLAWED FAMILY
I TIMOTHY 5

It's a glorious concept indeed, this whole idea of the church. The Bible describes it as a holy nation. A kingdom of priests. A vine bearing fruit. The temple of the Holy Spirit, with Christ as the chief cornerstone. A body, with each member a part, under the control of the head, the Lord Jesus Christ. A flock, presided over by no less than the Good Shepherd Himself. A bride, preparing herself for her wedding and awaiting her coming groom. What lofty terms God applies to this entity we call the church! But somewhere along the way, in every Christian's life, a harsh reality sets in. We become painfully aware that there are flaws in the church. We see sin in the membership, defects in the leadership, gaps in the stewardship, fractures in the fellowship, and even challenges to Christ's Lordship. Some believers conclude that the problem is with *their* church, and off they go to find another church that they think will better meet their expectations, but after awhile, they discover many of the same problems, or different ones, in the new church. When we find ourselves disappointed with the church, we should think of it not as an institution, but as a family. There are no perfect families. They all have their flaws, their quirks and their foibles, and the church is no exception. Paul speaks of family relations here, telling Timothy how to relate to various members of the congregation. He is to be careful first to *preserve an older man's dignity* (v. 1a). A rebuke is a reprimand, a verbal correction of wrong behavior. The

Greek word translated *"rebuke"* is only used here in the whole New Testament. There is another word for rebuke used in the Scripture, but this one is much harsher. The other word means "to mete out in due measure," the idea being that the rebuke must never be stronger than the offense, and it is to be given out with a desire to correct, not to punish. The word used here speaks of lashing out abrasively, hammering someone with scathing denunciations, really letting him have it. Paul tells Timothy that no matter how much an older man may deserve a real tongue-lashing, hold back and don't give in to that impulse. Approach him instead the way you would approach your own father, with dignity and respect and restraint. Second, Timothy is to **promote a younger man's equality** (v. 1b). *"Brothers"* carries the idea of equals, peers. Younger men can be approached with a little more directness and pointedness than older men, particularly if there is a relationship of trust and close fellowship. Timothy was serving in the church under the call of God and the direction of the apostle, and that gave him authority in the church, but not superiority. Even in the delivery of a rebuke, he must not come off as superior and condescending. Third, Timothy is to **picture an older woman's maternity** (v. 2a). In a Greek household, Daddy was respected, but Mama was loved. Therefore, Timothy was to approach older men with respect, and he was to approach older women with affection. If an older woman needed to be corrected, he was to do it in the same spirit he would speak to his own dear mother and in the manner he would want someone else speaking to his mother. Finally, Timothy was called to **protect a younger woman's purity** (v. 2b). His approach to a younger woman was to be like an older brother looking out for a younger sister and giving her the benefit of his wisdom and experience. And then Paul adds a word of caution: *"in all purity."* Timothy was to take special pains to make sure that such relationships did not cross the line into attraction and impurity.

PRAYER: Think of your church family. Who comes to mind when you think of older men, younger men, older women and younger women? Whoever the Lord brings to mind, lift them up in prayer.

FIVE MARKS OF FALSE TEACHERS
I TIMOTHY 6

As we have seen, false teachers had entered into the church at Ephesus and had infiltrated its leadership with their false teaching. Timothy's job was to confront the false teachers, show them their error, and urge them to repent. If they refused to repent, he was to remove them both from leadership and from the church itself. But how was he to recognize these false teachers? Paul outlines five symptoms in verses 3-5 that would alert Timothy to a false teacher. First, Timothy was to watch for *corruption in the teacher's doctrine* (v. 3). It seems rather obvious, but Paul says that the first characteristic of a false teacher is false teaching! The Bible is our standard, and every teaching, every claimed vision or revelation, and every later writing, is to be evaluated by its adherence to the truth we find in the Word. Not only was Timothy to watch for corruption in the teacher's doctrine, he was to watch for *conceit in the teachers demeanor* (v. 4a). Pride, egotism, arrogance, a "know-it-all" spirit, bragging, the drive for recognition and the need to be first are characteristics that often mark false teachers. Those who are truly spiritual, on the other hand, are marked not by pride but by humility. Third, Paul tells Timothy to watch out for *controversy in the teacher's delivery* (v. 4b). Anyone who teaches the truth of the Word of God will eventually run into some controversy over it, but Paul here is talking about those who have *"a morbid disposition for controversy and verbal disputes"*; in other words, those who go out of their way to stir up controversy and debates and who delight in getting people agitated. False teachers, in their arrogance, love to pick an argument, often over even the most nit-picky of details, because when they win an argument it makes them feel superior. But as Paul would write to Timothy later in II Timothy 2:24-25, *"The servant of the Lord must not quarrel, but must be gentle toward all people, able to teach, patient, in gentleness instructing those in opposition."* A truly godly teacher is more interested in winning a person over than getting a win over the person. Fourth, Paul tells Timothy to watch out for **chaos in the teacher's disciples** (v. 4c-5a). One of the ways to measure the validity of a teacher or a teaching is to look at the result of that teaching in the lives of its followers. Paul, back in 1:5, said that godly instruction leads to *"love from a pure heart and from a good conscience and from sincere faith."* Those who follow false teachers, on the other hand, are said here to be marked by *"envy, strife, malicious talk, <and> evil suspicions"* (NIV 84). True teaching brings people together in the bond of love. False teaching often pits them against each other in factions and divisions and arguments. Finally, Paul tells Timothy to watch out for **covetousness in the teacher's desires** (v. 5b). While ministers should be paid for their service, no minister should be in ministry for the money, and certainly no one should be using the ministry as a scheme to enrich himself. A true man of God, as Paul said earlier in the letter, is free from the love of money.

PRAYER: As you evaluate your church leaders in light of Paul's warnings here, I sincerely hope you are under the ministry of true teachers and not false ones. If this Biblical checklist indicates the latter, run! Pray about where the Lord would have you to go. If this Biblical checklist indicates that you are under the ministry of true teachers, pray for those teachers, and thank the Lord for them.

II TIMOTHY

SPIRITUAL ADVANTAGES
II TIMOTHY 1

As Paul opens his second letter to his beloved son in the ministry, he reminds Timothy of the many advantages he has in his service to the Lord. Timothy was blessed with godly forebears (v. 5), specifically a mother and grandmother who both had a sincere faith in the Lord, and had probably been won to the Lord during Paul's first missionary journey. He was also blessed with a godly mentor in the faith in the apostle Paul (vv. 1-2, 6), a mentor who had taught him the truth of the gospel (v. 13) and was continually holding him up in prayer (v. 3). Through the indwelling Holy Spirit (v. 14), he was given the treasure of spiritual gifting (v. 6), and also supernatural boldness, power, love and self-control (v. 7) by which he used that gifting. That supernatural power would sustain Timothy in any suffering he faced for the sake of the gospel (v. 8b), which would give him supernatural endurance in serving the Lord. Timothy also had a holy calling on his life, sovereignly placed there by his Lord and Savior (v. 9). These were powerful advantages indeed, but they are available to all of us! While we might not have the advantage of godly forebears (but if we have, we should be thankful) or close mentors, we do have the indwelling Holy Spirit, spiritual gifts, spiritual fruit, and the ability to endure for the cause of Christ. And while we often speak of ministers as being "called," there is a divine calling on all Christians' lives, including yours.

PRAYER: If you have godly ancestors and godly influences in your life, thank the Lord for them. If not, pray that you might find those older in the faith to mentor you, and pray that you will be a mentor and an example to future generations. Thank Him for the indwelling Holy Spirit and His gifts and fruit. If you don't know your spiritual gifts or the divine call upon your life, pray that He will reveal your area of gifting and how He would have you use that gifting in His Kingdom work, and pray that you might have endurance to stand strong against all opposition.

WORDS OF COMMAND
II TIMOTHY 2

Paul uses the image of a soldier in II Timothy 2, and in many ways, he's like a general giving orders to a subordinate. Note the imperatives (words of command) in the chapter. First, he commands Timothy to *"be strong in the grace that is in Christ Jesus"* (v. 1). Just as physical strength is a necessity for a soldier (and is therefore the focus of boot camp), so too is spiritual strength a necessity for the Christian soldier. Grace is not simply a one-time infusion of forgiveness by which we're saved; it is an ongoing power in our lives by which God supplies whatever we need in the moment we need it. Next, Paul gives Timothy his marching orders, commanding him to *"Share the things that you have heard from me...with faithful men who will be able to teach others also"* (v. 2).

Christianity is always one generation away from extinction. If any generation fails to win the next, it dies. Those who have been introduced to the faith have the responsibility of passing the faith along in an ongoing relay race stretching from the ascension to the Lord's return. To accomplish that task will require us to *"Endure hard times as a good soldier of Jesus Christ"* (v. 3), for there will surely be opposition, which all soldiers must expect. Paul commands Timothy to *"Remember Jesus Christ, raised from the dead"* (v. 8). A soldier in the midst of battle must remember what he's fighting for. We are fighting for the one who gave His life for us on the cross. Surely, the one who gave His all for us deserves our all! Verse 15 is a command to *"Study to show yourself approved by God, a workman who need not be ashamed, rightly dividing the word of truth."* The continual study of the Word of God is our training as Christian soldiers, and the truths of the Word will equip us as soldiers to wield the Word as a sword, doing damage to our enemy, the devil. In verse 22, Paul orders Timothy to *"flee youthful desires,"* in other words, to grow up and mature as a believer, pursuing instead that which makes for a mature disciple: *"righteousness, faith, love, and peace,"* and he is to do so in the company of *"those who call on the Lord out of a pure heart."* Rambo and the former Army slogan notwithstanding, no man is "an army of one." We need our fellow soldiers alongside us to be effective warriors for the Kingdom.

PRAYER: Which of the commands above most resonates with you? Which one do you find yourself most deficient in fulfilling? Pray that you might be a good soldier of Jesus Christ.

WHEN THE WARFARE IS INTENSE
II TIMOTHY 3

Verses 2-4 sound like a synopsis of a modern daily newspaper, a description of the *"perilous times"* (v. 1) we live in today. Of even greater concern than the actions of the world around us (after all, we shouldn't be surprised when sinners are sinful), are the words of verse 5, describing a compromised, impotent, all-form-and-no-substance church that is helpless (and likely has no desire) to make a difference in such a crumbling culture. Indeed, as verse 8 seems to indicate, this apostate church is more likely to bring its wrath to bear upon true believers than to engage a sinful society! How do true believers stand strong in such perilous times? First, we must recognize that *"all who desire to live a godly life in Christ Jesus will suffer persecution"* (v. 12). We must never be blind-sided by persecution; rather, we should live in constant expectation of it. Second, when the world encourages, then urges, then threatens and then demands that we compromise the truth of the Word of God or else, we must be steadfast to *"continue in the things that <we> have learned and have been assured of"* (v. 14), the things of *"the Holy Scriptures, which are able to make you wise unto salvation through the faith that is in Christ Jesus"* (v. 15). The whims of the world waver like the weather. The "convictions" of compromised churches and Christians shift with the cultural tide. But the inspired Word of God stands strong, a never-changing firm foundation, and those who stand upon it will be *"complete, thoroughly equipped for every good work"* (v. 17).

PRAYER: Where do you see the battle lines being drawn today between the truth of the Bible and the cultural whims of the world? Where do you see churches crumbling, trading in their Biblical birthright for cultural acceptance? Pray that no matter how intense the intimidation or how severe the persecution, you and your church will always stand strong on the truth of the Word of God.

A LIFE WORTH LEAVING
II TIMOTHY 4

As Paul writes this second letter to Timothy, he is facing the prospect of imminent death at the hands of a Roman executioner. How he faces that prospect of death is instructive for us. He displays no sense of panic, no fretting and no wringing of his hands. How could he face his death so calmly? He could face his death with calm first because he had prepared his successors. It has been said that success without successors is failure. As verses 1-5 indicate, Paul had prepared Timothy and others to carry on his mission after his death. He knew that his work would not die with him. Notice how Paul views his death in verse 6. He speaks of his impending martyrdom as a drink offering. A drink offering was a sacrifice of wine or some other liquid poured out before the gods. Paul pictures the shedding of his blood as a drink offering to God, one last act of sacrifice in a lifetime of service to his Lord. Paul was not afraid of death because he was already dead! He had died to self daily in his service to Christ. He also speaks of death as a departure, a nautical term that referred to weighing anchor, loosening the ropes, and preparing a boat to set sail. Paul had full confidence that death did not mean the end of life; he was merely setting sail to a much better destination. Paul could also face death because he had no regrets about his life. He could say with assurance in verse 7, *"I have fought a good fight, I have finished my course, and I have kept the faith."* He had left no task undone and had left no loose ends hanging. Beyond that, he could face death knowing that everything he had done, including his impending martyrdom, would be amply rewarded (v. 8). Paul could further face the prospect of death because he was holding no grudges. Even though

Demas had forsaken him out of love for the present world, Paul does not speak unkindly about him (v. 10). Alexander the coppersmith did him much harm, but Paul had handed him over to the Lord (v. 14). No one stood with him in his first defense, but he does not wallow in bitterness; rather, he prays that it not be charged against them (v. 16). Finally, Paul could face his impending death because his life was in the Lord's hands, and he knew that *"The Lord <would> deliver <him> from every evil work and <would> preserve <him> for His heavenly kingdom"* (v. 18).

PRAYER: The likelihood is that you are not facing imminent death right now, but one day you will be. How you've lived your life will determine how you face your death. What are you doing now that will impact your passing? Are you preparing your successors? Are you dying daily to sin and self? Are you faithful to every assignment given by your Savior? Are you living free from grudges? Are you trusting God with every aspect of every day? Pray about any of these areas where you see a deficiency.

TITUS

A NEGATIVE ENVIRONMENT
TITUS 1

The island of Crete was a difficult place to do ministry. The Cretan people, Paul wrote, had been described by one of their own prophets as *"always liars, evil beasts, and idle gluttons"* (v. 12). They were a lying, lawless and lazy people, and given that that prophet had written those words six hundred years prior to Paul, they had been so for multiple generations. Not only were the natives a difficult people, the church there was infested with false teachers who were defiant of authority (v. 10a), devoid of substance (v. 10b), deceivers in speech (v. 10c), disruptive of families (v. 11a), deviant in doctrine (vv. 11b, 14), desirous of money (v. 11c), and defiled in conscience (vv. 15-16). It was a difficult environment to be sure, but Paul calls Titus to a two-fold strategy to combat it. First, there was the need for sharp rebuke (vv. 9, 11, 13). There is a time for diplomacy and tact. When people are genuinely deceived, persuasion is the order of the day. But in the face of radical and intentional falsehood such as at Crete, firm, decisive action is called for.

The people leading others astray had to be silenced, refuted and rebuked. Second, there was the need for sound doctrine (vv. 9, 13, 2:1). The best cure for falsehood is to just keep piling on the truth, the truth of the Word of God that counters all falsehood and transforms lives. Titus had been sent into a difficult environment, but he was not to be intimidated by it; he was, instead, to transform that environment through his boldness and through the truth of the gospel.

PRAYER: You may find yourself in a difficult environment today, with difficult people and a difficult assignment, and your first thoughts may be "Lord, what did I do to deserve this?" and "How can I get out of this?" Change your thinking! When you find yourself in a wasteland, it's not always about you. Sometimes, it's about the wasteland. God wants to use you to transform your difficult environment through your godly presence, your committed prayers, and your bold proclamation of His Word. Pray today about how you can be an agent of transformation in whatever negative situation you find yourself.

GROWING OLDER IN GRACE
TITUS 2

One of the great challenges of the Christian life is growing older well and finishing strong. Paul here gives Titus some instructions for those in each stage of life: older men, older women, young women and young men. We'll focus just on the first two. First, he calls on the older men to practice *sobriety.* The word translated *"sober,"* when used figuratively, speaks of being clear-headed, not controlled by passions and emotion, but having the kind of sound judgment that comes from wisdom and experience. Used literally, the Greek word speaks of soberness in contrast to drunkenness, and certainly there is nothing that can hinder clear thinking and wise judgment more than alcohol or other mind-altering substances. Second, he calls the older men to practice **seriousness**. Seriousness is the middle ground between somberness and silliness. He is not calling them to be long-faced, dreary, and humorless, but to treat serious matters with appropriate seriousness. Paul then tells the older men to practice **self-control**, to be *"temperate."* Self-control speaks of subjecting our thoughts, attitudes, drives, desires, speech and behavior to the higher standard of godliness found in the Word of God. Fourth, Paul calls on the older men to practice **spirituality**. They are to be *"sound in faith."* To be sound in faith speaks of being doctrinally pure and Biblically knowledgeable, controlled by the truths of the Word of God. The word *"faith"* can also be translated "faithfulness," which speaks of fidelity to one's commitments and to the cause of Christ itself. Old age is no excuse to retire from the Lord's work; it can be an opportunity to give even greater focus to the things of God. Fifth, older men are called to practice **self-sacrifice**. They are to be sound in love, the Greek word *agape'*, which is love that always wants and only does the best for the other person, even at great personal cost. A person who is sound in love is willing to sacrifice, whether time or personal resources, to meet the needs of others. Finally, Paul calls upon the older men to practice **steadfastness**, being sound in patience or perseverance. Many are the men who start strong but fizzle before the finish line. Paul issues a challenge for the older men to keep going and finish strong! As for the older women, notice in verse 3, **older women and reverence**. The word for *"reverent"* is used nowhere else in Scripture, a Greek word that means literally "appropriate to the Temple." The idea is of a woman whose normal demeanor - the way she moves, the look on her face, the overall vibe she gives off - is what one would expect of a person in a place of worship, a woman whose whole life is one of consecrated holiness to God. Second, he speaks of **older women and** *rumors.* Older women must not be *"false accusers"* or *"slanderers"* (NIV 84). They are to refuse to speak, or listen to, slanderous words and demeaning accusations against others. Third, Paul speaks of **older women and restraint**. Paul says that the older women are not to be enslaved to much wine, but are to practice temperance in the same manner as the older men. Finally, notice **older women and their responsibilities**. The older women have the responsibility of teaching what is good and encouraging to the young women.

PRAYER: Are you an older man or woman? Pray that you might be a shining example for those younger, in your family and in your church family. Are you a younger man or woman? Read again the words to the younger men and women in verses 4-6. Who are the older, godly influences in your life? Pray that you might walk as they walk as you grow older.

ADJUST YOUR CONTRAST
TITUS 3

As we have seen already, the Cretan people were an aggressive lot - brutish, violent, and rebellious. It was an island of liars, cheaters and thieves. Paul suggests a game plan to win that island based upon a strategy of contrast: the Cretan Christians were to be so different from the unsaved pagans on the island, and indeed, so different from what they had been before they knew Christ, that the pagans could not help but take notice. That's a good word for us in our society as well. In our world of loud, angry, aggressive secularism, the path to victory is not through a louder, angrier, more aggressive so-called Christianity, a la Westboro "Baptist" "Church." The game plan for victory is not conflict, but contrast; not turning up the heat through responding in kind, but turning down the heat by responding in kindness. And when the heat gets turned down, that's when the light can often shine most brightly into the darkness of a secular world. Notice what Paul says about *the Christian's relationship to the state* (v.1a). The island of Crete had been forcibly annexed into the Roman Empire in 67 B.C., and had been fuming over it ever since. At best, the Cretans treated Roman officials with smoldering contempt; at worst, insurrections and assassinations were not unheard-of on the island. Paul tells Timothy to *"Remind them to be subject to rulers."* In most circumstances, Christians are called to obey the law of the land, to be respectful of those in power, to be model citizens and to pay their taxes. Only when the government tries to require of us what God forbids or forbid us to do what God commands do we have warrant to disobey, but only on those points where obeying man's law would require us to break God's law. Note also *the Christian's reactions to superiors* (v. 1b). *"Authorities"* would include government authorities, but it isn't limited to them. It would also include authorities on the job, in the home, in the classroom and in the church. The Cretan culture, with its me-first attitude, chafed under any expression of authority, much as our culture does, but Paul calls Christians to contrast that prevalent attitude by living in subjection. Third, notice *the Christian's readiness for service* (v. 1b). In that Cretan culture where everyone was trying to take advantage of everyone else, the Christians were to be known for doing good to others. They were to take every opportunity to do every good deed that presented itself. Fourth, notice *the Christian's rule of speech* (v. 2a). To speak evil of others is to slander or curse them and treat them with contempt. The Christian's speech was to be in stark contrast to such speech. Finally, notice *the Christian's rejection of selfishness* (v. 2b). Being uncontentious, gentle, and showing humility all evoke the replacing of selfishness - me first-ism - with selflessness, the *agape'* love that always wants and always does the best for the other person, even at great personal cost. And the fact that Paul calls us to do that for *"everyone"* tells us it's not just something we do for those who love us back, but even for our enemies.

PRAYER: Ask the Lord to show you today where you can live in sharp contrast to the prevailing worldly attitudes around you.

PHILEMON

INTERCEDING WITH A BROTHER FOR A BROTHER

The little New Testament postcard Philemon is a note from Paul to a friend and fellow believer in Colossae. Writing from prison, Paul urges Philemon to receive Onesimus, Philemon's slave, who had apparently stolen from him (v. 18) and then run away, which was punishable under Roman law by death if the slave owner so decreed. Since his departure from Philemon, Onesimus had come into contact with Paul and had become a believer. Now, he is returning to Philemon to make things right, and Paul writes Philemon, urging him to receive Onesimus not as a runaway slave, but as a newfound brother, a fellow believer in the Lord (v. 16). He states that it would be within his authority as an apostle to command Philemon in this matter (v. 8), but he doesn't want to do that; his desire, rather, is that Philemon freely choose to do the right thing by Onesimus (v. 14). Paul urges Philemon to see God's hand in what had happened (vv. 15-16). Had Onesimus not run away, he might not have come to know the Lord. Having been born again, Onesimus, who was once *"unprofitable"* (v. 11) or *"useless"* (NIV 84) (sounds like a troublesome slave indeed!) is now both profitable and useful, to Paul, to Onesimus, and to the Kingdom.

Philemon's response should not be anger over what had occurred in the past, but rejoicing in how God had redeemed the situation (v. 20)!

PRAYER: Are you aware of a dispute between two fellow believers? Pray about how the Lord might want to use you to bring reconciliation between them. If nothing else, intercede with the Lord for them to be reconciled.

HEBREWS

SUPERIOR TO ANGELS
HEBREWS 1

There was a time in the not-so-distant past when angels were all the rage. There were TV shows about angels, and any number of books about angelic encounters and contacting angels and even worshiping angels were populating the bestseller charts. While some of these books were sound Biblically (Billy Graham's excellent book comes to mind), most of them were written from a decidedly New Age perspective that either misinterpreted or ignored the Bible's teaching on angels altogether. No doubt, the one encouraging this "angel fixation" was none other than the chief of the fallen angels, Satan himself. The holy angels must have been appalled at this focus on them rather than upon the Lord Jesus. The first chapter of Hebrews shows that the He is infinitely superior to angels in every way. Jesus is the Son of God, whereas angels are the servants of God (vv. 5, 7). Angels are not to be worshiped, but God alone is to be worshiped; in fact, angels worship Jesus (v. 6). As the creator of all (v. 10), and the ruler of all (v. 8), Jesus is absolutely sovereign (v. 8); the angels, by contrast, are sent out on assignment, the assignment being to *"minister to those who will inherit salvation"* (v. 14).

PRAYER: Worship the Lord Jesus today as the eternal Son, as the Creator, and as the Sovereign Lord of all. Thank Him for His provisions for us, including the provision of angels to minister to us in the invisible, but oh-so-real, spiritual realm that surrounds us.

SUCH A GREAT SALVATION
HEBREWS 2

The author continues speaking of Christ's superiority over the angels, but he introduces another theme: the greatness of the salvation that Christ offers. Note the transition in verses 1-4: *"If the word spoken by angels* (which the author has already shown to be inferior to Christ) *was true, and every sin and disobedience received a just recompense, how shall we escape if we neglect such a great salvation, which was first declared by the Lord, and was confirmed to us by those who heard Him? God also bore them witness with signs and wonders and diverse miracles and with gifts of the Holy Spirit distributed according to His own will."* Jesus announced salvation, the apostles of Christ proclaimed His salvation, and their testimony was attested by God the Holy Spirit in His gifts and miraculous workings. If we refuse that offer of salvation, so powerfully offered, how shall we escape? We won't, for it is the only way of salvation. It is only through Christ alone that anyone can be saved. He is in control of this world and the world to come (vv. 5-9), and He offers not just forgiveness but a family relationship to those who receive Him (vv. 10-13). Through His death for everyone (v. 9), He has destroyed the one who has the power of death, the devil (v. 14), He has removed from those of us who believe in Him the fear of death (v. 15), and He has freed us, and progressively frees us, from bondage to sin (v. 16). Because He knows the pain of temptation personally, He is able to help us in our struggles with temptation (v. 18) and He is merciful to those who stumble (v. 17).

PRAYER: Are you struggling today with temptation? Call upon Him for help. Have you fallen to temptation? Approach Him for mercy.

DON'T LET YOUR HEART BE HARDENED
HEBREWS 3

It is amazing that many of the Exodus generation, who had seen the miracles God did in rescuing them from slavery in Egypt, still rebelled against Him and died in the wilderness without ever entering the Promised Land. It is even more amazing that many of those who have been redeemed from the bondage of sin (2:15) can become hardened through the deceitfulness of sin and lack of faith (vv. 13-14), to the point that they *"depart from the living God"* (v. 12). Such believers do not lose their salvation, any more than the rebelling Israelites were summarily returned to Egypt, but they do lose their usefulness to the Kingdom and their reward of service. The rebelling Israelites missed out on the Promised Land, a land of blessing flowing with milk and honey and a land of purpose in defeating their enemies and conquering the land, and instead were sentenced to live out their lives in what we might call God's Plan B. Oh, they still had the pillar of fire by night and pillar of cloud by day, they still had the manna each morning and the quail each night, and their clothes didn't wear out for the entire journey. Their needs were still met until they died, but what miserable, meaningless lives they lived: meander aimlessly in circles in the wilderness, pick up manna each morning, prepare manna, eat manna, stare at sand, attend funerals, grab a quail each evening, prepare quail, eat quail and manna, sleep, and repeat. Every day. For forty long years. No thrill of victory. No conquests by faith. No land of milk and honey. Not even a change of clothes. Nothing but dull, dry, meaningless, aimless sameness. It is likewise possible for those who are in Christ to miss out on their Promised Land. The Promised Land does not represent heaven, despite what many of our classic hymns would indicate, because there were still giants occupying the land and battles to be fought in the Promised Land, and surely there will be nothing of the sort in heaven. No, the Promised Land represents a victorious Christian life - going forward in faith, taking on giants, defeating the enemy, and taking ground for the Kingdom. That is an exciting life, a life of meaning and a life of reward. But for too many Christians, sin and lack of faith have sentenced them to wander through the wilderness of this world, enjoying just a small portion of God's intended blessings and accomplishing little of what God wanted for them; essentially, just waiting around to die. That is no way to live! It's not living at all, but just surviving, and God wants more for His children than that.

PRAYER: As you examine your life, are you like the Exodus generation, condemned by faithlessness and sin to less than God's best? Or are you like the Joshua generation, going forth in faith and obedience to defeat giants, take down walled cities, and take the territory of the enemy? Ask the Lord to reveal to you any area of your life where you are walking in less than His best.

RESOURCES FOR THE JOURNEY
HEBREWS 4

Living on this side of glory is tough. Even for the believer who is walking in faith and obedience, the Promised Land of spiritual maturity still brings with it high mountains (obstacles), giant warriors (opposition) and walled cities (challenges). We not only deal with the enemies without, but with the enemy within, our old sin nature that continues to plague us throughout this journey of life. Hebrews 4 shows us three powerful resources we have to give us victory in the obstacles, opposition and challenges of this life. The first resource is the Word of God. Far from being what the world tells us it is, an old, dusty book containing the obsolete wisdom of a bygone era, it is rather *"alive, and active, and sharper than any two-edged sword, piercing even to the division of soul and spirit, of joints and marrow, and able to judge the thoughts and intents of the heart"* (v. 12). The Bible is unlike any other book. In its pages we interact with God Himself. No doubt there have been times when you have been burdened, or confused, or guilty, or distressed, and you've come to your Bible reading for the day and found that it addressed exactly what you were dealing with in a powerful way. The words were, figuratively speaking, printed in neon. That's not a coincidence. That wouldn't have happened if you had read *Moby Dick* that day instead of the Bible. No, it was the living Holy Spirit, illuminating His living and active Word, that spoke to your heart. The author goes on to speak of the Word of God as a precision instrument, a surgical tool beyond the finest of lasers, so precise that it can separate our souls (our mind, will and emotions, which so often cloud our judgment) and our spirits (that part of us that communes with God), and to judge the thoughts and intents of our hearts. Even for believers, *"The heart is more deceitful than all things and desperately wicked; who can understand it?"* (Jeremiah 17:9), but the Word cuts through all of our internal clutter to show us God's truth, truth about Himself and truth about ourselves. Beyond the Word, we also have the resource of a great High Priest in Jesus, not *"a High Priest who cannot sympathize with our weaknesses, but One who was in every sense tempted like we are, yet without sin"* (v. 15). As the old hymn put it, Jesus knows all about our struggles. He has been there. He has felt the sting of temptation, and emerged victorious every time. He can give us victory, and He can pick us up when we fall. Finally, we have the wonderful resource of anytime, anywhere access to God in prayer. Verse 16 encourages us to *"come with confidence to the throne of grace, that we may obtain mercy and find grace to help in time of need."* Whether we're struggling with temptation, or laid low in the dust of failure, He is there for us. The devil will try to keep us from prayer because of embarrassment over our weakness and our failures (which will only lead to more weakness and failures), but this passage assures us that we can come boldly to the Lord in prayer. If we've failed, we will find mercy. In our weakness, we will find grace to help.

PRAYER: It's time to come boldly and confidently before God's throne! What do you need? Where are you struggling? How have you failed? Where do you lack wisdom? Tell Him now. Open your heart to His mercy. Rely in faith upon His strength. Open your eyes to His answers.

LEFT BACK
HEBREWS 5

When I was in elementary school, I was aware that there were some students who were "left back" in the parlance of the day. They had failed to master the curriculum at their grade level, and therefore had to remain at that grade level for the next school year while their classmates moved on to the next grade. What a terrible embarrassment it would be, I thought, to be left back. Unfortunately, many Christians, rather than moving on with the Lord, get left back, remaining at a level of spirituality they should have long ago mastered. The author speaks of them in verses 11-14, chiding his readers that they had been believers long enough to become teachers, but instead, they were still stuck in elementary school, needing someone to teach them the basics yet again, feeding on milk like babies rather than on solid food. Actual babies are cute, but 30 year-olds who act like babies are anything but cute, and Christians who should be mature but are still mired in carnality are likewise anything but cute. In fact, the author indicates that they are in a perilous position spiritually. They are *"hard of hearing"* (v. 11), *"unskilled in the word of righteousness"* (v. 13), and unable to discern between good and evil (v. 14). The mature, on the other hand, are *"those who through practice have powers of discernment that are trained to distinguish good from evil"* (v. 14). The key to maturity? Practice. Just as an athlete won't get better at his sport (and will in fact grow worse) without practice, so too the Christian who only hears the Word, but does not put it into practice, will not mature, but will degenerate in His Christian walk (James 1:22).

PRAYER: Not only were there students who were left back in my elementary school all those years ago, there were also students who were so advanced they skipped grades. I never heard of it happening, but I suppose it would have been possible for a "left back" student to really apply himself and get himself put back in the grade with his peers, or even to surpass them. The good news is that those who have fallen behind spiritually can go forward. Where are you in your walk with the Lord? Are you a hearer only, or are you putting into practice what you see in the Word? Pray that He might bring you to maturity, that you might be where He would have you to be as His disciple.

A MOST DIFFICULT PASSAGE
HEBREWS 6

One of the most difficult passages in the Bible is Hebrews 6:4-12. There are three primary ways of understanding it. Some teach that the people in question are genuine believers who lose their salvation. One must note, however, that if that is the case, it is impossible to renew them again to salvation, and most who teach that you can lose your salvation also teach that a person may be restored (born again, again?). In my mind, there are too many clear passages that teach that a person cannot lose his salvation to interpret this passage in this way (John 10:28 comes to mind; if even one person who has ever had eternal life perishes, that would make the Son of God a liar). Unclear passages are to be interpreted by clear ones, not vice-versa. A second understanding is that these were unsaved persons who had advanced to the very threshold of salvation, but had never committed themselves to Christ. They had merely *"tasted"* the Word of God, the heavenly gift, and the powers of the age to come. They had shared in the Holy Spirit in the sense that they had been enlightened by the Holy Spirit to understand the truth. They professed salvation, but they never possessed salvation, and they fell away, not from true saving faith, but from the fringes of faith. In favor of this understanding is verse 9. However, it is difficult to maintain its understanding of *"tasted,"* given that the same writer says that Jesus tasted death for every man (2:9). Further, the understanding of *"shared in the Holy Spirit"* seems strained. The third understanding fits best with the overall context: that these are true believers who stall completely and utterly in their Christian growth. In Romans 8:28-30, Paul sets up an unbroken chain: believers are foreknown, predestined, called to salvation, justified and eventually glorified. Curiously absent from this chain, however, is sanctification (spiritual growth). While sanctification is the work of God, the Bible indicates that cooperation and effort on the part of the Christian is necessary for sanctification (II Peter 1:5-7). What if this effort is not put forth, however? The passage here in Hebrews speaks of that possibility. The author gives a warning that there can come a point in which God places the believer "on the shelf," so to speak, at which point his heart will be so hardened (see the triple warning in 3:6, 3:15

and 4:7) that it will be impossible for him to repent of his condition (v. 6). Much as Paul feared in I Corinthians 9:24-26, such a believer has been effectively disqualified from any further usefulness to the Kingdom. The author elaborates on this teaching in verses 7-8. The land that drinks in the rain and then produces a useful crop receives the blessing of God. This is the believer who presses on to maturity, producing a crop of good works and the fruit of the Spirit. However, the author goes on to speak of land that produces only thorns and thistles. Such a land, he says, is *"near to being cursed"* and destined to be burned. This refers to the believer who does not press on to maturity. He is rejected (disqualified from future service), near to being cursed (but not in fact cursed!), and burned, not in the sense of hellfire, but in the sense of the testing of his works by fire at the judgment seat (I Corinthians 3:13), or in the sense of the discipline of God. When land is infested with thorns and thistles, burning the land burns off the thorns and thistles, but the land itself does not catch fire. Both God's discipline and the future testing achieve that same purpose. The believer is not burned (in the sense of losing his salvation), but the unfruitful works in his life are burned up.

PRAYER: However one interprets this passage, it is a dire warning, and it illustrates the importance of going on with the Lord. Is there an area of your life where you are lagging behind? Pray that you might drink in the rain from above and produce a harvest of righteousness.

THE ORDER OF MELCHIZEDEK
HEBREWS 7

In illustrating the superiority of Jesus over the Levitical priesthood, the author of Hebrews invokes an Old Testament type, a Messianic prophecy, and a complex argument drawn from them. A type is an Old Testament foreshadowing of a truth, usually about the person and work of Jesus, clearly taught in the New Testament. The type in question is the story of Melchizedek, the King of Salem and priest of Most High God whom Abraham encountered after his victory over the four kings (see Genesis 14:18-20). Melchizedek blessed Abraham, and Abraham gave him a tenth of the spoils of the victory. After this brief three verses in Genesis, Melchizedek is mentioned only once more, in Psalm 110:4, in a Messianic psalm declaring that the Messiah would be *a priest forever, after the order of Melchizedek.* Some have suggested that Melchizedek was in fact a preincarnate appearance of Christ, but that does not seem to be the case; Melchizedek is said to be like the Son of God (v. 3), not the Son of God Himself. How was Melchizedek like Jesus? Melchizedek was said to be both the King of Righteousness and the King of Salem (which means "Peace"). Certainly, those two terms are appropriately applied to Jesus. The Genesis account gives us no information about Melchizedek's ancestry, his birth, or his death. The Hebrews author takes that to be not because he had none, but because he is foreshadowing Jesus, who is eternal, and whose priesthood is eternal. He goes on to show that Abraham paid tithes to Melchizedek, and that Melchizedek blessed Abraham, both indicating that Melchizedek was Abraham's superior, and thus superior to Abraham's descendants, including his descendant Levi and all of his priestly descendants. If Jesus is of Melchizedek's order of priesthood, then He must be a superior priest to the Levitical priests as well. It is a complex argument, to be sure, but the point is given in verses 23-25: *"And the former priests were numerous because they were hindered from serving because of death. But He, because He lives forever, has an everlasting priesthood. Therefore He is able to save to the uttermost those who come to God through Him, because He at all times lives to make intercession for them."* The Levitical priests were mortal, weak, and sinful (vv. 23, 27-28), and they had to offer up sacrifices daily for their own sins and for the sins of the people. Jesus, the superior High Priest, offered up one sacrifice, a sacrifice of Himself *"holy, innocent, undefiled, separate from sinners"* (v. 26). The Levitical priests with their sacrifices could suffice to cover sin for a season, but only the perfect sacrifice of the perfect High Priest could take away sin forever and save us to the uttermost!

PRAYER: Praise Jesus today that He is our perfect High Priest, that He lived a sinless life, that He offered Himself as a perfect sacrifice in our place, and that He saves us to the uttermost, not giving us conditional life or probationary life, but eternal life through His eternal intercession for us!

A SUPERIOR COVENANT
HEBREWS 8

Having shown Jesus to be superior to the priests of the Law, the author now shows that Jesus is *"the Mediator of a better covenant, which was established on better promises"* (v. 6). The first covenant was faulty, not because of any fault in God, but because of the inability and failure of the Israelites to keep it (vv. 7-9). Under the old covenant, failure to keep the Law resulted in God's rejection (v. 9b). So a new covenant was necessary, one that would make allowance for the weakness and failure of human beings. This new covenant puts His laws in our minds and hearts (v. 10a), rather than on stone and parchment, and invites us into a personal relationship with Him (v. 10b-11). Beyond that, this new covenant provides mercy and forgiveness, rather than rejection, for the sinner (v. 12). The new covenant has superceded the old (v. 13). When I was in college, whenever a new catalog with new degree requirements came out, you had the option of continuing in the program as spelled out in the catalog you came in under, or you could adopt the new standards for your program. The same is true for the

Israelites that Hebrews was written to. With the coming of Jesus, a new covenant had been inaugurated. They could choose to remain under the old covenant, which would result in failure and condemnation, or they could receive the new covenant, resulting in forgiveness and mercy. That same choice faces us all. We can try to get to God through good works or religious ritual, but our failure is assured (Romans 3:23), or we can enter into the new covenant of grace through faith in Christ (Ephesians 2:8-9).

PRAYER: Thank God today that He was unwilling to keep the old covenant in force, the covenant of law, failure and rejection, but was willing to pay the price of the death of Christ to inaugurate the new covenant of grace, mercy and forgiveness.

JUST ONCE
HEBREWS 9

In continuing to assure his Hebrew readers of the superiority of the new covenant over the old, the author speaks of how the high priests of the old covenant must continually offer sacrifices, both for their own sins and the sins of the people, and then appear in the earthly Holy of Holies each year on the Day of Atonement with that blood (v. 25), but Jesus, as a far superior High Priest, has offered one sacrifice for all people for all time, appearing once in the heavenly Holy of Holies bearing the blood of His sacrifice of Himself (v. 26). There is no other sacrifice for sin, no other means of salvation, other than the shed blood of Christ on the cross of Calvary. Notice that there is another "once" in the passage: *"it is appointed for men to die once, but after this comes the judgment"* (v. 27). Contrary to the false claims of Eastern religions and New Age-ism and their promises of reincarnation, there are no second chances, no practice rounds, no "just keep running that play until you get it right" like some kind of cosmic football practice. There's one life, one death, and one judgment to follow. Obviously, the author is not talking about those times when someone is "clinically dead" and then resuscitated, but about the time when each of us will permanently exit this life, and when we do, we're not coming back; we're going to stand in the presence of God to be judged. The content of that one judgment is what we have done with the one sacrifice of Christ. Did we receive Him as our Lord and Savior, trusting His sacrifice on Calvary as the payment for our sins, or did we fail to receive Him during our lives? Hanging in the balance of that question is heaven or hell. Eternity is too long to get it wrong.

PRAYER: All of us have an appointment with death, but none of us knows when it will be. Are you ready for that appointment? Have you prepared for the judgment to come? Have you received Christ? If not, receive Him now! If you have, thank Him for His marvelous grace that fills this life with meaning and the future life with hope.

LET US
HEBREWS 10

In light of what he has been teaching about Jesus and His superiority as a High Priest forever, the author makes five "let us" statements in verses 19-25. First, he says, *"let us draw near with a true heart in full assurance of faith, having our hearts sprinkled to cleanse them from an evil conscience, and our bodies washed with pure water"* (v. 22). It is not enough merely to recognize who Jesus is, and what He has done in inaugurating the new covenant. We must enter into that covenant, drawing near to Him in faith. When we do, our hearts are sprinkled with His blood and we are cleansed from our sins. Having our bodies washed with water is a reference to the ordinance of baptism, the outward sign of our inward cleansing. Second, the author says, *"Let us firmly hold the profession of our faith without wavering, for He who promised is faithful"* (v. 23). From that beginning, we are to go forward with the Lord, standing strong in faith in Him and faithfulness to Him, unwilling to back down under the pressure of the evil world (see vv. 32-33). To do that, we need companions on the journey, fellow travelers in this Christian life, and so the author says, *"And let us consider how to spur one another to love and to good works"* (v. 24). Have you ever been "spurred" into doing something, only to be glad you did it? You only get "spurred" when it's something you're hesitant to do! When a fellow believer begins spurring you in some matter, don't get angry; consider that God may be using a fellow believer (even a prickly one!) to move you out of your comfort zone and into a place of greater blessing. Finally, the author says *"Let us not forsake the assembling of ourselves together, as is the manner of some, but let us exhort one another, especially as you see the Day approaching."* Recently, it was revealed that one of the fastest-growing statistical categories in terms of religious faith in America is what is being called "the Dones," people who haven't given up on their faith in Christ, but for whatever reason, have given up on the church. What a tragic mistake! The fellowship of the church is a necessity if believers are to stand strong, especially as times grow more perilous between now and the Lord's coming.

PRAYER: Have you drawn near by receiving Christ as your Lord and Savior? If so, have you followed up that personal commitment with the public demonstration of your faith in baptism? Are you standing strong, even under pressure? Are you standing with fellow believers in the church? Are you faithful in your attendance in the services of the church? If there is a disconnect between the commands of the Word here and your experience, ask forgiveness for your disobedience, and then pray about how you can make it right. Pray also that the Lord will show you ways you can spur your fellow believers to love and good works.

THE HALL OF FAME
HEBREWS 11

Hebrews 11 is the famous "Hall of Fame of Faith." The biggest display in this Hall of Fame is the one dedicated to Abraham. The Bible says that we walk by faith and not by sight (II Corinthians 5:7), or at least we're supposed to, and nobody embodies that walking-without-seeing faith better than Abraham. Notice here four truths that we're taught about walking by faith and not by sight in Abraham's story. First, *walking faith goes forward at God's command, even when the final destination is not revealed* (v. 8). The Bible tells us that God *knows* the end from the beginning, but it never says that He always *reveals* the end from the beginning. More often than not, He doesn't reveal the whole plan; He tells us to go and then gives us just enough light for the step we're on right now. Why is that? Because He wants us to trust Him, not the plan. If we've got to see how it's all going to work out before we are willing to obey, then we're not going to obey very often. God may not always reveal exactly what the end will be, or exactly what the means will be, but when He calls, and we go forward, He makes the way. Second, notice that *walking faith sacrifices current comfort for an unseen heavenly reward* (vv. 9-10). Abraham was apparently quite comfortable and settled in his home country. He had lived there for all of his 75 years, his family was there, and since he lived in a city, we can assume that he probably had a nice house to live in. He gave up all that to live in a tent, to wander from place to place in a foreign land among wicked people. Even though God promised him descendants and the land in which he dwelled, he was in the Promised Land 25 years before Isaac was born, and the only land he ever owned there was a cave in which he buried his wife. But verse 10 tells us why he was willing to give up the comforts of the Chaldees for the difficulties of Canaan; he was looking beyond this life to his heavenly reward. He was willing to give up his life in the city of Ur because he knew he would spend eternity in the city of God. He was willing to sacrifice in this life because he knew how great would be his reward in the next life. We are so tied so often to the things of this life, when God wants us tied to the things of the next life. We spend so much time seeking comfort here rather than reward there. We waste so much of our lives on things that we can see and feel and touch and enjoy only for a short time rather than laying up for ourselves treasures in heaven. Third, notice that *walking faith trusts God to do what is humanly impossible* (vv. 11-12). Sarah had been barren throughout their marriage, and now is long past child-bearing age, nearing 90. Abraham, likewise, is pushing 100. Every human, natural indicator said that there was no way these two were ever going to have any children. But God is a God of the miraculous, a God for whom nothing is impossible that is within His will and His nature, and He allowed them to conceive Isaac in their old age. The reason why many of us never see God move in miraculous ways is because we never commit ourselves to anything beyond what we can see or do in our own power. Lastly, *walking faith trusts in God's promise even when circumstances seem to contradict it* (vv. 17-19). We all know the story of how God told Abraham to take Isaac and sacrifice him. That set off a flurry of confusion in Abraham's mind. God had promised to bring descendants to Abraham through Isaac, but as yet, Isaac had no children. And now God was calling him to sacrifice Isaac as a burnt offering. How could this be? Finally, Abraham hit upon the answer. God must be planning to raise him from the dead! Of course, that was not what God had planned, as he didn't in the end require Abraham to sacrifice Isaac, but the point is that despite the circumstances, Abraham never wavered in his trust in God's promise, even when the circumstances seemed to contradict it. The big question in life is, what are we going to believe? What we see in our circumstances? Or what we read in God's Word? God is looking for people who will grab hold of his promises and hold on even while all hell breaks loose around them to try to break their grip. He's looking for people who will walk by faith, not by sight.

PRAYER: Pray today for an ever-growing walking faith, faith that will be strong in the toughest times of life.

LAY ASIDE THE WEIGHT
HEBREWS 12

Paul, who was apparently a sports fan, speaks of the Christian life in terms of a race, conducted in a stadium filled with all those great Hall-of Famers who have gone before (chapter 11). In verse 1, we are told to *"lay aside every weight and the sin that so easily entangles us."* What are the encumbrances that will slow us down and hinder us as we seek to run a good race in the Christian life? Think about a runner preparing to run in a race. Obviously, that runner is going to have to lay aside some things if he's going to be successful. First of all, he's going to have to lay aside *improper table habits*. A runner who is in training can't eat just anything and everything. He's got to eat the right foods with the right nutritional value in the right amounts. As Christians, our food is the Word of God, the Bible. It's got all the spiritual nutrients that we need to run the race of life in a way that pleases God. We need to be feeding on it regularly, on a daily basis, not just on a weekly or bi-weekly basis. Second, an athlete must also put aside *improper training habits*. Nobody ever became a great runner by skipping practice, watching other people run, or watching TV shows about running. To become a great runner, you've got to RUN! You've got to listen to the coach, and put into practice his training regimen. By the same token, nobody ever became a great Christian by skipping church or by sitting on the sidelines watching others serve the Lord. Going to church is not running the race. Going to church is practice. It is in church that believers are equipped to go out and do the work of ministry, running the race on the job, in their schools, in their neighborhoods and in their homes. Third, a runner who wants to compete at a high level most put aside *improper technique*. Running coaches are trained to watch as the runners run, to pick out any flaws in their stride that might be throwing them off and slowing them down. The Holy Spirit is our coach as we run this race. Through the Bible, through our consciences, through impressions, and through our fellow believers, He guides us not only in what He wants us to do, but in how He wants us to do it, and He alerts us to anything in our lives that might be throwing us off from doing His will or from doing it His way. Fourth, runners must put aside *improper teamwork*. Running is pretty much an individual sport, except for relay races, where each runner runs his leg of the race and then passes the baton to the next one. It doesn't matter how fast a member of a relay team is, if he can't work well with his teammates in receiving or handing off the baton, he is going to go home a loser, and his failure will result in his fellow team members losing as well. Our race of the Christian life likewise has both individual and team aspects to it. We need each other in the church if we are going to run well. It is only as each of us does his part, and only as we work together in harmony, that any of us can cross the finish line victoriously.

PRAYER: As you look over the above checklist, can you say that you are laying aside every weight in order that you might run the race in a winning manner? Pray about any encumbrances that may be weighing you down. Ask the

Holy Spirit, as your divine coach, to point out anything that may be hindering you.

REMEMBERING
HEBREWS 13

In this last chapter of Hebrews, the author calls his readers to remembrance on several fronts. The first call to remembrance is *"Do not forget to entertain strangers"* (v. 2). This call to hospitality is accompanied by a remarkable promise: *"thereby some have entertained angels unknowingly."* Imagine when such angelic encounters, of which we were totally unaware, are revealed to us in the next life! Second, the author calls us to *"Remember those who are in chains, as if imprisoned with them, and those who are ill treated, since you are also in the body"* (v. 3). As those who are relatively free from persecution, it is easy to become so consumed with our lives that we forget about those who are suffering for Christ in various corners of the world. Third, he calls them to remember their spiritual leaders: *"Remember those who rule over you, who have proclaimed to you the word of God"* (v. 7). Believers are called to follow the faith of their leaders, to look to them as examples of what a life of faith can accomplish. The author, after dealing with several other matters, returns to this subject in verse 17, where he tells his readers to *"Obey your leaders and submit to them, for they watch over your souls as those who must give an account. Let them do this with joy and not complaining, for that would not be profitable to you."* The word *"complaining"* carries the idea of a grievous burden rather than a joyful assignment. Adversarial relationships between churches and pastors lead to joyless ministries and faltering churches. No church will ever rise above the level of its pastor, and no pastor will ever be able to lead a church upward while being beaten down by it. Finally, the author tells his readers not to forget to do good and share with others, sacrifices that, along with the sacrifice of praise, are pleasing to God (v. 16).

PRAYER: Pray today for those who are being persecuted around the world, and for the pastor or pastors of your church.

JAMES

COUNT IT ALL JOY
JAMES 1

How can we react appropriately in the face of various trials we face? First, we must acknowledge the inevitability of trials. Notice that James doesn't say "if" you face trials. Trials are inevitable, part and parcel of living in a fallen world, and not only are Christians not exempt from them, we can expect extra trials that come from being Christians in a world hostile to Christ and Christianity. Second, we need to have the right attitude in the midst of trials. *"Consider it pure joy, my brothers, whenever you face trials of many kinds..."* (v. 2 - NIV 84). I don't know about you, but that's not usually my first reaction. Understand that James is not ordering some happy-face emotion during severe trials, nor is he demanding that believers somehow enjoy their trials, and he most definitely is not saying that the way to deal with a problem is to deny its reality. The word he uses, *"consider,"* has nothing whatsoever to do with the emotions; it has everything to do with the will. He is saying that we can make a deliberate decision to experience joy even in times of trouble, even when we don't feel especially joyful. Joy comes from knowing that God is in control, that suffering is temporary, that God only desires and does what is best for us, and that nothing can separate us from His love. Beyond our mindset, James goes on to give us two concrete actions to take in the midst of our trials. First, we should pray for God's wisdom (vv. 5-8), wisdom to manage the trial and to deal with it effectively, but most importantly, wisdom to get the full benefit of the trial. God never allows a trial into our lives except for a positive purpose. He uses trials to mold us and make us more like Jesus, to teach us things we need to know. Therefore, our first question when we find ourselves in trouble should be "God, what are you trying to teach me in all this?" Secondly, in verses 9-11, James encourages us to look at life from an eternal perspective. At first glance, verses 9-11 seem to have little relationship to what comes before it, but James is still developing his theme of dealing with trials. He speaks here of the Christian who is in humble circumstances, and of the believer who is rich in this world's goods. The believer in humble circumstances must remember that though he may not be blessed with great riches in this life, this life isn't all there is; it is but temporary, and there is a better home awaiting him in heaven. The rich Christian is likewise called to view life from an eternal perspective, realizing that what he has in this life likewise is temporary, and his main concern should be laying up treasure in heaven. When faced in this manner - with a proper attitude, a prayerful response, and an eternal perspective, trials reveal the genuineness and depth of our faith (v. 3), result in the growth of our faith (vv. 3-4), produce confidence in the God of our faith, and allow us to participate in the rewards of our faith (v. 12).

PRAYER: What trials are you currently facing? Pray for wisdom in the trial, and pray that you will receive the full benefit from it.

COUNTERFEIT FAITH
JAMES 2

Not all who believe they have saving faith actually have it. Many who profess faith in Christ in fact do not possess faith in Christ. In verses 14-19 James paints a picture of what counterfeit faith looks like. Notice that false faith is *totally ineffective* (v. 14). There are many who profess faith in Christ who have never shown any evidence of true conversion. They may have walked an aisle, and possibly continued on to baptism, but there has been no change in their personalities, their loyalties, their lifestyles, or their activities. When Christ truly comes into a person's life, when he is truly born again and regenerated to new life through the indwelling Holy Spirit, he cannot stay unchanged. There will be evidence of a changed life in that person. James is not saying that we are saved by works or saved by faith plus works; he is saying that we are saved by a faith *that* works. False faith is also *callously indifferent* (vv. 15-17). Where there is true faith, there will be concern for those who are hurting. But there will be more than concern, because true faith translates concern into concrete ministry. Third, false faith is *absolutely invisible* (v. 18). The argument James is advancing is this: if it were possible to have faith without works, a person who had faith without works would be at a complete loss demonstrate his faith to anyone else. The only way we can show our faith to others is through our actions, through our changed lives and through our compassionate ministry. Finally, notice that false faith is *merely intellectual* (v. 19). Just believing in the existence of one God is not enough to save. Oh, how many there are who think they are saved because they aren't rank atheists, but there's not even one demon of hell who is an atheist. They all believe in God, so much so that they shudder at their future fate. By the same token, there's not a demon of hell who doesn't believe in the deity of Christ, His virgin birth, His sinless life, His sacrificial death, His bodily resurrection or His triumphant return. The demons were confessing Jesus as the Christ in the gospels long before the disciples came to that conclusion. Obviously, true Biblical faith is more than believing the facts about Jesus; it is a personal turning from sin, an absolute trust in Christ to save you from your sins because of His sacrifice on the cross, and a personal decision to surrender your life to His Lordship. You can believe all the facts about Jesus on an intellectual level, but if you never make that personal decision, you will die lost, and spend eternity in hell with the demons who also believe all the facts about Jesus.

PRAYER: Is yours a true faith, or a false faith? Pray for those who are deceived into believing they are believers, when in fact, all they have is false faith.

SPEAKING OF TONGUES...
JAMES 3

It has been said that 99% of most problems in most churches would be solved if God's people would learn to control their tongues. James tells us that the tongue has great potential, both for good and for evil. Notice first that the tongue has *the power to discredit* (vv. 1-2). Leaders can do great damage if their speech is unbridled. Therefore, it is imperative that those who would assume the position of teaching be persons of controlled tongue and self-control in general. The tongue, uncontrolled, has the power to discredit our witness, our church, our message and our Savior. Second, the tongue has *the power to destroy* (vv. 5b-8). I can't imagine what ever led someone to coin the jingle "Sticks and stones may break my bones, but words will never hurt me." Most of us have never had our bones broken by sticks and stones, but few if any of us have made it through life without being grievously wounded by words.

Words may not break bones, but they do far worse than that. They break spirits. They diminish hope. They destroy reputations. James used two illustrations to show the incredible destructive power of the tongue. First, he spoke of fire. It only takes a small spark to start a fire, but once the fire is started, it takes on a life of its own. Likewise, even a few words can start a chain reaction that burns out of control. The second illustration is of venom. When a snake bites someone, it only injects a few drops of poison, but those few drops are enough to take his victim's life. So it is with words. It only takes a few words, ill-conceived, poorly motivated, wrongly spoken, to poison the fellowship and ministry of the church. Third, we see that the tongue has *the power to direct* (vv. 3-4). Two illustrations here show that the same power the tongue has to destroy, if properly harnessed, can be used to do great things. The first illustration is the bit in the mouth of the horse, and the second is the rudder that steers a ship. A horse is a powerful animal, far greater in weight and strength than any man, but with that bit in his mouth and a knowledgeable person in control, it can be controlled and its strength put to positive use. Likewise a ship without a rudder would be tossed aimlessly by every wind, but with that rudder, under the control of an experienced helmsman, the power of the wind is harnessed for a positive purpose. If we will allow Jesus to control our tongues, He will use those tongues to bring glory to himself and blessing to others. As destructive as the tongue can be uncontrolled, under His control, the tongue can be even more constructive, and as Christ directs the use of our tongues, they can be used to bring direction to others. A word of proper doctrine can cut through the lies and deceit of the enemy. A word of sympathy can soothe a troubled heart. A word of encouragement can make the difference between defeat and victory. A word of quiet rebuke can bring an angry person under control. A word of witness can redirect an entire life and even alter the course of history.

PRAYER: Pray that your speech might always be controlled by the Lord, that it might never discredit your testimony or be destructive, and that it might be used to bring blessing to others.

THE SUBTLE SINS OF THE SAINTS
JAMES 4

I am convinced that the greatest damage to the church is not that done by well-publicized scandals, but rather that done by the subtle sins of all the saints, sins that are not readily visible, but are deadly serious nonetheless. First, there is the sin of *selfishness* (vv. 1-2b). There's nothing subtle about church fights, but James tells us that behind the public spectacle of the church fight is the private, subtle sin of selfishness. Boil the pleasure-seeking, lust and envy he speaks of down to its essence, and you come up with one word: selfishness, a driving desire for one's own way that pushes everyone else aside, an inflexible attitude that seeks to conquer rather than compromise. Then there is the subtle sin of *prayerlessness* (v. 2c). Like selfishness, prayerlessness is subtle, but its results are far-reaching. Think of the power that is denied our preachers, the healing that doesn't come to the sick, and the comfort that escapes the bereaved because we don't pray. Most of all, think of the multitudes who remain lost because of the subtle sin of prayerlessness. Closely related to selfishness and prayerlessness is the subtle sin of *wrong motives* (v. 3). Notice that James doesn't say that they're praying for the wrong things, only that they're praying with the wrong motives. It is possible to pray for the right things, but because our motives are wrong, God refuses to answer the prayer. A fourth subtle sin is *worldliness* (vv. 4-5). The word *"world"* here refers to everything in the world that is opposed to God and the things of God. It refers to a world system that is under the control of the evil one that seeks to pull us away from our commitments to Christ. Many Christians want to keep one foot in the world and the other in Christianity, but James declares such an attitude as nothing less than adultery against our bridegroom, the Lord Jesus Christ. In verses 6 and 10, we see the subtle sin of *pride.* God is so opposed to pride because it blinds us to our need of Him and causes us to look down upon others, which often leads to the subtle sin of *slander* (v. 11a). We might think that our slanderous words are just between us and the person we're talking to, but in truth, anyone who is of low enough character to listen to gossip is seldom of high enough character to keep a confidence. Almost always, that slanderous, ugly speech will spread until it gets back to the person slandered. Along the way, it can destroy the person's reputation, and set a fire of interpersonal animosity that can burn down the fellowship of the church and poison its ministry. Closely related to the sin of slander is the subtle sin of *judgmentalism* (vv. 11b-12). The Scriptures do not forbid judgment - we need good, solid, sound judgment based on the Word of God. The Scriptures forbid judgmentalism, a critical spirit that judges everyone and everything from a perceived position of superiority and seeks to run others down. It is not the loving spirit that weeps over others' sins, but the condemning, merciless spirit that secretly rejoices in "getting the goods" on someone. Verses 13-16 speak of the subtle sin of *presumption.* James is not saying that there is anything wrong with doing business and making money. Nor was he saying that we should live day-by-day with no plans and goals for tomorrow. The whole scenario pictures someone who, even though he is a believer, is living his life, making his plans, and conducting his business with little or no thought to God's plans for his life, but in a believer's life, God and His will should be the primary consideration.

Finally, in verse 17, we see the subtle sin of *omission*. Sins of omission are those times when we know that we ought to do something, but we fail to do it. Imagine the ministry that goes undone, the words of encouragement that go unspoken, the witness that is never shared, and the growth that is stunted, not because we don't know what to do, but because we just don't do it.

PRAYER: Has the Lord shown you any of these subtle sins in your life? Pray that you might overcome it, and never fall prey to any of the rest of them.

LIFESTYLES OF THE RICH AND WICKED
JAMES 5

The Bible constantly points out the corrupting power of wealth, and James in this passage condemns the corrupt wealthy people of his day. First, he condemns those who *value money wrongly* (vv. 1-3). Even in James's day, there were those who saw the pursuit of wealth and possessions as the ultimate goal in life, but if you make riches your goal, you are in a precarious position for three reasons. Number one, the materialist is never secure. No matter how much wealth a person attains, he can never be truly secure, because it can be quickly taken away, by theft, by natural disaster, or by death. In James's day, there were three main ways people showed off their wealth: through stored up grain, extravagant clothes, and precious metals or coins. But James points out that grain can rot, clothes can become moth-eaten, and precious metals can tarnish. How quickly possessions can be taken from us! Not only is the materialist never secure, he is also never satisfied. In verse 3, James speaks of the rust consuming their flesh like the fire. Those who live for money and possessions find that there is no satisfaction in it. There is an endless push for more and more, and often people find that they cannot enjoy what they have in the all-consuming pursuit for more. Finally, if a person lives for money, he is in a precarious position because it is likely that he will never be saved. In verse 3, James speaks of storing up treasures in or for the last days. When the materialist stands before God in judgment, those treasures will testify that he has lived his life for gain, and not for God. The Bible doesn't teach that it is impossible for a rich person to be saved, but it does teach that it is impossible for an unrepentant materialist to be saved, because money for the materialist has become his god. Second, James condemns those who *acquire money wrongly* (v. 4). These rich landowners were refusing to pay their workers. After the day-laborers had worked all day, when they went to get their pay, they were laughed at. And what recourse did they have? Zero. The courts were for sale to the highest bidder, which is what verse 6 means. By their actions, they had destroyed the righteous man, but the righteous man didn't have the funds to resist. When money becomes a god, and the push for more and more becomes the ultimate goal of life, it's a very short step over the line into corrupt business practices. Third, James condemns those who *use money wrongly.* The people he speaks of used money wrongly first through extravagant luxury (v. 5a). The word in Greek speaks of wasteful, wretched excess that goes beyond any semblance of need. Secondly, they used money wrongly through personal indulgence (v. 5b). This was hedonism, the wanton pursuit of pleasure that indulged every desire, no matter how wrong or perverted it might be. Finally, they used money wrongly through wasteful hoarding (vv. 2-3a). It is not wrong to save and to have some funds set aside for emergencies. However, these rich people had gone beyond saving to hoarding. They had stored up so much grain that it mildewed before it could be eaten. Here was grain that could have fed hungry people, not the least of which were their own cheated employees, but they selfishly let it go bad rather than share it with anyone else. Their clothes didn't wear out from use; they were moth-eaten because they had so many clothes that they couldn't get around to wearing them all. And their coins had tarnished. Coins that are in circulation rarely tarnish; it's when they are hoarded and unused that they tarnish.

PRAYER: How is your relationship to money? Ask the Lord to point out any way you might be out of His will in this area.

I PETER

CLEAR THINKING
I PETER 1

Our mind is the key battleground in spiritual warfare. Even the word "demon" comes from two Greek words: *dia* meaning "through" and *mone'* meaning "mind." If you think a demon is going to come at you through a smoldering hole in your floor smelling of sulfur, you've been watching too much Hollywood and reading too little Bible. The main way demons disrupt our actions is by inserting falsehood into our minds. In verse 13, Peter shows us three danger zones that can derail our thinking if we're not careful. First of all, he warns us about ***dangerous deceptions***. The first phrase in the original language says literally that we are to gird up the loins of our minds, a strange image to the modern thinker to be sure. In the ancient world, everyone wore long flowing robes, but before running or going into battle, they would gird themselves by pulling the robe up between their legs and tucking it into their belts so that they wouldn't trip and fall. Peter tells us to square away our minds in that same manner, to do as Paul says in II

Corinthians 10:5 and *"<cast> down imaginations and every high thing that exalts itself against the knowledge of God, bringing every thought into captivity to the obedience of Christ."* We live in a world of error, and the error takes a multitude of forms. There is religious error, scientific error, philosophical error, and social and political error, and if we don't have a firm grasp on the truth, we can be tripped up by such error. The Word of God and the people of God today are questioned, ridiculed, disdained, dismissed and even attacked. To survive spiritually in such a climate, we must have our minds set on an unfailing standard of truth, and that standard must be the Word of God. The theories and philosophies of men are just grass that withers and flowers that fade, but the Word of the Lord stands forever (vv. 24-25). Peter not only warns us about dangerous deceptions, he goes on to warn us about **emotional excesses**. He tells us to be sober, or as it can also be translated, self-controlled. That means that we keep our emotions in check, not allowing them to cloud our judgment and our reasoning. Many people have literally ruined their lives because of bad decisions fueled by emotions not kept in check. Finally, Peter warns us about **current cares**. Sometimes, we can get so caught up in living in the here and now that we forget the big picture. As Christians, we are called to live with an eternal perspective, living our lives today based on the thought of standing before God one day and giving an account for our lives. When we look at life from a heavenly perspective, then we can think clearly, prioritizing the truly important rather than the merely urgent.

PRAYER: Which of these three avenues of attack are you most vulnerable to? Pray that the Lord will give you grace to shore up your defenses in that area.

SPIRITUAL BODYBUILDING
I PETER 2

Hardcore bodybuilders don't train their whole bodies every day; instead, they train one body part a day - Monday may be legs, Tuesday the back, Wednesday the arms and so on - and every exercise they do that day will target that one body part. In the first 12 verses of chapter two, we can see a parallel between bodybuilding in the physical realm and bodybuilding in the spiritual realm. Peter details five areas we need to develop if we are going to be built up in Christ. First, we must develop *a character that honors the name of Christ* (v. 1). Bodybuilders have to make sacrifices. They can't eat high fat foods, and they have to put in the time it takes to train. Likewise, if we are to be built up as individuals and as the body of Christ, the church, there are some things that we must put aside as well: wickedness, deceit, hypocrisy, envy and all evil speaking. Second, to be built up spiritually, we must develop *a craving for the Word of Christ* (vv. 2-3). Bodybuilders eat just the right foods to give them maximum energy to work out and attain maximum results from those workouts. Likewise, to be built up spiritually, we must feed on pure spiritual food, specifically, the Word of God, the Bible. Peter calls us to be like newborns again, longing for the pure milk of the Word, so that we might mature and grow up in Christ. Think of a newborn who has gone without a bottle for awhile. We should have that kind of desperate longing for God and the things of God, that longing for Bible Study, worship and prayer, that kind of insatiable hunger to feed on His Word and grow and mature in Him. To develop that craving, start eating. Feed on the Word as a matter of discipline, and before long you'll be doing it as a matter of delight. With physical food, the more you eat, the less you want, but with the spiritual food of the Word, the more you eat, the more you hunger for more. Third, if we're going to be built up spiritually, we must develop *consecration to the Lordship of Christ* (vv. 4-8). Bodybuilders have to have a single-minded commitment to the program of building their bodies. By the same token, the Christian is to have a single-minded focus on the Lordship of Christ. Jesus is spoken of here as the cornerstone. The cornerstone of a building is the first stone laid, and the whole building is built and oriented from the location of that cornerstone. Jesus Christ is our cornerstone, both as individuals and as the church. When we say that He is Lord, that means that He is the orientation point in our lives. Every aspect of our lives centers on Him and revolves around him. Fourth, to be spiritual bodybuilders, we must develop *communion with the body of Christ* (v. 9a). Bodybuilding is an individual sport. Nobody can lift those weights or maintain that nutrition or make those poses for you. But the more successful bodybuilders have training partners, and they work out together and hold each other accountable. By the same token, we come to Christ as individuals. Each individual must make a personal decision to receive Christ as his personal Savior and Lord by turning from his sins in repentance, placing his faith in Christ and His sacrifice on the cross, and surrendering his life to His Lordship. But we live out the Christian life in the fellowship of other believers in the body of Christ. Finally, if we're to be built up spiritually, we must develop *compassion that reflects the nature of Christ* (vv. 9-12). Bodybuilders train in order to show off. Not so with spiritual bodybuilders. They train to bring people out of the kingdom of darkness and into the Kingdom of God. Peter says that we received mercy when we were saved; now God calls us to be channels of His mercy and grace to others. We are to have the same compassion for the lost that Jesus did, the compassion that caused Him to weep over the lost and give His life for them. We are to proclaim the excellencies of our Savior to a lost world, all the while living as aliens and strangers, maintaining a separated lifestyle and keeping our behavior excellent so that they can see the difference that Christ makes in our lives.

PRAYER: Are you a spiritual bodybuilder, or a spiritual 98-pound weakling? Which area above most needs work? Pray that you might be built up in Him.

YOU WANT ME TO DO *WHAT*?
I PETER 3

The word *"submissive"* in verse one is often highly misunderstood and woefully misapplied in our culture. The word *"Likewise"* connects this passage with the one before. As Peter begins his words to the Christian wives, he says that in the same way Christ was submissive to the Father, humbling Himself so that we might be saved, so Christian wives are to be submissive to their husbands so that others, especially their husbands if they are unbelievers, might be saved. The word translated *"be submissive"* is a Greek military term that means literally "to order under." It speaks of an entirely voluntary and totally uncoerced ordering of oneself under the authority of another person. When a person joins the military, he agrees to order himself under those of higher rank. It's not that those people are superior human beings, but for the smooth functioning of the military, that chain of command has to be in place with someone taking the lead and others following. Likewise, the call of wives to submit to their husbands does not indicate that God considers women of lesser value than men. If women were somehow intrinsically inferior to men, it would read, "Women, be submissive to men," which is unfortunately how some read it. But that's not what it says. It says, *"Wives, be submissive to your own husbands."* All women are not called to submit to all men, just wives to their own husbands. It has nothing to do with gender, but with the proper functioning of the marriage relationship. The way God has designed the marriage relationship is that the husband is to be a spiritual, servant leader under God, and the wife is to submit to and support her husband's leadership. Anytime the subject of submission comes up, all kinds of cultural fog rolls in to obscure what it's supposed to look like in real life. Some think that the Bible authorizes the husband to live as a king and the wife to live as a slave, catering to his every whim. In truth, the Bible nowhere calls for women to submit to unfair, unjust, unloving, or unkind treatment on the part of their husbands, or anyone else for that matter. As in all kinds of submission, if the husband tries to coerce his wife into disobedience to God, obedience to God comes before any human relationship, even that of husband and wife. What is being established here is who has been given the final authority, and thus the ultimate responsibility and the ultimate accountability before God, to lead the family to be all that it should be under God. That responsibility and authority have been given to the husband, and he will one day give an account for that God-given responsibility. Does the wife play a part in that? Absolutely! She was created to work side-by-side with him in the fulfillment of God's will. Does the husband make all the decisions without consultation and discussion with his wife? He's crazy if he does! Any man who makes major life or financial decisions without his wife's input is wrong for at least two reasons. Number one, that's not the kind of loving servanthood that God commands. There is nothing loving or servantlike about a man imposing his will unilaterally on his wife. That's a bully, not a servant. Number two, any man who makes all the decisions without his wife's input is depriving himself of a precious resource that God has put into his life to give him a different perspective to help him make wise decisions. The husband will answer to God for the family's proper functioning, and the wife will answer for whether she has supported her husband in that role or whether she has undermined him in that role. When a wife submits to the loving leadership of her husband, she is not a doormat under his feet, but the wind beneath his wings.

PRAYER: Pray for your spouse today. If you are unmarried, pray for your future spouse. If you are a husband, pray that you might be the kind of loving servant God has called you to be. If you are a wife, pray for your husband, and pray that you might be the submissive helpmate God has called you to be.

WHEN THE HEAT IS ON
I PETER 4

There was a time when the Christian faith and Christian people were respected in our nation. That time is no more. Persecution against the righteous grows daily, and is likely to get worse over time. Therefore, it is imperative that believers know how to respond when the heat of fiery ordeals come upon us. Peter tells us that we shouldn't be surprised by such treatment, thinking it strange (v. 12). What is strange, from a Biblical and historical perspective is how *little* persecution Christians in America have faced throughout the years. He tells us that when suffering for the faith comes, as it surely will in lesser or greater intensity, we are to *"rejoice insofar as <we> share in Christ's sufferings"* (v. 13a). None of our sufferings for Him can compare to what He endured to secure our salvation, and all of our earthly sufferings will be richly rewarded when this earthly life is over (v. 13b). Beyond that, our being *"reproached for the name of Christ"* is a blessing in that it serves as evidence that *"the Spirit of glory and of God rests upon <us>"* (v. 14a). Those who attack us are in fact blaspheming our Lord, but we, in our willingness to endure that ill-treatment for the sake of His name, are glorifying Him (v. 14b). Obviously, we should not suffer as evildoers (v. 15), but if we suffer for doing right, we should not be ashamed (v. 16), nor should we back down.

Rather, we should *"entrust <our> souls to a faithful Creator, while continuing to do good"* (v. 19).

PRAYER: Where have you experienced persecution for the sake of Christ? Pray that you will keep the proper perspective in such fiery ordeals, and that you will continue to do right in spite of the consequences.

RUN TO THE ROAR
I PETER 5

In verses 8-9, we can see three of the devil's favorite tactics. First, we see his tactic of **intimidation**. He has a frightful roar. If you've ever heard a lion's roar, it is paralyzing in its volume; it shakes you to the core of your being. Satan often attacks us with all manner of threats and dire warnings, and, if we don't know the truth about ourselves, our Lord and our enemy, those threats will paralyze us from going forward to do him harm. Then there is his tactic of **inaccuracy**. The devil is a master of deception, but the best antidote to falsehood is truth. That's why we must *"resist him firmly in the faith"* (v. 9). When the New Testament talks about *the* faith, it's not talking about saving faith, that initial investment of trust in Christ by which we're saved, nor is it talking about walking faith, that ongoing trust by which we live and serve the Lord. No, *the* faith is that body of doctrinal truth that came through Christ and has been recorded by His apostles and prophets in the Word of God. We can only resist the enemy by holding firmly to the truth of the Word of God. A final tactic is **isolation**. The devil loves to make us feel like we're alone in this battle, that no one else is going through what we are, but Peter tells us that our fellow Christians are suffering the same things and fighting the same battles. The devil wants to keep us isolated because lone believers are easy prey, just as lions hunt the stragglers, the weak and the slow on the periphery of the herd. As Dr. Tony Evans once pointed out, lions don't roar when they're hunting their prey; they sneak up on their prey. Lions only roar when they've already made the kill. They let out that intimidating roar because they themselves are intimidated. What could intimidate a lion, you ask? Nothing, one on one. In one-on-one conflict, the lion is the king of the jungle, but lions are terrified of hyenas and jackals, who travel in packs and will come in overwhelming numbers to take away the lion's prize. The lion doesn't want to fight a whole pack of hyenas or jackals, so he roars to scare them off. If they only knew how frightened the lion was of them, and if they only knew not to be scared of the roar but to stay together and keep coming toward him, he would back off and they could take from him what he had destroyed. Christians, the same principle holds true for us. If we will ignore the roar, and march out together, we can take back from him the homes, the schools, the communities, the culture, and the nations that he has destroyed. We have the greater power, because as verse 11 tells us, all of the dominion and power belongs to our God.

PRAYER: Through prayer and through the Word, marching together with our fellow believers, we resist the devil. Where do you see him at work today? Pray that the Lord will open your eyes to anywhere he is sneaking in to destroy, and pray against anything you see him doing in your life, the life of your family, the life of your church, the life of your community, or the life of our culture.

II PETER

GROW UP!
II PETER 1

Peter tells us to *"make every effort"* to grow spiritually (v. 5). Spiritual growth is not something we do for ourselves; it is something that God does in us, but it is not something that comes automatically. We must cooperate with Him and yield to Him, and He will bless our efforts with success. Peter shows us in verses 5-7 the areas we need to be expending our efforts in the Christian life. He begins with faith, because faith in Christ is the entry point of the Christian life, and therefore faith becomes the foundation upon which all Christian growth rests. He says to add to that saving faith *"virtue."* God is not pleased with Sunday-morning-only Christianity that doesn't make us better people, better citizens, better spouses, better children, better parents, and better workers. As Christians, we are to strive for moral excellence, because if the world can't see that Christ has changed our lives, how will they ever believe that He can change theirs? He goes on to say that we are to add to our moral excellence *"knowledge."* Once we come to know Christ personally, we need to get to know more about Him, His Word, His will and His ways, and the source of that knowledge is the Bible. In the Bible, we have all the knowledge we need to come to life in Christ and to live in a godly manner (vv. 3-4). Peter says next to add to our knowledge *"self-control."* Self-control means keeping our passions, our desires and our drives under control. It can refer to any such passions and desires, but it is generally used in Greek literature to refer to control over one's sex drive. The people Peter wrote to were, like we are, immersed in a sex-obsessed culture, a world where the immoral was not only not condemned, but was celebrated as normal, right and good. Peter's message of self-control is every bit as needed today as it was then, if not more so. Next on Peter's list is *"patient endurance,"* which is the ability to face great amounts of opposition without quitting, and *"godliness,"* which is a commitment to Christ that puts Him first and foremost in our lives. Then we are to strive for *"brotherly kindness,"* which is the Greek word *philadelphia*. That word speaks of the love of family, and the love of those with whom we have something in common. It is the love we have for one another in the church because we share a common family relationship - God is our Father, and that makes us brothers and sisters. No Christian can grow outside that family commitment to the local church. Next, Peter mentions *"love,"* which is the Greek word *agape'*. That is the highest form of love, the divine kind of love. It is love for the unlovable, the unlovely, and the undeserving, love that extends not only to fellow believers but also to unbelievers, an unconditional love that always wants and only does the best for the other person, even at great personal cost. I'm convinced that one reason many churches are not more effective in reaching the lost is because they only feel our condemnation, and they don't see any love in us. The church must be a place where people are loved unconditionally, a place, to be sure, where sin is hated and confronted with a holy passion, but where sinners are welcomed, accepted and loved.

PRAYER: Are you growing up in Christ, or just growing old in Him? Pray about what needs to be "added" to your life to move you onward to maturity.

BEWARE FALSE TEACHERS
II PETER 2

Whenever a contagious disease enters our bodies, it has the potential to injure, incapacitate, or even kill us. The same is true when false teaching enters into a believer's life or in the life of the church. Peter warns that just as there were false teachers and false prophets among the people in Old Testament times, so too there are false teachers that arise within the church (v. 1a). Peter is not referring to those believers who might have an unusual or mistaken interpretation of a particular Scripture; he is referring rather to those who *"bring in destructive heresies, even denying the Lord who bought them"* (v. 1b). Some introduce these destructive teachings because of greed (v. 3), while others are motivated by the *"the pursuit of unclean desires"* (v. 10), particularly of a sexual nature (v. 14). Others are driven by their disdain for proper authority (vv. 10b-12). While some of them are genuinely deceived themselves (v. 13), others, like Balaam, know the truth but *"<love> the wages of wickedness"* (v. 15). Still others are driven by their own arrogance and vanity (v. 18). The ones most in danger from these false teachers are *"those who barely escaped from those who live in error"* (v. 18), the young (or perhaps just immature) in the faith who could be easily deceived. The teaching of the false teachers, while promising much, delivers nothing positive (v. 17). Peter details the fierce judgment that awaits such false teachers who lead others astray (vv. 3b-10, 12b-13a).

PRAYER: Pray for any young believers you know, that they might be protected from falsehood and grounded in God's Word.

LIVING IN THE LIGHT OF HIS COMING
II PETER 3

Unfortunately, when the subject of the Lord's coming is broached, many Christians give vent to all manner of wild speculation. Peter tells us in this chapter a better way to live today in the light of Christ's future coming and the end of the world. First, the knowledge of the Lord's coming should lead us to *expectation* (v. 13). As we look at the chaotic world scene all around us, we could surrender to hopelessness, but as Christians, there is no need for despair. We recognize that what is happening in the world is merely what is to be expected in a fallen world under the control of the evil one, a world that has largely rejected God's Word and God's standards. And we realize with joy that the world will not always continue this way. Rather, *"according to His promise, we are waiting for new heavens and a new earth, in which righteousness dwells"* (v.13). That phrase *"waiting for"* can also be translated *"looking forward to"* (NIV 84). We live in a world filled to the brim with unrighteousness, but when Christ returns, this wicked world will be done away with, replaced by a world in which righteousness dwells, a world governed by Christ Himself. Christ's coming should also move us to *purification* (vv. 11, 14). The main theme of the New Testament in regard to Christ's future coming is that it should inspire is to holy living in the here and now. Third, Christ's coming should motivate us to *evangelization* (vv. 12, 15). To understand verse 15, you have to back up to verse 9, where Peter explains why the Lord's coming is delayed: so that more people can be saved. God's desire is not for any to perish, but for all to come to repentance, and He is holding back the events of the end as long as He can for more to be saved. But in order for the lost to be saved, the saved have to reach them with the gospel. Christ's coming is also a motivation to *continuation* (v. 16), *separation* (v. 17), and *maturation* (v. 18). The Bible is clear that the closer we get to the end, there will be an alarming rise in false teaching. To counter that rise in falsehood, we must continue in the Word of God, anchored in the truth of the Bible. We must be so familiar with the Word that we recognize and expose error and separate ourselves from those who propagate it. Finally, we must be growing in Christ, becoming spiritually mature, growing in grace and knowledge of Him daily, and walking closely to Him. By living in this way, we will not be ashamed when Christ returns.

PRAYER: Thank the Lord that the world will not always be like this. Thank Him for the promise of His future coming.

I JOHN

THE CHRISTIAN AND SIN
I JOHN 1

Try as we might (and obviously, we ought to try with all our might), sinless perfection will elude us in this life. We need to understand that while sin as believers will break our fellowship with God, it does not break our relationship with Him, any more than a child who misbehaves is cast out of the family. No, such a child is corrected and taught how he ought to live as a member of the family. Likewise, when we sin as Christians, we are still God's children and He is still our Father. As our Father, He convicts us (and disciplines us) when we sin in order to return us to a right fellowship with Him, because it is only in that unhindered fellowship that we experience the abundant life He wants for us. How do we respond when we've blown it as Christians, whether in word, in thought, in attitude, or in action, and the Holy Spirit has put His finger upon our sin? I John 1:9, sandwiched between two verses that tell us how *not* to respond, tells us. Verses 8 and 10 may be speaking of those believers who insist that they've reached sinless perfection in this life, or, more likely, they are speaking to the situation of a believer who has sinned and is being convicted through the ministry of the Holy Spirit. To deny that divine conviction, to insist either that we haven't sinned or that what we've done isn't really sin, is serious business. It indicates that we are self-deceived, walking in falsehood rather than God's truth, and we are in fact calling God a liar for His accusation of us! Many are those who respond in this way, either denying the Bible's teaching on sin, or rejecting the Spirit's moving in their lives, or both, and they remain in broken fellowship with God, becoming even more alienated over time. Verse 9 calls us to another response. When we become aware, through the Word of God or through the still, small voice of the Spirit, that we have sinned, we must confess that sin to God. The word for *"confess"* means literally, "to say the same." We are to agree with God's assessment of our sins, not just admitting our guilt, but saying the same thing about it that God does: that it's wrong, that we shouldn't have done it, and that it should have no place in our lives as believers. That response brings the blessing of cleansing from the sin and the blessing of being restored to fellowship.

PRAYER: Is there some sin in your life that the Holy Spirit has put His finger on? Confess it now!

CHILDREN, YOUNG MEN, FATHERS
I JOHN 2

In verses 12-14, John addresses some comments to three distinct groups of people: children, young men and fathers. He is not using these as literal terms, but figurative terms for young believers, more mature believers, and older believers in the church, no doubt including the female believers as well. He says to the children, the young believers, that *"your sins are forgiven for His name's sake"* (v. 12) and that *"you have known the Father"* (v. 13). Knowing God in His forgiveness and knowing Him as our Father - such are the marks of a young believer, who may know little else of theology or Christian living at that point. But as that young believer matures, he becomes a young man: strong and energetic, full of the Word of God, willing and able to do battle with the evil one, in the front lines of Kingdom advance (vv. 13-14). Then, over time, the young men become fathers, those who *"have known Him who is from the beginning,"* a statement repeated verbatim in both verse 13 and verse 14. At first glance, that comment about the fathers seems a lesser one than the others, but it most assuredly is not. The knowing of the fathers is a long-term knowledge, a knowledge that comes from personal experience in seeing God work from the beginning of their Christian lives and through the battles of their Christian lives over the course of many years. Such experience develops not just a head knowledge of God, but a die-hard faith in God. Such people become "fathers" to the younger, both in bringing new converts into the Kingdom, and in training the young men for spiritual warfare through their example, their faith and their experience.

PRAYER: Where are you in your Christian walk: child, young man, or father? If a child, what are you doing to mature in your walk with the Lord? It is the Word of God living in us that moves us into maturity and victory (v. 14). What "fathers" are you looking to as mentors? What "young men" are you looking to mentor?

SNAPSHOTS AND MOVIES
I JOHN 3

I John at times seems to be a study in contradictions. In the first chapter, John established clearly that sinless perfection is impossible in this life. Then, in this chapter, he seems to be teaching the exact opposite - that sinless perfection is the very proof of our salvation (vv. 6, 9). So, which is it? Well, if sinless perfection is necessary for salvation, I don't know anyone who's saved, including me! The key is in the verb tenses, which the translators try to capture in English by using the word *"practice"* (vv. 8-9). There is a huge difference between falling into acts of sin and practicing ongoing sin as a lifestyle that one excuses as not sinful, despite what God says about it (1:10). If you were to look at a snapshot of certain moments of a Christian's life, you would be convinced that he couldn't possibly be in Christ, but if you were to then see a movie of that Christian's life, you would see that, while there are some slips and falls in the process, the overall motion of his life is onward and upward toward becoming more like Christ. That "onward and upward" lifestyle reveals itself in increasing righteousness (vv. 7-10), increasing purity (v. 3), and love for the brethren (v. 14) revealed in tangible acts of ministry (vv. 17-18). When we have fallen into the muck and mire of sin, our hearts, spurred on by the accusations of the evil one, will often condemn us (vv. 19-20), causing us to question our salvation. It is in those times that we must review the movie of our lives, and recall the basis of our salvation: not sinless perfection or good works that we have done, but faith in Christ as our Savior and Lord (v. 23).

PRAYER: Have you slipped and fallen into the muck and mire of sin? Don't wallow in it! Get up! Go immediately to I John 1:9! Receive His cleansing, and get back on the path of righteous living.

THE LOVE CHAPTER
I JOHN 4

It is this chapter, probably above all others, that earned John the nickname "The Apostle of Love." John has come a long way from his days as a "Son of Thunder," angrily desiring to call down fire on a Samaritan village that rejected Jesus! At that time, Jesus rebuked him and his brother James, telling them *"You do not know what kind of spirit you are of"* (Luke 9:55). Now, he knows exactly what Spirit he is of, and it's not the same spirit as he was of then! The change in him from angry disciple to apostle of love has come about because of the indwelling Holy Spirit (v. 13), and that same indwelling Holy Spirit creates love in us as well. The angry, the hateful, and the mean-spirited show no evidence of that indwelling Spirit (vv. 20-21). God, who is love (v. 8), cannot help but create love in those who are in relationship with Him, those who are in fact indwelt by Him (v. 16). God loved us before we loved Him or even knew Him (v. 10). Even when we were at our most unlovable, lost in our sins and rejecting Him, He loved us enough to send Jesus to be our atoning sacrifice (v. 9). Now, *"We love Him, because He first loved us"* (v. 19), and we love others for that same reason (v. 11). God's love is revealed as a love that is extended even for those who don't return that love, love for the unloving and unlovable, and love that is willing to sacrifice greatly to do the best for the person loved. We are called to love with that same kind of love. That love always transforms the giver of that love (v. 12), and has the potential to transform the recipient of that love (v. 16).

PRAYER: Do you know someone who is difficult to love? Pray that you might be a conduit of God's love to that person, and that he or she might be transformed by God's love.

CLOSING THE CIRCUIT
I JOHN 5

John makes clear that the only way of salvation is through Jesus, the Son of God: *"God has given us eternal life, and this life is in His Son. Whoever has the Son has life, and whoever does not have the Son of God does not have life"* (vv. 11-12). From there, he speaks of yet another "proof" of our salvation: answered prayer. We can pray with confidence, knowing that *"if we ask anything according to His will, He hears us"* (v. 14). Some Christians adopt a kind of fatalism about prayer, an attitude that says, "Well, God's going to do what He wants to do whether I pray or not." That is simply not so. God not only wills the result; He wills the means to the result, and part of the means to His will being done on Earth is the prayers of His people. God desires for us to cooperate with Him in bringing His will to Earth (Matthew 6:10) through our prayers. Think of prayer as a light switch. In your home, there are wires going through the walls, into a fuse box, and out to the pole, and those wires eventually go back to the power station. Coursing through those wires is far more than enough power to run the light bulb in your room, but until you close the circuit by flipping the switch, none of that potential energy is accessed, and there is no light. Likewise, God has innumerable things He desires to do in our personal worlds and in the world around us. Everything is set. He has built the infrastructure for it. He certainly has the willingness and the power to do it. But He is waiting for someone to close the circuit through prayer according to His will. When we pray according to His will, there is no power shortage. His will will be done (v. 15). When we get to heaven, only then will we see the multitude of prayers that were never answered...because they were never offered (Ezekiel 22:30).

PRAYER: Where can you close the circuit of God's will being done through prayer today, either for yourself or for someone else? Some Christians worry about praying wrongly, about praying something outside of God's will, so they are hesitant to pray at all. Most of us at some point have heard someone whisper in conspiratorial tones, "Be careful what you pray for...*you just might get it!"* No! God is not some malevolent genie waiting for us to ask wrongly so that He can "stick it to us." He is a loving Father who only gives us what is best for us (Matthew 7:11). Don't ever be afraid of praying wrongly; even if you don't fully know God's will in a matter, the Spirit of God does, and He will intercede for you according to God's will (Romans 8:26-27). You can't lose when you pray!

II JOHN

LOVE AND DISCERNMENT

John speaks much about the subject of love, both in his first letter and in this little postcard, but true love must also include discernment. This is an important truth in our day, when so many, even in the church, encourage a "live and let live" philosophy, a "let's all just sit around and sing 'Kum Ba Ya' together without regard to doctrine" stance. The overwhelming philosophy of the secular world, a kind of radical tolerance that accepts nothing as absolute truth and everything as relative, that says that it's all just opinion and anyone's opinion is as good as anyone else's, has crept into the church. To point out that someone's doctrine is unbiblical or their lifestyle is immoral is to risk pointing fingers and shouted accusations of "Unloving!" In the first century church, there were teachers and missionaries who traveled about from church to church, many times collecting money or goods to take the gospel where it had not gone before. It was important to support such men, as we'll see in III John, but also important not to be led astray into supporting those who were spreading a false gospel. Scholars are divided about whether *"the elect lady"* (v. 1) is an individual or John's term of endearment for a church of his acquaintance, but it little matters. Whether he is speaking of a woman opening her home to false teachers, or the church opening its pulpit to them, he makes it clear that love requires neither the approval of falsehood nor the facilitation of its spread. Indeed, a person who welcomes a false teacher with hospitality *"takes part in his evil deeds"* (v. 11). True love confronts and stands against falsehood, so that the children (either literal children or used figuratively of young believers) walk in the truth, and are not led astray into falsehood (v. 4).

PRAYER: Are you careful to support only those ministries that walk in and teach the truth of the Word of God? Pray for such ministries, and pray that those believers led astray into falsehood would see the truth.

III JOHN

THE WRECKING CREW

By the time III John was written, John was a very old man, the last of the apostles still alive. He was living in Ephesus, unable to travel about like he once did, but he was training and commissioning younger men and sending them out to preach the good news of Christ. These younger men would travel to the established churches, stay with them a short time to teach and edify them, and then receive from the church an offering of money and goods to send them on their way to the next church. When they came to the end of the line, they would take the final offering and launch out into the unknown, taking the gospel to places where it had not gone before. That whole system of missions support was being threatened by one man, a church leader named Diotrephes who rejected the authority of John and refused to support these young missionaries. As we look at John's description of Diotrephes, we can see the tools of the wrecking crew that the enemy often unleashes in a church. First, there is *self-centeredness.* John says that Diotrephes *"loves to put himself first among them."* The church may have met in his home, or he may have been a heavy contributor to the finances of the church, or he may have just had a forceful personality, but for whatever reason, Diotrephes had power, and he used it not to do good, but to exalt himself. A second tool of the wrecking crew is **rejection of authority**. Diotrephes rejected John's authority as an apostle. Many today reject the apostles' authority by questioning or ignoring the apostles' teaching as found in the Bible. A third tool of the wrecking crew is **slanderous words**. The Greek word is *phluareo*, which means literally "to babble on and on incoherently." His words had no basis of truth in them, but when gossip is repeated often enough, no matter how absurd it may be, it will come to be believed. A fourth tool of the wrecking crew is **isolation**. Diotrephes would not receive the brethren, and in that refusal he was cutting off the church from cooperative missions with other churches. While it is important for each church to make its own decisions under God without any outside pressure, it is also important for churches to cooperate with other churches in the larger work of the Kingdom. Another tool of the wrecking crew is **intimidation**. Not only would Diotrephes not receive these men; he intimidated others into refusing them lodging and help. And then there's the tool of **misused power**. Diotrephes put out of the church those who gave aid to the missionaries. No one person, and no small group within the church, should have that kind of power. Decisions about the membership, the mission and the money of the church must be made by the congregation at large, and not by one or two influential members.

PRAYER: Compare John's words about Diotrephes with his words about Gaius and Demetrius (vv. 1-4, 11-12). Pray that you might always be on the building crew, and not the wrecking crew, in your church.

JUDE

CONTEND FOR THE FAITH

Jude had hoped to write about *"the salvation we have in common"* (v. 3) but instead felt compelled to warn the church against false teachers and their spurious doctrines. Jude speaks of four areas of doctrine that are usually either blatantly attacked or gradually eroded by false teachers. First, they pervert *the doctrine of grace* (v. 4b). The so-called "Libertines" in the early church taught that when Jesus saved us, He saved us from all of our sins, past, present and future. We can't lose our salvation, they said, so it doesn't matter what we do. And beyond that, God delights in forgiving our sins, so therefore, let's continue in sin so that God's grace may abound. When Paul dealt with that faulty theology in the book of Romans he was absolutely appalled by it, condemning it in the strongest possible terms (Romans 6:1-2). A true believer cannot wallow in continual, unbroken, unrepentant sin like the unbeliever does. He may fall into sin sometimes, and there may be pockets of carnality and strongholds that he struggles with, but the true believer's main desire will be to overcome sin and please Christ, not to indulge sin and please self. When he sins, he will be miserable as he comes under the conviction of the

Spirit and the burden of the Lord's discipline. That seems to be the point of verse 5. Not everyone who left Egypt was a true believer, as their later actions would show, and not everyone who claims Christ is truly in Christ either. We should beware of any teacher or preacher who de-emphasizes the importance of holy living, who treats salvation as just a transaction between a sinner and God that brings no changes in the life of the sinner. Second, Jude says that these false teachers pervert *the doctrine of Christ* (v. 4c). We are to beware of any teaching that takes away from the Biblical portrait of the person and work and uniqueness of Christ. The Bible teaches that Jesus is both fully human and fully divine. He is not a created being, but He is fully God, the second person in the Trinity, co-equal and co-eternal with both the Father and the Holy Spirit. He came to Earth, was born of a virgin, grew to manhood, lived a sinless life, died on the cross for our sins, rose again from the dead, ascended to the Father, and is coming again one day to planet Earth. The Bible also teaches that there is no salvation apart from Him. It is only by repenting of our sins, placing our faith in Him and surrendering our lives to His Lordship that we can be saved. We must hold tenaciously to that great core of gospel truth. Anyone who rejects that truth is a false teacher, peddling lies and heresy. False teachers also often attack *the doctrine of salvation* (v. 11). What was *"the way of Cain"*? Cain tried to approach God his own way, rather than God's way. He brought the work of his hands, his crops, rather than the God-appointed blood sacrifice of a lamb. There are those today who teach salvation by the work of our hands - good works or religious ritual - but the Bible is clear that the only way to God is through the blood of the Lamb, Jesus Christ. Finally, false teachers often attack *the doctrine of authority* (v. 8, v. 10a). Our final authority as believers is the Word of God, the Bible, but in our day, the Bible has come under sustained, aggressive attack by those outside, and unfortunately, by those inside the church.

Teaching that contradicts or attacks the Word of God is to be rejected.

PRAYER: Pray that you might always have the wisdom to discern, and the courage to confront, false doctrine.

REVELATION

REVEALER, REDEEMER, AND RULER
REVELATION 1

Throughout Christian history, no book of the Bible has so fascinated and challenged Bible students as the book of Revelation. One of the keys to understanding Revelation is to look at it through the lens of its first verse. Although it deals with the future, it is not primarily a book about the future. It is a book that reveals Jesus in all of His heavenly glory. Notice what is revealed about Him just in this first chapter. We see *His revelation* in verses 4-5a. Verse 5 says that Jesus is *"the faithful witness."* He is the highest revelation of God, who most clearly revealed God as a God of grace and mercy, but also a God of justice and judgment. It was Jesus who clearly unfolded the mystery of God as triune in His nature. The word "Trinity" is a word that means "three-fold unity." As Christians, we believe there is one God, revealed eternally in three persons: God the Father, God the Son and God the Holy Spirit. This passage testifies to that great truth, as we see the Father on the throne, described as *"the one who is, and who was, and who is to come"* (v. 4), which speaks of His eternal nature. There was never a time when God was not, and there will never be a time when He is not. Jesus describes Himself in the exact same words in verse 8, testifying to His nature as fully and completely God. The Holy Spirit is described here as *"the seven Spirits"* or as it could also be translated "the seven-fold Spirit." The number 7 in Revelation is symbolic of deity; to describe the Spirit this way is to attribute God-status to Him as well. Second, we see **His resurrection** in v. 5b. Jesus is described as not only the faithful witness, but the firstborn from the dead. The resurrection is of absolute importance to Christianity; indeed, the whole of the Christian faith rises or falls on that one point. I Corinthians 15:17 says that if Christ is not risen from the dead, then our faith is vain and we are still in our sins. Because He has conquered death, we know that He can conquer death for us as well. Third, we see **His reign** in verses 5c and 6a. These verses speak of Jesus as the great sovereign Lord of all. According to verse 6, He is Lord over His church. He has made us to be a kingdom, and as His subjects, and we are to be submitted to His will in all things. And notice that Christ is not only sovereign over His church, He is sovereign over the kings of the earth as well (5c). As Christians, we are to submit to man-made laws, but when any kind of earthly government tries to forbid us to do what God commands, or command us to do what God forbids, at that point we must recognize that we are under a higher authority than an earthly government, and refuse to submit in that matter. Our first priority is to serve the King of kings and Lord of lords. In verse 5d, we see **His redemption**. Jesus came to pay the price for our sins so that we might be forgiven and have eternal life. The method of our redemption was His shed blood. The motive for our redemption was His love for us. Finally, in verse 7, we see **His return**, a return that will be both visible and victorious! The first time, Jesus came as a Lamb to be slaughtered; when

He returns, He comes as a Lion to judge. If there is one theme that comes through loud and clear in the book of Revelation, it is this: when the dust settles and the smoke clears at the end of time, the ones left standing are the Lord Jesus Christ and those who are His!

PRAYER: The return of Christ is a terrifying prospect for those who don't know Him, but for those who do know Him, His return is called the blessed hope. Look at what John says at the end of verse 7. The unsaved may mourn His coming, but John says, *"Even so. Amen."* *"Amen"* means "Let it be so!" Thank Him today for the glorious redemption of His first coming, and for the glorious hope of His future coming.

SATAN'S SINISTER STRATEGIES, PART 1
REVELATION 2

Jesus gives John messages to relay to seven churches that were located in Asia Minor. Each of those churches was under attack by the evil one, and in Jesus' words to them, we can see some of the ways the devil attacks churches (for a more thorough treatment of the seven churches, see the author's book *Churches in the Crosshairs*, available from the author or from Amazon.com). As we look at the church at Ephesus, we see that *he douses the church's devotion.* The Lord commends much in the church, but He states that they had left their first love. What exactly it was that had waned? Their love of the Savior? Their love of the lost? Their love of their fellow saints in the church? If this were a multiple choice exam, my answer would be "D - All of the Above," because they're all interrelated. When we lose the intensity of our love for Christ, our love for each other and for the lost will naturally dim as well. In the church of Smyrna, we see a second strategy: *he drives the church's detractors.* Smyrna was a persecuted church, a church that was being hit from all sides with harsh words from the Jewish religious establishment and with pressure to conform from the culture at large. That's what that word *"tribulation"* means in the original language; it refers to unrelenting pressure, to being squeezed into a mold. In the church at Pergamum we see a third strategy: **he drains the church's discernment.** Satan had first run the persecution strategy against the church at Pergamum, but they had stayed strong, even when one of their members, possibly the pastor, had been martyred. So he went back to the drawing board and came up with a much more subtle and indirect approach. Having failed to crush them, now he sought to corrupt them through compromise with the world. There were members of the church who had bought into the Nicolaitan heresy that you could worship God yet still indulge in the sins of the pagan temples, but God is not just interested in a people who give him lip service on Sunday; He's called us to be a holy people who live for Him every minute of every day, even when nobody's watching. The devil wants to drain our discernment, to so dull our hearts that we are in a position of excusing and defending sin rather than exposing and decrying sin, because when we tolerate sin in our lives and in our church, we grieve the Holy Spirit and we quench His power among us. At Thyatira, we see a fourth strategy the devil uses against the church: **he dilutes the church's doctrine.** There was at Thyatira a festering cancer in that otherwise healthy body, a false teacher whose teaching threatened to infect the whole body. This Jezebel was combining the worship of God with the false doctrines of the pagan cults around them, and the result was something with a veneer of Christianity, but in fact far removed from the true faith. That was bad enough, but Jesus was most upset that the church as a whole, even those who were not participating in this obscene perversion of doctrine and worship, was tolerating it! They knew it was wrong, but they were unwilling to confront her and stop her.

PRAYER: Have you left your first love? Has there ever been a time when you were closer to Jesus than you are now? Jesus calls on the church at Ephesus first to remember. Remember what it was like when that first love of Christ was in full bloom. Next, He calls them to repent. It is sin not to love the Lord with passion and enthusiasm, sin that must be repented of. Finally, He tells them to redo, to go back and do again what they were doing at first. Wherever you lost your first love, that's where you'll find it. If you left it by not spending time in the Word or in prayer, you'll find it there. If you left it by falling out of the fellowship of the church, you'll find it there. If you left it by allowing other things to take precedence over the Lord, you'll find it there. But wherever it is, you need to find it quickly, lest as verse 5 says, the lampstand of your witness and effectiveness be removed. Pray that your first love might always burn brightly for Him.

SATAN'S SINISTER STRATEGIES, PART 2
REVELATION 3

As we move to the church at Sardis, we see Satan's fifth strategy against the church: *he disguises the church's deadness*. The church at Sardis had a great reputation. Other churches envied them, and the people of their community admired them. Of all of the seven churches, it had experienced the least persecution. It was known as a "happening" church in the eyes of men, but in the eyes of the Lord, it was a dead church, totally devoid of any spiritual energy and vitality. It was a church that had grieved the Spirit through their immoral activities, staining the white garments they had been given at conversion with post-conversion sins that had gone unforsaken and unrepented-of, and as a result, the Spirit's power in their lives, their ministries and their church had been quenched. It is possible for a church to have a busy schedule of activities, a large population of members, an impressive facility, and good singing and preaching, and yet accomplish nothing of eternal value for the Kingdom. Looking at the church at Laodicea, we see a sixth strategy of Satan: *he diminishes the church's dependence.* Of all the seven churches the Laodicean church was the most materially prosperous, but it was also the most spiritually bankrupt. Its membership came from higher strata of society than the others, and financially, they were well-off both as individuals and as a church. They were so well-off, in fact, that they had fallen into the trap of satisfied self-sufficiency. They thought that they were rich and had need of nothing, which might have been true in the material realm, but in the spiritual realm, Jesus says that they were wretched and miserable and poor and blind and naked. He goes on in verse 18 to tell them that it is only through dependence on Him that we can truly become rich, only through dependence on Him that we can be cleansed from sin, and only through dependence on Him that we can have spiritual insight. The devil came against the church at Laodicea by diminishing the church's dependence, and thereby destroying its power and influence. Those are six strategies of the enemy, but in the church at Philadelphia, we can see that *he is defeated by the church's determination.* Philadelphia had been victorious over his nefarious schemes. What were the keys to that victory? The first key is divine power. They recognized that they had a little power, but when they stepped out on faith and depended on the power of God, God did in them and through them what they could not do alone. The second key is doctrinal purity. They kept the Lord's Word, not getting sidetracked by false teaching and its attendant immoral actions. A third key was dedicated proclamation. They did not deny the Lord's name, but boldly proclaimed His saving power to their lost, pagan, and sometimes hostile community. Finally, the fourth key was their determined perseverance. They faced hardships and opposition in their stand for their Lord, but they would not back down. Because they would not let the devil sidetrack them or intimidate them off the field, they were being victorious over him in the battle for human souls. They had an open door of opportunity that no one could shut, and Jesus promises them victory over the persecutions and hardships they faced.

PRAYER: Pray for your church today, that it might never be taken in by the sinister strategies that crippled the other churches, but that it might always be a victorious church like the church at Philadelphia.

IN THE THRONE ZONE
REVELATION 4

(Adapted from chapter 14 of the author's book *Observations of Worship*, available from the author or from Amazon.com).

The key word in chapter 4 is *"throne,"* a word that appears 12 times in 11 verses. God's throne is the center of the scene, and everything in the passage is seen in its relationship to His throne. Likewise, the key to worship is in our recognition of God's place as sovereign and center. He is the Sovereign Lord of the Universe, but even more personally, if we are His children, He is the Sovereign Lord of our lives, the center around which every other aspect of life revolves and finds its place. In worship we establish a "throne zone" wherever we are and whatever we're going through. We enthrone Him anew and afresh as Lord of our lives, renewing our commitment to Him, and expressing our submission to Him. No wonder the psalmist told us that the Lord sits enthroned on the praises of His people! The first thing John sees when he is in the Spirit is the throne of God. Whenever John talks about being in the Spirit in Revelation, he is talking about going into a trance and having a vision.

When he is in the Spirit, the Isle of Patmos, where he has been imprisoned by the Roman government, fades, and the spiritual realities of life under Christ's spiritual rule come into focus. I seriously doubt that any of us will have the kind of visions that John experienced, but I don't think it's stretching the text to make the point that the more we are in the Spirit - filled with the Spirit, walking according to the Spirit and not according the flesh - the less the world will allure us and the more the throne of God and the Lordship of Christ will be our supreme focus. As the great old hymn put it, "the things of Earth...grow strangely dim in the light of His glory and grace."

PRAYER: Imagine yourself in the scene depicted in Revelation 4. Enthrone the Lord on your praises today. Focus on His Lordship, and watch the things of this earth, the things that may have kept you awake last night, grow strangely dim.

WORTHY!
REVELATION 5

The scroll, as I understand it, represents the Day of the Lord judgments (the trumpets and bowls), and the seals represent the course of history from the Lord's first coming to the time of the end. John was told to *"Write the things which you have seen, and the things which are, and the things which will take place after this"* (1:19). *"The things which you have seen"* refers to his vision of Jesus in chapter one; *"the things which are"* refers to the seven churches that Jesus addressed in chapters 2-3, which were then in existence in Asia Minor; and *"the things which will take place after this"* refers to the remainder of the book, which brings history to its conclusion. From this point on, Revelation is set up in a cascade effect: the seventh seal of the scroll contains the seven trumpets, and the seventh trumpet contains the seven bowls of God's wrath.

John wept when it seemed that no one was worthy to take the scroll. That would mean that history is under no one's control, that this world we live in is merely spiraling downward into ever-greater chaos, which, admittedly, it sometimes seems to be. John certainly might have been tempted to think so. He was the last of the apostles still living, the rest of his compatriots having died as martyrs. Roman persecution was growing daily and coming aggressively against the churches he loved so dearly. John himself had survived being boiled in oil and was now exiled to the barren rock of Patmos in the middle of the Mediterranean, far removed from the people he loved. For us, just looking at the news channels for a few minutes would be enough to convince us that chaos reigns supreme. But that is only from our perspective. In heaven, the Lamb is on the throne, He reigns supreme, and He has all things completely "in hand." He is worthy to take the scroll, worthy to unroll it, and worthy to shepherd time and history - marred as they are by human sin - to their best possible conclusion. He is worthy because of His death on the cross as the sinless sacrifice for the sins of the world (v. 9), and His worthiness is recognized and celebrated by the 24 elders and the four living creatures (vv. 5-10), by thousands upon thousands of angels (vv. 11-12) and by all of creation (v. 13). Knowing that history was in good hands - the nail-scarred hands of His perfect Savior - John's weeping could stop. And so can ours.

PRAYER: Praise the Lord today! Because of His sacrificial death on the cross for our sins, He *is* worthy of all *"blessing and honor and glory and power, forever and ever!"* (v. 13), and He has all things - in the world and in our lives - completely under control.

THE SEALS
REVELATION 6

The scroll is described as being sealed with seven seals, and Jesus begins opening those seals one by one. Different interpretations have been given to the seals, but my understanding is that the first six seals represent the course of this age, stretching from Jesus' first coming until His coming to rapture His church (compare verses 1-2 to Matthew 24:4-5, verses 3-4 to Matthew 24:6-7a, verses 5-8 to Matthew 24:7b, and verses 9-11 to Matthew 24:9-14). Jesus said that *"all these things must happen, but the end is not yet"* (Matthew 24:6). All of the things He mentioned - false Christs, wars and rumors of wars, famines, epidemics, earthquakes and persecutions - which are also the subject of the first five seals, are just part and parcel of life on this fallen planet. The sixth seal (vv. 12-14), which corresponds to Matthew 24:29-31, represents Christ's return, not in secret as some have taught, but in a highly public revelation of Himself such that *"every eye will see Him, even those who pierced Him. And all the tribes of the earth will mourn because of Him"* (1:7). That mourning is spelled out further in verses 15-17. God's children have experienced much of the wrath of sinful human beings throughout history (vv. 9-11), but now He has come to their rescue, and those who have inflicted wrath upon them now know that the wrath of God is about to be poured out upon them (v. 17). Indeed, with the opening of the seventh seal, the great time of God's wrath, represented in the trumpet and bowl judgments, will come upon planet Earth.

PRAYER: Thank the Lord today that though we live in troublesome times, there is a rescue coming and a grand vindication for His cause and His children! Thank Him for the promise of His future coming, and for the assurance that you will be caught up to meet Him in the air at His coming.

BEFORE THE WRATH FALLS
REVELATION 7

Before the opening of the seventh seal, which contains the judgment of God, there are two further scenes associated with the sixth seal. The first is the sealing of the 144,000 children of Israel in verses 4-8, 12,000 from each tribe. The Bible in other places hints at a great turning of the Jewish people to Christ in the end times, and connects this turning to His visible coming (Zechariah 12:10-13:2; Romans 11:25-27). With Christ's coming, the times of the Gentiles will be fulfilled (Luke 21:24) as the fullness of the Gentiles will have come in, and the partial hardening which now afflicts Israel will be removed (Romans 11:25). While the Gentile world, seeing the returning Christ, mourns over its impending judgment, the Jewish world mourns in repentance. Given that the number twelve in Biblical numerology is the number of completion, some speculate that this is not a literal 144,000, but a number signifying the entirety of Israel being saved (Romans 11:26). Because of their repentance, they are sealed, and thus protected from the judgments to come, much as the Exodus generation was sheltered from the plagues that fell on Egypt. The other order of business before the wrath of God falls? The removal of the church from the earth, which we see in verses 9-17, where suddenly, there appears in heaven a great multitude beyond counting, dressed in white robes and singing praises to the Lamb for their salvation. While some have postulated that these are "converts" of the 144,000 "Jewish evangelists" of the previous verses, who are then summarily martyred for the faith, it is difficult to believe that such a multitude could be won to Christ in such a short time, particularly in the midst of the kinds of world-shaking judgments to come. Besides, we've already met the martyrs in 6:9-11, and beyond that, these believers all appear in heaven at one time, not scattered out over time as they would if they were being martyred. No, this is nothing less than the resurrected and raptured church of all the ages, believers of all time glorified and taken to heaven at Christ's appearing. But, some may argue, they *"came out of the great tribulation"* in verse 14. Indeed. But what is the great tribulation? While that term is often applied to a seven-year period of God's wrath between the rapture of the church and His coming to Earth, there is no Biblical passage that speaks of that period as "The Great Tribulation." I believe the great tribulation that is spoken of here and in Matthew 24:29 is in fact another term for the church age, the period covered by the first five seals, a long period of time in which God's people have been under continual tribulation (John 16:33). With Christ's coming, the tribulation is over (vv. 16-17) and the celebration begins!

PRAYER: Are you experiencing the tribulation (a word that means "pressure") of the world as it attempts to squeeze you into its mold of thinking, believing and acting? Pray that you might never be conformed to this world, but rather transformed by the renewing of your mind (Romans 12:2).

SILENCE, THEN FURY
REVELATION 8

"When He opened the seventh seal, there was silence in heaven for about half an hour" (v. 1). I suspect that the silence is in recognition of the magnitude of what is about to happen: God's final judgment on planet Earth and its unregenerate inhabitants. It is a judgment that comes in ever-increasing waves, building to a tsunami of wrath. How long the half-hour pause in heaven translates to time on Earth, we do not know, but the remaining inhabitants of Earth have seen Christ's return and the snatching away of His people, and they know that judgment is coming (7:15-17). Yet, even their worst expectations cannot match the reality of what is to come. The seventh seal, as aforementioned, contains the

seven trumpets, and with those seven trumpets, devastating judgments rain down upon the earth and its people. These are not natural occurrences that might be blamed upon "climate change" or such, but clearly supernatural plagues that no one would doubt constitute the wrath of God being poured out. Imagine the horror of *"noises, thunder, lightning, and an earthquake"* (v. 5), followed in rapid succession by *"hail and fire mixed with blood"* (v. 7), a plague that primarily impacts the trees and the green grass. Reeling from that, *"something like a great mountain, burning with fire, was thrown into the sea"* (v. 8), perhaps a reference to a large meteor strike. The results are that one-third of the seas turn to blood, one-third of the sea creatures die, and one-third of the ships of the sea are destroyed. Then there comes *"a great star from heaven, burning like a torch"* (v. 10) which impacts a third of the rivers and springs of waters. For the first time, we read about human casualties, as *"many men died from the waters, because they were made bitter"* (v. 11). Then, with the sounding of the fourth trumpet, one-third of the sun, the moon and the stars are darkened. Could this be the result of the smoke or dust from a meteor strike obscuring the atmosphere? As horrible as all this is, in verse 13, the angel flying through the midst of heaven announces that it's only going to get worse with the last three trumpets.

PRAYER: Reading about the coming judgments should both fill us with relief that we will not be here and subject to God's wrath, and concern for those who will be. Pray for anyone you know who is unsaved, and pray that God will open up opportunities for you to share your faith with that person.

TORMENT, THEN DEATH
REVELATION 9

Obviously, the previous plagues have caused no small degree of distress upon the inhabitants of the earth, including the death of some of them from contaminated water, but with the sounding of the fifth and sixth trumpets, the plagues begin to fall directly upon human beings. Indeed, the demonic locusts of the fifth trumpet are specifically commanded *"not to harm the grass of the earth, or any green thing, or any tree, but only those men who did not have the seal of God on their foreheads"* (v. 4). Their job is not to kill, but to torment, and their torment is so severe that *"men will seek death but will not find it. They will desire to die, but death will elude them"* (v. 6). With the sixth plague, four angels at the river Euphrates are released to kill one-third of what's left of humanity, putting them out of their human misery but sending them to a torment far worse than the stings inflicted by the locusts. Lest anyone think God is being too harsh, keep in mind that the plagues have been progressive, and yet, as bad as they have gotten to this point, *"The rest of mankind, who were not killed by these plagues, did not repent of the works of their hands. They did not cease to worship demons, and idols of gold, silver, brass, stone, and wood, which cannot see nor hear nor walk. Nor did they repent of their murders or their magical arts or their sexual immorality or their thefts"* (vv. 20-21).

PRAYER: Pray for those who need to repent of their sins and turn to Christ in faith, that they might do so before God's judgment falls.

THE SEVEN THUNDERS
REVELATION 10

Between the sixth and seventh trumpets, a mighty angel cries out, and seven thunders sound their voices. John is about to record the content of those seven thunders, but he is forbidden to write it down, leaving us with a mystery. The knowledge of the seven thunders should fill us with a great deal of humility in dealing with end times scenarios and teachings. Throughout history, disagreements about the sequence of end-time events have caused rifts in fellowship among believers, but for those who have their charts all ready and are absolutely certain they've got it all figured out, I would point out that they're trying to put together a jigsaw puzzle without having all the pieces! I suspect that most, if not all, of the many end-time scenarios people put forth have some degree of truth in them, and I would equally suspect that none of them have it down perfectly. As someone I heard once put it, Jesus came the first time exactly as the prophets predicted, but like no one expected, and it's likely His second coming will be the same. In hindsight, we will look at His coming and the events surrounding it, then we will look at the teachings of Revelation and other prophetic books, and we will say, "How did we miss that?" It's best not to be too dogmatic on this side of His coming about the details, but we should hold on tenaciously to the main truths of His coming: He IS coming, to bring salvation to those who are His and judgment upon those who are not. Let us not waste time in fruitless speculation and disputing about the details, but spend our time getting people ready for His coming (see Acts 1:7-8)!

PRAYER: Thank Him today that though He has not revealed all the details of the future to us, we can trust that He holds the future, and our future, in His hands.

THE TWO WITNESSES
REVELATION 11

Even in the midst of the pouring out of His judgments, God is a merciful God who continues to offer grace. In spite of humanity's ongoing, unrepentant sin (9:20-21), God sends two supernatural witnesses to offer His forgiveness to whoever will listen. The description of them has led some to identify them as Moses and Elijah, while others reference them as Enoch and Elijah, two prophets of God previously taken from the world without dying. All this is speculation. All we know for sure is that they come on the scene with amazing powers and supernatural protection until their testimony is finished (it has been said that all God's people are immortal until God's purposes for them are fulfilled). After 1260 days, they are put to death in Jerusalem by *"the beast that ascends from the bottomless pit"* (v. 7), and their bodies are refused burial for three and a half days. Amazingly, the world will react to their deaths like it is Christmastime; they will *"rejoice over them and make merry and send gifts to one another, because these two prophets tormented those who dwell on the earth"* (v. 16). It is a testimony to how far gone a person is in sin when he considers the one who tells him the truth about God and offers him God's forgiveness to be a tormentor! We see that dynamic in our world today, as those who are deep in sin of various kinds do everything in their power to silence the preaching of the gospel. After the three and a half days, though, the breath of life returns to these prophets, and they are caught up to heaven in the sight of all those who had celebrated their deaths. With the inhabitants of Earth having again spurned God's grace, the judgments will continue, and indeed, will intensify. With the sounding of the seventh trumpet (which contains the seven bowls), God's judgment will be complete.

PRAYER: Pray for those who preach the gospel in difficult, and even hostile, situations, and pray for the hostile, that God's Spirit will overcome their hostility so that they might be saved.

THE WOMAN, THE DRAGON, AND THE CHILD
REVELATION 12

The seventh trumpet has sounded, but just as there was a delay between the opening of the seventh seal and the sounding of the seven trumpets it contains (see chapter 8:1-5), so too there is a delay between the sounding of the trumpet and the pouring out of the seven bowls it contains. As part of this interlude, there is a vision of *"a woman clothed with the sun, with the moon under her feet, and on her head a crown of twelve stars"* (v. 1). This woman is in the process of giving birth to a male child, *"who was to rule all nations with an iron scepter"* (v. 5), and a great red dragon waits to devour her child as soon as He is born. The symbolism here is not difficult to interpret. The woman is Israel (compare the description of the woman to Joseph's dream in Genesis 37:9), the child is the Lord Jesus Christ, and the red dragon is Satan, who, through Herod the Great, did indeed attempt to destroy Jesus soon after His birth (see Matthew 2:13-18). This attempt fails, and the child is caught up to God and to His throne, a shortening of the story that curiously leaves out the cross and resurrection and goes right to the ascension! Verse 4's reference to the dragon's tail sweeping a third of the stars from the sky has been long interpreted as meaning that Satan took one-third of the angels with him in his fall; those fallen angels are now known as demons. War breaks out in heaven, with Michael the Archangel battling against the dragon and his demons, resulting in the dragon and his demons being expelled from heaven and cast down to Earth. The Bible has previously hinted that Satan has had some degree of access to the throne room of God up to this point (see Job 1-2, Zechariah 3:1-2), but that access will be no more. The devil is furious, exuding *"great wrath, because he knows that his time is short"* (v. 12). He seeks to take out his fury upon Israel, but she is supernaturally protected (vv. 13-16; see also 14:1-5), so he turns his attention to *"the remnant of her offspring, who keep the commandments of God and have the testimony of Jesus Christ"* (v. 17). Who are these targets of the evil one? If we understand Satan's expulsion as coming at the ascension of Christ, then there is little doubt that the scene is describing the persecution of both Jews (who have been supernaturally preserved throughout history) and Christians during the entirety of the church age. If we understand his expulsion as coming in the end times, these are those few (only a remnant) who have come to Christ after the rapture of the church during the 3 ½ year ministry of the two witnesses. Like the martyrs of old, this remnant will be persecuted and even overcome, from every earthly perspective (see 13:7), but in fact, they will overcome the enemy by the blood of the Lamb and the word of their testimony, loving not their lives even unto death (v. 11).

PRAYER: Pray today that whatever opposition or persecution comes your way, you will stand strong, proclaiming the blood of the Lamb as the salvation of the world, not shrinking from testifying of your faith in Him, and not backing down, even under threat of death.

THE UNHOLY TRINITY
REVELATION 13

It is hard to imagine the social and political chaos that will come upon the world in the end times. First, there is the sudden departure of all the believers. Then come the horrific judgments detailed in the first six trumpets. Now, a political leader arises to unite the remaining inhabitants of the earth under one government, a government hostile to

God (vv. 5-6) and the remaining people of God (v. 7). This leader is described as *"a beast rising out of the sea"* (v. 1). We might be dubious that a world leader and a world government could arise out of the chaos of such times, but in such times, people desperately look for a leader to bring order, and keep in mind that there has been an interim of at least 3½ years since that last trumpet judgment (11:3), enough time, it would seem, for some relative degree of normalcy to return. Keep in mind also that this leader is empowered by Satan himself, who gives him *"his power and his throne and great authority"* (v. 2), not to mention that the unregenerate people of Earth at this time will be under a strong delusion (see II Thessalonians 2:9-11). This leader is further allied with a *"beast rising out of the earth"* (v. 11) who has a superficial resemblance to a lamb but who speaks with the voice of the dragon. Some interpreters see in these two beasts a reference to Imperial Rome of the first century, the first beast representing the Roman government and the second one the false religions of Rome (particularly emperor worship) that supported the Roman government. In ancient Rome, those who would not declare "Caesar is Lord" and burn incense to his image were often ostracized, fired from jobs, denied business, forbidden to own land, or even jailed or killed. Christians declared that they would pray for Caesar, pay taxes to Caesar, and obey the laws of Caesar that did not contradict with God's laws, but they could not and would not declare "Caesar is Lord," for Christ alone is Lord! The economic pressure the early church was under to conform to this "beastly" system was immense. Other interpreters see these beasts as symbolic of a future Antichrist and false prophet, empowered by Satan and ruling the earth just prior to Christ's return to Earth. Still others see the beast imagery here as symbolic of political, social, religious and economic pressure put upon believers in all times and places to deny Christ and conform to the world system under the control of the evil one. So, which is it? My answer would be "D - All of the Above." Certainly, there is no doubt that John's first readers would have understood the pressure they were under from Rome as a beastly system of corrupt government, false religion, and demonic opposition. The Bible certainly indicates elsewhere that there will be a future man of lawlessness who will do incredibly blasphemous things just prior to Christ's return to Earth (see II Thessalonians 2:3-12). And certainly, in all times, and in our time, the forces of overreaching government, false religion and economic pressure have come against the church.

PRAY: How do you see corrupt government, false religion and economic pressure coming against the church today? Pray that you, and other believers, will stand strong against these powerful forces.

GRACE AND JUDGMENT
REVELATION 14

Once again, we see the 144,000 Israelites who were sealed in chapter 7, standing with the Lamb on Mt. Zion in Jerusalem, still protected from the chaos happening around them and the evil machinations of the beast kingdom. The final judgment is about to fall in the seven bowls, but they will still be protected from it. Yet, before those final plagues fall, grace is still offered to the unregenerate world in the form of three angels flying in the midst of heaven. The first angel calls upon the lost world to *"Fear God and give Him glory, for the hour of His judgment has come"* (v. 7). The second angel warns that Babylon, a term for the beast kingdom, is about to be utterly destroyed. The third angel warns against receiving the mark of the beast or worshiping his image. For the remnant few who have come to Christ after the departure of the church, they must not give in to the pressure, which will undoubtedly be immense, at this time.

They must stand firm, even unto death, which will come to many of them (vv. 13-14). Those who think they can wait to be saved after the rapture would do well to heed these verses. The suffering of those who come to Christ after the departure of the church will be horrific (12:17, 13:7). *"Blessed are the dead who die in the Lord"* (v. 13) at this time, and their reward will be great for their suffering (v. 14), but how much better would it have been to be part of the great catching away of the church? Verses 14-16 seem to be a flashback to the earlier rapture of the church, placed here to emphasize that very point, and to contrast the harvesting of the earth of believers with a second harvest, the harvesting of the grapes of wrath to be thrown into *"the great winepress of the wrath of God"* (v. 19). Or perhaps, given that these martyrs of the beast appear in heaven in the next chapter, verses 14-16 are a symbolic representation of their reception into heaven.

PRAYER: Pray for those around the world today who are facing pressure to conform to the evil world system. Pray for those who are even facing death as martyrs, that they will stand firm to the end.

VICTORY AND JUDGMENT
REVELATION 15

In this short chapter, we see *"those who have the victory over the beast, over his image, and over his mark and over the number of his name, standing on the sea of glass"* (v. 2) in heaven, singing praises to the Lord God Almighty. Truly, *"They overcame him by the blood of the Lamb and by the word of their testimony, and they loved not their lives unto the death"* (12:11). They have received the grace of God, and experienced the temporary wrath of the evil one as a result, but now they are experiencing the eternal reward of the Lamb. Now, those who have rejected the grace of God, and experienced the temporary reward of the evil one as a result, will experience the eternal wrath of the Lamb. Once again, there is an announcement of the upcoming final plagues. Even in the writing of the book, God seems to be hesitating, almost reluctant to pour out His final judgment. But pour it out He will, beginning in the next chapter.

PRAYER: There is no middle ground. A choice must be made, a choice that will affect both time and eternity. Pray for those who are hesitating to make that choice because of the temporary costs involved. Pray that they might see past the temporary to the eternal before it is too late.

THE SEVEN BOWLS
REVELATION 16

"It is what they deserve!" (v. 6b). It is hard to imagine that anyone could deserve such punishment, but we must keep in mind that *"true and righteous are <His> judgments"* (v. 7), and that nothing has been spared to give these people grace, but they wouldn't receive it. Even though they had *"shed the blood of saints and prophets"* (v. 6a), God still would receive them if they would only repent. In the midst of earlier judgments, they had refused to repent, and even in the midst of these final, more intense judgments, they are settled in their rebellion, and indeed, overflowing in their hostility toward God. Three times, in verses 9, 11, and 21, we're told that these inhabitants of Earth blaspheme God. Not only this, they seek to attack God the only way they know how, by attacking His people, the 144,000 of the Jewish nation that have been protected through the plagues and protected from the wrath of the beasts. Inspired by demonic spirits (vv. 12-14), the armies of the whole world gather together at Armageddon. Given how staggered they must have been by the first five plagues, it rather reminds me of the situation in Sodom when the men of that wicked city, already struck blind, were still trying to find Lot's door to get at the angels!

Surely, this degree of wickedness, demonic deception, and hostility toward God is deserving of such intense judgment.

PRAYER: Of course, all of us are deserving of God's judgment. Thank Him today for His grace, for the price He paid for your free gift of forgiveness and eternal life, and for how He drew you to Himself that you might receive it.

THE GREAT HARLOT
REVELATION 17

Chapters 17-18 give further details of the destruction of the final beast kingdom afflicted with the seven plagues of the previous chapter, but it applies to more than a future Satanic kingdom. By giving it the name of Babylon, and by including features of Rome (such as verse 9; Rome sat upon seven hills), this kingdom can be seen as symbolic of all evil, godless, Satanic regimes of all time, all of which culminate in that final apocalyptic kingdom. Certainly, John's first readers would have seen in this description a portrait of Rome, for Rome was certainly *"drunk with the blood of the saints and with the blood of the martyrs of Jesus"* (v. 6), but Rome was not the first, nor has it been the last power to come against God by persecuting His people. Every such kingdom, down through history - Egypt, Assyria, Babylon, Greece, Rome, Nazi Germany, the Soviet Union - has fallen, and we can be assured that whatever kingdoms, both present and future, who oppose God and attack the people of God will meet the same fate.

PRAYER: Pray for those believers who are currently dwelling under oppressive, anti-God, anti-Christian regimes. Pray that they might stand strong under persecution. Pray for the fall of such regimes and the vindication of God's people.

BEAUTY AND HORROR
REVELATION 18

The description of the great harlot in 17:3-6 is a study in contrast.   She is sitting on a hideous beast full of blasphemous names, but she is described as quite beautiful: *"arrayed in purple and scarlet, and adorned with gold and precious stones and pearls, having in her hand a golden cup."* But yet, upon closer examination, that cup is *"full of abominations and the filth of her sexual immorality,"* her name on her forehead reveals the horror of her wickedness, and she is *"drunk with the blood of the saints and with the blood of the martyrs of Jesus."* Isn't that how Satan works? He does not come to us as the blasphemous beast he is, but in the guise of something beautiful, something pleasant, something valuable - everything we've ever wanted and more. It is only when we drink of the cup that we taste the filth inside; only when we embrace the woman that we see her for the prostitute and cannibal she is. That dynamic is not only played out on a personal level with temptation and sin, but on a national and international level, as we see in chapter 18. The final beast kingdom, like all those before, was *"a dwelling place of demons, a haunt for every unclean spirit"* (v. 2), but it did have its splendor: *"she glorified herself and lived luxuriously"* (v. 7). Blinded by her glory, *"the nations have drunk of the wine of her sexual immorality, the kings of the earth have committed adultery with her, and the merchants of the earth have become rich through the abundance of her luxury"* (v. 3). When that kingdom falls, it is the merchants who most mourn. How many times throughout history have nations (including ours) looked the other way as brutal regimes committed all manner of atrocities because of economic/trade considerations (oil comes immediately to mind)? How many times have we personally been tempted (or given in to temptation) to compromise our integrity because of financial/job/economic considerations? Verse

9's call is not simply a call to some future people of God, but to us: *"Come out of her, my people, lest you partake in her sins, and lest you receive her plagues."*

PRAYER: Where in your life might something seemingly beautiful be blinding you to something simply horrible? Where might you be tempted to compromise? Pray for clarity of vision, to be able to see past the splendor to the horror, and pray for willingness to do the right thing, no matter the cost, knowing that the cost of doing the wrong thing will always be greater.

THE RETURN!
REVELATION 19

What a contrast to the judgments falling on Earth we see in the Marriage Supper of the Lamb, as God's people, both the raptured believers of all time and the believers who stood strong against the final beast kingdom and paid for it with their lives, celebrate and worship the true and righteous judgments of God. The final scene of God's purging wrath comes with the return of Jesus and His saints to Earth. The armies of Earth have gathered at Armageddon in a futile effort to attack the 144,000; they are met by a far more mighty army commanded by the *"KING OF KINGS AND LORD OF LORDS"* (v. 16), and quickly destroyed by the sharp sword proceeding from His mouth (vv. 15, 21; see also II Thessalonians 2:8). In contrast to the magnificent, heavenly Marriage Supper of the Lamb comes the horrific, earthly *"supper of the Great God"* (v. 17), as the birds of the air *"eat the flesh of kings, the flesh of commanders, the flesh of strong men, the flesh of horses and their riders, and the flesh of all men, both free and slave, both small and great!"* (v. 18). The beast and false prophet are not killed but captured, and *"thrown alive into the lake of fire that burns with brimstone"* (v. 20), a fitting end to those who had deceived the entire world as the devil's primary agents.

PRAYER: In the ancient world, most marriages were arranged marriages, arranged by the families of the couple. Once an announcement was made, there would be a betrothal period of one year, during which time the couple would get to know each other better, and the groom would prepare a home for the bride. Then came a week-long marriage feast, followed by the ceremony. This is our betrothal period. The Bridegroom is preparing a place for us (John 14:2). Pray that you might come to know the Bridegroom better through the Word and prayer. Thank Him for your future at the Marriage Supper.

WHY THE MILLENNIUM? AND WHY THE FINAL JUDGMENT?
REVELATION 20

Chapter 20 of Revelation has always raised a couple of questions for me (not that *every* chapter of Revelation doesn't raise significant questions for me!). The first question surrounded the need for the thousand-year Millennial Reign of Christ on Earth. What is the point? Why not just go into the final state? I think the Millennium serves as one last vindication of God, and one last indication of man's stubborn sinfulness. God has, throughout history, answered every objection that man could offer to excuse his sin. "But God, if we only knew what you wanted from us..." so God gave the Law. "But God, if you would speak to our current situation..." so God gave the prophets. "But God, if you would only come down to our level and speak to us personally..." so God sent His Son. The result? Human beings broke the Law, rejected the prophets, and crucified the Son. In the Millennium, God answers the objection, "But God, if you would only give us a perfect environment to live in..." While the raptured saints and the martyrs of the beast kingdom will enter the Millennium in glorified bodies, there will be many who will not: the 144,000, and the believers who managed to escape martyrdom at the hands of the beast. Yes, they are believers, but they are still possessed of a sin nature, and they and their offspring will reproduce for many generations over that thousand-year period, passing that sin nature along. All of those generations will live in a perfect environment: a world without Satan ruled over by the perfect government of Christ Himself, but yet when the thousand years has ended, and Satan is removed from his prison, he will find many ready and willing to follow him. Once and for all, it is shown that the fault for our sin is not in God, and not in our environment, but in ourselves. The second question that arises is the need of the Great White Throne Judgment at the end of time. Why an end-of-time judgment? Why dredge up those who are already in Hades for another judgment? Why not just judge people fully when they die? I suspect that the reason is because it is only at the end of time that the full measure of a person's evil (or righteousness, for that matter) can be measured. Just as the good of the Apostle Paul did not die with him, but continues to resonate to this day, so too the evil that other men, such as Charles Darwin, Karl Marx, Adolph Hitler, etc., have done also tends to resonate long after their deaths. Each person's judgment (and each believer's reward) will be 100% just and right, and just as there will be degrees of reward in heaven, so too there will be degrees of torment in hell.

PRAYER: One day the Lord Jesus will rule over planet Earth. Recommit yourself to His rule over your life right here and now (Matthew 6:10).

ALL THINGS NEW!
REVELATION 21

The beauty of the new heavens, the new earth, and the new Jerusalem is beyond imagining. We would expect it to be, given that God tossed off the current heavens and earth in a mere six days, and even marred by sin, this world we live in still takes our breath away with its beauty. He's been working on "Version 2.0" of creation for almost 2000 years now; how magnificent it will be! The things we think of as most precious here - gold, pearls, and precious stones - are used for pavement and building materials there (vv. 18-21)! What is most significant, though, is not what *is* there, but what is *not* there. There is no separation between God and man, because *"the tabernacle* ("dwelling-place") *of God is with men, and He will dwell with them"* (v. 3). There is no more death, no more sorrow, no more crying and no more pain (v. 4). There are no more cowardice, unbelief, abominations, murders, sexual immorality, occultism, idolatry or lying there (v. 8), and no more temples, *"for the Lord God Almighty and the Lamb are its temple"* (v. 22). There isn't even a need for a sun or a moon, because *"the glory of God is its light, and its lamp is the Lamb"* (v. 24). *"No unclean thing shall ever enter it, nor shall anyone who commits abomination or falsehood, but only those whose names are written in the Lamb's Book of Life"* (v. 27). What a marvelous future for the children of God!

PRAYER: Praise Him today that your name is written in the Lamb's Book of Life, and you will one day take your place as a citizen of that final, heavenly home.

COMING SOON!
REVELATION 22

Three times in chapter 22, Jesus proclaims, *"I am coming soon"* (vv. 7, 12, 20). Christ's coming could be at any time, even before you finish this sentence! What are we to do in the meantime? 1) We are to *"Worship God!"* (v. 9). 2) We are work in such a way as to receive His reward at His coming (v. 12). 3) We are not just to know His commandments, but *"do His commandments"* (v. 14, see also James 1:22). 4) We are to issue His invitation, in the power of the Holy Spirit, to those who do not know Him (v. 17). 5) We are to live by and proclaim the Word of God faithfully (vv. 18-19). 6) We are to look forward in eager anticipation to His coming (v. 20). For now, we must pursue righteousness and pursue the lost, but a time is coming when the righteousness of the saints will be absolute, and the evil of the lost will be forever entrenched (v. 11). Some have questioned the justice of God in punishing someone forever for a short lifetime of sin, but we need note that for the lost, their sin does not end at death; their sin goes on forever, and therefore, so does their punishment.

PRAYER: Pray that you might be faithful in pursuing the tasks Jesus has left to us until His coming. Jesus says, *"I am coming soon!"* Our response should be, *"Amen* ("let it be so"). *Even so, come Lord Jesus!"* That can only be our response if we're walking in accord with His Word and laboring in accord with His will. If His coming were today, would you have regrets over tasks left undone, righteousness not fully pursued, and witness not uttered? Pray about how you can be fully ready for His coming.

Made in the USA
Charleston, SC
19 March 2016